D0425123

WITHDRAWN

364.106 SELIGMAN
Seligman, Scott D. author.
  Tong wars : the untold story of
vice, money, and murder in New York's

TONG WARS

Scott D. Seligman

TONG WARS

The Untold Story of
Vice, Money, and Murder
in New York's
Chinatown

VIKING

VIKING

An imprint of Penguin Random House LLC

375 Hudson Street

New York, New York 10014

penguin.com

Copyright © 2016 by Scott D. Seligman

Penguin supports copyright. Copyright fuels creativity, encourages diverse voices, pro-
motes free speech, and creates a vibrant culture. Thank you for buying an authorized
edition of this book and for complying with copyright laws by not reproducing, scan-
ning, or distributing any part of it in any form without permission. You are supporting
writers and allowing Penguin to continue to publish books for every reader.

ILLUSTRATION CREDITS

New York World-Telegram and Sun Collection, Library of Congress: pages 15, 54, 128,
145, 193, 216, 219, 253; Library of Congress: pages 25, 108, 131, 213; Manuscripts and
Archives Division, New York Public Library: pages 28, 73; Museum of the City of New
York: page 31; National Archives and Records Administration: pages 41, 47, 187; Prints
and Photographs Division, Library of Congress: page 45; © Bettmann/Corbis: page 60;
Detroit Publishing Company, courtesy of Shorpy.com: page 63; Detroit Publishing
Company Photograph Collection, Library of Congress: pages 68, 177; George Grantham
Bain Collection, Library of Congress: pages 79, 114, 159, 173, 208; Wikimedia Com-
mons: page 101; courtesy of Scott D. Seligman: pages 122, 226; *Brooklyn Daily Eagle,*
Oct. 12, 1899: page 132; New York *World,* March 6, 1906: page 140; Russel Crouse,
Murder Won't Out (Garden City, N.Y.: Doubleday, Doran & Co., 1932): pages 161, 169;
Annual Report of the Police Department, City of New York, 1922: page 221; © Underwood &
Underwood/Corbis: page 249

ISBN 9780399562273 (hardcover)
ISBN 9780399562297 (e-book)

Printed in the United States of America
1   3   5   7   9   10   8   6   4   2

Set in Columbus MT Std
Designed by Francesca Belanger
Map by Daniel Lagin

CONTENTS

INTRODUCTION

Nothing had worked. Not threats, not negotiations. Not shutting down Chinatown's gambling halls and opium dens nor exiling its unmarried white women. Not house-to-house searches for weapons nor arrests. Not throwing Chinese offenders into prison nor even *executing* them. The situation seemed hopeless and out of control, and the New York County district attorney, Joab H. Banton, was running out of ideas.

Despite his best efforts, tong men in New York were still killing one another.

There had been reason for hope. The most recent treaty, signed five months earlier in March 1925 by the tong kingpins, was supposed to have provided "for lasting peace between the On Leongs and Hip Sings in all parts of the United States." Senior tong men not seen in public for months had emerged from their hiding places, newly confident they would not be mown down on the streets of the Chinese quarter by an enemy gunman. But like the seemingly endless series of peace accords negotiated over the three decades in which the tongs had been at each other's throats, this one hadn't lasted.

Distrust ran so high that any incident could prove incendiary. When a Boston On Leong decided a Hip Sing had been too attentive to his wife, he picked up his gun, and so did tong men throughout the East and the Midwest. Dozens of Chinese were slaughtered.

Banton's predecessors had been able to sit the heads of the New York tongs down together and read them the riot act with some expectation that calm would be restored if and when they willed it. But over the previous couple of decades, the organizations had spread out to dozens of cities, most of the founders had passed from the scene, and lesser men had filled their shoes. Because the bosses had not *authorized* the most recent outbreak, it was far from clear that they had the stature or the clout to *stop* it. And the stakes had never been higher: more people were dying as the weapons of choice evolved from hatchets and meat cleavers to pistols, automatic weapons, and even bombs.

On September 8, Banton assembled the leaders of the warring factions to deliver a "final ultimatum." If the killing didn't cease, he warned, he was prepared to call in the federal government. It was no empty threat: Federal officials had already vowed to deport imprisoned tong men after their sentences were up. They were now poised to up the ante. And so when two Hip Sings were brutally assassinated the very next day—one shot, another bashed in the skull—Washington decided it was time for drastic action.

The U.S. attorney Emory R. Buckner announced that four federal departments would cooperate to deport every Chinese in New York who lacked a certificate permitting him or her to remain in America. Because securing certificates hinged on one's ability to demonstrate that one had entered the country legally, Buckner knew that many couldn't qualify; they were out of status and vulnerable. Never mind that there was no evidence that these were the people who were wielding the guns or that their expulsion would do much of anything to bring peace to Chinatown.

In raids carried out over several days, local police imposed a dragnet as federal agents swooped in on Chinatown. They rounded up everyone they could find who looked Chinese, some of whom were citizens and most of whom were legal residents. Without warrants, they raided restaurants, gambling houses, laundries, theaters, tenements, and shops. They dragged people from their beds. If wiping out the scourge meant running roughshod over individual rights and playing fast and loose with the law, they proved alarmingly eager to step up.

Detainees by the hundreds were ferried by paddy wagon to the Federal Building, where they were herded into a large room and examined through interpreters, one by one, by immigration officers in impromptu hearings. Those with papers were released. Those without documents were placed under arrest, arraigned, and sent to the Tombs—lower Manhattan's jail—or to Ellis Island. Men who had never brandished a weapon in their lives wept as they were held without bail to await certain deportation.

No other immigrant group had ever been targeted the way the authorities were going after the Chinese. Italian and Irish émigrés had fought their share of brutal gang wars, but nobody had ever rounded them up for wholesale expulsion. Yet this time, the government was acting as if the only way to bring peace to Chinatown was to get rid of its Chinese, through whatever means necessary.

How it came to this is the story of four bloody wars and countless skirmishes fought intermittently over more than three decades in New York's Chinatown and the Chinese quarters of several other cities in America's East and Midwest, with their attendant casualties, peace parleys, and treaties. It is the story of a clash of mismatched cultures, of misunderstandings, naïveté, and bigotry. It tells of stubborn men willing to fight and die not only for concrete rewards like money and property but also for intangibles like loyalty and "face"—that Asian notion so closely tied to reputation, dignity, and prestige. And it is the story of a veritable army of precinct captains, detectives, and uniformed officers bound and determined to stop them.

Or at least to line their pockets.

The warriors were men from south China, most of whom had come to the West Coast to seek their fortunes and eventually headed east, but who planned to return home at some future date. Most were manual laborers, but some built businesses, amassed substantial wealth, and planted roots in America. The tongs were their secret, sworn brotherhoods organized ostensibly for social purposes but very much involved in criminal activity. (The Chinese term carries no negative connotation and can be used to describe any of a variety of organizations, but for clarity's sake its use in this book will generally be limited to those secret societies.) Their weapons were cleavers and knives, then guns, and eventually explosives. And their primary battleground in New York was a triangular parcel of land not much larger than an acre adjoining the seedy Five Points neighborhood of lower Manhattan. Bounded by Mott and Pell streets, Chatham Square, and the Bowery, and including the whole of crooked Doyers Street, it was then—and remains today—the heart of New York's Chinatown.

In my many years of living and working in China, studying the Chinese language, and doing research on early Chinese American history, I had heard frequent mention of the tong wars, but most of what I had read about the tongs was highly sensationalized, as indeed was much of what was written about all Chinese in America before about thirty years ago. Many writers were more interested in conjuring up Oriental mystery and lurid intrigue than presenting real history, because that is what most people wanted and expected to read.

I also knew that many Chinese Americans simply wished to forget about the tong wars, because they don't reflect well on early residents of Chinatown, but I wanted to know the truth. I was reasonably sure there was more to the story than simply bad, greedy men slaughtering other bad, greedy men for lucre. Surely the clash of cultures and the way in which the Chinese were treated in America—disenfranchised, marginalized, objecti-fied, and often denied justice—had had *something* to do with it. So I set out to understand what had happened and why, to demystify the stories, and to look at them in the broader context of the early Chinese experience in America, and especially in Tammany-era New York.

This book is the result. The characters depicted in it have not in any way been fictionalized. The events really occurred at the times indicated. All dialogue that appears between quotation marks was recorded at the time. And no thoughts have been placed into the heads of people who left neither diaries nor letters behind, nor have emotions or motives been as-cribed to them that were not made explicit or at least strongly suggested by their actions.

All that being said, the sources that survive are far from unimpeachable, and there are gaps in the record. Most of our knowledge of early China-town comes from the major New York newspapers, which covered the goings-on there in surprising detail and never more intensively than when the battles among the On Leongs, the Hip Sings, and the Four Brothers, a third combatant, were in full throttle. They provide a serviceable chronol-ogy, but their coverage was mostly the work of white journalists whose observations were sometimes astute, often superficial or naive, and more than occasionally demonstrably false. Because none spoke Chinese, they had to rely on Chinese informants for many of their stories, but they couldn't always distinguish fact from fiction and could be oblivious when they were being played by one faction or another.

The early residents left few written records in any language, but I have had the benefit of other contemporary sources. Massive digitization has made thousands of old newspapers keyword searchable, which has permitted a truly comprehensive inventory of available articles from New York and beyond. Extensive indexing of federal and state census records, passenger manifests, and conscription and vital records now permits researchers to verify facts about individuals. Court records, though mostly not digitized, can often be obtained with a little effort. And the Chinese exclusion era case files in the National Archives, collected long ago by the government for questionable purposes but tremendously helpful and enlightening to researchers today, provide rich detail about many of the figures mentioned in the text. They have been of immeasurable help in creating a fresh assessment that confirms some popular impressions, discredits others, and brings some new, compelling stories to light.

Two English-language books written by Chinese authors in the 1930s deserve special mention: *Tong War!* by Eng Ying "Eddie" Gong and Bruce Grant and *Chinatown Inside Out* by Leong Gor Yun. The former is an as-told-to memoir of a Hip Sing kingpin who witnessed much of the later action of the book and was written shortly before the end of the conflict. The latter is an account of Chinatown life with a section on the tong wars attributed to Y. K. Chu, the editor of a liberal Chinatown newspaper called the *Chinese Journal,* who teamed up with an unnamed American journalist. The pseudonym used is likely a pun, "Leong Gor Yun" being a plausible rendering in Cantonese of a phrase meaning "two people." Both books tend toward the anecdotal and, in places, the sensational. But they were useful for insights and character descriptions.

Lack of understanding and abject prejudice characterized some of the writing, so I occasionally had to take what I read with a grain, and sometimes a lump, of salt. I dismissed articles in which reporters made patently ridiculous claims about Chinese customs and practices. For example, in 1904, the *New York Telegram* related the ostensible cause of a tong feud this way:

About 6000 B.C., when Confucius' great-grandfather had just perfected the dish of chow mein, the feud may have started. The Hep Sing Tong in those historic days wanted chow mein to be declared the national dish, but the conservatives, the Gon Sing Tong, clung to chop suey. There was a clash. Armed from head to foot, the Hep Sing Tong and the Gon Sing Tong made deserts of Shanghai and Canton, and even Pekin felt the effects of the unrelenting warfare.

Or this absurdity on the same subject, from a New York *World* columnist, a quarter of a century later:

Two Chinamen were shot in Newark, N.J., for drinking Lipton's tea instead of Formosa-Oolong. One thing led to another and another Chink bit the cobblestones in San Francisco for wearing rubber heels on his sandals. . . . Things have quieted down a little now, but you will notice every Chinaman always wear [*sic*] a black silk suit so he will be shot down in his mourning clothes.

Such drivel, unfortunately, often passed for journalism, even in respected newspapers.

I also had to reject some very appealing tales much favored by other writers that either did not appear in primary sources or struck me as improbable. For example, Herbert Asbury, in his famous 1928 *Gangs of New York,* recounted that the On Leong comedian Ah Hoon was shot in his bed through the window of his fourth-floor room by a Hip Sing gunman lowered in a chair by a hoist from the roof of the building. It was a compelling image, but I found no corroborating evidence for it and much to contradict it. The newspapers agreed he had died in the hallway outside his room; there was no mention of a hoist. And his assassin was probably not even a Hip Sing.

A persistent and baffling stereotype that appeared in the press was that Chinese desperadoes were terrible shots and that in gun battles they typically crouched down, shut their eyes tightly, and fired in all directions until they ran out of bullets. This struck me as ludicrous, and the relatively small number of innocent bystanders shot during the years the tongs preferred guns over hatchets suggests its fallaciousness. I also rejected a press account of Mock Duck's wife angrily dragging her husband by his hair queue from the apartment of a mistress. The anecdote was catnip to writers eager to suffuse contemporary Chinatown women with the spirit of the suffragettes and make the dreaded Mock Duck appear henpecked, but I don't believe many Chinese American females dared behave that way in 1908, still less Mock Duck's wife, who was treated as little more than chattel and whose favors were apparently offered up to other men on more than one occasion.

Sorting out who was who was a major challenge. There was no standard romanization system for Chinese names during this period. They were spelled haphazardly and often differently over time, even in the same publications. Was the Joe Gong who was treasurer of the On Leong Tong in 1897 the same person as the Chu Gong who testified as a witness in a 1904 trial? Was he also the Ji Gong who was attacked on Mott Street in 1905? I concluded that he was and have harmonized the spellings accordingly. On the other hand, I satisfied myself that the Lee Sing who shot Mock Duck in 1904 couldn't have been the same Lee Sing who beat Tom Lee up in a street brawl in 1880, because census records proved that he would have been only nine years old at the time of the earlier incident.

The exact Chinese characters for these names, if they were known, might have provided clarity, but unless documents were signed in Chinese or people were mentioned in the few Chinese-language sources that do survive, these are impossible to discern a century later. To add to the problem, many Chinese went by more than one name or were known by nicknames, truncated versions of their given names, or even the names of their business establishments. Reporters often couldn't tell surnames from given names, and some Chinese actually *reversed* the order of their Chinese names to follow the American convention of putting the surname last. So it's easy to see that parsing spellings might have introduced some inadvertent errors. To aid the reader, a Dramatis Personae section to help sort through the most important characters can be found on page xvii.

I undertook this project mindful of the danger of reinforcing prejudices and stereotypes that go back more than a century. Chinatowns have long suffered from tabloid-style coverage that portrays them as dangerous places run by inscrutable, all-powerful villains, their streets washed in the blood of the victims of the evil tongs. But the Fu Manchu stereotype belies the reality that most of the restaurateurs, laundrymen, cooks, grocers, cigar makers, street peddlers, and other Chinese in New York at the turn of the twentieth century were decent, law-abiding people trying to make their way in a society that might have offered them a living but leavened it with a large measure of discrimination and abuse. It was also a highly corrupt culture in which the power that police and other government officials exercised over them went mostly unchecked and in which Chinese could not count on fair treatment, even from the courts.

The image of the Chinese quarter as a dangerous neighborhood perilous to outsiders has, to some extent, persisted even to this day, and it is, in the main, an injustice. Even during the height of the tong wars, the number of "highbinders"—a generic, and now archaic, term for Chinese desperadoes— was small, and the real dangers posed were to members of rival tongs, seldom to Chinese civilians, still less to non-Chinese tourists.

One other caveat is worth mentioning. Tongs battled in Chinatowns in many cities across the United States. The skirmishes were arguably fiercer in the cities of the West Coast where Chinese, and tongs, were far more numerous. In focusing on the New York tongs exclusively, I have consciously told only part of a larger story. I have included events in other locations, but only insofar as they were relevant to what was going on in New York, the center of gravity for Chinese in the East and the Midwest. I leave telling the story of the West Coast tong wars to others.

In his 1902 portrait of local Chinese residents, *Bits of Broken China,* William E. S. Fales, sometime attorney for many members of New York's Chinese community, decried the tendency of Western writers to represent the Chinese as "monsters of iniquity and marvels of Machiavellian craft." I have kept this danger squarely in mind and tried my best to present the various characters as they were: human beings with virtues and foibles who were trying to eke out a living in a foreign country with its own set of rules often at odds with their own values. Some were upright and others wicked; like people everywhere, most fell somewhere in between.

Scott D. Seligman

A NOTE ON ROMANIZATION
AND CHINESE NAMES

Nearly all the Chinese people mentioned in this book were of Cantonese origin, most hailing from the Pearl River delta—generally the Taishan or Guangzhou area. In China, of course, their names were written in Chinese characters. But when they reached America, some form of latinized spelling was required. Although a standard romanization system for Chinese, the Wade-Giles system, was coming into popular use in the twentieth century, it was a transcription of Mandarin, a northern dialect very different from the ones spoken by these immigrants and therefore not of much use to them. There has never been a widely accepted spelling system for either the Taishan or the Cantonese dialect.

Rendering the names in letters was generally left to ship captains, immigration officers, court clerks, preachers, and journalists, few if any of whom spoke Chinese. The result was a hodgepodge of spellings, some more, some less true to the Chinese pronunciations. For purposes of clarity, I have adopted one consistent spelling for each name in this book, but I have not changed how the names are rendered in the quotations from historical documents that appear in these pages.

For personal and organizational names, I have employed spellings used during the period covered in the book. Where known, the equivalent in Pinyin—the modern, standard, Mandarin-based romanization system for Chinese—is noted in the Dramatis Personae section that follows for people and in the Glossary and Gazetteer section at the end for organizations. For Chinese place-names, names of dynasties, and other terms, I have generally relied on Pinyin, exceptions being traditional renderings like "Hong Kong" and "Manchu" and Cantonese terms such as *boo how doy* and *pi gow*. These are listed with Pinyin equivalents in the Glossary. Both sections also include the standard Chinese characters associated with the Chinese names and terms, where known. Simplified characters were not yet in use during the period covered in the book.

DRAMATIS PERSONAE

All names appear in alphabetical order by presumed surname (or, if the surname is unclear, a given name). "Aliases" are listed for people called by more than one name or whose names were spelled in more than one way. Dates, organizational affiliations, standard Chinese characters, and Pinyin equivalents are provided where known.

Au Yang Ming (歐陽明; *Ouyang Ming*)
(1838–1902)
First Chinese consul in New York. Served between 1883 and 1886.

Joab H. Banton
(1869–1949)
New York County district attorney from 1922 to 1929.

Theodore A. Bingham
(1858–1934)
New York City commissioner of police from 1906 to 1909.

Charlie Boston (李觀長; *Li Guanzhang*)
(1863–1930)
On Leong officer convicted of conspiracy to smuggle opium in 1911 and imprisoned at the U.S. penitentiary in Atlanta. Alias: Lee Quon Jung. Affiliation: On Leong Tong.

Bow Kum (probably 包金; *Bao Jin*)
(1888–1909)
China-born consort whose brutal murder caused a 1909 war between the On Leong Tong and the Four Brothers' Society.

Nicholas Brooks
(1842–1925)
Captain of the Elizabeth Street Police Station from 1891 to 1892.

Emory R. Buckner
(1888–1941)
U.S. attorney for the Southern District of New York from 1925 to 1927.

Warry S. Charles
(1857–1915)
Senior Hip Sing functionary who headed the New York branch before decamping to Boston. Convicted of murder in the first degree in 1908. Affiliation: Hip Sing Tong.

Chin Jack Lem
(1884–1937)
On Leong kingpin who joined the Hip Sings and caused a multicity tong war in 1924. Affiliations: On Leong Tong, Hip Sing Tong.

Chin Lem
(1878–1914)
Laundryman who brought Bow Kum to New York and helped cause a 1909 war between the On Leong Tong and the Four Brothers' Society. Affiliation: On Leong Tong.

Tai Yow Chin
(1878–?)
First wife of Mock Duck.

Chu Fong (趙晃; *Zhao Huang*)
(1864–?)
Proprietor of the Doyers Street Chinese Theatre. Affiliations: On Leong Tong, Four Brothers' Society.

Chu Gong (趙昂; *Zhao Ang*)
(1869–1907)
On Leong Tong treasurer nearly assassinated by Hip Sing hatchet men in 1905. Aliases: Joe Gong, Ji Gong. Affiliation: On Leong Tong.

Chu Lock (趙樂; *Zhao Le*)
(1869–1919)
Gambling house owner who attacked Mock Duck in 1897 and who was sent to Boston in 1909 to hire hatchet men in the Four Brothers' War. Affiliations: On Leong Tong, Four Brothers' Society.

Thomas C. T. Crain
(1860–1942)
Court of General Sessions judge from 1906 to 1924; district attorney of New York County between 1930 and 1933.

Dong Fong
(1873–?)
Bayard Street merchant and interpreter charged with felonious assault in 1897 who pleaded guilty to wounding On Leong Lee Yu in 1905. Affiliation: Hip Sing Tong.

William Eggers
(1867–?)
Acting police captain who headed a bureau charged with investigating police corruption and who was given jurisdiction over Chinatown briefly in 1905.

Eng Hing
(1894–1915)
Hip Sing gunman convicted and executed for the 1912 killing of Lee Kay, Tom Lee's nephew. Affiliation: Hip Sing Tong.

Eng Ying Gong
(1885–after 1935)
National Hip Sing Tong officer who authored a tell-all book on the tong wars in 1930. Alias: Eddie Gong. Affiliation: Hip Sing Tong.

Richard E. Enright
(1871–1953)
Acting captain of the Elizabeth Street Police Station in 1910 and New York City commissioner of police from 1918 to 1925.

John L. Falconer
(1873–1945)
Captain of the Elizabeth Street Police Station from 1913 to 1915.

Ah Fee
(1857–1900)
Newark tailor murdered by Hip Sing operatives in New York in 1900. Affiliation: On Leong Tong.

Warren W. Foster
(1859–1943)
Court of General Sessions judge who mediated disputes between the tongs in 1906, 1910, and 1913.

Michael J. Galvin
(1870–1910)
Captain of the Elizabeth Street Police Station in 1909.

Gin Gum
(1863–1915)
Longtime right-hand man to Tom Lee and stepfather-in-law of Mock Duck. Aliases: Jim Gun, Charlie Lee. Affiliation: On Leong Tong.

Ha Oi
(1901–?)
Half-Caucasian adopted daughter of Mock Duck and Tai Yow Chin who was removed from their custody in 1907. Alias: Helen Francis.

William H. Hodgins
(1856–1912)
Captain of the Elizabeth Street Police Station in 1910. Alias: Big Bill Hodgins.

Ah Hoon
(1874–1909)
Chinese Theatre comedian shot to death in 1909. Affiliations: Four Brothers' Society, On Leong Tong.

Huie Fong
(1864–1905)
Hip Sing operative shot to death on Mott Street in 1905. Affiliation: Hip Sing Tong.

William T. Jerome
(1859–1934)
Associate counsel to the Lexow Committee between 1894 and 1895. New York County district attorney from 1902 to 1909.

Francis J. Kear
(1858–1908)
Captain of the Elizabeth Street Police Station between 1904 and 1905.

Ko Low
(1880–1922)
National president of the Hip Sing Tong in the early 1920s. Affiliation: Hip Sing Tong.

Lee Dock
(1882–1915)
Hip Sing gunman convicted and executed for the 1912 killing of Lee Kay, Tom Lee's nephew. Affiliation: Hip Sing Tong.

Frank William Lee (李錦綸; *Li Jinlun*)
(1884–1956)
Son of Tom and Minnie Lee. An ordained Baptist minister who immigrated to China, where he worked as a missionary and government official.

Lee Loy (李來; *Li Lai*)
(1860–?)
Secretary of the On Leong Tong and cousin of Tom Lee. Affiliation: On Leong Tong.

Minnie Rose Kaylor Lee
(1860–1917)
Tom Lee's wife, an American of Scotch-German extraction.

Lee Sing (利勝; *Li Sheng*)
(ca. 1848–after 1929)
Boardinghouse keeper who bested Tom Lee in a street brawl and testified against him in an extortion case. Affiliation: Hip Sing Tong.

Lee Sing
(ca. 1872–?)
Massachusetts laundryman who shot Mock Duck on Pell Street in 1904. Affiliation: On Leong Tong.

Tom Lee (李希齡; *Li Xiling*)
(ca. 1849–1918)
Merchant and longtime "mayor" of New York's Chinatown who headed the On Leong Tong and was a deputy sheriff of New York County. Alias: Wung Ah Ling. Affiliation: On Leong Tong.

Lee Toy (李彩; *Li Cai*)
(1852–after 1906)
Nephew of Tom Lee who served as his enforcer. Alias: Black Devil Toy. Affiliation: On Leong Tong.

Sam Lock
(1850–?)
President of the Four Brothers' Society. Affiliation: Four Brothers' Society.

William McAdoo
(1853–1930)
New York City commissioner of police from 1904 to 1906 and later chief of the city magistrates' courts. Defended the police department against sniping from the Parkhurst Society.

Thomas L. McClintock
(1865–after 1940)
Longtime superintendent of the Parkhurst Society, Hip Sing ally, and critic of the New York Police Department.

John H. McCullagh Jr.
(1842–1893)
Captain of the Elizabeth Street Police Station between 1883 and 1891.

Douglas Imrie McKay
(1879–1962)
New York City commissioner of police for five months between 1913 and 1914.

Mock Duck (麥德; *Mai De*)
(1879–1941)
Head of the Hip Sing Tong, with a reputation for cunning and brutality. Aliases: Mock Sai Wing, Mark Tuck. Affiliation: Hip Sing Tong.

Frank Moss
(1860–1920)
Attorney and reformer who served the Parkhurst Society, the Lexow Committee, and the district attorney's office. Champion of, and sometime counsel for, the Hip Sing Tong.

Edward P. Mulrooney
(1874–1960)
New York City commissioner of police from 1930 to 1933.

Reverend Dr. Charles H. Parkhurst
(1842–1933)
Presbyterian minister and social reformer who headed the Society for the Prevention of Crime and launched an attack on Tammany Hall and government corruption.

Eugene A. Philbin
(1857–1920)
District attorney of New York County between 1900 and 1901.

Edmund E. Price
(1834–1907)
Attorney who represented Tom Lee and other On Leong Tong defendants.

Dominick Riley
(1874–1930)
Captain of the Elizabeth Street Police Station in 1913.

Theodore Roosevelt
(1858–1919)
New York City commissioner of police from 1895 to 1897 and governor of New York State from 1899 to 1900. Later vice president and president of the United States.

Sin Cue
(1862–1901)
Suspect in a 1900 murder and potential witness against Mock Duck before his own assassination. Affiliation: On Leong Tong.

Sing Dock
(1862–1911)
Hip Sing gunman involved in massacres in New York and Boston. Alias: the Scientific Killer. Affiliation: Hip Sing Tong.

Meihong Soohoo (司徒美堂; *Situ Meitang*)
(1868–1955)
Founder of the Boston chapters of the Chee Kung Tong and the On Leong Tong and longtime national president of the On Leong Tong.

Sue Sing
(1861–after 1914)
Gunman condemned to life in prison for the 1900 murder of Ah Fee. Affiliation: Hip Sing Tong.

Joseph C. Thoms (譚作舟; *Tan Zuozhou*)
(1861–1929)
Chinese physician and courtroom interpreter who worked with police to crack down on Chinatown gambling. Alias: Tom Ah Jo.

Frank A. Tierney
(1869–1936)
Captain of the Elizabeth Street Police Station from 1911 to 1913.

Patrick J. Tracy
(1867–1926)
Captain of the Elizabeth Street Police Station from 1905 to 1906.

Tuck Hop (黃天; *Huang Tian*)
(1855–?)
Mott Street grocer and early antagonist of Tom Lee's. Alias: Wong Tin. Affiliation: Hip Sing Tong.

Rhinelander Waldo
(1877–1927)
New York City deputy commissioner of police from 1906 to 1910 and commissioner of police from 1911 to 1913.

James Wang
(1848–?)
Former Methodist lay reader and high-ranking Hip Sing functionary. Alias: Jim Wang. Affiliation: Hip Sing Tong.

Charles S. Whitman
(1868–1947)
Magistrate who became district attorney of New York County between 1910 and 1914 and later governor of New York.

Wo Kee
(1849–?)
Early Chinatown merchant and community leader. Aliases: Wong Ah Chung, Wong Achon.

Wong Aloy
(1868–1922)
Hip Sing who provided information on Chinatown vice to the Committee of Fifteen. Affiliation: Hip Sing Tong.

Wong Chin Foo (王清福; *Wang Qingfu*)
(1847–1898)
Chinese American journalist, editor, lecturer, and social activist. Close ally of Tom Lee's.

Wong Get (黃傑; *Huang Jie*)
(1869–after 1927)
Hip Sing strategist, merchant, and interpreter who testified against Tom Lee before the Lexow Committee. Alias: Wong Gett. Affiliation: Hip Sing Tong.

Yee Toy (余才; *Yu Cai*)
(?–1912)
Hip Sing gunman indicted for the 1906 murders of two On Leongs and involved in the massacres at the Chinese Theatre and Oxford Place, Boston. Alias: Girl Face. Affiliation: Hip Sing Tong.

Robert Young
(1836–1898)
Acting captain, and then captain, of the Elizabeth Street Police Station between 1895 and 1898.

Frances Toy Yuen
(1894–1945)
Second wife of Mock Duck.

TONG WARS

Chapter 1

An "Army of Almond-Eyed Exiles"

New York's Chinese colony was just finding its permanent home in lower Manhattan when Tom Lee arrived in 1878. Although small numbers of Chinese immigrants had reached New York earlier in the century, they began to come in a steady stream only after 1869, when work was completed on the transcontinental railroad and the laborers had to look elsewhere for work. The flow increased dramatically throughout the 1870s, because many white men out west, hobbled by economic recession and threatened by cheap Chinese labor, took to doing whatever they could to make the Chinese among them feel unwelcome and unsafe.

When California enacted laws in the late 1870s preventing Chinese from working in public projects and authorizing municipalities to relocate Chinese residents outside their city limits, and hoodlums in Washington, Oregon, Wyoming, California, and elsewhere in the West attacked Chinese businesses and homes in the 1880s, Chinese got the message. Many returned to China, but others headed east, where work might be found and where there was little violence against their kind. Most set their sights on the larger cities of the Midwest and the East like Chicago, St. Louis, Philadelphia, Baltimore, and Boston. New York, America's largest and most important metropolis, was the favorite destination.

The New York that greeted these new arrivals was developing briskly. Heady economic growth had followed the recession, though its rewards were distributed unevenly among the city's million residents. The ruling class, in their tony Murray Hill and Gramercy Park mansions, occupied themselves with lavish parties, fashion, theater, and tours of Europe. The working class, far more numerous, crowded into the tenements of the Fourth Ward—lower Manhattan's East River waterfront—and the Sixth Ward's Five Points neighborhood, named for an irregular intersection where Anthony (now Worth), Orange (now Baxter), and Cross (now Mosco) streets converged and which was notorious for its saloons, gambling halls, cathouses, and gang wars. Newly arrived Chinese, their numbers still minuscule, joined Irish, English, Jewish, Italian, and German immigrants and blacks in a struggle for survival in a quarter known for vice, crime, and grinding poverty.

There was bias against all newcomers, but the Chinese were in a class by themselves. Although they were not widely viewed in New York as an economic threat, it didn't take long for anti-Chinese stereotypes, honed in California, to make their way eastward. Chinese were derided in the press as inferior, dishonest, immoral, indecent, unsanitary, and disease-ridden. They were called clannish and criticized for their unwillingness to assimilate—as if they were in any way welcome to do so. They were godless heathens with sordid habits, it was said, like smoking opium and eating rats and dogs. These very prejudices led Congress to pass the Chinese Exclusion Act in 1882, halting further immigration of Chinese laborers for ten years and rendering those Chinese already here ineligible for citizenship.

In Manhattan, many early migrants were met at the railway station or pier by Wo Kee, a Hong Kong–born merchant who delivered them by horse-drawn coach over rutted streets to 34 Mott Street. There he ran a general store and a boardinghouse with accommodations for two dozen men sleeping two to a bunk. There he briefed new arrivals on life and business opportunities in New York. And there they might remain until they got established.

Wo Kee—his real name was Wong Ah Chung, but he was popularly known by the name of his store—was the de facto leader of the tiny Chinese community when Tom Lee arrived. In 1873, at age twenty-four, Wo Kee had staked out the predominantly Irish neighborhood south of Canal Street that would become the permanent home of Manhattan's Chinese community. There was little to recommend the unsavory district, but rents were cheap.

Wo Kee's shop carried just about everything a Chinese émigré might need. His front parlor, chock-full of merchandise, could barely accommodate four customers at a time. Waxen ducks, desiccated mushrooms, nuts, sweetmeats, dried sharks' fins, and a variety of teas filled his shelves, barrels, and crates. Pasteboard boxes spilled over with seeds, roots, herbs, and barks, remedies for various ailments that gave the place a decidedly pungent odor. But there were also sweet-smelling incense sticks and altars for use at funerals and religious rituals. Jade bracelets, sandals, Chinese garments, porcelain teapots, tobacco, opium pipes—and opium itself—rounded out his inventory. The sallow-skinned, mustachioed Wo Kee, a stout man who stood five feet four and spoke reasonably good English, served tea to all comers, totaled purchases on an abacus, and kept his accounts with a writing brush.

Out of the same location, he also ran an underground gambling parlor and a mutual aid association called the Polong Congsee (which probably translates as "Conscientious Protection Company"). One of a pair of benevolent societies serving the small community, it collected dues and met monthly in his basement. Boasting seventy-five members and assets of several thousand dollars, the Polong Congsee functioned in part as an immigrant depot, helping newcomers open laundries or secure other employment.

In 1875, state census takers had enumerated only 157 Chinese in all of New York City, and the federal census five years later still tallied fewer than 1,000 in the entire state. This was likely a severe case of undercounting, however. The *New York Times* was probably closer to the mark in its 1880 estimate of 4,500 Chinese in the metropolitan area: about 2,000 in Manhattan, another 1,000 in Brooklyn, and 1,500 in New Jersey.

The discrepancy arose because census takers found it especially problematic to get an accurate count. A *New York Herald* reporter gave a flavor for the obstacles: "A person unacquainted in the district might easily enough ask one of the Chinamen all the questions, and then, ten minutes afterward, meeting the same Celestial in another house, innocently endeavor to repeat the examination." This was true, he explained, because "they all look alike"—a generalization with which most New Yorkers would have readily agreed. Then, too, Chinese crowded a lot more people into a given dwelling than did other immigrants. It would have taken several trips to any given address and a good measure of patience and perseverance to interview all of its residents.

Most of New York's Chinese lived in boardinghouses. Some had been built as tenements, with their cheerless railroad flats and gloomy hallways, jammed up against one another without so much as a narrow alley in between to let in a little light. Others had once been stately private residences but had deteriorated over time. Enterprising landlords fitted high-ceilinged rooms with makeshift, intermediate floors, doubling their profits even as they turned their properties into firetraps. Front rooms were typically given over to retail businesses, while rear chambers, attics, and cellars were used for housing. Many men could sleep, cook, and eat in one large, unheated dormitory, rudely furnished with a stove, a table, stools, and rows of shelves that served as bunks, some wide enough to accommodate three sleepers.

Most of the early arrivals had been peasants or small shopkeepers in China, and most intended to make some money in America and then return home to a comfortable retirement. Many were literate in their own language, but few spoke much English, so even if they had not been shut out by white Americans, they had no choice but to fraternize exclusively with other Chinese. As a rule, they had little to do with outsiders and lived, ate, slept, and relaxed with their own kind. They dressed in traditional Chinese robes, blouses, flowing pantaloons, and wooden-soled slippers ill-suited to New York's muddy streets. And they sported the signature hair queues worn at the time by all men in China. They could scarcely have appeared more foreign to their New York neighbors.

Diligent laborers with few deadbeats among them, the Chinese were closely associated with the laundry business, which permitted a hard worker to put away $10 to $14 per week, about what an average white grocery clerk or letter carrier made. None of these men would have dreamed of washing clothes back in China; there it would have been a job for their women. But it was an occupation that needed little capital—they could set up shop for as little as $75—and it did not put them in competition with white males, which would have spelled trouble. By 1879, the city already boasted more than three hundred Chinese laundries.

But Chinese worked in other trades as well. Skilled cigar makers—not a few of whom had logged time as coolies in Cuba's tobacco fields before sailing to New York—found employment in tenement cigar factories. They were paid by the piece and could take home as much as $27 a week. More than seventy-five Chinese worked as domestics and were paid $18 to $25 a month plus room and board. Fifty Chinese-run groceries, twenty tobacco shops, ten drugstores, and six Chinese restaurants were operating in the Chinese quarter in 1879. And these didn't include enterprises in Brooklyn or New Jersey.

By early 1880, Chinese had leased nearly every building—sixteen in total—on lower Mott Street, just up from Chatham Square. But the influx of what the *New York Herald* called an "army of almond-eyed exiles" arriving from the West—at the rate of twenty per day, by one count—soon overtaxed the boardinghouses. More space was needed, but there was opposition to expansion of "Little China."

When the Rutgers Fire Insurance Company was offered a large advance on the rent for a property it owned at 3 Mott, the company asserted that it would sooner pull the building down than allow a "Chinaman" to live in it. The owner of two cramped houses on nearby Pell Street refused $60 a month from a would-be Chinese tenant, even though the properties had not previously fetched anywhere near that amount. And another Mott Street landlord vowed to allow his property to sit idle rather than accept a generous offer of $1,000 for the year from a Chinese.

In May, Chinese tenants in five of the quarter's residences—including 34 Mott, which housed Wo Kee's establishment—suddenly received eviction notices. The landlords blamed opium-smoking Chinese for the fact that their properties' market value had plummeted and vowed to enjoin future lessees from subletting to Chinese or to blacks. When an offer by the Polong Congsee to buy two of the buildings was refused, Wo Kee tore down his sign, packed up his wares, and headed for nearby Park Street. In due course, however, he would be back, and he would bring his countrymen with him.

Tom Lee, a crafty man with no small level of ambition, came to New York with four goals: to impose order and organization on its Chinese colonists; to build bridges for them to the white establishment; to make himself rich and successful; and to start a family. He saw no conflict among those objectives and wasted little time in pursuing all of them at once.

His name wasn't *actually* Tom Lee; that was just the identity the courtly emissary from San Francisco's more established Chinatown assumed shortly after his arrival. Born about 1849 near Guangzhou, Lee—slender at five feet six inches—had come to America at age fourteen. He had worked in San Francisco as a labor contractor, supplying white-owned companies with low-paid Chinese workers, and had ingratiated himself there with powerful figures in the Chinese community. He had readily picked up serviceable English, although it was always somewhat broken and he forever retained an accent. He was a man on the move, up the economic ladder and east across the continent.

By 1876, Lee had reached St. Louis, where he opened a barrel-making business and took out citizenship papers—one of the first Chinese in America to do so—under his original name, Wung Ah Ling. And after a short stint as a merchant in Philadelphia, he moved on to New York, where he petitioned Manhattan's Court of Common Pleas for a new moniker, explaining that Americans had too much trouble pronouncing the old one. The judge assented, and Wung Ah Ling became Tom Lee forever after.

Although Lee adopted Western dress earlier than most, he still sported a queue in the late 1870s, as did nearly all Chinese. The wearing of hair queues had been imposed on all Chinese males as a sign of subjugation when the Manchus, a minority tribe from the Northeast, conquered China and established the Qing dynasty in 1644. The penalty for noncompliance was death. After a couple of hundred years, however, the pigtails came, paradoxically, to be accepted as a symbol of national pride, and even many Chinese living abroad refused to part with them, especially if they expected to return home. To appear more Americanized, however, Lee tucked the long plait into the crown of a stiff derby hat, which caused the hair on the back of his head to stand out, someone once said, "like the quills of an angry porcupine."

The olive-skinned Lee wore a wispy mustache under his flat nose, and a sparse goatee obscured his pointy chin. Dapper, urbane, and distinguished looking, he dressed fashionably, a diamond stickpin securing his tie and an elegant, eight-ounce gold watch chain dangling from the third button of his waistcoat.

Just before coming to New York, Lee, nearing thirty, had wed the comely Minnie Rose Kaylor, a buxom Philadelphia brunette of Scotch-German heritage who was more than a decade younger and quite a bit larger than he was. Marriage between Chinese men and women of other races was unusual in this era, but it was not illegal. A Lutheran minister performed the ceremony, even though Lee was not baptized. He moved his new bride to 20 Mott Street shortly afterward, and they lost no time starting a family.

Minnie bore two daughters who died in infancy and then two sons— Tom junior in 1882 and Frank William in 1884. A huge celebration followed the birth of young Tom: *Two* traditions were honored, mirroring his mixed heritage. He was baptized and was feted at a "head shaving" party held, according to Chinese custom, thirty days after the birth of a male. The elder Lee did not stint on the festivities. On April 1, 1882, he closed both of his stores—he now had two of them—for a huge party.

It took two restaurants to accommodate the three hundred guests from Manhattan, Brooklyn, and New Jersey. Three diplomats from the Chinese legation made the journey from Washington; the local representatives of the Manchu government had an interest in seeing to it that there was order among their countrymen in America, so they wanted to signal their approval of Lee's assumption of the leadership of the New York colony. VIPs were entertained in the parlor of the Lee home, where banners inscribed with good wishes adorned the walls. Lee had also invited American friends, some of whom attended. But he received regrets from several who found the idea of a party to celebrate a haircut so odd that they mistook the invitation for an April Fools' joke.

Tom Lee's arrival in New York had been no accident. He had been sent there by the Six Companies, San Francisco Chinatown's supreme governing body. A fraternal organization that sat at the apex of Chinese society in the United States, it was, as its name implied, an umbrella group of about half a dozen associations.

From the moment they arrived in America, Chinese immigrants organized mutual aid societies, which fell into three broad categories. The first type—regional societies—consisted of organizations set up by and for people from a specific district in China who spoke a common dialect. Men from Taishan, for example, who made up the majority of Chinese residents, generally belonged to the Ning Yeung Society. Those from three counties nearer Guangzhou joined the Sam Yup Benevolent Association.

The second category was clan societies, where membership was available to Chinese from anywhere who happened to share a surname and were thus presumed to be kin. Most everyone named Moy paid dues to the Moy Family Association, for example, and there were similar circles for the Lee, Wong, Ng, and other families with sufficient numbers to sustain them. In one case, four numerically small clans came together under one umbrella to form the Four Brothers' Society.

Membership in both the regional and the clan organizations was close to automatic. These groups established New York chapters as soon as the city had a critical mass of landsmen. Dues were used to help new immigrants get settled, find housing, and get established in business. The associations made loans to aspiring businessmen and provided bail and legal fees for any who got arrested. They offered protection from harm and mediated disputes among their members. And they also served immigrants in death, organizing funerals and providing welfare for their families. In due course, when resources permitted, the bones of departed members would be exhumed, scraped clean, and shipped home to be reinterred with those of their ancestors.

The third category consisted of sworn brotherhoods generally known by the term "tong," meaning "chamber," with no geographic or family requirements and generally with fewer members. Sometimes called triads and sometimes secret societies, these were open to Chinese from anywhere who paid dues and underwent initiation. Although they, too, were ostensibly benevolent associations and some of their services overlapped with those of the regional and clan groups, they came to be associated with a variety of underworld activities.

The Six Companies was the congress of the major regional societies, and it stepped in when issues crossed jurisdictional lines. Its chairmanship rotated among its member associations, and its authority derived in part from a clever arrangement struck with the Pacific Mail Steamship Company, the dominant transpacific shipping line. Pacific Mail required certification from the Six Companies that a would-be return passenger had paid his dues to one of its constituent groups and had discharged all his debts before it would sell him a ticket home. Most Chinese in America were thus stuck there until the Six Companies cleared them for departure.

Later known as the Chinese Consolidated Benevolent Association (Chung Hwa Gong Shaw) and more or less overseen by Chinese diplomats, the organization also served as the voice of the Chinese community and, inevitably, as a lightning rod for criticism of the Chinese. Its role was much misunderstood by white America. It was accused, among other things, of ordering the execution of malefactors and of importing Chinese coolies to work at slave wages. In truth, the Six Companies played a constructive role in maintaining peace and order in San Francisco and other American cities where Chinese settled. It had already begun to speak out on the single biggest issue they faced: the prospect of legislation to exclude them.

In the late 1870s, the leading lights of New York's nascent Chinese colony had petitioned the Six Companies to send an emissary to Manhattan. They wanted someone who could provide the young community with services already available to Chinese in California and elsewhere: governance, discipline, protection, and representation. The assignment was given to Tom Lee, whose relationships with the group's bosses dated to his stint in California. With their backing, he assumed leadership of New York's Chinese upon his arrival.

That most local Chinese accepted his authority stemmed from a strong penchant for hierarchy on their part. Chinese in America naturally sought to re-create communal structures familiar from the old country, where rank had always been important. The men's strong sense of social order dictated that someone play the part the village patriarch had played in China. This involved providing leadership, settling differences, presiding over ceremonies, solving problems, and looking out for the general welfare.

Tom Lee relished the role and established himself in grand style. He rented 20 Mott Street, occupying the entire three-story, brick residence—an unheard-of amount of space for a Chinese family. He decorated the house with plush carpets and rosewood furniture, large porcelain vases, colorful Chinese paintings, and even a piano. The quarters were intended to be impressive and to serve not just as a home but as a symbol of power and prestige.

No sooner had Lee settled into lower Mott Street than he began his outreach to New York's white power elite. The Six Companies had been doing the same in San Francisco for more than a decade. Late one August afternoon in 1878, he hosted a dinner for Edmund E. Price, a well-known criminal attorney; Colonel George H. Hart, Price's partner; and a *New York Herald* reporter. Also present was Wong Chin Foo, a lecturer and journalist who was a prominent member of New York's Chinese colony, a fluent English speaker, and already a good friend of Lee's. Always gracious, the soft-spoken Lee produced fine cigars from a humidor and ushered his guests to a table laid with "snowy napkins and silver service that would not have disgraced a *petit souper* on Murray Hill," the reporter later wrote.

Lee pulled out all the stops. He greeted guests on the front stoop in a high silk hat and engaged two white maids to serve tea and slice bread; male Chinese servants prepared and served the food. A roast suckling pig nestled in herbs was brought to the table, followed by sauces, salads, stewed chicken, fruit, and cake. Lee himself provided musical entertainment; he sang and accompanied himself on two traditional Chinese instruments. And he hosted more American guests at an even more lavish repast at the dawn of the Year of the Rabbit early in 1879. The *New York Herald* dazzled its readers by publishing the entire menu.

Tom Lee quickly became the spokesman for the Chinese colony. In November 1878, he opined to a New York *Sun* reporter on the virtues of citizenship for Chinese, naming several who had already naturalized. The following January, he sounded a similar theme with a *New York Telegram* reporter. He dismissed Chinese who returned home as "disappointed and homesick," noting proudly, if not grammatically, that "this country good enough for me."

Indeed it was. Tom Lee was home. He had an American wife and no intention of ever living in his native land again.

It didn't take long for Lee to realize that if he wanted to build bridges to New York's politically powerful, most roads led to Tammany Hall. The Society of St. Tammany—named for a leader of the Native American Lenape tribe—had gotten its start as a social and fraternal organization in the late eighteenth century and had dominated New York politics since the middle of the nineteenth century. Over time, it had developed into a well-oiled political machine that kept Democrats of its choosing in power in the city and sometimes the state. Through an intricate system of political patronage and kickbacks, Tammany bosses had acquired functional control over government, and they used it for many decades to lucrative advantage.

Tammany Hall's hold on power depended on securing enough votes on Election Day to keep its candidates in office, thus enabling them to profiteer from public works projects, offer employment, dole out gifts to friends and allies, and bribe political rivals. Once a nativist movement, it had begun to reach out to the growing number of immigrants from Europe, especially Ireland and later Italy, who were flooding the city. Many were unemployed, broke and desperate, and more than willing to pledge their loyalty to whoever would provide them with a livelihood.

Earning their allegiance required a complex grassroots organization able to reach deeply into the city's neighborhoods. Ward bosses oversaw a network of precinct captains who built relationships with the families in their jurisdictions. Many were first- or second-generation immigrants themselves who could speak with newcomers in their native tongues. They helped new arrivals secure food, clothing, shelter, and jobs, either with government or with companies beholden to the bosses. They also assisted in securing emergency loans and solving minor legal problems. Most important, they facilitated immigrants' applications for citizenship, which, of course, was necessary to turn them into voters. In exchange for all of this, those who received patronage were expected to vote the Tammany ticket. It was the responsibility of those same captains to make certain that the men showed up at the polls for city, state, and even federal elections and knew exactly whom to choose. They also stuffed ballot boxes when necessary.

Chinese were not of much interest to the machine in this regard because most could not vote, and after 1882 the Exclusion Act ensured that they couldn't become citizens. But there were other ways Chinese could support friends in the political firmament, and Tom Lee soon figured them out. The most obvious was through offering financial support, which he did regularly. Another involved hosting grand outings worthy of any Tammany boss.

On September 15, 1881, he arranged a picnic on Staten Island for fifty of his countrymen and a handful of invited guests. Among the white guests were some powerful figures: Maurice Hyland, a saloon keeper and Sixth Ward party boss; James Cowan, a well-connected civil and criminal attorney; and the Fourth District Court judge John A. Dinkel, who routinely heard cases involving Chinese claimants and defendants.

The guests assembled on Mott Street, festooned with flags to mark the occasion. As a bugler from New York's Sixty-ninth Infantry Regiment sounded a call, everyone boarded horse-drawn coaches. The parade proceeded to the Battery without incident, save some heckling from lower-class whites, who derided the Chinese travelers loudly as "haythen" and "yaller rat eaters." When they arrived at the pier, the police held back other passengers to allow the Chinese to board the ferry together.

They arrived to a Western breakfast of ham and eggs, clam fritters, fried eel, potatoes, bread, and coffee, and—with a bit of instruction from the American guests—the Chinese consumed it with knives and forks, in what the *New York Times* approvingly deemed "a thoroughly Christian manner." There was swimming, a tug-of-war, and a hundred-yard race: Lee, playing the patriarch, awarded a $2.50 prize to each winner. There was music from Chinese percussion, wind, and stringed instruments. A caricature artist sketched attendees. And those who had brought opium wafers partook of the narcotic with impunity. After dinner, the guests departed for home, where they were welcomed by an explosion of Chinese firecrackers and Roman candles.

Truth, a New York daily, hailed the event as a signal that New York's Chinese were learning to do and act as Americans: "Not only are they assuming the manners of Americans, but they are rapidly becoming thorough New Yorkers."

And, indeed, many were. In at least *some* sense of the term.

Lee quickly eclipsed Wo Kee as head of the Chinese colony, and early in 1880 he established a new organization. The Loon Yee Tong, whose name translates as the "Chamber United in Friendship," was part trade union, part social club, part fraternity, and part political advocacy group. Although it was portrayed to the outside world as a Chinese Masonic lodge, in no sense was it organically related to traditional Freemasonry. It was, however, an outgrowth of a venerable Chinese institution. The Loon Yee Tong was the New York incarnation of a much larger and older organization sometimes called the Hongmen.

The Hongmen had gotten its start in China early in the Qing dynasty as a sworn brotherhood cum gang of outlaws committed to restoring the earlier Ming dynasty, which had been Chinese rather than Manchu ruled. It had arrived in North America with the earliest Chinese immigrants. It went by different names in different cities: it was known as the Chee Kung Tong, or "Chamber of Universal Justice," in San Francisco and elsewhere in California and by the turn of the century would assume that name in New York as well.

Broadly speaking, the Loon Yee Tong served fraternal functions in the Chinese community similar to those of the Freemasons or the Elks. It charged an initiation fee of $10 and levied annual dues of $5. Within days, 150 men had signed up, and within a month it had amassed several thousand dollars. A year later its membership doubled to 300, and it had entirely eclipsed Wo Kee's Polong Congsee. But there were apparently no hard feelings; Wo Kee would become a staunch Lee ally.

The Loon Yee Tong soon occupied sumptuous quarters at 18 Mott. Its "Joss" Hall—the term, a corruption of the Portuguese *deus,* meaning "God," described a Chinese idol—was decorated with banners and Chinese paintings, including one of Confucius and one of the emperor. At one end stood a shrine, ten feet high and six feet wide, with an altar where offerings to Guan Gong, a virtuous third-century general and hero, were made on certain days of the month and important Chinese festivals and whenever someone needed divine intervention in a life event or good fortune for an evening of gambling.

Rooms in the rear were given over to members in need, whether ill or out of work. Because nearly two-thirds of the fellows were laundrymen, the organization paid special attention to their interests. Its bylaws, for example, did not permit any member to start a laundry within two city blocks of an establishment owned by a brother.

Like all Hongmen chapters, the Loon Yee Tong had secret rites. Initiations involved suspending a sword over a neophyte's head as he recited thirty-six oaths of allegiance. The candidate's finger was pricked and a drop of his blood spilled into a cup of wine, which was then drunk by all to symbolize his admission into a blood brotherhood. And a rooster was ritually decapitated as an illustration of what would befall him if he broke his oath to obey tong leaders without question. Loyalty and obedience were valued above all else.

From the start, it was clear that the Loon Yee Tong would also have a political agenda. One officer predicted to a *New York Herald* reporter that "before the next Presidential election we will have over five hundred Chinese voters in New York, and then we can speak not only as residents, but as citizens." His dream was not to be realized, however, because in 1882 the passage of the Chinese Exclusion Act ended any further naturalization of Chinese.

Shortly after the Loon Yee Tong was established came a startling announcement: Under Sheriff John B. Sexton, a powerful Tammany Hall figure, had appointed Tom Lee a deputy sheriff of New York County. Lee's relationship-building efforts had paid off handsomely: he had asked for—and certainly *paid* for—the nomination. Although not a member of the police department, a deputy sheriff was a civil law enforcement officer authorized to make arrests, issue summonses, and carry firearms, and the appointment was ostensibly made to help keep order in Chinatown, where Chinese were sometimes taunted and assaulted by Americans and where fights occasionally broke out among the residents themselves.

Lee was the first Chinese to hold *any* government office, appointive or elective, in New York's history. And he wore his new title, quite literally, as a badge of honor, affixed to his suspenders. The *New York Herald* reported that "the Celestials are delighted over the success of his application, and feel sure that they will not be molested in their own neighborhood."

But not all of New York's "Celestials"—a term that meant "Chinese people"—were so delighted with one of their own strutting around flashing a badge. Vesting so much power in one individual—first by the Six Companies and now by municipal authorities—caused resentment, and it did not take long for the new deputy sheriff to be tested. Soon after he took office, a fight broke out in a gambling house at 17 Mott after a sailor claimed to have been cheated out of $2.50. He appealed to a local boardinghouse keeper named Lee Sing for help, and the dispute quickly grew into a general riot that spilled out onto Mott Street.

Tom Lee, named deputy sheriff of New York County in 1880, was the first Chinese to hold any government office, appointive or elective, in New York's history.

The two beat policemen stationed nearby were unequal to the task of breaking up the brawl, so when one spied the new deputy sheriff, he called on him for assistance. Aided by Loon Yee Tong members, Tom Lee attempted to restore order, but he and several others were knocked to the pavement by Lee Sing, a bulky man with a considerable weight advantage. He blackened both of Tom's eyes and kicked him as he fell.

The police overcame and arrested Lee Sing, but the Court of General Sessions later acquitted him of felonious assault, infuriating Tom Lee. Irritated at the lack of respect shown him and his position, he sued Lee Sing for $10,000 in damages. It was highly unusual to involve civil authorities

in an altercation between two Chinese; such disputes were normally adjudicated within the Chinese community. But because Tom Lee *was* the authority within the community, he was hardly in a position to mediate.

When the case was heard, both the plaintiff and the accused appeared
in court in Western dress. The New York *Sun* noted that the portly Lee Sing
was as big as *two* Tom Lees. Lee Sing persuaded the jury he had acted in
what he believed was self-defense. He not only won the case; the judge
assessed Tom Lee $100 to cover Lee Sing's legal fees.

Although no one could have known it at the time, Lee Sing's assault
was the first blow dealt between the two Chinatown factions that would
eventually become the Hip Sing Tong and the On Leong Tong.

There was nothing professional about the New York Police Department of
the 1880s. There were no accepted hiring standards beyond the requirements that officers be citizens of the United States, residents of the state
for at least a year, and free of criminal convictions. The longshoremen,
teamsters, and other blue-collar workers who became officers, many of whom
were Irish immigrants, were not well educated, but they were well connected, because it took a politician to appoint them. The job of policeman
was much sought after; for most, it was considered a step up in the world.
By the mid-1880s, recruits were required to submit to examination by a
board before they could be hired, but it still took a $250 payment to a local
politician to seal the deal.

New York's police were governed by a board of four Tammany-approved
commissioners. These were appointed by the mayor with the advice and
consent of the Common Council—later the Board of Aldermen—for stag-
gered terms of six years and were paid $5,000 per year. One superinten-
dent, 4 inspectors, 34 captains, 126 sergeants, 142 roundsmen, more than
2,000 patrolmen, and 73 doormen made up the force. The city was divided
into thirty precincts led by captains, each under the jurisdiction of an inspector.

There were also detectives, twenty-five at headquarters and one to four
in each precinct, who investigated crimes. Like roundsmen and patrolmen,
detectives earned $800 per year. Sergeants, assigned four to a precinct,
earned $1,250 annually; captains were paid $1,800 and inspectors $3,000.

Police officers were a step above longshoremen and on their way toward middle-class wages. Neither seniority nor merit brought salary adjustments; promotion was the only path to a raise.

The commissioners exercised broad powers over internal discipline, appointments, and promotions. They also had charge of the Bureau of Elections and the power to choose election inspectors and poll clerks. Both sets of responsibilities offered myriad opportunities for graft and abuse, however, and it was well understood that the department was corrupt, from the commissioners on down. In 1875, a select committee of the state assembly had found that

> one of the greatest difficulties experienced in procuring an efficient Police has been . . . the continual intermeddling of politicians with the government of the force. Patrolmen have generally been appointed through political influence; promotions have been made on the same ground, and even details for duty have frequently been regulated in the same manner.

Tammany Hall demanded standard fees for promotions, payable to political bosses. An officer could become a roundsman for $300; a roundsman could advance to sergeant for $1,600, and a sergeant to captain for $12,000 to $15,000. Because such payments were normally beyond the reach of the individuals involved, many of whom struggled just to make ends meet, most of those hopeful of advancement had to find backers to raise money.

The obvious sponsors, apart from friends and family, were the merchants who operated within their jurisdictions. They had the most to gain from good relations with local police, and those with resources were often willing to "invest" in a promotion or were pressured into doing so. Payback was expected not only in cash over time but also in other ways. When the lenders were gambling bosses, saloon owners, or brothel keepers who operated outside the law, they expected to be permitted to continue to do so on a wink and a nod.

Looking the other way was easy for a new sergeant or a captain. Raising the money to repay lenders was more challenging. An accepted way to amass funds was to shake down smaller merchants in exchange for "protection." In Chinatown, however, this was problematic because most Chinese couldn't speak English very well and no one on the force could speak Chinese. There was, therefore, a gap between the police and the Chinese merchants. Whoever filled it would be well positioned for lucrative rewards.

The idea was not lost on Tom Lee.

Chapter 2

The Gamblers' Union

Tom Lee's businesses in San Francisco, St. Louis, and Philadelphia had earned him enough to rent and furnish his first New York home at 20 Mott. By 1880, he had also leased buildings at 2 and 4 Mott Street, where he opened a variety store and a tobacco shop and sublet the rest of the space. With Chinatown growing quickly, his businesses—legitimate and otherwise—prospered over the next several years, and by 1883 his net worth was estimated at $200,000.

Even if that was an exaggeration, he had amassed enough to *purchase*, rather than simply rent, real estate in the nascent Chinese quarter. In 1880, when four Mott Street properties had become available, only the Polong Congsee, a collective, had had the resources to make an offer on them. But by 1883, at least four Chinese capitalists, Lee among them, were in a position to buy property in their own right, albeit with mortgages.

In early April, it was suddenly announced that Wo Kee—who had started with $10 but was now worth an estimated $150,000—had bought 8 Mott for $8,500. Other Chinese merchants bought No. 10 for a similar amount and No. 15 for $5,000. Tom Lee purchased the best property—No. 18—for a princely $14,500.

All these premises were occupied by Chinese storekeepers, restaurateurs, laundrymen, and cigar makers who immediately became alarmed. They saw in this rash of furtive activity a scheme to drive them out of business, believing the purchasers to be clearing the way to establish their own shops. And sure enough, lessees soon received notice to accept a 40 percent rent increase or vacate by May 1.

The day after the announcement, the tenants met to decide on a course of action. Wong Tin—known by the name of his business, Tuck Hop— was one of the organizers, even though his grocery at No. 17 was not affected. Although he would not speak openly about what was decided—he was no fan of Tom Lee's, but neither he nor anyone else dared take Lee on publicly—the group had resolved to fight the move in court and had raised $3,000 for legal defense.

When the new landlords heard this, they realized they had overplayed their hand, and they attempted to calm the angry tenants at a meeting of their own. The matter was ostensibly settled according to a principle laid down by the Six Companies in San Francisco: whenever premises occupied by Chinese were purchased by another Chinese, rent was to remain unchanged for a full year.

But in fact nothing was really settled at all. Despite the agreement, the frightened lessees went ahead and retained counsel. And their attorney, Charles Meyers, went to the authorities with a broadside against Tom Lee. Meyers accused Lee of extortion, alleging he had abused his deputy sheriff position by shaking down Chinatown gambling houses. Lee, Meyers said, was collecting $5 per week for each *fan tan* table as a "license fee," the quid pro quo being that the establishments would not be molested by the police, with whom Lee was sharing the receipts. Meyers asserted that Lee earned between $12,000 and $20,000 per year from thirty-seven such establishments. To corroborate his charges, he filed fifteen affidavits by Chinese merchants with the district attorney's office. And for good measure, he accused Lee of running a gambling house of his own.

In Tammany-era New York, police were *assumed* to be on the take. But such accusations had never been aired publicly about Tom Lee, and they constituted the first serious challenge to his rule. Before the month of April was over, his deputy sheriff commission was revoked.

Although the threat of eviction had been the apparent trigger, the men of Chinatown had other reasons to be wary of the rise of Lee and the other merchants. Some were suspicious of any who could speak English well; such people could improve their lots with the white establishment in numerous ways at the expense of their language-challenged brethren. Others were envious, believing Lee and his cronies to have prospered on the backs of their countrymen and to be intent on squeezing them out. The New York *Sun* went so far as to tar Tom Lee as "the Chinese Jay Gould."

Meyers handed a list of five "known" Chinatown gambling establishments to Captain Jeremiah Petty of the Sixth Precinct's Elizabeth Street Police Station, which had jurisdiction over Chinatown, and pressured him to shut them down. At least four—and probably all five—were properties owned by Tom Lee and his allies. A forty-two-year veteran with a reputation as a strict disciplinarian, Petty had been given command over the seventy-nine men of the brand-new station the year before, and a few days later he did order a raid on a Chinatown business. But it was Tuck Hop's at 17 Mott that was hit, not any of the houses on Meyers's list.

Meyers protested that Tuck Hop, one of his clients, had been compelled by Lee to pay $5 a week, even though he allegedly ran only a grocery store and played only dominoes for private amusement. According to Meyers, Tuck Hop had recently refused to make additional payments to Lee, which was why he was targeted by the police.

Both Tuck Hop and his friend Lee Sing, who was on the premises at the time of the bust, were arrested. The message was clear: Cross Tom Lee and you cross the New York City Police Department. And you do both at your peril.

If New York was a moral cesspool of gambling houses, saloons, brothels, and opium dens, it was not without those who wanted to clean it up. The late nineteenth century saw the formation of many organizations dedicated to leading sinners back to the light. One such group was the New York YMCA's Society for the Suppression of Vice. Chartered by the state legislature to "supervise the morality of the public," it was led by a zealot named Anthony Comstock. A do-gooder best known for agitating against pornography, premarital sex, and adultery, Comstock had taken affidavits from Tom Lee's accusers that corroborated Meyers's accusations. He claimed four had personally witnessed Lee accepting illegal payments.

Armed with these allegations, the New York County district attorney, John McKeon, put the matter before a grand jury. Among his charges were the following:

When Chinamen come to New York City and open businesses in Mott Street and vicinity, this man Tom Lee would go to them and say that he was a Deputy Sheriff and would show to them his badge of office. He would tell them that he knew all about the American law and advise them to open gambling places and that they would have the right to do so provided they paid him five dollars a week in advance for every Fan Tan and other gambling table they would use. He told them that for this payment they would have a license and right to play and that as he was a deputy sheriff no one would molest them.

To defend himself, Lee enlisted his friends the attorneys Edmund E. Price and James Cowan, who in turn retained a former assistant district attorney and justice of the superior court. On April 25, the grand jury handed down an indictment against Lee and then adjourned, leaving it to the district attorney to work out the exact language.

While both sides waited for formal charges to be filed, they made their cases in the press. Lee implausibly disavowed any knowledge of gambling and asserted it was jealousy that motivated his detractors. He had made his money, he said, from his various businesses, all legitimate. He also reminded reporters of his own generosity toward his fellow Chinese: he regularly handled insurance and court matters for them, either free of charge or for whatever they could afford. Furthermore, he averred—disingenuously— that his rank as deputy sheriff had been of no value to him and had only exacerbated the enmity of his compatriots.

Meyers described his clients as "respectable Chinese merchants who desired to see all gambling done away with for the sake of the poorer classes of their countrymen who thus squandered their earnings," an assertion that also strains credulity, because these men would have had no issue with Tom Lee had they not been running illegal establishments of their own. It was a foreshadowing of the ruse the Hip Sing Tong would later use to recruit allies in its war against Lee's On Leong Tong.

On May 1, Lee was arraigned. He was accused of extorting money from the keepers of a gambling house at 17 Mott and of maintaining a betting parlor himself. The more serious charge—that he had paid off the police— was dropped for lack of evidence. The district attorney asked for $2,000 bail for each charge, but the judge fixed bond at just $750. Lee immediately dispatched a messenger to his bank and, when the funds were produced, handed the cash to the clerk and left the courtroom smiling. Tuck Hop and

Lee Sing, among his accusers, were also indicted for keeping gambling establishments. Both would continue to be thorns in Lee's side for years to come.

Then, on May 12, Ah Chung, who had also been arrested, confessed in writing to keeping an opium joint at 18 Mott Street—Tom Lee's building. He declared he had paid Lee $10 per month as a "license fee" and agreed to turn evidence to this effect. Ah Chung was no savory character; he had been arrested the previous year for keeping a brothel on Pell Street. But armed with this new accusation, Meyers went before the police court three days later to obtain a second warrant for Lee's arrest, and the case was heard the following day.

Meyers's delay proved costly, however, because in the intervening days Ah Chung experienced a change of heart. On the witness stand, he denied ever lodging a complaint against Tom Lee and maintained he had no idea why he was even in court that day.

Meyers angrily brandished Ah Chung's earlier affidavit and demanded, "Did you swear to the truth of this statement?"

"Yes, I did," the Chinese man replied.

"Has anybody representing Tom Lee seen you since you signed this affidavit?"

Ah Chung replied that no one had seen him or spoken with him about the matter.

"Did Lung Chung speak to you about it?"

"I don't know those who spoke to me," he replied, glancing at Lee and contradicting himself.

Ah Chung explained that anything to which he might have attested was said because Meyers told him that doing so would get him out of trouble. According to the *New York Times,* someone had warned him that if he testified he had ever paid a cent to Tom Lee, Lee would "make it hot for him." With Ah Chung recanting, the case against Lee fell apart, and the judge had no choice but to dismiss the indictment.

One upshot of the whole affair was that Lee moved his family uptown, out of Chinatown entirely. But the *Boston Herald*'s observation that "Tom has lost his badge . . . and his power in Chinatown is a thing of the past" would prove to be dead wrong on both counts.

❖   ❖   ❖   ❖   ❖

The attack on Tom Lee left Chinatown irretrievably divided. On June 6, 1883, a few weeks after the Manchu government established a New York consulate, some local Chinese entertained the new consul general, Au Yang Ming, at a dinner in the Chinese quarter. Although it was a lavish banquet, several merchants refused to attend, claiming it was an insult to invite the diplomat to Mott Street and that an uptown banquet would have been more appropriate. Six boycotters were named in the newspaper, including Wo Kee and Tom Lee.

In an interview with the *New York Herald,* however, the journalist Wong Chin Foo revealed that the dispute ran far deeper than the appropriate location for the reception. "Au Yang Ming . . . came to New York utterly ignorant of the fact that the Chinese here are divided into two factions, each one fighting bitterly against the other," he said. Wong was explicit in naming Tuck Hop and Lee Sing as heads of one and Tom Lee as the boss of the other.

Not all of Lee's Loon Yee Tong members were loyal to him, either. On July 15, there was a secret meeting to consider ousting him from the leadership, to no avail. But popular or unpopular, Lee continued to be a force to be reckoned with. He played a prominent role in the community, spoke for it to the outside world, and had close relations with the police and the political establishment. Newspapers quoted him as the "Mayor of Mott Street." He continued to look out for his allies and to discharge his responsibilities to those from whom he accepted payoffs, friend or not.

Those remunerations came not only from gambling bosses but also from those who ran bordellos and opium dens; most forms of vice existed in the Chinese quarter. Lee bailed out Chin Tin, whose wife ran a brothel into which young girls were allegedly lured and then drugged. Chin was no friend of Lee's, but he was being assessed $60 a month for police protection and was thus entitled to it. Lee also posted bond when Wo Kee was charged with running a gambling house and selling illegal lottery tickets. And when twenty-nine opium smokers were arrested in a raid on an Elizabeth Street den, Lee hastened to the Tombs, lower Manhattan's jail, to reassure the fourteen Chinese among them that his attorney would soon secure their release.

Formally known as the New York City Halls of Justice and House of Detention, the Tombs got its nickname from its resemblance to an Egyptian mausoleum but earned it in other ways as well. Constructed in 1838, the massive granite quadrangle occupied an entire city block and housed the police, the courts, and jails for men, boys, and women. The gloomy structure had been built for two hundred prisoners but was forced to accommodate many more than that. Built on marshland, it had a well-deserved reputation for being dungeon-like: damp and unsanitary and poorly ventilated and lit.

A working relationship with the Tombs' warden would be an important asset for the leader of the Chinese community. Lee saw his opportunity and stepped up. In late 1885, together with two other naturalized Chinese, he attended a meeting of the Second Assembly District's County Democracy

The "Tombs," lower Manhattan's jail, earned its nickname because of its resemblance to an Egyptian mausoleum. Built in 1838 and demolished in 1902, it also housed the city's police court.

Campaign Club. It was a gathering organized to support Thomas P. "Fatty" Walsh, a Tammany ward leader who would soon be appointed warden.

Getting favors out of any official was no easy task for the largely disenfranchised Chinese community, but offering financial support was the best way available to them to build relationships. Tom Lee not only gave Walsh a sizable donation; he worked assiduously to curry favor with New York's power elite more generally. He even raised eyebrows on a cruise up the Hudson organized by the Second District assemblyman, Tommy Maher, a liquor dealer, when he plunked a fistful of money on the counter to buy drinks for a crowd of Fourth and Sixth Ward residents. Seeing this, Maher's brother wondered under his breath whether Lee himself planned to run for office in the district.

"Of the 9,000 Chinamen in New York, only 50 have taken the trouble to become citizens and voters. Deputy Sheriff Tom Lee is the unopposed leader of this small band," the *San Francisco Bulletin* reported, omitting the fact that naturalization had not been an option for any others since passage of the Exclusion Act. "He is a political power in the Fourth and Sixth wards, for these 50 voters will, to a man, support any candidate that he favors. The politicians know this, hence Tom's importance." But giving them money didn't hurt, either.

If the intent of charging Tom Lee with operating a gambling house had been to warn him off the business, it was an abysmal failure. By early 1884, he was rumored to "control" sixteen such establishments in Little China, although he did not *own* them so much as *tax* them.

Apart from prostitutes and opium, gambling was the chief form of recreation for the men of Chinatown, who were mainly bachelors or married men whose families had remained in China. Few wives came to America, and single Chinese women seldom made the journey unless betrothed or—more commonly—recruited or sold into the sex trade. Lacking access to spouses, children, and grandchildren, lonely immigrant men turned to games of chance, both for entertainment and in the vain hope they might strike it rich and stage a triumphant return home. Gambling, although illegal in America, carried no stigma among the Chinese.

In what little leisure time they had—generally evenings and Sundays—they enjoyed three popular games of chance: *fan tan*, the "spread and turn over" game; *pi gow*, a dominoes-like pastime; and *pak kop piu*, the "white pigeon ticket" lottery that Americans referred to as policy. All were illegal and subject to police raids, so games were organized clandestinely and played in cellars and back rooms. Chinese learned of them through word of mouth or from Chinese-speaking street touts who beckoned them inside.

The gaming rooms were cheap to set up; a table, some stools, and a sign that spelled out the rules were all you needed. *Fan tan* was played on a mat and required only a cup, a square tin, a pointer, some slips of paper or chips, and about four hundred copper or brass buttons or coins. *Pi gow* and policy required even less—thirty-two Chinese tiles in the first instance, and a bowl and slips of paper in the second. Only a small staff was required to run the games, keep the accounts, and man the door, both to troll for customers and to sound early warning if a policeman was sighted.

Fan tan was a simple game of chance. The dealer sat on a stool, a cashier by his side, and gamblers stood around the flanks of the table or perched on wooden stools. The four edges of the tin were labeled with the numbers 1, 2, 3, and 4. The dealer would grab a handful of coins and place them under the cup, and each player would select one of the four numbers on which to place his money or his marker, a slip of paper or a chip. The choice represented his guess as to how many coins would be left after the dealer removed them with his pointer, four at a time, until four or fewer remained.

A dollar placed on the winning number would fetch $3, less 7 percent for the house. Losers were not necessarily required to settle immediately; if they were known to the house, they could pay up the next day if they wished.

Pi gow, once dubbed "dominoes with Chinese complications," was fairly straightforward. Players were dealt four dominoes, which they used to create a "front hand" and a "rear hand" of two tiles each. The goal was for the dots on the two tiles to total nine or something close to it and to beat the house in the process. And policy was a numbers game. Eighty Chinese characters

A used policy slip from Lone Tai (*Lian Tai*), a gambling establishment at 18 Mott Street at the turn of the century. Policy— or *pak kop piu*—was a popular Chinese lottery game.

taken from a classical text were written on slips of paper and placed in a bowl, and twenty were removed. Gamblers guessed which would be drawn by marking them off in red on a sheet of paper. A dollar bet would fetch $20 if one successfully guessed six characters, or $200 if one guessed seven, and so on. Two drawings took place per day.

Gambling offered a far faster, if unlikely, pathway to riches than working in a laundry. It was a compulsion in the humdrum lives of many Chinese men. "The Celestial is a shameless and inveterate gambler," wrote George Washington Walling, a former New York police chief, in 1887, and he got no argument from the journalist Wong Chin Foo, who wrote, "Lock up the Fan Tan players, chain them with heavy chains, gag and blindfold them, place half a dozen millstones upon their necks, give them nothing but water and tea to eat—they will bet with their fingers or toes in the dark cells, just as if nothing had happened." Whites and Chinese alike felt the generalization was justified.

The promise of profits that greatly exceeded anything a merchant could earn from legitimate business made many willing to risk arrest and punishment by running illegal games. Typically, such ventures were partnerships: about ten men would get together, each investing a nominal amount. Equipment, rent, and wages had to be paid, with the rest of the cash used to back the bets. But because the operations were subject to police closure and harassment, the gambling bosses soon recognized the need to band together for mutual protection.

By 1886, Tom Lee had organized the Chinese Gamblers' Union, headquartered at 18 Mott and funded by dues. The organization regulated the number of games in the quarter and adjudicated disputes among owners. But it did far more than that. It also defended its members if they were arrested, bailed them out of jail, paid the police for "protection," and dealt firmly with informers.

When social reformers provided the *Commercial Advertiser* with a list of gambling parlors in Chinatown the following year as a means of pressuring the police to shut them down, it so alarmed their owners that the Gamblers' Union raised $5,000 to neutralize whoever had provided the reporter with the list. It turned out to be Tom Ah Jo, a Brooklyn medical student and enthusiastic Baptist who had anglicized his name as Joseph C. Thoms. The Gamblers' Union offered him $1,800 not to testify against them. When that failed, they had him arrested by putting a laundryman named Moy Park Sue up to accusing him of larceny. And they were said to have put a bounty of $3,000 on his head.

Thoms believed the threat was real. At his trial in Tombs Police Court, his attorney announced that "Dr. Thoms is now in the custody of this court, and any attempt to molest or injure him will be visited with severe punishment. I make this statement at this time knowing that efforts have been made to kill him or kidnap him."

The court proceedings bordered on the farcical. They began with the crowing of a cock. Proclaiming that heathen Chinese would not be bound by any oath sworn on the Bible, Thoms's attorney insisted they be sworn "in the Chinese way," which he suggested meant burning paper with a "horrible Celestial oath" written on it and chopping off the head of a cock. And he actually had an officer of the court produce a large brown rooster and a cleaver for the ritual, together with a strip of yellow paper emblazoned with Chinese characters for "Supreme Heaven, if I tell a lie may a thunderbolt strike me dead."

The idea of beheading the rooster was an improvised takeoff on the Hongmen initiation ritual, and the judge overruled the motion, noting wryly that if he permitted such a thing, he would be guilty of cruelty to animals. The witnesses were compelled to kiss the Bible and swear to tell the truth, even though it is highly doubtful non-Christian Chinese witnesses felt bound by such an oath.

Thoms pleaded not guilty, and $1,500 bail was posted on his behalf. But the defamation continued. Several other Chinese came forward with accusations, surely untrue, that Thoms had been selling police protection for illegal business activities—precisely the same accusations that had been leveled against Tom Lee four years earlier. Lee himself told a reporter that Moy Park Sue had offered him $500 to secure the same premises, lending credibility to what was undoubtedly a false accusation.

Thoms's ordeal was an object lesson. The Gamblers' Union was willing to use carrots, but it was not averse to using sticks. If Thoms wasn't prepared to play ball, the gambling bosses had the means and the motivation to deal severely with him—and anyone else who dared challenge their franchise.

Like gambling, opium was a far more profitable business than cigar making or washing clothes, and like gambling it was illegal. Keeping an opium den, selling the drug, and smoking it were all against the law in 1880s New York, which meant such enterprises were subject to police raids. So Tom Lee also found profit in running interference for those who owned illegal dens. His job was to keep the police away or, failing that, to warn proprietors when a raid was in the offing. Failing *that,* he was expected to post bail for any dealer who got arrested.

Although opium was an ingredient in many patent medicines Americans took for nervous disorders and other ailments, Chinese were widely blamed for importing and popularizing the far more potent, smokable variety. By the 1880s, the authorities had become alarmed because the narcotic was being smoked by *non*-Chinese.

The federal government had not outlawed opium—that would come later—but it did tax it heavily. Raw opium was assessed at $10 per pound in 1884. Because Canada taxed it at half that rate, much of the substance entered the United States illegally over the northern border. The drug, imported from Asia, was often processed in British Columbia and smuggled

A New York Chinatown opium joint, photographed ca. 1895
by the muckraking photojournalist Jacob A. Riis.

in, depriving the American government of the duty. Much of New York's opium came across the St. Lawrence River into upstate cities and towns. But it was also shipped directly into U.S. ports under the false bottoms of packing crates, in the folds of sails, in the soles of Chinese shoes, in barrels of pickled fish, and in a thousand other hiding places.

The reporter Wong Chin Foo wrote that a couple of dozen Chinese firms in New York dealt in refined opium, wholesale and retail, and sold it to whites and Chinese alike. He also counted eleven private "joints" where Chinese might smoke it for $2.25 an ounce. Many of these declined to admit whites in hopes that a lower profile might make it less likely that the police would molest them. One such shop could sell ten to twelve four-ounce cans on a Sunday—when business was best—at a profit of several dollars per can. According to Wong's arithmetic, the place grossed nearly $250,000 in a year.

Although opium could be smoked in the privacy of one's quarters, dens were popular because they offered all the equipment and comforts a smoker could desire. A typical opium den was a dim room with any windows covered, because the drug rendered one sensitive to light. The chamber was divided into stalls, each furnished with a mat, a pillow, and a tray to hold the necessities: a wooden pipe about two feet long, a needle, a jar, and an oil lamp. A sweet, musky, vaguely floral aroma would hang in the air.

A hop fiend—as someone with an opium habit was called—would purchase a lump of the drug, already boiled into a dark, molasses-like mass. He would wind it around the needle and suspend it over the flame from the lamp. After a couple of minutes, when it took on a rich, amber color, he would stuff it into the pipe. Then he would recline and suck in the smoke, holding it in his lungs as long as possible before exhaling. Within a minute or two, the portion would be exhausted, and the process would be repeated; intoxication required several rounds. In a little while, he would fall into a deep, trancelike stupor. If he had come in the evening after work, he would probably sleep until daybreak.

It was easy for the police to turn a blind eye when only Chinese were involved, but even payoffs couldn't protect the dens in the spring of 1883 when the Young Men's Association of Mott Street's Catholic Church of the Transfiguration alleged that lecherous Chinese men were plying young white girls with it and then forcing them into prostitution. It was a false charge, but local papers took it at face value, and the police had no choice but to act. The crackdown that followed placed Chinatown under siege. The opium dens were forced to close, or at the very least to admit only Chinese men known to the owners. Things eventually cooled off, but Chinatown opium resorts continued to be raided from time to time, which meant ongoing business for Tom Lee and his associates. Securing the release of dealers who were arrested was part and parcel of his responsibilities as Chinatown's grafter in chief.

Citywide, more than $3 million was paid by gambling house keepers each year for protection. It was done through the so-called Gambling Commission that included municipal officials and state senators. The commission met weekly, and the *New York Times* believed there wasn't a betting parlor in the city unknown to it. A would-be proprietor would approach his precinct captain with a request to open and an initiation fee of $300. The captain would investigate whether the applicant was likely to be able to pay promptly, and a week later would notify him of the commission's decision. If the application was approved, the captain would keep the money. In the rare instance in which one was denied, the deposit was refunded. It was all very businesslike.

Gambling parlors were charged monthly fees on a sliding scale, with poolrooms at the top of the heap, assessed at $300 per month, all the way down to policy shops, which paid $50. By one estimate, there were more than two thousand gambling halls in New York. Any could be closed for nonpayment on short notice by police officers who owed their jobs to city officials and took their orders from them.

When it came to the Chinese community, however, the powers that be were hard-pressed to regulate the games unaided. *Fan tan* and *pi gow* parlors came and went without notice. Intelligence was not forthcoming from close-mouthed Chinese patrons, and there were no Chinese on the police force to serve as undercover informants. The police didn't really understand the nature of the games at all. This was the gap Tom Lee and his men filled. They stood between the gamblers and the authorities, able to communicate and do business with both. And for this service, they earned their tribute.

Using the trappings of power and the prerogatives of one's office to line one's pockets was a time-honored Chinese tradition. Tom Lee would have found little about this system unfamiliar, even on his first day in town. Lee and his contemporaries would certainly have been acquainted, for example, with the story of He Shen, a Manchu who won the favor of an eighteenth-century Qing emperor, received several titles, and enriched himself and his family through graft and extortion of public funds. Or those of Wei Zhongxian and Liu Jin, eunuchs who rose to high rank during the Ming dynasty and became fabulously wealthy by using their positions for personal gain. These were historical figures. But Chinese literature and theater were also chock-full of stories of corrupt officials. Such people were not admired, but they were certainly feared, and they felt little shame in their actions. Indeed, in China, one might be thought a fool *not* to use one's position to enrich oneself, one's family, and one's cronies.

Tom Lee provided a valuable service. For a modest fee, he offered the gambling bosses a way to operate illegally and yet avoid arrest. If that meant compromising underpaid police officers or paying off corrupt political bosses in the higher echelons of Tammany Hall, it was certainly no moral concern of his.

For the balance of the 1880s, Lee consciously pursued the image of a well-connected, law-abiding pillar of New York society. The less attention paid to his relationships with gamblers and opium merchants, the better. He used his influence in myriad ways to improve the lives of New York's Chinese. He participated in politics, adopted charitable causes, entertained the rich and powerful, and played the patriarch in the life events of the Chinese community.

In 1888, he worked energetically for the election of Benjamin Harrison as president. Although Lee was very close to Tammany Hall Democrats, he and the rest of the Chinese community had a strong reason to back the Republican in this national election. President Grover Cleveland, running for reelection, had lobbied for, and signed, the Scott Act, which prohibited Chinese laborers who left the country from returning. General Harrison, on the other hand, had voted against the Exclusion Act and other anti-Chinese measures while in the Senate. Still hopeful that the political will could be found to repeal the hated Exclusion Act, Lee arranged to place collection boxes in Chinese restaurants and laundries to raise funds for Harrison's campaign. He also joined the community's wealthiest merchants and ponied up $10,000 of his own money, and he personally delivered the funds to Republican Party headquarters on Fifth Avenue.

In early 1889, when flooding of the Yellow River decimated the wheat crop in China's Shandong Province, Lee raised more than $1,200 for famine relief. He topped the list of New York Chinese donors with a personal contribution. But his philanthropy wasn't limited to Chinese causes. Two months later, he helped drum up support in Chinatown for victims of the Johnstown, Pennsylvania, flood by translating and disseminating news to ensure local Chinese understood the extent of the disaster. Here, too, he headed the list of subscribers.

When Yuet Sing, a wealthy merchant, decided to take a young bride in 1888, it was Lee who toasted the couple at their wedding ceremony at the new Joss House. Lee was one of four Loon Yee Tong dignitaries who led the cortege at the funeral of a retired general who had fought the French in Tonkin (Vietnam) in the early 1880s. On another occasion, he appeared astride a white horse in the elaborate funeral procession of the secretary of the tong.

When Lee took sick in 1887, felled by a pulmonary hemorrhage—he was a chronic smoker, though of cigars and cigarettes rather than opium—his infirmity merited a report in the *New York Times*. A stream of well-wishers called at his home. Under the care of a Columbia-educated physician and nursed by his wife, however, he made a full recovery.

The New York *World* observed that Tom Lee was "a powerful Republican factor in the affairs of the Twenty-First Assembly District." Indeed, he was, although he always maintained strong ties with Democrats as well. At the dawn of the 1890s, there was no more influential person in New York's Chinese quarter.

Chapter 3

"A Clear Case of Corruption"

Captain John H. McCullagh Jr. had a well-deserved reputation for being tough on crime.

As a rookie policeman, the Irish-born McCullagh had cut his teeth in some of Manhattan's toughest neighborhoods and had built an impressive résumé by breaking up street gangs. He had left his father's farm to join the force in 1864—hence his nickname, "Farmer John"—and was seen as a rising star in the department. He was promoted to sergeant two years later and made captain in 1872. And in 1883, he had been given command of the still-new Sixth Precinct, which he took over from his mentor, Captain Jeremiah Petty. In his seven years there, he brought a measure of order to the vice-ridden cesspool that was widely known by the sobriquet "the Bloody Sixth."

None of this meant that McCullagh himself was actually honest. He was a creature of his times. He had surely paid for his promotions, and during earlier assignments he had been tried twice for misconduct, both times for attempting to blackmail brothel keepers to pay him off if they wished to remain open. When he got to Chinatown, he proved all too ready to enter into a sweetheart arrangement with Tom Lee's Gamblers' Union, which, the *New York Herald* observed, considered him a "good fel-lee" because he was willing to play ball.

Members of the Gamblers' Union had recently been paying $8 per table per week on the understanding that a third of the money would go to Tom Lee, with much of the balance handed over to the police to prevent raids, or at the very least to ensure advance notification of searches so they might clear their tables and lock up their cash before the police arrived. The reporter Wong Chin Foo estimated that this franchise netted Lee up to

$10,000 a year. How much of the rest was going into McCullagh's pocket was never clear, but it was surely a considerable sum. When Farmer John died suddenly in 1893, his estate was valued at more than $100,000—none too shabby for a man whom the city paid only $1,800 a year.

After the *New York Herald* printed an embarrassing report in January 1891 alleging that street gambling in Chatham Square was going on directly under the noses of the local police, McCullagh's tenure in the Bloody Sixth was abruptly cut short. He was hauled before the publicity-averse police commissioners, who felt compelled to act against him. In less than a week, he was exiled to a command in the Bronx, trading places with Captain Nicholas Brooks, who became the new overseer of the Elizabeth Street Station in his stead.

Brooks, for his part, was something of a prig. A twenty-year veteran when he was promoted to captain in 1887, he was said by the *New York Times* to make "an honest, conservative and urbane police captain," and by all accounts he did. His worst offenses during his long career were sitting while on patrol and conversing while on duty. Although Tammany Hall approved of Brooks—the *Tammany Times,* its in-house paper, praised him as "proof of what may be accomplished by attention to business and fidelity to duty"—there was never a hint of scandal about the man.

Tom Lee immediately sought authorization from the gambling bosses to spend $1,500 from their $10,000 treasury to get on a "pleasant footing" with the new captain. He called on Brooks and was received politely, but the latter made it clear he would not be party to any such arrangement. He was determined to be a *bad* "fellee." He later denied ever meeting Lee. Unable to come to terms with the new captain, Lee ordered Chinatown's betting parlors temporarily closed, lest they be raided.

They stayed shuttered for several months, and when they reopened later that year, a few changes had been mandated in the rules that governed them. An October 1891 circular that survives suggests strongly that an accommodation was reached with the police or the Tammany higher-ups, probably an upward adjustment in the amount of protection money they received, although there is no evidence Brooks was in on it. The notice mandated new rates the casinos were to collect from their gamblers. It read, in part:

Readers: Because of cheating and excessive expenses, we hereby propose that for payouts of more than 25 cents, commissions will be doubled, as customary. Any gambling hall that fails to follow this regulation will be fined $10. Whoever reports the violation will receive a $5 reward, with the balance given to our organization. . . . This announcement is posted to avoid any future misunderstanding. Your cooperation is appreciated.

Given under our hand and seal in the ninth month of the 17th year of the reign of the Emperor Guangxu.

Although the circular was signed by the New York Bin Ching Union—a name meaning "Upholding Fairness" not heard before or afterward—it was surely another term for the Gamblers' Union, and even *that* name soon fell into disuse in favor of the On Leong Tong, which translates roughly as the "Chamber of Peaceful Conscientiousness." The new moniker was derived from a Chinese proverb about "eliminating despots and bringing peace to the people" that had been used by rebels in China for many generations.

Peace, however, would turn out to be the last thing the On Leong Tong would bring to the people of Chinatown. With the profitable monopoly it enjoyed from its perch between the law and the vice dens, the tong itself was the only "despot" in sight. The task of eliminating it—or at least sidelining it—would be taken up by an entirely different organization: a new brotherhood from the West that had appeared in New York and that had cast a jealous eye on the On Leongs' lucrative franchise.

There was an odd math at work. The Exclusion Act had caused the overall Chinese population in the United States to decline by more than 15 percent in the 1890s, and it would continue to diminish for another two decades. But New York, by contrast, saw heady growth in its Chinese inhabitants. According to the federal census, the number of Chinese in New York City more than tripled in the last decade of the century—from just over two thousand to more than six thousand—and this didn't count those in the suburbs or those missed by the census takers. And what was happening in New York was also happening in Chinatowns throughout the East and the Midwest.

Although more New York Chinese were marrying and starting families than had previously been the case, this alone could not account for such a dramatic rise. What was really driving the growth was continued migration from the West Coast, on the one hand, and a robust smuggling industry, on the other.

Smuggling Chinese into the United States was widespread and lucrative. The going rate for illegal entry was about $200 per head, and it was widely believed that Chinese criminal syndicates involved in the illegal business had put government officials at various entry points on their payrolls. Chinese were entering from Canada—where they were still welcome but subject to a "head tax"—as well as from Mexico. Chinese from Cuba were also evading the law; many entered on Spanish passports, ostensibly in transit to other destinations, but quickly disappeared once they had landed. The journalist Wong Chin Foo commented in late 1889 on the appearance in New York of as many as three hundred "strange Chinamen," mostly from abroad.

One underworld syndicate deeply involved in the trafficking was a sworn brotherhood called the Hip Sing Tong, which had gotten its start in San Francisco and quickly expanded in the West. The organization, whose name translates as the "Chamber United in Victory," emerged in the mid-1880s. The *Oregonian* reported in 1887 that San Francisco had become home to "organized bodies of men . . . who set the laws completely at defiance, and who do not hesitate even at murder. . . . Their organizations are supposed to be for mutual aid, but they are in reality combinations for criminal purposes." Citing the Hip Sings by name, the paper continued, "The members are bound together by the most solemn oaths . . . to do unquestioningly and unhesitatingly what the society orders. Briefly they are organized criminals who make their own laws and defy those of America." There was probably little exaggeration in the newspaper's report.

The tong began to establish beachheads in the East in the late 1880s. When Joseph Thoms, the medical student, gave the authorities the names of gambling parlors in Brooklyn and Manhattan in 1887, his source had been a Hip Sing, whom Tom Lee and company later paid to leave town so he wouldn't be available to testify against them. In 1888, Wong Chin Foo reported on "a Chinese organization of so-called anarchists," already one hundred strong, that was forming on Pell Street, though he didn't call them by name. And in Philadelphia, Hip Sings tried to bribe and blackmail witnesses in an 1889 court case against three of their number. They also threatened a merchant who identified their gambling bosses to a reporter.

In New York, the fault line between the Hip Sing upstarts and the more established On Leongs soon began to express itself geographically. Mott Street and Chatham Square merchants like Tom Lee, Wo Kee, and Yuet Sing, On Leongs all, were men of means who dominated the governance of Chinatown and dealt with the wider community, including the political establishment, on its behalf. In contrast to "clean, quiet and orderly" Mott Street, however, was Pell Street—the preserve of the Hip Sings:

> Here is the headquarters of the Highbinders, the famous secret society of thugs and murderers, who caused so much terror in San Francisco, and who have been at the bottom of not a few desperate crimes in New York. There are probably three hundred of these criminals and outcasts, who haunt the dirty basements and tenements . . . gambling, drinking, smoking opium and carrying on wild orgies, which sometimes end in fatal affrays. The respectable element in Chinatown looks down upon these ruffians, but it also fears them. They are known to hold life lightly, and for the smallest sum will hire themselves out to do any desperate deed.

This informal division of Chinatown's turf would continue for decades. But the establishment of the Hip Sings in New York was very bad news for Tom Lee and his allies. They would become permanent—and deadly— nemeses.

In addition to being Tom Lee's nephew, Lee Toy was his right-hand man. He ran a gambling hall at 18 Mott, one of his uncle's properties. And he managed his uncle's business with the other betting parlors and the police.

Sometimes known as Black Devil Toy, Lee Toy was nearly six feet tall, broad shouldered, and muscular, with the sinews of a cat. A tough, rough-hewn man, he had served seven years for larceny in a California penitentiary before coming to New York. He was said to have leaped from a fourth-floor

Lee Toy, Tom Lee's nephew and enforcer,
ca. 1896.

window to escape pursuing police, using an umbrella to break his fall. And he sported a makeshift coat of mail under his tunic to protect him from the bullets and knives of those who wished him ill, who were many.

Lee Toy was Tom Lee's enforcer.

When the gambling bosses got word that two important Hip Sing men had informed New York newspapers about the locations of Chinatown casinos, they wasted no time going after the pair. On October 9, 1891, Lee Toy and an associate confronted one of them, Chin Tin, on the corner of Pell and Doyers, cursed him, and struck him repeatedly. When the other, Warry Charles, came to his aid, he too was beaten up. Charles managed to break free and summon two policemen, but as soon as the officers recognized Lee Toy, they dismissed Charles, insisting he was not seriously hurt. Nor, at Elizabeth Street, was Charles able to persuade the sergeant on duty to issue a warrant for Lee Toy's arrest. As his uncle's number two, Lee Toy was well-known to the police, who gave him wide berth.

Charles was assaulted a second time when he unwisely passed in front of 18 Mott that same week. This time he was hit with a slingshot by another of Tom Lee's associates, Lee Quon Jung, a.k.a. Charlie Boston—a nickname derived from his earlier residence in that city. Charles was taken to the hospital, where a surgeon sewed up a wound over his eye and a gash in his scalp. Boston was locked up and in court the next day was represented by Edmund E. Price, Tom Lee's lawyer. Price had also defended Boston earlier that year against a charge of opium smuggling, one of his main businesses.

But the On Leongs weren't done with Chin Tin, either. Just as they had done to Joseph Thoms three years earlier, they found someone to accuse him of extortion—in this case, a fruit vendor who did business in front of 20 Mott, where Chin Tin leased the ground floor. Chin was arrested, and at trial, in consideration of a $1,000 payment from the On Leongs, the peddler testified that Chin had demanded $4 from him and told him he couldn't sell there anymore if he didn't pay up.

The defense alleged a conspiracy against Chin and Charles. It also put up a witness who testified that Lee Toy had offered $3,000 for Charles's murder, $2,000 for killing Chin Tin, $1,000 if Chin Tin was imprisoned for ten years, and $500 if the prison term was less than that. The judge was convinced, and he dismissed the charges against the supposed extortionist.

On April 8, 1894, police raided a gambling house at 14 Pell. Most of the patrons fled, but twenty-five-year-old Wong Get had too much money on the table to give it up easily. As the officer seized the cash and ordered him out of the room, Wong protested in English that there were other Chinatown establishments that never seemed to be molested and that he was willing to lead the officer to one.

Wong had emigrated from China in 1882 at age thirteen. A quick study, he had learned to speak English fluently in San Francisco. After nearly a decade there, he had come to New York, joined the Hip Sings, and quickly set about opening a gambling house of his own.

Wong led the policeman around the corner and brought him to Tom Lee's building, where there were three games going on. As they approached, however, a crowd of gamblers emerged and, sizing up the situation, began thrashing and kicking him. The officer just looked on without interfering. As Wong fled for his life, Lee Toy chased him down Mott Street, beating him mercilessly with a blackjack—a leather-wrapped iron club. When they got to the corner, however, another bluecoat grabbed Lee Toy and arrested him.

Wong had been pummeled all over his body, and blood flowed freely from cuts in three places. Even after several days, he was in too much pain to appear in Tombs Police Court, and so Lee Toy's hearing was postponed. It was finally called for April 23, and that day Lee and his attorney— Edmund E. Price, of course—appeared in court promptly at 10:00 a.m. When the plaintiff failed to appear, the judge dismissed the charges.

Wong Get's attorney, however, had been told the hearing had been called for 2:00 p.m., so when he arrived with his client, the case had been thrown out and the judge had gone home. The lawyer naively assumed a miscommunication, but there had been no mistake. It had all surely been a setup. And a prominent attorney and social reformer named Frank Moss, who had come to court that day, declared as much.

"It is a clear case of corruption," Moss told a New York *World* reporter. "Tom Lee controls the police in Chinatown. He orders them to make arrests or raids as he pleases. This case of Wong was dangerous to them, and it was necessary to use every trick to get [Lee] Toy off. There is a system of corruption in Chinatown as deep as in Tammany's strongest districts," he declared. "Gambling is carried out under police protection."

Moss's presence in court that day had been no coincidence. He was looking for someone who might help expose that "system of corruption" whereby the police protected, rather than shut down, Chinese gambling houses. It would have to be an insider, someone who understood the seamy underside of Chinatown. And he thought he had found just such a person in Wong Get.

The rotten system that Tammany Hall had built, in which politicians, police, and criminals were interconnected and mutually dependent, cried out for reform. And one of the first to sound the cry—loudly, and for all to hear—was the Reverend Dr. Charles H. Parkhurst, who, in 1891, had been drafted to head the Society for the Prevention of Crime. Cleaning up the political leadership of the city and cracking down on widespread police corruption were the principal goals of this civic group, which had been organized in 1877 but had not made much of an impact in its first decade and a half.

A minister of New England Puritan stock called to serve Manhattan's Madison Square Presbyterian Church as pastor in 1880, the goateed Parkhurst was a firebrand. Certain that God was squarely on his side, and supported in his crusade by the attorneys Frank Moss and William T. Jerome, both reformers, Republicans, and opponents of vice, he was unafraid of taking on the Tammany establishment. From his pulpit, Dr. Parkhurst launched a full-frontal attack on Tammany politicians and their henchmen. His personal influence was so profound and his imprint so deep that his group soon became known popularly as the Parkhurst Society.

Parkhurst's opening salvo was an 1892 sermon that startled his congregation and shocked the city with its brazenness. "The mayor and those associated with him are polluted harpies," he declared. "Under the pretense of governing the city they are feeding day and night on its quivering vitals. They are a lying, rum-soaked and libidinous lot. While we fight iniquity they shield and patronize it; while we try to convert criminals they manufacture them; and they have a hundred dollars invested in the manufacturing business to every one invested in converting machinery. Police and criminals all stand in with each other. It is simply one solid gang of criminals," he added, "one half in office and the other half out."

Challenged for proof, Parkhurst resolved to experience Manhattan's vice district firsthand. Exchanging his clerical garb for a pair of loud trousers and a flannel shirt—the disguise was necessary, lest he be arrested and intentionally embarrassed by the police, whom he had already thoroughly alienated—he visited brothels and saloons, tattoo parlors and rathskellers. For a week, he surveyed New York at its lowest and most desperate. He even spent an evening in the Chinese quarter, observing "dope fiends" splayed about on cots in a Doyers Street opium den and watching a dozen *fan tan* players wager their earnings in a gambling house on Pell.

Armed with firsthand observations of the hell that was New York's underworld and ably assisted by the portly Moss and the energetic Jerome, Parkhurst ratcheted up the pressure for reform through his sermons and

The Reverend Dr. Charles H. Parkhurst,
ca. 1896. The Presbyterian pastor
spearheaded a hard-hitting attack
on Tammany Hall politicians.

writings. He made no headway with the Democrats in Albany, but in late 1893, after Republicans gained control of the legislature, he provoked the state senate into investigating municipal police corruption.

The vehicle created for this purpose was a special committee of the senate chaired by the Brooklyn-born Clarence Lexow, a Republican attorney and a Progressive. It was popularly known simply as the Lexow Committee. Moss and Jerome were recruited to serve as associate counsels, and beginning in 1894, the body heard lurid testimony on police involvement in extortion, election fraud, bribery, voter intimidation, and counterfeiting. All of New York watched as the newspapers cheerfully trumpeted news of the hearings.

One piece of the puzzle was the nexus between the police and New York's Chinese, and it was the search for a witness who might testify about the unholy alliance between officers of the Sixth Precinct and Tom Lee and his men that had brought Frank Moss, in his capacity as counsel to the Lexow Committee, to Tombs Police Court on April 23. When the judge dismissed the charges against Lee Toy, Moss approached Wong Get, whose body still bore the bruises he had received at Lee Toy's hands. Moss knew exposing Tom Lee would require a fearless and credible witness who knew his way around Chinatown and had enmity for Lee and his henchmen. Wong Get seemed made to order for the task.

Wong, too, sensed an opportunity. He easily persuaded Moss that he had repudiated his former dissolute life and shared his desire, and that of the committee, to rid the Chinese quarter of vice. Here, ostensibly, was a "good Chinaman," a reformer who would make an excellent witness. And the fact that he was quite handsome, spoke good English, and was known for Sunday psalm singing at Chinatown's Christian missions only added to his allure and credibility.

Moss so fervently wished to expose Tom Lee and the police that he was more than willing to overlook the fact that Wong Get's abandonment of his former life, which had conveniently taken place just about a month or two earlier, might not be sincere. He arranged for Wong to testify as the star witness at the committee's thirty-third hearing, the only one that would touch on the Chinese community. But Wong hadn't needed much persuading. He was more than happy to bear witness against Tom Lee, who had been reappointed deputy sheriff early in 1894. And there was much to tell.

The Albany-based Lexow Committee needed a location in New York City for its hearings, and it was given the use of one of thirty opulent hearing rooms at the New York County Courthouse at 52 Chambers Street. The room was unusually packed on June 27, 1894. The spectators included women, uniformed police officers, and even Chinese men in their native attire, all anomalies among the usual collection of white men in frock coats and starched collars one saw at the courthouse. Wong Get, the only Chinese witness and the only one slated to testify about Chinatown, sat in the front row, just behind the rail, in anticipation.

There was considerable irony in the choice of venue. The neoclassical confection of pediments and pilasters that had taken twenty years to com-

Wong Get, longtime secretary, consigliere,
interpreter, spokesman, and peace
negotiator for the Hip Sing Tong, ca. 1906.

plete and cost taxpayers more than $10 million had been dubbed the Tweed
Courthouse, in homage to William M. "Boss" Tweed, who had headed Tammany Hall for nearly two decades. Ten years into the building's construc-
tion, the *New York Times* had exposed how Tweed and his cronies had
skimmed millions of dollars off civic projects like 52 Chambers, whose
original budget had been a mere $250,000. In 1873, in a hearing room in
the still-unfinished structure, Tweed himself had been tried, convicted, and
sentenced to twelve years in prison. His "palace of plunder" had become not
only a symbol of his unethical rule but also the setting for his demise.

Wong Get, who did not require an interpreter, took the stand after
lunch. Frank Moss asked most of the questions.

"Is not Tom Lee generally considered or called the boss of Chinatown?"
Moss asked the witness.

"They all call him the boss; he is captain for Chinatown. They call him
mayor and captain," Wong replied.

"What do they do in Chinatown Sundays?"

"Oh, they have a lot of games; Fan Tan games, I know."

"How many games have there been running there during this year, do you know?"

"Sometimes 50 or 60, or less."

"Do you know whether there are or have been any games running in Tom Lee's house?"

"On 18 Mott Street, on the second floor; one game in his office room."

"What is Hip Sing Tong?"

"That is what they call the Workingman's Society."

"Is that Tom Lee's society?"

"No, no. . . . That society the On Leong Tong."

"Are the two societies friendly?"

"No, no."

"Did you pay any money to Tom Lee in January?"

"He asked me $16."

"What was he to give you for that?"

"He say, 'Anybody want to run a game have to give me that. You see, I got a badge. I got a gold badge. I am the Deputy Sheriff.'"

"Tom Lee said he had a gold badge, he was Deputy Sheriff?"

"Yes; stuck on his suspender."

"Did you want to run a game?"

"I start a game at 18 Doyers Street, where I live, downstairs in the rear room, and the next morning he come to my room. He said, 'You give me money.' I said, 'How much I have to give you?' He said, '$16 a week.'"

"Did he tell who he gave the money to?"

"He tell me he got to pay somebody."

"Who came to collect the money?"

"Tom Lee. Sometimes he come with Lee Toy; sometimes he come without, and with—"

"With an officer?"

"He was some policeman downstairs; I didn't go downstairs looking."

"You mean to say he left the police officer downstairs?"

"Yes, sir."

"And came up?"

"Yes, sir; to collect the money."

Then Wong told a story of a police raid on his *fan tan* parlor that had taken place despite his payments to Tom Lee for protection. He described a comical scene in which a police detective tried to undo his error.

"I ran that game four weeks, and on Monday evening at 9 o'clock, [John] Farrington, the detective, he come up. My doorkeeper holler, 'Policeman.' We shut the door. Farrington pushed the door in, chucked the things all out of the window, smashed up the table, and chased me out."

"You had paid your money to Tom Lee?"

"I did. Right after that I go to Tom Lee. I say, 'I pay you all the time. What is the matter? Policeman come in, bust in my house. Toss them people out and send them people out.' He says, 'What one?' 'Farrington.' 'I go see him right away.' Then, after a while Farrington come back, take some screw driver, and fix that door on again."

Wong supplied the committee with the names and addresses of several Chinese who ran gambling houses. And finally, Moss made a point of announcing publicly that if anything untoward happened to Wong as a result of his appearance, the committee would protect him.

Everyone got what he wanted out of Wong Get's testimony. Moss and the committee got on the record one piece of the much larger, citywide puzzle of rampant corruption within the police force. And shining the light of day on Tom Lee and his On Leong Tong was just as useful to Wong and his allies, who hoped more than anything to shunt him aside and take over his empire.

Wong Get was determined that Lee Toy face justice for the beating he had received at his hands, especially after Lee's shenanigans had cheated him out of testifying against him. Wong's legal team, which now included Frank Moss himself, appealed to a second judge, who issued a bench warrant for Lee Toy's rearrest.

By that time, the man had disappeared, however, and he remained at large for two months. But one day, when he was seen entering 28 Mott to visit his wife and daughter, Wong's Hip Sing brothers quickly posted twenty-one-year-old Dong Fong, one of their interpreters, in front of the building. After watching all night, Dong went to the Tombs the following morning to demand that the police apprehend Lee. Although they had declined to arrest him in the past, they were obligated by the warrant to apprehend him this time.

When they knocked, Lee Toy's wife shouted that he was not there. So the officers set about prying the door open with a crowbar, at which point Lee ran to a window and briefly considered a reprise of his famous San Francisco leap. But on the pavement below stood a Hip Sing who threatened to beat him up when he landed. While Lee Toy hesitated, the police broke in, and as the terrified women looked on, he was apprehended and taken to the Tombs. Bail, fixed at $1,000, was quickly furnished.

That night, it was the Hip Sings who celebrated. With Moss's help, they had trumped the On Leongs *and* the police by compelling Lee Toy's arrest through the courts. But it was a minor victory. Far more important was the fact that after Wong Get's testimony before the Lexow Committee, the Hip Sings had begun to acquire a reputation as "the reformers of Chinatown." The New York *Sun* described their members as "the respectable element among the Orientals who are anxious to prevent the spread of vice among their fellow countrymen." The Hip Sings were touted as the best hope for change in the squalid Chinese quarter.

And, in a perverse way, they probably were.

In the summer of 1894, while the Lexow Committee was in recess, the two tongs fought a proxy war. It was mostly nonviolent, with both managing to get others to do their dirty work. It began in early July, when the New York *Sun* reported that Tom Lee was in danger of losing his "lucrative and influential job" in Chinatown.

According to the *Sun,* Lee had become unpopular, and his position was shaky because he had cast unwelcome light on Chinatown and failed to prevent the raid on Wong Get's *fan tan* parlor, a lapse that showed him ineffective in keeping the police at bay. The paper claimed a large poster had appeared on a Chinatown bulletin board casting aspersions on Lee's character and declaring that when he attempted to collect "rent"—which surely meant protection money—he had begun to meet with resistance.

The *Sun*'s source was undoubtedly a Hip Sing. The Lexow Committee was not the only organ of the white establishment that could be co-opted to strike a blow against Lee and his On Leongs; the press worked just as well, if not better, and the story smacks of having been planted. Nor was it credible. The idea that Lee's control stemmed from his popularity was preposterous. For all the picnics and fetes Tom Lee organized, it was not admiration that kept him in power. It was fear.

Two could play at the public relations game, however, and the resentful On Leongs resolved to show the world it was the Hip Sings who were dirty. Three weeks later, Lee hosted a *Sun* reporter in his office, where he and several fellow merchants told the journalist that the Hip Sings had issued a schedule of fees by which protection would be purchased from *them* during the summer. According to the subsequent article, they were already players in the extortion game and wished to get in even deeper.

They planned, the *Sun* wrote, to charge gambling parlors $16 per week, opium joints $10, and brothels $3, but there was no pretense that any of *this* money would go to the police. The Hip Sings were simply threatening to release to the Lexow Committee the locations of those establishments that refused to pay, confident that the committee, in turn, would press the police to shut them down despite their arrangement with the On Leongs. This was extortion, plain and simple, not a fee for service.

Then, in early August, another group of merchants told a journalist that the Hip Sing Tong was a society "organized for the sole purpose of levying blackmail." The New York chapter, which numbered about a hundred, it was said, was composed of professional hit men, "available for hire to punish any Chinaman's enemy." Their price for "doing up"—that is, beating up—a man was $25. Another of their practices was to demand money from reputable Chinese merchants "under threat of personal violence and looting and wrecking his place of business."

In other words, the On Leongs were selling protection from the *police;* the Hip Sings were selling protection from *themselves.*

According to these merchants, the Hip Sings now boasted that they had become the "Lords of Chinatown," more powerful than the On Leongs and even the police. "We are determined to break up their power," they vowed, "if it takes every cent in Chinatown."

Chapter 4

The Chinese Parkhursts

New York's newspapers covered the Lexow Committee's hearings in lurid detail throughout 1894, and the picture that emerged was a wholesale indictment of the New York Police Department. Those sworn to serve and protect were charged with rampant corruption, extortion, blackmail, and worse.

The committee accused police of condoning and profiteering from prostitution and gambling. It revealed the gratuities demanded by officers from brothel and gambling hall owners. It exposed abuses in the electoral process whereby officers had arrested, intimidated, and even brutalized Republican voters, poll watchers, and workers, all in the service of electing Tammany candidates. And it placed blame squarely at the feet of district leaders and police commissioners who abused their authority over appointments and assignments and enriched themselves in the process.

Tammany Hall, while powerful, was not unassailable, and occasionally during its long rule, which would continue well into the twentieth century, New York voters tossed Tammany men out of office. The election of 1894 was such a case. Against the backdrop of bad economic times, the allegations of the Parkhurst Society, coupled with the revelations of the Lexow Committee, were enough to drive voters to clean house. A reformer, William L. Strong, was chosen as mayor. He was the first Republican to occupy the office in two decades.

Mayor Strong set to work cleaning up the city, systematically going after corrupt officials. When it came to dealing with law enforcement, he was presented with a blueprint by the Lexow Committee, whose ten-thousand-page report, conveniently issued on January 17, 1895, in time to be useful to him, contained recommendations for reform.

The committee favored making the Police Commission bipartisan and concentrating executive power in a single commission head. It also called for a civil service system to oversee promotions. Mayor Strong heeded the call and wasted little time ousting the four sitting commissioners, especially after three of them came out against reform. He made new appointments early in 1895.

The most prominent was the U.S. Civil Service commissioner Theodore Roosevelt, a longtime champion of civil service reform. A Manhattan-born aristocrat who had served in the state assembly, he had campaigned unsuccessfully for the office of mayor of New York in 1886. Since 1889, he had put Washington's new Civil Service Commission, just six years old, on the map. He filled federal jobs according to merit instead of the spoils system. He also took steps to professionalize the federal workforce, despite considerable opposition from Congress, especially when it came to firing patronage employees for corruption or misconduct.

It is easy to understand why Mayor Strong wanted someone with this kind of experience—not to mention someone of Roosevelt's stature—to transform the discredited police department. For his part, Roosevelt saw the position as a political stepping-stone: he was eager for another opportunity to make his mark against patronage and corruption and to be seen as doing so, especially in his home state. Roosevelt accepted the mayor's offer, returned to New York, and was sworn in on May 7. He would serve as president of the new police board.

Although technically only first among equals, Roosevelt, because of his outsize personality, was credited with many reforms designed to modernize the operation. His first task was to purge it, as much as possible, of political influence. "I was appointed with the distinct understanding that I was to administer the Police Department with entire disregard of partisan politics, and only from the standpoint of a good citizen interested in promoting the welfare of all good citizens," he wrote later.

During his relatively brief tenure in the job—by 1897, he had returned to Washington to accept an appointment as assistant secretary of the navy—Roosevelt raised hiring and promotion standards by emphasizing merit and ability over patronage. He punished misconduct without regard to political connections. He became known for late-night rounds to check up on his officers—always with reporters in tow—in which he exposed

Theodore Roosevelt, ca. 1896, during his tenure as
New York police commissioner.

and disciplined policemen caught sleeping on the job. He also championed
modernization efforts such as training officers in marksmanship, establishing a bicycle squad, and installing police call boxes on city streets to allow
beat cops to contact their station houses on the fly. His chief misstep—
which cost him and the mayor a good deal of popular support—was to
shut down city saloons at 1:00 a.m. and on Sundays, enforcing blue laws
that had been on the books for years but widely ignored.

Roosevelt made short work of the detective bureau chief, Thomas
Byrnes, a thirty-two-year veteran whom Dr. Parkhurst had called as "criminal as any other member of the force." Byrnes was permitted to retire without facing personal corruption charges. An acting chief was appointed, and
acting inspectors were made of Nicholas Brooks—the "bad fellee" who had
refused a gratuity from Tom Lee—and John McCullagh—the "good fellee"
who had preceded him at the Sixth Precinct and somehow flown under
Roosevelt's radar. And down at Elizabeth Street, Sergeant Robert Young
was named acting captain.

The Hip Sings, sensing an opportunity, approached Roosevelt soon after he took office. On July 19, 1895, Warry Charles, who spoke excellent English, complained to him that Elizabeth Street police were not cracking down on Chinatown gambling houses because they were in the pay of the On Leong Tong. He said he could fix the problem if Roosevelt would place two headquarters detectives at his disposal. But he also warned Roosevelt that if he did not cooperate, Charles would provide information to the Parkhurst Society, which would certainly use it to embarrass the police into action.

Roosevelt was having none of it. He might have bristled at the threat, he might have been told Charles was a bad egg—the Chinese man had been indicted for bribery and extortion a couple of years earlier—or he might have felt he had already addressed the problem with the appointment of Young. He referred Charles to an assistant who, in turn, bucked him to someone even lower down. No action was ever taken on the Hip Sing offer.

In March 1895, Lee Toy finally went on trial for assaulting Wong Get the previous year. Although charges against him had been dropped by two judges and a grand jury had declined to indict him, Frank Moss, now a member of Lee's legal team, was hell-bent on bringing him to justice. Moss saw corruption in all of the maneuvers that had kept Lee Toy from a conviction. Accordingly, he had gone to a third judge, and this time succeeded in getting him tried. On March 23, Lee Toy was convicted of assault in the third degree, but the jury recommended clemency. He was fined $250, which he paid immediately from a thick wad of bills he kept on his person.

"The conviction of Lee Toy is a victory over the gambling and police ring of Chinatown," Moss crowed after the verdict. "A man quite prominent in some political movements in this city got to Wong Get and his friends, and by various promises and threats endeavored to induce them to abandon the case, but they would not. The influences [in] back of Lee Toy in this case were surprising, and have demonstrated the power of the gambling ring in Mott Street."

Tom Lee—who surely had everything to do with any high-level

intervention that might have taken place on Lee Toy's behalf—then threw a banquet for him. Afterward, the guests, treated to the biggest cigars that could be had, blew smoke into the windows of Hip Sing headquarters.

Despite mounting evidence to the contrary, in the eyes of the Lexow Committee and those of many journalists, Wong Get was a courageous do-gooder who had abandoned his sinful gambling ways. He had placed himself at substantial risk in exposing Tom Lee. And if Wong was a good Christian devoted to ridding the Chinese quarter of vice, then his Hip Sing Tong must be a worthy organization.

This rise to respectability of the Hip Sings—who became known as the Chinese Parkhursts—was telegraphed for all to see when Mayor Strong visited Chinatown on April 4 and became the first mayor ever to make an official visit to the Chinese quarter. Although Strong went at the invitation of Chu Fong, the wealthy On Leong proprietor of the Doyers Street Chinese Theatre, just before dinner, at a posh restaurant at 24 Pell called the Mon Lay Won, it was a Hip Sing who took center stage.

In a small room adjoining the banquet hall decorated with flowers and carved ebony furniture, a slim young Hip Sing gave a welcome speech and ushered the mayor onto a bunk covered in finely woven matting. He then deftly cooked an opium pill and showed the mayor how it was smoked. He even offered him a pipe, though His Honor politely declined to take it.

The young man's name was Mock Duck. Although he was already well-known to the customs inspectors as "one of the most active smugglers of Chinamen in the city," it was surely the first time the mayor or any other politician had ever heard his name. It would not, however, be the last. It was a name New Yorkers would hear—and fear—for many years hence.

For the balance of the 1890s, the tongs struggled with each other, but not yet in deathly fashion. Although there were skirmishes, the short-term prizes were an advantageous position with the police and the favor and respect of the larger community.

In August 1895, officers raided Wong Get's place at 12 Pell on the suspicion *fan tan* was being played there. The tip probably came from On Leongs, but by this time the local police had built up enough resentment against Wong Get, who had disparaged them before the Lexow Committee, that they didn't need any excuse to harass him.

A week later, Wong, who had concluded he would never get a fair shake from the Sixth Precinct, bypassed Elizabeth Street entirely and went directly to police headquarters on Mulberry Street to report a *fan tan* game at 30 Mott being run under On Leong protection. He claimed his repeated complaints to Captain Young had been ignored. His implication, of course, was that Young and his men were in the pocket of Tom Lee. It was a brilliant assault against both the On Leongs *and* their police partners, and it had its desired effect. Central Office police, who had no ties to the On Leong Tong, raided the game on August 10, and twenty-eight men were arrested.

Captain Young had not been told of the raid, and when he saw Wong Get at the station house, he became enraged.

"You lie when you say you can get no satisfaction here," he said.

"I say I don't," Wong Get replied sharply. "I have reported gambling places to you, but you never made a raid."

"What right did you have to go to Police Headquarters? You can't prove these Chinamen were gambling. You're mad because I won't let you run a game," he said accusingly, adding, "I'll fix you."

Even though Wong Get identified seven of the arrested men as Hip Sings who had been not gambling but merely gathering evidence, Young insisted on locking up *all* the men without bail, a spiteful move that infuriated Frank Moss.

"I am not through with Captain Young yet," Moss declared threateningly.

The Hip Sing Tong continued its quest for the appearance of respectability. In late 1896, its attorney submitted articles of incorporation to the Brooklyn Supreme Court, where they were approved on November 5. According to the articles, the organization's objects were

to establish and maintain a permanent place of meeting for the members away from the baneful influences of the opium den and gambling joint, where religious observances, social amusements, recreations and intercourse may be enjoyed and the study of the English language pursued.

To further the suppression through lawful means of gambling, Policy selling, vice and immorality generally among the Chinese of the Cities of New York and Brooklyn, and such other places as the corporation, through its Directors, may hereafter decide to add; and to prosecute through the proper authorities such violations of the laws relating to order and morality as may come to its notice, and in general to raise the tone of the resident Chinese.

In other words, the charter specified goals that were more or less the polar *opposite* of what the group actually stood for. Three hundred men were said to have joined, and an organizational meeting was set for January.

Not to be outdone, the On Leongs secured a charter from Albany as the Chinese Merchants Association on February 4, 1897, two days after Chinese New Year. Boasting more than two hundred members, the On Leongs occupied the top floor of 14 Mott and named Tom Lee as their president, Charlie Boston as their vice president, Lee Loy as secretary, and Chu Gong as treasurer.

To mark the occasion, the On Leongs secured a permit to set off fifty thousand firecrackers, strung from their building to another across the street. The popping lasted for a full ten minutes and was audible for half a mile. Then the officers appeared, dressed in their finest silk robes, and presided over a seventeen-course dinner at the clubhouse for members and guests, followed by musical entertainment.

In the following months, the Hip Sings wrapped themselves in the Parkhurst flag at every turn. In April 1897, Dong Fong, the Hip Sing interpreter who had helped secure the arrest of Lee Toy three years earlier, was detained after a fight. Dong assaulted an officer and was arrested for disorderly conduct. In the station house, he threatened to have the policeman dismissed from the force.

"I know Commissioner Moss," he boasted, "and I'll have him broke."

Dong might have overestimated Moss's power, but he wasn't lying about the relationship. He was, indeed, close to Frank Moss, who mentioned him in a book he published that year:

> He is bold, plucky, resolute and true. His heart is generous, and he would sacrifice himself to serve a friend. . . . In the days of the Lexow Committee, when I pursued my inquiries into the ways and methods of Chinatown, I felt safe when Dong Fong was at my right hand. . . . Dong, I like you, I trust you, I know you will not betray me, and I am not afraid of Chinese blackjacks or daggers in dark hallways when you lead the way.

In court, the attorney George W. Glaze accused the policeman of arresting Dong precisely *because* he was a member of the Parkhurst Society. He also defended Dong's honor, such as it was.

"Your honor, this man is fighting crime in Chinatown, and is not the kind of a man to get mixed in a brawl," Glaze assured the judge.

"Well, I believe the officer," the judge rejoined, "and I'll fine Fong $5. And officer, if any trouble is made at Police Headquarters, you may call on me for help."

But there was dissent in the Hip Sing ranks. A tong meeting on August 29 degenerated into violence. To all willing to see it—and Frank Moss was not among them—the veil of respectability so useful to the Hip Sings was slipping.

"There is trouble in the Hip Sing Tong," the New York *Sun* warned. "The organization is composed of Chinamen who pose as reformers, but who, the merchants of Chinatown say, are not reformers. The society was organized for the purpose of suppressing vice, but it seems to have a rocky road to travel, its members being continually in hot water and quarrelling with one another." But the *Sun,* which offered the most in-depth reporting about Chinatown of all the New York papers during this period, was on both sides of the argument about the Hip Sings. Later the very same month, it published a paean to Mock Duck, calling him "a shining light in the Hip Sing Tong" who "is a regular Parkhurst."

❖   ❖   ❖   ❖   ❖

Young Mock Duck, who was rising rapidly in the Hip Sing hierarchy, claimed to have been born in San Francisco in 1879, though there are no records to prove it. He was slim and delicate, almost girlish in demeanor, with a wide face, slender shoulders, and a flat, narrow torso. He wore size 6 shoes, weighed 125 pounds, was under five feet six, and looked anything but menacing. But his benign, youthful appearance belied what one observer warned was "the spirit of a tiger."

The "shining light" was actually spearheading a drive to consolidate Hip Sing control over Pell Street, which his tong viewed as its rightful territory. He knew it would have been foolhardy to take on the On Leongs directly in light of the latter's strong relationship with the police department, so he sought out an easier mark: the Four Brothers' Society, which was a clan association rather than a secret society. Most such organizations were set up by and for people with one surname; the Four Brothers' Society was unusual in that it brought four numerically small families together under one umbrella. In New York's Chinatown, the Chu family dominated its leadership.

On September 21, Mock Duck visited a gambling house at 22 Pell Street to shake down Chu Lock, the owner. The Hip Sings were demanding $10 a week in protection money. When Chu's henchmen kicked him down the stairs and into the street, Mock Duck went to the police to report the establishment. But by the time officers reached Pell Street, Chu had removed all incriminating evidence from the premises.

The following week, a brawl ensued at the same location, and knives were drawn. Chu Lock's brother was wounded in the fray, as was Mock Duck himself. He sustained a large gash in his left leg, and another Hip Sing was stabbed in the shoulder. A spate of court cases followed: Chu Lock was accused of felonious assault, and he, in turn, accused the Hip Sings of perjury; a grand jury also handed down an indictment against Mock Duck, Dong Fong, and a third man for felonious assault. But no convictions followed.

◆　◆　◆　◆　◆

OPPOSITE: Iconic turn-of-the-century photo portrait of the Hip Sing kingpin Mock Duck.

Late in 1897, Tom Lee gave a dinner for Tammany Hall. It was a clever move, because Tammany operatives were poised to retake the city government. Local government's reach was also about to grow significantly: to ensure the metropolis's continued economic and commercial primacy, voters had approved, and Albany had mandated, the consolidation of Manhattan, Brooklyn, Queens, Staten Island, and the Bronx into the City of Greater New York. The new entity would be born at the stroke of midnight on New Year's Day.

Mayor Strong, who had opposed the consolidation, had not sought reelection. His replacement was Robert Anderson Van Wyck, a Tammany man who had campaigned on the slogan "To Hell with Reform" and defeated his Republican opponent handily. Van Wyck declined Lee's invitation, but some seventy others spent the evening of November 23 in Chinatown. The *New-York Tribune* explained that the leading lights of the Chinese quarter, weary of having their vice dens raided, wished to get off on the right foot with the new administration. And because Tammany was returning, they had every reason to expect an easier time of things.

The guests were given royal treatment. They were greeted by firecrackers and treated to dinner at the Mon Lay Won. Popularly known as the Chinese Delmonico, it was the grandest eatery in the Chinese quarter. They sampled shark's fin and bird's nest soup and three kinds of Chinese spirits. And afterward, they were treated to a performance at the Chinese Theatre.

But Lee did not neglect his Chinatown constituency. A year later, renovations bankrolled by the Lee family were completed on the Joss House in Chinatown's City Hall at 16 Mott. The new worship space was richly decorated with paintings and tapestries and appointed with carved ebony altar fittings and furniture. At a $20-a-plate celebration, Tom Lee delivered a paean to his adopted country and to the position of the Chinese within it: "We are living here in the new white light of freedom, enlightened, yet not

OPPOSITE: Lower Mott Street, ca. 1900. At the far right is 14 Mott, headquarters of the On Leong Tong, whose sign is visible on the top floor. Next to it is No. 16, the headquarters of the Chung Hwa Gong Shaw, also known as Chinatown's City Hall, which included the Joss House. To its left, an awning protrudes at No. 18, a property owned by Tom Lee.

enthralled. We are of this great people a part, a body; we will never bring them harm, nor trouble, nor disgrace, but happiness."

In the public relations war against the Hip Sing Tong, the On Leongs struck a major blow with the 1898 publication of a book called *New York's Chinatown*. Its author, Louis J. Beck, a white journalist and private detective, set out to provide an impartial look at the everyday life of the city's Chinese. Beck had a keen eye for detail, and he presented a comprehensive account of the people, customs, and institutions of the Chinese quarter, including descriptions of opium dens and *fan tan* houses, an accounting of Chinatown organizations, and profiles of its leading lights. Nothing like it had ever appeared before.

Beck's principal sources, however, were On Leongs, whom he portrayed in glowing terms, making no mention of their association with vice. Not so the Hip Sing Tong, about whom he had no illusions. He had no doubt that it was little more than a criminal enterprise and gave no credence to the idea that it stood for reform.

The Hip Sings, Beck reported, had about 450 members in 1898, "every one of whom is an expert in crime, as understood in this country, and fully eligible to a residence in state's prison or a seat in the chair of electrocution." But he allowed that some Chinese had a different view of them. "They are not looked upon as criminals by the Chinese whose moral ethics differ so widely from those of Western civilization. They go and come among their countrymen with entire freedom, though well-known and their nefarious business thoroughly understood."

Beck called highbinders like the Hip Sings "cold-blooded, pitiless and cruel," with "no hesitation at shedding blood, or even committing murder." He added, "In fact, for pay, the highbinder is ready to perpetrate any villainy, from perjury up to murder, and his oath-bound fellows, under pain of death, must protect him should he fall in the meshes of the law in the practice of his unholy vocation."

Beck didn't so much exaggerate the Hip Sings' faults as ignore those of their rivals. The On Leongs were certainly guilty of graft and adept at trumping up charges and bearing false witness against their enemies. Although they preferred to pay hired guns to do their dirty work—the Hip

Sings were more likely to rely on their own members when blood was to be shed—the only real difference was that the On Leongs cut the police in on the booty to ensure protection of their clients, while the Hip Sings reported those who refused to pay to the Parkhursts or else threatened nonpayers with violence they would inflict themselves.

Both strategies were effective, and both were profitable. Whose would prevail remained to be seen, but getting there would cost both tongs dearly in treasure, angst, and carnage. The bloodbath was about to begin. Where it would end was anyone's guess.

Chapter 5

The War Begins

Shortly after the turn of the century, the killing began.

The first to die was Lung Kin, a Hip Sing. An Amsterdam Avenue laundryman paying his usual Sunday visit to Chinatown, he fell victim to a pistol shot by thirty-one-year-old Gong Wing Chung, also a washerman, on the evening of August 12, 1900, in the dreary hallway of a tenement at 9 Pell.

With a bullet lodged in his abdomen, Lung Kin was rushed to Hudson Street Hospital, where he bled to death. His assailants—Sin Cue and three others, in addition to Gong—were promptly arrested and found in possession of revolvers, blackjacks, brass knuckles, daggers, and other deadly weapons. Police spirited them off to the Elizabeth Street stationhouse as a large crowd of whites massed on Pell Street, shouting "lynch the Chinks" and scorning the prisoners as "Boxers," a reference to the violent, antiforeign militiamen then in rebellion in China whose killing of Americans and other foreigners had recently been trumpeted in the newspapers.

According to the rumor mill, Gong had lost heavily at *fan tan* that evening and claimed Lung had cheated him. But this was no gambling row. It was a well-planned execution of a Hip Sing by a member of what the papers called the "Mongolian Order of the Masons." Although strictly speaking that was a reference to the Loon Yee Tong, what was surely meant was the On Leong Tong. The confusion was easy to understand: both organizations were under the thumb of Tom Lee.

The plan, police learned, had been to kill four Hip Sings, but the others had escaped. And the confiscated weapons were all brand-new, leading them to believe that the On Leongs had been gearing up for battle. No such group of armed criminals had ever been caught in Chinatown before.

Lung Kin's assassination initiated the First Tong War, a battle for control of graft in Chinatown. It would be fought with revolvers, truncheons, and cleavers on Pell and Mott streets, on the Bowery, and in the Doyers Street theater. The combatants would use ambushes and arson and would make threats against jurors and attacks on witnesses. And the conflict would last for six long years.

Charged with homicide, Gong was remanded, although he never actually stood trial. While incarcerated in the Tombs, he was judged mad and was committed to New York State's Matteawan Asylum for Insane Criminals. The others, charged with felonious assault and carrying concealed weapons, were released on bail.

Just over a month after Gong's arraignment, the Hip Sings took revenge. When Sin Cue visited Pell Street on September 21 with his friend Ah Fee, a Newark tailor who was also an On Leong, the pair stopped at the Wo On Chinese Merchandise Shop at the corner of Pell and Doyers to buy wrapping paper. Emerging from the store at 4:00 p.m., they were ambushed by half a dozen armed Hip Sings waiting on Pell. One threw pepper in Sin Cue's face, and another began to beat him with an iron bar.

Sin Cue and Ah Fee fled up Pell Street, hotly pursued by Sue Sing, a thirty-eight-year-old Hip Sing laundryman, and by Mock Duck. The latter chased Sin Cue, who was short and stout, into No. 23, firing at him through the double doors with a six-shooter. He missed his target, but a stray bullet struck a bystander, twenty-four-year-old Mary Mazzocci, who was sitting on the front stoop with two children who were also slightly injured.

Sue Sing fired at Ah Fee as he chased him up Pell. One bullet struck the On Leong in the back and passed through his right lung before it exited. Ah Fee managed to stagger around the corner onto Mott Street, but when he got to No. 24, he dropped to the pavement. A nearby policeman ran to him; as he lifted the man's coat and vest, blood gushed out.

"I go die," Ah Fee cried out.

The officer ran to one of the call boxes installed by order of Commissioner Roosevelt and summoned an ambulance. Most of the assailants had scattered, but Sue Sing, who had discarded his empty six-shooter—standard tong practice was to get rid of evidence as soon as possible—was captured by another bluecoat and placed under arrest.

Ah Fee had no pulse when the ambulance arrived. He was revived at

Pell and Doyers streets, 1900. Ah Fee was shot after he emerged
from the Wo On Chinese Merchandise Shop at 19 Pell Street,
whose sign and doorway are visible at the far right.

Hudson Street Hospital, but when the police learned the surgeons didn't
think he would last the night, they dragged Sue Sing to the hospital. Ah
Fee identified him as the man who had shot him, although he declined to
explain why. Nor was Sue Sing, arraigned the next day and held without
bail, talking. Ah Fee died at half past ten.

Tom Lee confirmed to the press that the murder stemmed from discord
between the two Chinatown societies but claimed ignorance of the reason
Ah Fee had been targeted. Lee was surely being disingenuous. Both men
were on the Hip Sing hit list, Sin Cue for his role in Lung Kin's murder and
Ah Fee because he was an alibi witness for Gong Wing Chung, Lung's
shooter. Ah Fee's assassination was a calculated Hip Sing effort to ensure
Gong's conviction by eliminating a witness who could place him elsewhere,
and Tom Lee certainly knew it.

❖ ❖ ❖ ❖ ❖

After two years on the Police Commission, Theodore Roosevelt had been drafted by President William McKinley to serve as assistant secretary of the navy, a position he held for a year before resigning in 1898 to serve with the Rough Riders, which is when he led their famous charge up Cuba's San Juan Hill. Later that year, he was elected governor of New York. And although he had a good deal on his gubernatorial plate, his antipathy toward Tammany Hall was undiminished, and he still managed to keep an eye on law enforcement in New York City. He took note when Asa B. Gardiner, who had become New York County district attorney when Tammany returned to power in 1898, was hauled up on charges of corruption. Roosevelt removed him from office and appointed the attorney Eugene A. Philbin to the post at the end of 1900.

Philbin had a reputation for rectitude and vowed to make his administration a "strenuous" one. He told reporters he hoped to be guided by Roosevelt's example, and he didn't waste time. Within days, he had fired many senior members of the staff he inherited and announced a war on vice, and within months he began indicting gambling bosses and bookmakers and going after corrupt police captains.

Philbin inherited the Chinatown murder cases from his predecessor. The newspapers had made a great deal of them. Gambling and running opium dens were bad enough, but now the Chinese had also begun to kill one another. A strong response was needed, and Philbin decided to use Sue Sing's trial to go after the Hip Sings, whom he fingered as the source of all the trouble.

One of his deputies, Francis P. Garvan, a twenty-five-year-old Yale-educated attorney, claimed they had amassed evidence that showed that Hip Sings had murdered Ah Fee and allowed that they had gotten help in gathering it from none other than Tom Lee, a "good Chinaman." Sue Sing pleaded guilty to murder in the second degree to avoid the possibility of a death sentence and was sent to Sing Sing prison for life. But Philbin, convinced the killing had been the work of a syndicate, vowed to go after his cohorts as well.

In the meantime, the Hip Sings put a $3,000 bounty on Tom Lee's head. After Sue Sing's sentencing, Lee told Garvan, four Chinese men had begun tailing him, not only at his place of business on Mott, but also at his home on 161st Street. They had even pounded on the door one evening and, after being sent away by Lee's wife, lurked in the shadows until after midnight. Garvan promised Lee police protection.

"They are after me now," Lee told a friend. "Some day I go like that," he added, with an ominous snap of his fingers. Soon afterward, he received a warning from a friend, or perhaps an enemy, in Los Angeles who signed his name only *W.* The note read, "Be on your guard. Five men, members of the H., are on way to New York to assassinate you."

Tom Lee knew exactly what *H* meant. He didn't stop aiding the new district attorney. But he did take to carrying a loaded gun at all times.

Philbin and Garvan pursued the Hip Sings relentlessly. Sue Sing gave no help; bound by a blood oath, he refused to implicate any of his associates. But the district attorney's office got all the information it needed from Tom Lee and company. Philbin issued indictments for felonious assault for the wounding of Mary Mazzocci and the children and for first-degree murder for the killing of Ah Fee. Apart from Sue Sing, now in prison, five Hip Sings, including Mock Duck, were charged.

The men bolted when they learned of the charges; the electric chair, introduced in New York in 1888, was a real possibility if they were convicted of murder. Tom Lee and Sin Cue were determined to track them down, however. Police managed to capture three of the five—one was never apprehended and Mock Duck fled to Buffalo. Tom Lee had him shadowed there and provided information on his whereabouts to the police, whereupon his arrest became a foregone conclusion. So much so that more than two months after the warrant was issued, Mock Duck surrendered himself.

He was already on the judge's docket for assault when he appeared to answer the charge of first-degree murder, prompting his attorney, Abraham Levy, to ask for a stay of two days before submitting his plea.

"I've been working hard to get him tried on the assault charge," Levy complained to Judge Rufus B. Cowing, "and all that's resulted is an indictment for murder."

"You keep on," Cowing warned before granting the request, "and you'll get him hanged."

But before any trials could begin, just after 7:00 a.m. on June 3, a fire broke out at 16 Pell. A pan of grease ignited in the kitchen of the Hung Far Low Restaurant on the second floor and spread rapidly to the two upper floors of the rickety old structure, which housed the sleeping quarters of several On Leong Tong members. Firemen were summoned, and sleepers were roused. Most managed to escape, but three men died in the fire. The first two were found prostrate next to their bunks; the third had managed to get to the balcony of the third floor before being overcome by heat and smoke. To the horror of those gathered outside, he then plunged headlong into the street, landing squarely on his skull. He died instantly.

The man was thirty-nine-year-old Sin Cue, Ah Fee's companion and one of Lung Kin's attackers. He was also the district attorney's principal witness against Mock Duck.

The authorities believed the fire had been an accident, but the On Leongs knew better. The Hip Sings needed Sin Cue out of the way so he couldn't testify against their brothers. And indeed, when Wong Get saw his dead body that morning, a broad smile crossed his face.

Assistant District Attorney Garvan acknowledged that the loss of Sin Cue dealt a serious blow to the case but not, he believed, a fatal one. "I think we can convict the prisoners, but it will not be without considerable difficulty," he told the press.

He had no idea how difficult it would prove to be.

The election of Mayor Van Wyck in 1897 had signaled a return to Tammany business as usual. Although it posed a setback to the reformers, it didn't stop their efforts to combat corruption. In 1900, at a meeting of prominent New Yorkers, the "Committee of Fifteen" was established to investigate the citywide rise in prostitution and gambling and propose legislative remedies.

The nonpartisan, blue-ribbon panel of men-about-town was chaired by William H. Baldwin Jr., president of the Long Island Rail Road, and included luminaries like the bankers Jacob Schiff and George Foster Peabody. They hired investigators and dispatched them to brothels, opium dens, and gambling parlors across the city. Acting on tips from concerned citizens, the sleuths gathered a great deal of detailed information.

When it came to Chinatown, however, they found it quite as opaque as earlier reformers had. Unable to pose as Chinese or speak their language, they had little means of penetrating the inner sanctums of the Chinese quarter on their own. Fortunately for them, however, a couple of would-be Virgils were more than happy to take their inspectors by the hand and guide them in their descent into Chinatown's version of hell.

One was Wong Get, the darling of the Parkhurst and Lexow committees. The Hip Sings' alliances with these groups had paid off in spades, and they weren't about to pass up yet another stick with which to bludgeon the hated On Leongs. Together with Wong Aloy, an associate who also spoke English quite well, he offered the investigators information about Chinatown vice and a guided tour.

Among the places Wong Aloy led Arthur E. Wilson, one of the committee's undercover investigators, was Mike Callahan's saloon at 12 Chatham Square. Although not run by Chinese, it catered to many Chinese patrons. In a rear chamber, where young women were known to "expose their limbs using vulgar and profane talk," Wilson was solicited by a Miss Annie Gilroy, who lived at 11 Mott, an On Leong hangout owned by Charlie Boston. Later he reported,

> This woman solicited me to go there with Mr. Wong Aloy and my friend Rogers, telling me that there I could have sexual intercourse for $3 each man. She said that she would have some very pretty girls from the age of 18 to 20 years of age. She stated to me that the police received protection money from each girl who occupied rooms in the above named houses. All the protection was generally paid to wardmen or somebody deputized by the Captain or wardman to collect. They pay from $12 to $20 per month each girl. She told me that if I wished to call there any night she would have the girls who lived in rooms at the same address, 11 Mott Street, call in her room and have a good time. She would also have a Chinese girl there and would have her strip and show me what a Chinese woman looked like.
>
> This Miss Gilroy stated to me her nerves were all racked and her nervous system gone from the excessive use of opium. She said she had cohabited with four different Chinamen of high rank. She also told me

that if I wanted to go to an opium den where society women from uptown districts—some of them were women from families of refinement—she would be pleased to take me and my friends there providing Wong Aloy would be with the party. She said I could see the women reclining on couches under the influence of opium and generally they had the bosoms of their dress open and also I would be able to observe the familiarity often and Chinamen who visit this opium den with these women.

Most of the women involved in the trade Miss Gilroy and her friends were plying were white. It could hardly have been otherwise, because the ratio of Chinese men to Chinese women in New York State in 1900 was nearly five thousand to one, a consequence of the Page Act, passed by Congress in 1875 specifically to deny entry to prostitutes from Asia. The few Chinese prostitutes who made it to America would typically work in bordellos for four or five years until the fees for their passage, payments to those who brought them, and any disbursements made to their parents to "purchase" them were all repaid and a profit had been earned at their expense. After this, if they had not died of venereal disease or succumbed

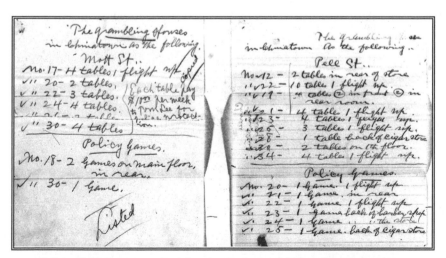

A list of Chinatown gambling houses provided to the Committee of Fifteen by the Hip Sings Wong Get and Wong Aloy, 1901.

to some other dread ailment, they would be free to wed, work elsewhere, or return to China. Many did remain and marry, their fortunes somewhat improved by the overall paucity of Chinese women in America.

According to Leong Gor Yun in *Chinatown Inside Out,* as a rule, the Chinese prostitutes "are owned by powerful tong members, and even if independent, have to be on good terms with them. In general they have to give right of way to tong men to avoid trouble," he added, meaning they had to service their Chinese keepers before anyone else. "Prostitution yields a sufficient income (though much less than gambling) to keep the tongs interested and in control," Leong observed, "but on the whole it is only a secondary cause of war."

Freelance white hookers plied their trade on the streets of Chinatown, visiting laundries early in the mornings, when the washermen were not busy, or cheap restaurants, where they might score a meal and a tip in exchange for their favors. But there were also brothels, and some were run by Chinese. The pimps charged $1 per call: fifty cents for the bed and fifty cents for the house. The girls kept anything they could get over that amount.

Wong Aloy took Wilson to see the bawdy houses up close. Wilson described how all were protected by Chinese guards whose job was to sound warning at the first sign of danger. The services rendered by the tong men included only protection against harassment from rival gangs and rowdies, however, not from the police. The payoff to the authorities, according to Wilson, came directly from the girls.

Wong Aloy did as fine a job of duping Committee of Fifteen investigators as Wong Get and Mock Duck had done earlier with the Parkhursts. "Wong Aloy is a man who can be depended upon as he showed enthusiasm and a zealousness on these visits last night," Wilson cooed. "He said his main object was to destroy the gambling houses and stop his countrymen from being robbed by Chinese expert gamblers, also of having police levy tribute and blackmail upon gambling houses and houses of prostitution."

What he *didn't* say was that if the On Leongs' hold on the gambling parlors could be broken, the way would be clear for Wong's Hip Sing brethren to pick up the slack.

The Committee of Fifteen's report did not name specific establishments.

It focused broadly on the overall problem and possible solutions and did not result in the closing of any Chinatown vice dens. But it did shine more light on the nexus between the police and the underworld, and its findings—like those of the Lexow Committee before it—helped put Tammany Hall out of office again.

A former mayor of Brooklyn and more recently the president of Columbia University, the reformist Seth Low was chosen mayor of New York in 1901 with the support of his own Republican Party and anti-Tammany Democrats. His administration took office on New Year's Day 1902. The Chinese New Year celebration that followed by a month offered the On Leongs a made-to-order opportunity to entertain the newly powerful. On February 17, they hosted a banquet at their headquarters and invited just about everyone they could think of who might prove useful.

Vilified in the 1890s as the evil lords of Chinatown, Tom Lee and his On Leongs were making progress in the new century reclaiming their reputation as upstanding citizens. It was the Hip Sings who were now generally identified as highbinders—that is, gangsters. The On Leong Tong, otherwise known as the Chinese Merchants Association, was coming to be seen more as Chinatown's chamber of commerce. Its members were said to be the most respectable and well-to-do men in the community, so their banquet was well attended.

Although Mayor Low, who had accepted their invitation, failed to show up, the attendees constituted a veritable *Who's Who* of local law enforcement and the judiciary, including a few surprising guests whose pasts suggested they might be less than friendly to Tom Lee. Among those from the police department were Colonel John N. Partridge, newly appointed to the office of police commissioner, and his deputies. There was Judge Warren W. Foster of the Court of General Sessions, who was destined to play a major role in mediating the tong wars. Also present was the Parkhurst and Lexow Committee alumnus William T. Jerome, who replaced Eugene A. Philbin as New York County district attorney. These men had been no lovers of the On Leong Tong. The Chinese consul general was also on hand. And Tom Lee had graciously invited the four attorneys defending Mock Duck as well, though all declined.

The dinner was inaugurated with a fusillade of 100,000 firecrackers strung across Mott Street. The more than one hundred guests were seated at small, round linen-draped tables and served a twenty-seven-course meal. Tom Lee's son Frank gave a speech, and the elder Lee followed Chinese custom and made the rounds of the room, toasting guests at each table. Attendees received small preserve dishes as favors; the most honored got ivory chopsticks. And after the meal, Colonel Partridge and his party were given a tour of Chinatown.

The evening was a roaring success. "When the city officials separated," the *New-York Tribune* noted, "they did so with the feeling that they could teach the yellow man little of the art of hospitality."

The day after the banquet, Mock Duck went on trial for the murder of Ah Fee. Assistant District Attorney Arthur C. Train, one of Jerome's deputies, appeared for the People. He, too, had been a guest of the On Leongs' the night before.

The Hip Sings were willing to pay for top legal talent to defend Mock Duck, who had emerged as leader of the New York branch of the tong, now outranking even Wong Get. The attorneys Abraham Levy and George W. Glaze were on the defense team, as was the redoubtable Frank Moss.

The first hurdle was swearing in a jury. During hour after hour of voir dire, each prospective juror was asked whether he had any "objections to Chinamen," and many did. Adolph Bauch was excused after he admitted his prejudice would influence his verdict. John French quoted Bret Harte: "For ways that are dark and tricks that are vain, the heathen Chinee is peculiar." He, too, was discharged, as were a Mr. Dougherty, who felt there should be a law keeping "Chinamen" at home so there would be more work for American washerwomen, and George Carter, a tailor who disdained all Chinese as heathens. Frank Fisher, a divinity student, on the other hand, said he would "believe a Chinaman a great deal sooner" than some white men he knew. He was accepted.

"If this jury business keeps on," one of the weary prosecutors quipped, "we may have to hire Mr. Duck to plead guilty or commit suicide."

The jury box was eventually filled, but on February 21 a white prosecution witness named Emma Wing reported she had been threatened. When she appeared in the Criminal Courts Building, she said, a man named Lee Lang told her he would cut out her heart if she dared testify she had witnessed the killing. Lee, in the courtroom as a spectator that day, was immediately taken into custody and held on $500 bond and was eventually convicted of witness tampering.

Nor was that the only such case. Another white witness, a wrestler named Leo Pardello, handed Train a note he had received whose upper half was saturated with blood. It bore the dateline "Hell, February 21" and read,

> You last Friday make witness for the District Attorney against my brother, Mock Duck. You lie; police lie; District Attorney lie; everybody lie. You when go for witness you make big mistake. You die, die today. Pepper in your eyes and bullet in your heart. You no go alive. Chinese and Chinese fight: that is our business. No good business for white man. Well, best thing you die so you make no more witness for Chinese.

The letter was signed, simply, "One, Two Three," which might have been triad-related code words, and the district attorney's office pledged to investigate its origins. Whether any jurors received similar threats is unknown. For whatever reason, however, Mock Duck's trial ended in a hung jury. After deliberating for seven hours, the panel, which favored conviction by a vote of 10–2, was deadlocked.

But it wasn't over for Mock Duck. He was sent back to the Tombs to await a new trial.

Less than a month later, Mock Duck was tried for murder a second time. No one accused him of pulling the trigger on Ah Fee, but he was believed to have masterminded the operation.

Prosecution witnesses placed him at the scene, waiting for Ah Fee and Sin Cue to emerge from the Wo On shop at 19 Pell. Several reported seeing him point to the store and hearing him tell the others to "wait until they come out." Some recalled he had fired a gun. Mary Mazzocci identified him as her assailant. And his next-door neighbor remembered seeing him remove a bulletproof vest and take a gun from his pocket when he returned to his room shortly after the shooting.

In all, twenty-seven witnesses were called to make the prosecution's case or rebut the testimony of defense witnesses. Even Frank Lee, Tom's younger son, took the stand, ostensibly to confirm that Sin Cue was dead and thus unable to testify, but really to hint that he had been murdered to prevent his appearance.

Frank Moss cross-examined many of the witnesses, but it was the attorney Glaze who presented the defense's theory—or rather *theories*—of the case. His principal argument was that Mock Duck had an alibi: he and a friend were at Fulton Street Market at the time of the shootings. They had gone to buy a terrapin—highly prized in Chinese herbal medicine for its alleged disease-curing properties. As a backup, however, Glaze blamed Sin Cue and Ah Fee for shooting first, which, if true, would have made Sue Sing's killing of Ah Fee a case of self-defense rather than murder. And if no murder had been committed, then even if the jurors believed Mock Duck had been present on Pell Street, he could not have been an accessory to murder.

The prosecutor asked several defense witnesses who had recruited them to testify, and the answer was generally Wong Get. Similarly, the defense attorneys pointed the finger at the On Leongs. The implication, of course, was that testimony was induced or compelled in some other way, through threats or blackmail. By the end of the trial, it was impossible to escape the conclusion that many of the witnesses had been bought.

Moss, clearly worried for his client, revealed his flair for the melodramatic in his summation, painting as gruesome a picture of the death penalty as he could. He enjoined the jury,

> If it be so, that, within a few months from now, in the grounds of Sing Sing, the electric current be turned on, and the blood of Mock Duck be made to seethe in his veins, and his tissues to melt with heat, and his tortured nerves to be wrung in anguish, and his spirit to be sent, unbidden, to the presence of his Maker, will it be, think you, the hand of the jailer that turns on the current, that really does that act? I tell you, gentlemen, that, if that thing happens to this living man, it will be you that will do it, it will be the foreman, Mr. Wolf; the second juror, Mr. Bixby; and the third, Mr. Paspary; and the fourth, Mr. Pine; and every one of you.

The attorney and social reformer Frank Moss, longtime ally of the Hip Sing Tong, who served the Parkhurst Society, the Lexow Committee, and the district attorney's office.

He also attempted to neutralize any anti-Chinese prejudice felt by the jurors by owning up to his own bias:

> I declare to you that, were Mock Duck a white man and the testimony the same, I should submit this case to you without argument. But Mock Duck is not a white man. . . . I realized this morning as I came to court to perform my duty by this man that I had not put out my hand to him, as I would have done, if he had been a man of my own color. . . . I admit it, and yet it is not right, and yet it is in the antagonism of the races. . . . I dwell upon these things because the same God that made you made him, and because there is the same sort of soul that dwells there.

In his summation, Assistant District Attorney Train made much of the fact that Moss and company had presented two incompatible defenses and two sets of witnesses with conflicting stories to support them. He noted that Mock Duck had initially fled from justice and had not come up with his alibi until seven months after Ah Fee died. He did what he could to discredit the alibi witnesses, dismissing one as immaterial, another as in-toxicated, and a third as opium addled and suggesting that others were paid for their testimony.

Train actively *played* to latent racism among the jurors, dismissing one Chinese witness as "the chattering Chinaman" and attempting to impeach a white witness who placed Mock Duck at the Fulton Market by stooping to the "they-all-look-alike" argument:

> Could any man, any living man, remember the face of a Chinaman, to whom he had sold a terrapin after eighteen months, when . . . they have a great many Chinese customers?

He also predicted retaliation against the prosecution's witnesses if the jury voted to acquit:

> If this man is guiltless, turn him out. . . . Send back to Chinatown this man and the other man. Well, if we do, I do not think that I would give much for the lives of the People's witnesses in this case. There has not been a shot fired in Chinatown since the 21st of September, 1900. If this man is acquitted, I imagine you will hear more shots.

In his instructions to the jury, the judge dealt a blow to one of the defense's two theories—that Sue Sing had acted in self-defense. He stated simply that if the jury accepted that Ah Fee was fleeing from Sue Sing when he was shot in the back, then it had been murder, plain and simple. This left only the alibi defense. But the judge also made clear that a guilty verdict would require the jury to conclude that Mock Duck had aided and abetted Sue Sing in the killing of Ah Fee. They were told if they found he had not been on Pell Street when the murder was committed, they must acquit.

After nearly two weeks of directly conflicting testimony, the jury could not agree that Mock Duck had planned the assassination. After an overnight session that ran for twenty-one hours, this jury, too, was deadlocked, their vote standing at 11–1. This time, however, the majority favored acquittal.

Mock Duck was released, but there was still the matter of the assault charge for the shooting of the bystanders. A third trial was scheduled for April 28, but Assistant District Attorney Train decided to drop the charges against all the defendants. Mock Duck had already been tried twice at great expense, and because the evidence for murder and assault was substantially the same, he knew securing a conviction would be difficult. Besides, the accused men had already spent nine months in the Tombs, which was deemed a fair sentence for assault. There was no need for another trial.

Two weeks later, a banquet for more than a hundred was thrown at the Hung Far Low Restaurant to celebrate the release of Mock Duck and his cohorts. The singing could be heard on the street, and the flag of the Hip Sing Tong was hoisted in front of the building.

It was the very building at which Sin Cue, whose testimony had been expected to convict Mock Duck, had met his maker.

Chapter 6

"A Regular Highbinder, Six-Shooter War Dance on the Bowery"

At 1:30 in the morning on November 3, 1904, as Mock Duck ascended the steps from the basement of 18 Pell, an assailant emerged from a doorway across the street. Without a word, the gunman crossed and fired two bullets at him at close range. One only grazed him, but the other lodged in his stomach and he collapsed. Had the second missile not been partially deflected by his belt buckle, he would surely have died.

The drama continued when a policeman, alerted by the shots, grabbed the fleeing attacker. He dragged the man back to Mock Duck, who, though lying in the gutter in agony, was conscious and able to finger him as his assailant. Suddenly they were surrounded by three Hip Sings with revolvers drawn, intent on vengeance against the enemy who had felled their leader. The policeman quickly pulled his prisoner into a doorway for protection, however, and kept the gunmen at bay until a dozen reinforcements arrived and they fled.

At Hudson Street Hospital, Mock Duck's wound was deemed serious. One paper even jumped the gun with the headline "Chinaman Murdered." His shooter was identified as thirty-two-year-old Lee Sing. This was not the portly Lee Sing who had blackened Tom Lee's eyes in the 1880s; this Lee Sing, a laundryman from Dedham, Massachusetts, was a recruited assassin. He was locked up at Elizabeth Street pending arraignment. Near the scene of the shooting, police found a six-chambered, .32-caliber Smith & Wesson revolver with a twelve-inch barrel and two empty chambers. They also discovered a hunting knife with an eight-inch blade.

At the arraignment, Lee Sing refused to say a word. But Thomas L. McClintock, superintendent of the Parkhurst Society, appeared and asked that as an obvious flight risk he be remanded. McClintock told the court he believed the attack had been carried out in revenge for aid Mock Duck had provided the Parkhursts in recent raids of policy games.

Using information gleaned from Mock Duck and his Hip Sing cohorts, McClintock had goaded the new commissioner of police, William McAdoo, into raiding several Chinatown gambling houses. The Irish-born McAdoo, a former Democratic congressman who had served as assistant secretary of the navy, had taken the job early in 1904. He had been a strong supporter of the mayoral candidate George B. McClellan Jr., a Tammany man and son of the Civil War general and onetime Democratic presidential candidate of the same name. McClellan had beaten Seth Low, who ran for reelection in 1903, when the coalition that had elected Low in 1901 fell apart. Tammany Hall was back in the driver's seat, where it would remain for a decade.

McAdoo had actually been a controversial choice, because the machine's political bosses, who always benefited from lax enforcement of the vice laws, feared he might not consent to play the game. Their instincts were correct. McAdoo wasted little time in declaring his intention to purge the force of extortion and bribery and quash the system that permitted the purchase of promotions and appointments. This would seem to align him with the Parkhursts, who had similar goals.

Armed with warrants they had persuaded a magistrate to issue, the Parkhursts had demanded that McAdoo bypass the Sixth Precinct police, who always seemed to pull their punches when it came to Chinese gamblers, and dispatch headquarters police to accompany them on raids. McAdoo had cooperated. On July 21, 1904, together with a dozen Central Office officers armed with crowbars, axes, revolvers, and billy clubs, six teams of Parkhursts raided policy joints at 20 Doyers Street; 20½ and 23 Pell; and 17, 18, and 30 Mott. The axes came in especially handy at 18 Mott—Tom Lee's building—where officers had to destroy *four* sets of doors to reach the inner sanctum. Fifteen Chinese men, all On Leongs, were arrested.

But the interests of McAdoo and the Parkhursts were actually anything but aligned. "We are after the police in this business," McClintock revealed to the press. "They not only know nothing about our raids, but they have not been doing anything about these gambling places, and more than that, have actually been 'in' with these people. But we will get them in a short time."

The Sixth Precinct police were especially embarrassed at this, which had been McClintock's aim. Captain Francis J. Kear, who had taken command of Elizabeth Street that year, attempted to shift the blame, protesting that his men had arrested more than a hundred Chinese gamblers over the previous six months but had been unable to secure convictions. Nor did McAdoo enjoy being made to look bad. He was no less responsible for the Sixth Precinct than he was for police headquarters, and he quickly became defensive about the insinuation that officers under his command were on the take.

McAdoo demanded proof. After a tour of Chinatown, he declared, "If Mr. McClintock has any evidence whatever to that effect and will bring it to me, I will take pleasure in bringing the machinery of this department at once against the offender, and if they are proven guilty, I will gladly cooperate with the District Attorney in having them brought to justice and properly punished."

Newspapers across the country had a field day with the attack. Most persisted in portraying the Hip Sing as the familiar reformer who desired to clean up Chinatown, and they blamed the assault on nefarious gambling interests intent on foiling his efforts. Others were agnostic as to Mock Duck's motives but quick to label the episode a gang shooting.

Several papers suggested the shooting had been retaliation for the deaths of Ah Fee and Sin Cue, but McClintock suggested a more proximate cause: Mock Duck was slated to appear in court that month as chief witness against the gamblers arrested in July, and he had kept out of sight because he knew the On Leongs were determined to stop him. At a secret meeting of the On Leong Tong, McClintock said, lots had been drawn to determine who would make the hit, and Lee Sing and two associates were selected. Out-of-towners were preferable to locals, because they could more easily disappear after a shooting.

For the first time, the clash between the Hip Sings and the On Leongs was being portrayed as a "tong war" and the highbinders compared to organized criminal gangs of other ethnic groups. "Quite as deadly as the Italian 'Mafia' and 'Black Hand' and even more thoroughly organized, are the secret Chinese societies," the New York *World* explained in something of an overstatement.

Mock Duck was transferred to Bellevue Hospital, and he eventually recovered. But "somewhere in the dark labyrinths of Chinatown are two cutthroats with .44-caliber revolvers and long, keen knives waiting for Mock Duck to leave the hospital," the *World* warned ominously.

By 1904, some sixty *fan tan* parlors and thirty lotteries were operating in Chinatown. Tom Lee and his On Leong Tong had raised their rates and were now assessing the *fan tan* halls $15 per table per week and the policy shops $20. The funds went into a kitty, where they did much more than simply provide insurance against police harassment.

Fifty cents of each payment was earmarked for the Chung Hwa Gong Shaw, the Chinese Consolidated Benevolent Association. Headquartered in the Joss House at 16 Mott, it was the de facto governing body of the community and largely a New York branch of the Six Companies, though it was bankrolled locally. It was an authoritarian organization whose officers were not popularly elected but rather chosen by Chinatown's rich and powerful.

Another half dollar went to the On Leong Tong, the gambling proprietors' guild, and seventy-five cents went to support the Chinese Hospital on nearby Park Street. A fifty-cent cut was also paid to the Merchants Association. Although the On Leongs often went by this English name, this was a different group.

And, of course, untold sums wound up in the pockets of Tammany higher-ups and New York's Finest.

The system amounted to what George Washington Plunkitt, a Tammany Hall ward boss and sometime armchair political philosopher, liked to call "honest graft." A New York state assemblyman and senator who became a millionaire by buying up property based on insider information and reselling it after it had appreciated, Plunkitt drew a distinction between "looters" and "politicians." "The looter goes in for himself alone without considerin' his organization or his city," he said. "The politician looks after his own interests, the organization's interests, and the city's interests all at the same time."

Tom Lee had never been guilty of considering only his own interests. He was certainly intent on personal enrichment; he didn't get to be one of

Chinatown's wealthiest men solely by selling cigars. And he was not above ordering hits on his enemies when his interests were challenged. But he also had the greater good of the Chinese community in mind and had since his arrival in the late 1870s.

Mock Duck and the Hip Sings, by contrast, appear to have had more in common with Plunkitt's looters. They were out *only* for themselves, and any protection money they collected from illegal businesses went nowhere but into their own treasury; nothing was earmarked for the Chinese Hospital. As the "good Chinamen" mask slipped further from the organization's public face, the image emerged of a gang of blackmailers and desperadoes interested in little more than self-enrichment.

The trouble in New York's Chinatown was beginning to raise alarms in several quarters. In San Francisco, the Six Companies discussed appointing a tribunal to resolve the feud and considered asking the Chinese legation in Washington to intercede. The Chinese consul in New York posted a placard calling on both camps to lay down their arms. And the New York *World* even suggested the federal government get involved.

McClintock quoted to the New York *Sun* a missive the On Leongs had sent the Hip Sings a month earlier, in October 1904:

> We invite you to meet and talk over our trouble together at the Chinese Joss House on the ninth day of the present month at 7 o'clock. We want to stop the trouble and enjoy peace. We want a committee of six merchants representing your society to come to the Joss House and make a settlement regarding this trouble so that gambling in Chinatown can proceed as usual and the percentages can be received by the Joss House to enable us to raise the bones of the dead Chinamen here and return them to China as heretofore.

He—and the Hip Sings—saw the statement as a damning acknowledgment by the On Leongs that they were indeed involved in gambling and a bald-faced tactic aimed at obtaining a roster of Hip Sing members, ignoring the possibility that it might actually have been a good faith effort to stop the conflict. In all likelihood, the On Leongs *were* prepared to make concessions in exchange for peace. They had more to lose than the Hip Sings did, and war was costly.

If it was an olive branch, it was a failure. It elicited no response. And later that month, the night after Mock Duck was released from the hospital, the Hip Sing Tong banner that flew outside the brotherhood's headquarters at 12 Bowery was torn from its moorings and stolen. There was no mistaking the provocative nature of the act. It put the Hip Sings on high alert as they anticipated another move against Mock Duck, who, in addition to earning On Leong enmity for past acts, had become a double threat as the chief witness against Lee Sing, his shooter.

They didn't have to wait long. In the wee hours of November 26, pistol shots, shrieks, and cries were heard as the two factions exchanged gunfire in what the New York *Sun* branded "a regular highbinder, six-shooter war dance on the Bowery." The fracas, played out in front of Hip Sing headquarters, occurred as several Hip Sings returned from the Chinese Theatre. Mock Duck, the likely target, was not there, but his absence did not stop the attack.

The fusillade lasted only a couple of minutes. Police immediately arrested four Hip Sings and held two On Leongs as witnesses. Because the On Leongs were the provocateurs, however, this was further indication of their sweetheart arrangement with the law. Officers confiscated an imposing array of battle armor from the Hip Sings. Four coats of armor—two of steel mesh, one of cloth, and one of human hair—were seized. One vest, made of steel rings woven in a lattice pattern, weighed seventy-five pounds, and while it made its wearer invulnerable to bullets, it also rendered him more or less immobile, which in turn made it easy for the police to nab him. The collection of paraphernalia so unnerved the magistrate at Tombs Police Court the next day that he ordered it removed from his sight.

None of the Chinese involved sustained injuries, but three white bystanders were hurt. One was wounded in his hip, and another lost part of his ear. But it was John Baldwin, a white man who had been drinking at Kelly's Saloon at 10 Bowery and had failed to duck for cover, who suffered most. He took a bullet in his abdomen and later died of his injuries.

For his part, Mock Duck, now recovered from his near-death experience, decided to leave town for a while. In due course, however, he would return. And when he did, he would come girded for battle.

Because of Baldwin's death, the four Hip Sings, charged initially only with felonious assault, were now accused of murder. And because the life lost was that of a white man, everyone was feeling the heat.

The Parkhurst Society, according to the New York *World,* was "prepared to spend every penny in its treasury" to protect the accused Hip Sings and to "expose the alleged conspiracy to send them to the electric chair." For first-class legal talent, they had to look no further than Frank Moss, still in their corner. Moss continued grandstanding in the same vein as McClintock. In court, he predicted more killings, reserving his most pointed invective for the district attorney and the police:

> There will be murders, shootings and troubles without end if a stop is not put to gambling in Chinatown, and I want the District Attorney's office to realize it. The control of the gambling privilege is a bone of contention between two great Chinese secret societies, the Hip Sing Tong and the On Leong Tong. The only way to stop this contention is to eliminate the gambling houses in the whole Chinese quarter. I am amazed to see the police and the District Attorney's office apparently protecting the gambling syndicate in this section.

Assistant District Attorney Francis P. Garvan, who handled the case for District Attorney William T. Jerome, predictably took umbrage at Moss's diatribe and challenged him to provide evidence for his accusation. "You appear here in behalf of the On Leong Tong as though you were a paid attorney of that infamous organization," Moss retorted, oblivious to the fact that precisely the same could be said about his own relationship with the Hip Sing Tong.

Moss blamed the police for the Bowery shootings, claiming they had ensured an advantage for the On Leongs by a dragnet they had imposed on the Hip Sings. "For a week, every Hip Sing in Chinatown was searched by policemen and plainclothesmen for weapons. The On Leongs pointed them out to the police. Not an On Leong was searched, mind you," he added.

This so-called advantage was belied by the veritable arsenal the police had discovered at Hip Sing headquarters, but Moss didn't mention that. He also faulted the police for failing to guard the building on the night of the row, claiming they had had ample reason to expect an attack.

The Parkhursts felt responsible for the whole affair. "In the present crisis we got these Chinamen into trouble," Moss told the *World,* "and we are going to stand by them." But Moss's Parkhurst colleagues were beginning to get defensive about their reflexive support for the Hip Sings, whose reputation had been taking a drubbing. McClintock assured a New York *Sun* reporter that the society had not been "taken in" by the Chinese organization. He went on to explain that the Parkhursts had begun their raids at the urging of many Christian Chinese alarmed at the effects of gambling on the Chinese community and who "kindly volunteered to act as gambling house spies." And then he added, incredibly, that "one morning, the society found that these spies all happened to be Hip Sings."

That, of course, was *not* the way it had happened, and McClintock surely knew it. The Parkhursts had been aware from the very beginning, when Frank Moss recruited Wong Get, that they were working with the Hip Sing Tong. They had simply refused to acknowledge the true nature of their partners. The *Sun* went on to point out that although McClintock was aware that Hip Sings *elsewhere* were "thugs, murderers, dealers in slaves and blackmailers," he believed the New York variety were "worthy persons." The newspaper wasn't buying it. "Something in the Atlantic breeze may soften the nature of the sternest Hip Sing and make his heart pure," it wrote sardonically.

In fact, the cozy relationship between the Hip Sings and the Parkhursts had just about run its course. McClintock and his reformers would stick with the tong for the next couple of years, but their support would recede noticeably and eventually disappear entirely. To most observers, the Hip Sings had shown their true colors. Only Frank Moss would stubbornly remain a friend and a true believer.

"I do not want to say that the police can't stop gambling among the Chinese," District Attorney Jerome said in response to Moss's allegation, "but it would be an exceedingly difficult task." He had good cause for this observation. Police corruption notwithstanding, the fact was that obtaining convictions of Chinatown gambling bosses was fraught with difficulty. Infiltration of the betting parlors was impossible; there were no Chinese on the police force to do it. Chinese stool pigeons could sometimes be recruited, but they often had their own agendas, and besides, judges and juries tended to devalue or discount the testimony of Chinese, much of which was assumed to be bought and paid for. Convictions usually required testimony by the arresting officers that they had actually seen money change hands, and the cash had usually vanished by the time the police came in.

The next move belonged to the Hip Sings, and they saw their opening when the On Leongs ventured outside the jurisdiction of the Elizabeth Street Station. In late 1904, an On Leong rented a room on the fourth floor of 34 Bayard Street. He claimed to represent a group of Chinese Christians who needed a meeting room and paid a month's rent in advance, and then he proceeded to fit the hall out, which included stringing a wire from the fourth floor down to the front entrance to permit a security guard to send a signal upstairs if he spotted trouble. Nobody thought to ask what a group of praying Christians would need with an early warning system.

The Hip Sings got wind of the arrangement and immediately informed McClintock. He, in turn, staged the raid with officers from the Eldridge Street Station, which had authority over Bayard Street and no known relationship with the On Leongs. It took three round-trips of a patrol wagon to shuttle all fifty-six On Leong gamblers who were arrested to court, where all but two were discharged—the guard and the gamekeeper.

The newspapers declared that the Hip Sings now had the On Leongs on the run, having made it extremely difficult for them to keep protecting gambling parlors. The *Sun* observed that, going forward, the On Leongs had only two choices: cut the Hip Sings in on the graft or continue the shooting. It was an astute analysis. Unfortunately, they would choose the latter before they got around to the former.

Two weeks after the Bayard Street raid, the On Leongs were out for revenge. But their plans did not call for assault or murder. What they had in mind was humiliation: a simple prank slated for Christmas night.

Ah Lah and two other On Leongs disguised themselves as out-of-town laundrymen and lured fifteen Hip Sings into a *fan tan* game. They had secured the basement of 5 Mott, and they watched in silence as the Hip Sings took the necessary precautions—setting up a trip wire at the top of the cellar stairs to slow intruders and warn gamblers of imminent danger.

At about 2:00 a.m., a confederate reported the game to Elizabeth Street, and a squad of policemen was dispatched to break it up. The wire did its job, causing two plainclothesmen to stumble down the steps and alerting the gamblers to their presence. Money and *fan tan* accoutrements went flying as the gamblers searched frantically for a way out. Then one of the On Leongs helpfully pulled on an iron ring and opened a trapdoor in the floor. Without a word, the Hip Sings plunged through the opening, one by one—into two feet of standing water.

As the last man disappeared down the hatch, Ah Lah banged the trapdoor shut, and he and his two brothers stood on top of it, confining the captive gamblers below. When the police finally entered, they noticed the hatchway. They assumed it was an opening to an escape tunnel—Chinatown was rumored to be honeycombed with such passageways—and figured anyone who had fled the game was probably long gone. They decided to have a look anyway, however, and when they opened the hatch, they discovered a pit about five feet deep, filled with fifteen angry Hip Sings, dripping and cursing.

All eighteen men were arraigned in Tombs Police Court the next day, but because the officers had not actually seen money change hands, all but the one who had acted as "banker" were released. But the attorney engaged by the Hip Sings predicted, "There'll be three On Leong Tong gamblers who will lay pretty low for a while."

As Lee Sing cooled his heels in the Tombs waiting to be tried for shooting Mock Duck, the On Leongs did everything they could think of to get him released. Late in November 1904, Detective Michael Powers, who, with Detective Patrick Carr, had apprehended him, received an anonymous letter warning him not to testify at Lee's trial:

> You can never convict Lee Sing. Before he would be convicted one hundred Chinamen would be killed. Mock Duck would never testify against him. And if Carr and Powers persist in their attempt to convict this man they would be done away with.

But death threats weren't the only tactic the On Leongs employed. In early December, they attempted to sow enough doubt about Lee Sing's guilt as to obviate the need for a trial. Their strategy was to blame a man named Lu Chow, who had a bad reputation and who had conveniently already returned to China, for the shooting. They provided witnesses to swear that Mock Duck had been quarreling with Lu over a white woman just prior to the shooting and that Lu had drawn a revolver and shot him twice before disappearing.

The trial went on in January, with Frank Moss appearing for the Hip Sings and Edmund E. Price representing the defendant. Mock Duck wasn't in town to testify, and the other prosecution witnesses were not convincing. The defense put enough people on the stand to corroborate the presence—and motive—of Lu Chow to plant seeds of doubt in the judge's mind. In the end, after eight hearings, he threw the case out.

It was surely a case of abject perjury, but who could prove it? Unaccustomed to the rule of law—the legal system in their home country was eminently corruptible—the Chinese tong men saw the courtroom less as a forum for the dispassionate administration of justice than as an opportunity to score points against their enemies. They could hardly be blamed for doubting a system in which their testimony was distrusted and in which judges and juries alike often held deep-seated prejudices against them. Recruiting, coaching, and paying witnesses posed no moral dilemma for them. At the end of the day, it was just another cost of doing business.

Chapter 7

A Price on Tom Lee's Head

At 1:00 a.m. on the last day of January 1905, another Hip Sing fell.
A cold wind was blowing down Mott Street, and all was quiet,
save the sound of a Chinese flute emanating from a third-floor window
above the Joss House. But just as forty-year-old Huie Fong, a Hip Sing,
rounded the corner from Chatham Square, the melody changed abruptly. It
was a signal.

A man swiftly emerged from a candy shop in the basement of No. 16,
headed up the stairs to the pavement, crossed the street, and followed Huie
Fong into No. 17. It was an odd place for a Hip Sing to be headed at such
a time of night, because No. 17 was an On Leong preserve, but someone
apparently was expecting him. Suddenly the music stopped, and three
staccato gunshots were heard.

A police detective two doors away rushed to the scene and found Huie
Fong gasping for breath and "flopping like a landed trout," blood gushing
from two holes in his chest. He spotted a Chinese man fleeing the scene
and managed to restrain him. Reinforcements came, and Huie was carried
to the street, but, unable to talk, he could not identify his attacker. He
perished before the ambulance arrived. The man in custody admitted
nothing; he just repeated the sentence "They wait for him!" suggesting that
Huie had been lured there by someone else. He volunteered that his name
was Yee Lee and that he was an On Leong laundryman.

Smarting from the Bayard Street incident, the On Leongs had declared
that "for every raid, there would be a dead Hip Sing." There had been raids
in the neighborhood two days earlier, and the police believed Huie Fong's
assassination was retribution. They arrested Yee Lee, who was unarmed,
and charged him with complicity in a murder.

At Yee's arraignment the next day, Lee Loy, secretary of the On Leong

Tong and another of Tom Lee's cousins, testified for the defense. Lee Loy, forty-five, had come to America at age nineteen, lived in Oregon for more than fifteen years, and then made his way eastward, working as a laundryman in small upstate towns before moving to the city. And in open court, he accused the Hip Sings of putting a price on the heads of the leaders of the On Leong Tong.

It wouldn't have been hard to see this coming. The On Leongs had been brazen in their attempt on the life of Mock Duck, now at the apex of the local Hip Sing pyramid. So it was only fair for the Hip Sings to return the favor. In early February 1905, immediately before the Chinese New Year, Chinatown had been plastered with red signs once again offering a $3,000 reward for Tom Lee's demise.

"Four highbinders from Boston are here to kill Tom Lee and to earn the reward," Lee Loy told the court. "Not only is a price put on Tom Lee's head, but a price of $1,000 each is paid for me to be killed and three others, all officers of our society." The others, identified later, were Charlie Boston, Chu Gong, and a man named Gin Gum.

China-born Gin Gum had appeared in New York around 1900 after he was released from jail. He had worked as a cook in San Francisco before being sentenced to three years at San Quentin for passing a forged check. When his appeal was finally heard by the California Supreme Court, he had already served most of his sentence in Alameda County Jail, so he was released. He joined the On Leong Tong in New York and rose quickly in its ranks. A proficient English speaker, he had already become indispensable.

Tom Lee applied to his friends in the police department for protection. Three officers were detailed to guard On Leong headquarters at 14 Mott, and four were posted in front of Lee's office at No. 18, in addition to the four Chinese bodyguards already there. But Lee didn't let the threat interfere with Chinese New Year festivities, and the On Leong open house was held as usual on February 3. Chinatown was draped with the customary colorful pennants, and the crackling of firecrackers and the beating of gongs and drums could be heard as Chinese exchanged visits, presented youngsters with red envelopes stuffed with "lucky money," and offered New Year's greetings to friends and acquaintances.

Lee even sat for a holiday interview with the New York *World*. He made several points, mostly about the tactics and methods of the Hip Sings, which the paper quoted, using spellings intended to mimic a Chinese accent:

The 'Melican people blame all the Chinese for the deaths in our village. Only a few highbinders and Hip Sing men are responsible, and I try to keep the highbinders out of our village. The Hip Sings have a "system," which is to watch where a Chinaman opens a laundry. Then they open one next door by paying a month's rent and threaten to cut down prices unless $100 is paid for them to move. They say, "I washee shirt seven cents, you chargee ten. I dlive you out. I stay. You pay hundled dollals I leave."

He continued:

We have clubs where the laundryman who works six days can go one day and play games like what you call checkers and dominoes. If some of our clubs do have a game like white clubs, the Hips demand one-half of the receipts or they will tell the Parkhurst Society.

Of course, Lee made no reference to the fact that his On Leongs had been doing the same thing for years, the only differences being that the tax was far less than 50 percent and that the police got a cut of the take. But if the reporter had any doubt about the resolve of local police to protect Tom Lee from harm, he needed only to look out the window at the swarm of officers outside the building.

The *Sun* reported a rumor that the Hip Sings had offered to stop inform-ing in exchange for a lump sum payment of $10,000. Such an arrangement would ostensibly put the entire conflict to rest. But the On Leongs, who could have afforded it, didn't trust them to live up to their word. "They ar-gue that if they pay up, the Hip Sings will be back again in a few months for another payment," the *Sun* wrote, and they were surely correct.

Four days into the Year of the Snake, at 8:00 a.m., Ching Gong's nephew found his uncle's body lying across the threshold of the door that led to the sleeping cubbyhole in his Bronx laundry. His skull had been crushed.

Like most of New York's Chinese by this time, Ching didn't live in Chinatown. Of the estimated seven thousand Chinese in Greater New York in 1905, fewer than two thousand now resided in the Mott Street area, which had been evolving from the home of the Chinese community to its marketplace. Chinese visited at night and on Sundays to purchase supplies and foodstuffs, patronize the restaurants and opium dens, attend club meetings, and gamble, but most didn't live there. Laundrymen in particular had to set up shop where their customers lived, and this meant spreading throughout Manhattan, the other boroughs, and New Jersey.

Ching Gong, a Hip Sing, had been driven out of Chinatown after being discovered to be a police informer. He had not been seen for two days. There were signs of forced entry through a broken rear window, but no weapon was found. He appeared to be the latest victim of the "one life for every raid" policy of the On Leongs.

In retaliation, fifty-eight-year-old Lee Yu, another of Tom Lee's cousins and a senior tong member, was felled on Pell Street by a bullet through his head. Lee Yu had been high on the Hip Sings' hit list because he had had a hand in the attempted murder of Mock Duck and the November Bowery clash and was strongly suspected of having planned the January killing of Huie Fong. His alleged shooter was Dong Fong, the favorite of Frank Moss. As it happened, the Parkhurst Society superintendent, Thomas L. McClintock, was walking with Dong at the time—or so he claimed—and McClintock denied Dong had been involved. The police didn't buy his story, however, and they arrested Dong anyway.

Although they had no corpse to show for their efforts—Lee Yu didn't die of his wounds—the Hip Sings were nonetheless jubilant. For the moment, they felt they had the upper hand over their antagonists.

If the On Leongs were depressed at the latest downturn in their fortunes, March 1905 brought even more ominous news: Mock Duck was back in town.

The fearsome Hip Sing blackguard had left New York late the previous year after his release from the hospital. Some said he had headed for China, but he had actually gone only as far as California. Word on the street when he reappeared was that he had returned with four San Francisco Hip Sing desperadoes in tow and a determination to exact revenge on Tom Lee and company.

Sure enough, a scant three days later death warrants for Tom Lee, Gin Gum, and other senior On Leongs appeared again on several Chinatown walls. And Gin Gum noticed he was being followed. He and Tom Lee asked District Attorney William T. Jerome—a guest at the recent On Leong Chinese New Year celebration—for protection. Immediately, Captain Kear of Elizabeth Street dispatched all the Sixth Precinct's plainclothesmen to Chinatown.

The *New York Telegraph* summed up the situation on its front page with some lighthearted doggerel:

> When Mock Duck ducked to 'Frisco
> Tom Lee was mighty glad;
> But now he's back in town, alack,
> And Tom Lee, he is sad.
> For Mock Duck is no mocker
> When he goes out for blood,
> And Tom Lee sees his finish
> In a dull and sickening thud.

The Hip Sings were serious. When Chu Gong, the On Leong Tong's treasurer, was walking down Pell Street at dusk on March 18, three men emerged from the shadows at No. 11, including Mock Duck himself. At the sight of Chu, he beckoned to twenty-seven-year-old Louie Way and thirty-one-year-old Lung Gow, who pulled out their revolvers. Had it not been for timely intervention by a plainclothesman, Chu would have been shot. The two hatchet men were arrested on the spot. Mock Duck, however, managed to disappear.

Tom Lee vanished as well, appearing only, with Gin Gum and Lee Loy, before Magistrate Charles S. Whitman at the arraignment of Louie Way and Lung Gow. The subject turned immediately to Mock Duck, who Lee insisted had masterminded the assault. Tom Lee tarred him as "very much worse than Monk Eastman," a reference to a colorful and dangerous gangster who led one of the most powerful street gangs in New York and who was, at the time, serving a ten-year sentence for assault at Sing Sing. "He no 'fraid of police, and like killee white man," the *New York Times* quoted Lee as saying, in an article the paper tastelessly chose to title "Mock Duck, He Velly Bad." Mock Duck had never killed a white man, but Lee probably calculated that the authorities would find that far more alarming than if the victim were Chinese.

Louie Way and Lung Gow were held on $2,000 bail, and the following day Mock Duck was arrested at Hip Sing headquarters. Although he was accused only of assault for the Chu Gong incident—a charge that would have permitted his release on bail—District Attorney Jerome decided to indict him once *again* for the 1900 murder of Ah Fee, an accusation that had resulted in two hung juries and that Jerome himself had finally withdrawn. Jerome didn't really intend to try him a third time for that crime; the charge was simply a ruse that made it possible to hold him without bail, which the district attorney felt would help keep the peace in Chinatown.

In a moment of candor, Jerome asserted, "I don't care as long as the members of that society stick to playing Fan Tan, but when they take to murder then something must be done to stop their practices." He added, "And for this purpose it is principally that I have had this man arrested."

Mock Duck's reemergence gave the newspapers an opportunity to reintroduce him to the reading public. "The vengeful Mock Duck . . . is a short, fat little Chinaman, with a round, smiling face that shows no guile," the *Cleveland Plain Dealer* reported, although in surviving photographs Mock Duck always appears slender. "Duck is a mild-mannered Celestial, wearing a pigtail and an enormous diamond ring," the *New York Post* declared. "He is only about twenty-six years old," the *New York Times* observed, "and is even more youthful looking."

"I don't want to kill anybody," Mock Duck said, in perfect English, from his jail cell after the hearing. "It isn't true that I came here to kill Tom Lee, and I had nothing to do with the proclamation offering $3,000 for his death. I was not in San Francisco, and I did not bring with me any persons who want to break the law."

But only after Mock Duck was safely behind bars did Tom Lee emerge from hiding, and then the On Leongs celebrated. Guests were well fed at the Mon Far Low Restaurant downstairs from On Leong headquarters, and nobody left without a cigar.

The next day, when Frank Moss appeared for Mock Duck at the Court of General Sessions, he and Jerome nearly came to blows. A decade earlier, the two had been colleagues, associate counsels for the Lexow Committee. But since 1903, when they found themselves on opposite sides of a manslaughter trial, enmity had prevailed between them. In the wake of relentless and withering criticism of the district attorney's office by the Parkhursts, there was now no love lost between the onetime comrades.

Moss filed a motion to discharge Mock Duck from custody, arguing that the murder indictment had been dismissed eleven months earlier at the recommendation of Jerome himself. He did not ask for dismissal of the assault charge but contended it was an offense that certainly warranted bail. Asserting that "Duck is the most inoffensive person in Chinatown," the ever-loyal Moss went on to say,

> A few months ago he was shot twice as he was leaving a gambling house where he had secured evidence. The man who shot him was arrested, but in spite of six witnesses to the crime, he was discharged in the police court. Duck saw that he could not get justice here and went to Chicago, where he lived a decent life. On going away, however, he had forgotten a trunk containing many valuable things, and as he heard that the case in which he was shot was about to be laid before the Grand Jury he decided to come back and testify if wanted and also get his trunk.

Of course, nobody *else* believed Mock Duck was the upstanding paragon Moss conjured, and Jerome's response dripped with sarcasm:

> This simple, angelic creature, as counsel would have it appear, has been twice tried for murder. The first time the jury stood ten to two for conviction. There are at least ten men who believe he is guilty of murder. It is true that I consented to the dismissal of the indictment charging murder because I had doubts if it would ever be possible to get a conviction. I still have those doubts. But when valuable information is laid

before me to the effect that he intended to come back to New York bent on murder, I don't think one should pick and choose his methods.

Then, unable to resist a dig at the Parkhursts, he went on,

I might add that until a certain society in this city began to "monkey" and "butt in" around with Oriental affairs we heard of nothing but gambling in Chinatown among the classes there. Since that certain society interfered, plenty of shooting scrapes have been there.

Jerome acknowledged that there would not, in fact, be a third murder trial and offered to dismiss even the assault charge if Mock Duck would agree to leave the jurisdiction. "I want to get him out of town and away from here," he explained.

The judge refused to discharge the defendant. He even commended Jerome for causing Mock Duck's arrest, adding that "he has done so to keep peace and quiet in that part of the city." He fixed bail for the assault charge at $1,000 but did warn that if Mock Duck were not tried on that charge within a reasonable period, he would dismiss it.

The two former associates left court without speaking. Outside the courtroom, Jerome ran smack into Gin Gum and Tom Lim, a high-ranking Hip Sing. It was fortuitous, because the exasperated district attorney had a message for both tongs. He grabbed Lim's embroidered shirt with one hand and hooked a finger of the other through Gin Gum's buttonhole and announced, "I am very glad to see you, gentlemen, and particularly glad to see you together in peace. Now listen to me for a few moments.

"Please tell the head men of your societies or gangs or tongs or whatever you call them, that I want to see them, and that they had better accede to my request. That is, I mean—I *callee* and they *comee*. I am going to send for them a week from Wednesday or Thursday. Keep that date in mind so that there can be no excuses. Tell them that they have got to come to an agreement to stop that shooting fest that has been going on in Chinatown.

"Then, when we have had our little talk, you will have to put a stop to some of your gay practices. Play Fan Tan by all means. That is none of my

William T. Jerome, associate counsel to the
Lexow Committee and later New York
County district attorney, ca. 1905.

business. It is wrong, of course, but it is up to the police to look after it. But
don't murder. It goes beyond the line I have drawn. You must stop that
kind of thing yourself, or I will stop it. I shall not call in the police. No, I
shall send a few of my own men over to Chinatown. There won't be any
great number of arrests made, either, but I promise you that there will be a
great number of Chinese in that region who'll discover that this world is
not all peace and joy. Have you understood?"

They said they had. Then they left the building, like the two attorneys,
without a word to each other.

It took five days, but Mock Duck was finally bailed out of the Tombs.
And, surprisingly, not by his Hip Sing brethren, nor by the Parkhursts, but
by a white poultry dealer who supplied Chinatown restaurants, probably

including the one of which he was a co-owner. The merchant put up $1,000 and Mock Duck was once again at liberty. Given Jerome's comments at the discharge hearing, many thought he might seize the opportunity and leave the city.

Jerome wasn't the only one fed up with the shooting in Chinatown. Although gambling there was a fact of life, that certainly didn't mean most Chinese took the killings with equanimity. Law-abiding residents suffered when Chinatown was not at peace. Most merchants would have been delighted to see betting stopped entirely; the trouble it brought was bad for business. And according to some, it siphoned money out of Chinatown and demoralized the population.

"These shops pay money to gambling society, and where does all the money go to? It goes to someone uptown—I know not where—who helps to keep gambling going on," one of them complained to a New York *Globe* reporter. He was surely correct, although it's hard to pinpoint precisely who, apart from the police, was receiving it. Tom Lee hadn't spent so much effort cultivating Tammany higher-ups for nothing. Inspectors and officials further up the food chain were benefiting from Chinatown vice as much as the local police were.

An equally critical Chinese described the problem from a different angle in a letter to the police commissioner, William McAdoo. Although it was written in halting English, its thrust was clear. The writer was protesting arbitrary and corrupt behavior of police detectives on the take. The note read,

> At present time the Detective of Chinatown terrorize and arrest every Chinaman by they feel alik [sic]. I know so many Chinamen victim by them and take their money away if refuse arrest follow one Chinamen reading a letter in his room they grab him and arrested and took away and other one was reading a book in 12 Pell St. They go in the room brake [sic] the draw [sic] and take all the money away and other one they don't like his face get arrested if you give them money let go. The month of March about a hundred case like this. This is real hell treat worse then [sic] dogs. If you don't remove them they be rich men sure

the police men alright [*sic*], but the detective is real thief black mailer and bruet [*sic*] and cruel. I am swear to God what I saying is true.

McAdoo released the letter without naming its author, but he defended his men with the claim that it was impostors, and not true police detectives, who were shaking down the Chinese. "Of course any man with a badge has every opportunity in the world to take advantage of these poor creatures down there," he protested. "They do not know the difference between a policeman and a blackmailing faker."

A New York *Sun* reporter went to Chinatown to find the writer. Although he was unsuccessful, he did happen on one English speaker who summed up the situation beautifully. "The detectives who do the thieving and holding up are not fakers," he said flatly, putting to rest McAdoo's lame defense.

The trouble has been going on for many years. Whenever a policeman-detective needed money he would pretend to raid a gambling house. Everybody must give him money or be arrested. If he got his money—he always got his money—then nobody was arrested and was the wiser, because people down here are apart from the rest of the world and nothing is said.

But then came the quarrel between the societies. The police worked with the gamblers. The other society, which is all cutthroats, tried to get a share of the money. . . . The Parkhurst Society took sides with the cutthroats. There has been nothing but terror here. It is as the man in the letter says—nothing but hell. Peaceable men like myself who wish that all the members of the societies could be taken out to the ocean and drowned—we dodge bullets.

Now all this is good for the detectives. They have excuses for many raids. In every raid they catch a lot of Chinamen from out of town, laundrymen mostly, who have come in for one night's social pleasures among their own people. They eat, they play cards. Is it a crime to play cards with your friends? Not unless you are a Chinaman. The detectives break in. Unless you pay them money, you go to the police station. The Magistrate knows you are a liar, because you are a Chinaman. So he will punish you anyway. Why not pay the policeman and save time and trouble? That is how it works.

Like the letter writer, the speaker more or less exonerated the uniformed police, reserving his invective for the detectives. And he described a more direct form of graft than had previously been described. As he told it, some police detectives had taken to extorting money straight from their victims, without any need for a middleman. These were damning accusations that surely contained much truth. Police corruption was a part of daily life in Chinatown. The letter should have given pause to anyone inclined to place blame solely at the feet of the Chinese immigrants. There were others with a strong, vested interest in maintaining the status quo.

A *New York Post* reporter found Tom Lee on the steps of On Leong headquarters dressed in a mustard-colored herringbone overcoat and puffing on a cigar. He asked his view of the letter. As reported, Lee replied in broken but serviceable English.

"You think it was written by a member of the Hip Sing Tong?"

"Not think at all; know him," said Lee.

"And it is not true?"

"Him damned true."

"Explain what you mean, Tom," said the reporter.

"Very simple to explain him. Twenty, maybe fifteen years ago, Chinaman play him domino game, not make trouble for anybody. Policeman on Mott Street go him home play with baby. No shoot Italian man, no shoot Tom Lee. Then come highbinder. Me good 'Melican citizen, good Christian, but highbinder not American citizen. Bad Chinaman; plenty bad. He make plenty trouble very soon. No work, no washing. Him grafter.

"Me work very hard, sell tea much plenty. Presently come highbinder: 'Tom, you give ten dollar.' I give him. Presently: 'Tom, you give twenty dollar, me start laundry.' Him damn big liar. Never start laundry, just grafter. Pretty soon me get mad. No more ten dollar, twenty dollar. Then he begin shoot revolver. Kill white man, white woman; kill more white man, bring Mock Duck here.

"Mock Dock, him king grafter. Make policeman grafter, too. Him work together. Make domino game good graft, everything graft. Him policeman learn business pretty damn quick. . . . Mock Duck hide self; very much afraid Mr. Jerome. Him snake; come wiggle on tummy, shoot 'em revolver at ol' Tom Lee, kill 'em two white men. Him bad man. Him frighten decent Chinaman, graft him until decent Chinaman give him up business."

"But how would you stop the police graft, Tom?" the reporter interjected.

"Kill 'em Mock Duck, or put 'em Sing Sing twenty years. . . . Very bad man, Mock Duck, but him not too big for Mr. Jerome."

Chapter 8

The Chinese Theatre Massacre

At a quarter to eight in the evening of April 23, 1905, what appeared to be a wedding procession rolled up Mott Street from Chatham Square and halted opposite the Church of the Transfiguration. Twelve closed, horse-drawn coaches led the way, followed by a large automobile. The only thing that seemed missing was a carriage for the bride.

But it was Easter Sunday, and no one was getting married. Each vehicle carried not wedding guests, but half a dozen policemen and one Chinese informant, and each one was assigned to a particular gambling hall. On command, officers wielding crowbars and axes emerged from nine coaches and headed down Mott Street; the rest were dispatched to Pell and Doyers. At the rear, supervising the operation, was the former detective sergeant William Eggers, a twelve-year veteran whom McAdoo had promoted to acting captain and installed as head of a Central Office vice squad.

Once inside, the officers quickly apprehended the lookouts before any could warn the gamblers, then smashed their way through doors that were several inches thick and heavily reinforced. They hacked holes around the locks, stuck revolvers through them, and forced the Chinese men to let them in.

The invasion had deliberately been scheduled for a Sunday, when Chinese from outside Manhattan came to town to shop. Many typically stayed on to gamble, so it was a sure bet the *fan tan* and *pi gow* parlors would be humming. And the plan had been a well-kept secret. Eggers had not revealed the assignment until all the officers had boarded the coaches and had not let anyone disembark until they had arrived. In other words, there was no possibility that Tom Lee would be warned and able to get word to the gambling bosses to close up shop. The whole maneuver was executed flawlessly and took only about ten minutes from beginning to end.

A dozen paddy wagons carrying all available police reserves from south of Fourteenth Street were positioned in front of the selected establishments. The reservists quickly disembarked and cordoned off the streets. As hundreds of people, mostly Chinese and Italians, watched from their windows, balconies, rooftops, and fire escapes and white sightseers in several "See Chinatown by Night" coaches gaped, more than two hundred men were detained. Together with a large collection of gambling paraphernalia, a vast cache of revolvers and knives, and wads of cash seized as evidence, they were ferried to seven different Manhattan station houses.

It was the largest and most spectacular raid ever carried out in Chinatown. In fact, police said, it was the largest of any kind in New York City history.

The Parkhurst superintendent, Thomas L. McClintock, whose relationship with Commissioner McAdoo was strained in the best of times, crowed that the crucial evidence had been gathered by James Wang, one of "his" Chinese detectives, who had worked hand in glove with Eggers's staff. Wang, a Methodist lay reader, was a senior Hip Sing with a criminal record, though McClintock didn't mention that latter fact. But McAdoo wasn't about to let the Parkhursts claim even partial credit. He insisted they had had nothing to do with the operation. "The initiative was taken here and every movement was planned here. No society or individual outside the Police Department cooperated with, or had anything to do with, this office," he declared flatly, although this was clearly untrue. Each coach had included a Chinese stool pigeon.

McAdoo reiterated that he had seen no evidence that any money paid by Chinese gambling lords ever wound up in the pockets of the police. While that might have been technically true, there was the matter of the letter he had received accusing the local detectives of rampant corruption. For that reason, no one at the Sixth Precinct had been told of the foray in advance, even though all the joints raided were under their jurisdiction. Nor were any of those arrested taken to Elizabeth Street.

Mindful of the ever-present possibility of retaliation, Eggers ordered that two uniformed patrolmen be placed outside Hip Sing headquarters as a precautionary measure. The raid amounted to a major victory for the Hip Sings, but not because all those arrested were On Leongs. Most were surely

The New York police commissioner William
McAdoo, later chief of the city magistrates'
courts, ca. 1910.

gamblers not affiliated with either of the secret societies. What the bust had
demonstrated was that Tom Lee and company couldn't be counted on to
deliver the protection for which they were charging the gambling halls.
The On Leong franchise had therefore been severely undermined.

But anyone naive enough to think that the gambling problem had been
solved would be sadly mistaken. Two hours after the arrests, some of
Eggers's men returned to one of the Mott Street establishments that had
been closed down. Gambling had already resumed.

A circus-like atmosphere prevailed at Tombs Police Court the next day.
Assistant District Attorneys Frank A. Lord and Arthur C. Train appeared
for the People, with the attorney Daniel O'Reilly, a former congressman
and friend of Tom Lee's, retained by the On Leong Tong to represent the
defendants. Nearly every seat in the courtroom was filled with Chinese
men, some prisoners, some spectators.

If the police operation the day before had been an exercise in military precision, the arraignment was pure bedlam. The immediate problem was trying to figure out who was who. The various name lists compiled by the detectives did not agree with one another, and at least forty men granted bail the previous day did not return to court. Some even sent paid stand-ins. The magistrate turned in despair to James Wang for help identifying the prisoners, and he, in turn, invited Chow Yong, a middle-aged Hip Sing, to assist as the defendants were called up according to the addresses at which they had been arrested. As they marched in single file to the front, each was scrutinized by Chow, who provided names and addresses for some, including Lee Sing, the On Leong accused of shooting Mock Duck.

When the seven or eight who had been arrested at 17 Mott came to the front, however, the magistrate looked away for a second. The accused men met Chow's gaze, and each drew a finger across his throat. Chow blanched and immediately proved unable to identify any of them.

Twenty-one prisoners were named in this way; most were employees of the gambling houses. The others were dismissed, but in the commotion that followed, even three of those identified managed to disappear. The remaining eighteen were held by the judge on $500 bail. After the hearing, Chow was escorted by police to Hip Sing headquarters, and as the New York *Sun* noted, the Hip Sings celebrated with "two white women of blondine complexion."

But their joy didn't last long. By noontime, placards had been posted on Chinatown buildings placing a $6,000 bounty on the lives of Chow Yong and James Wang.

The Parkhursts, on a roll, decided to go for broke. They quietly secured a warrant for Tom Lee's arrest on the charge that he had collected $15 a week from a man named Tom Wing to permit him to run a *fan tan* game at 21 Pell. Then the Parkhurst superintendent, McClintock, trapped Commissioner McAdoo into taking Lee into custody by telling him only that he had a warrant for the arrest of a Chinese gambler without specifying who it was. He asked for two officers from headquarters to help him capture the man, and McAdoo assigned two of Eggers's vice squad detectives to the task. In this way, Lee was detained on April 26, 1905, and released on $500 bail to await trial.

Later that day, McAdoo summoned Lee and Mock Duck, who had not left town as expected after his release from jail, to police headquarters on Mulberry Street. He proceeded to have the talk with the men that District Attorney Jerome had threatened a month earlier. Captain Eggers was also present, as was Gin Gum, but McClintock was pointedly not invited. McAdoo wasn't about to give the Parkhursts any further opportunity to steal his thunder.

"I told them that gambling had to cease in Chinatown, that I did not care for their factions, and that the same law must apply to them as applies to others," McAdoo said later. "I told them that the practice of carrying pistols had got to cease," he continued. And McAdoo also mentioned one other significant fact: he had remanded the detectives at Elizabeth Street to patrol duty elsewhere in the city and had put Chinatown under the direct jurisdiction of Captain Eggers and the Central Office.

Both Mock Duck and Tom Lee came out of the meeting smiling, but Mock Duck had more reason to do so. McAdoo's decision meant that none of the officers on the On Leong gravy train would be patrolling Chinatown. It also guaranteed that the new policemen assigned to Mott and Pell streets would be dependent on informants for the lay of the land. The Hip Sings quickly stepped in to try to fill the vacuum.

Then it got even worse for the On Leongs. At 1:00 a.m. the following day, two of Eggers's men broke into 18 Mott, one of Tom Lee's properties.

"What do you want?" Gin Gum demanded.

"We want to search this place," they said. And then they began pulling down boxes and overturning furniture.

Gin Gum, who understood English and knew something of the law, was not about to be railroaded. "Where's your search warrant?" he demanded.

"Je-rusalem! Hear that Chink talking about warrants!" was the only reply. And then violence broke out. Two tong members trying to protect their premises were pummeled with blackjacks until they bled. The police found guns on two others and arrested them all.

"This is one of the most unwarranted and unprovoked assaults I ever heard of," protested the attorney David Frank Lloyd, who had stepped down from his position as assistant district attorney and was now in private practice, appearing as an attorney for the On Leongs. "Two officers of the law have entered private property without warrant and have beaten two inoffensive citizens. I intend to bring a charge of felonious assault against these men. I have five white witnesses who say that it is the most uncalled for outrage they have ever seen in Chinatown," he added, mindful that testimony of white witnesses always carried more weight than that of Chinese. By way of defense, the policemen insisted they had seen two "highbinders" sneak into 18 Mott and that Gin Gum and his colleagues had made "threatening gestures" in their direction.

On Tuesday, May 9, the magistrate made progress in clearing his docket. He dismissed the case of the eighteen On Leongs left over from the Easter Sunday arrests after District Attorney Jerome asserted it would be difficult to secure convictions. He also dismissed the cases against the two On Leongs arrested at their headquarters for possessing guns. The third case heard that day was Tom Lee's, which was also dismissed, probably for lack of evidence.

Dong Fong, the Hip Sing who had shot Tom Lee's cousin Lee Yu, was not so fortunate. He had been incarcerated at the Tombs since his arraignment at the end of February. He finally went on trial in mid-May, charged with shooting with intent to kill. The Parkhurst Society superintendent, McClintock, had provided an alibi, claiming he had been with Dong at the time of the shooting and that Dong hadn't been involved. Dong, however, pleaded guilty, possibly in exchange for a lighter sentence but otherwise casting serious doubt on McClintock's rectitude. He was sent to Sing Sing for not less than one and a half, nor more than five, years.

Tom Lee had lain low since the disastrous Easter raid and his subsequent arrest, but he hadn't been idle, and he was nothing if not resourceful. The Hip Sings had benefited when authority over Chinatown was transferred from Elizabeth Street to the Central Office; any relationships Lee had with Sixth Precinct detectives were useless under such a regime. But cooperating with the police had been Lee's idea in the first place, and if Chinatown had new overlords, he wasn't about to cede them to Hip Sing upstarts without a fight.

Accordingly, he sent Chu Gong and Lee Loy out to gather evidence the police might use. They peeked through gratings and keyholes and amassed a list of a dozen gambling houses in Hip Sing territory. And then he sent Gin Gum to police headquarters to tell Eggers and his men all about them.

Eggers saw his mission as cleaning up Chinatown; he didn't much care where he got his information or whose ox was getting gored. He certainly had no loyalty to the Hip Sings, who regularly provided the Parkhursts with ammunition they used to bludgeon Commissioner McAdoo, his boss, and the police generally. So he was perfectly willing to sit down with Tom Lee, who suggested timing the next raid for Decoration Day, as Memorial Day was then called, because legal holidays always brought more gamblers than usual to Chinatown.

In the afternoon of May 30, 1905, Eggers dispatched twenty-five plainclothesmen to Chinatown and put them in charge of fifty uniformed officers. Squads of police borrowed from seven precincts surrounded Pell Street, the Hip Sings' preserve. Then they tightened their cordon and invaded several gambling halls. Gambling and opium paraphernalia were seized. Eggers ordered that every table, chair, and piece of equipment not needed as evidence be destroyed, so after the prisoners were taken into custody, ax-wielding officers reduced the contents of the gambling halls to kindling. This had never been done to the On Leongs, and the Hip Sings were especially resentful over it. At one point, Chu Gong asked an officer if he might borrow an ax and inflict some of the damage himself.

In the end, sixty men, including James Wang, were arrested in the largest daylight raid Chinatown had ever seen. Most were discharged, but twenty-six of them, identified as proprietors by On Leong informants, were locked up at the Sixth Precinct.

Tom Lee made it his business to be far away as all of this took place. A reporter found him at his uptown home. Asked if he had had anything to do with the events of the day in Chinatown, he replied obliquely, "Fine day for Decoration Day; fine day to plant flowers on graves."

Less than a month later, the On Leongs struck a second blow at James Wang, on whose life they had earlier placed a bounty. They accused him of extortion. As part and parcel of his role as stool pigeon in the Easter operation, Wang had assisted in identifying the arrested Chinese. Two of them, both On Leongs, later told Assistant District Attorney Frank A. Lord that

Wang had shaken them down. After their arrest, they said, he had offered to guarantee their freedom by failing to identify them at the arraignment. For this service, he had demanded, and received, $40 a head. Lord had Wang arrested again. The On Leongs had succeeded in turning his most cherished victory—the Easter Sunday raid—into a resounding personal defeat.

The police did not often visit the Doyers Street Chinese Theatre, also known as the Chinese Opera House. There was no need, because bad things didn't happen there. No vice was associated with it, and there had always been a tacit understanding that it constituted neutral ground where Hip Sing and On Leong alike could enjoy a Chinese play after a day's work. Americans visited from time to time, but few were drawn to what one called the "strange, curious and grotesque mixture of barbaric costumes, wild contortions and horrible sounds" that characterized Chinese opera.

On August 6, 1905, the all-male troupe presented a Cantonese drama called *The King's Daughter*. It was very popular, so the performance in the four-hundred-seat theater that Sunday night was standing-room only. Nobody in the all-Chinese audience paid much attention when several Hip Sing men quietly took seats in both the front and the back of the hall before the performance began. Nor would anyone have suspected that concealed under their garments were .44-caliber revolvers.

Suddenly, during a dramatic moment in the play, a Hip Sing jumped from his seat near the front, lit a string of firecrackers, and tossed them onto the stage. The startled actors fled immediately, at which point four Hip Sings in the back rose simultaneously, drew their guns, and shot into the crowd. Panic-stricken theatergoers crawled under seats or dashed for the doors. Their mission accomplished, the men fled, still brandishing their weapons. Thanks to the angle in Doyers Street, they were quickly out of sight.

The fusillade of more than a hundred bullets shattered windows, knocked plaster from walls, and splintered benches. And although it ap-peared as though the gunmen had fired indiscriminately, they had actually selected their targets carefully. When police forced their way into the smoke-filled auditorium, they discovered four On Leong men lying on the

A view of the outside of the Doyers Street Chinese Theatre—
a.k.a. the Chinese Opera House—ca. 1908. In 1905, it was the scene
of a Hip Sing massacre of On Leong enemies.

floor in puddles of their own blood and a score of others cowering under
the benches.

The officers summoned two ambulances to ferry the wounded to
Hudson Street Hospital. A forty-one-year-old restaurateur, shot in the right
temple, died on the way, as did Yuck Li, a thirty-nine-year-old grocer shot
in the chest. Yuck's brother, Yuck Yu, a thirty-seven-year-old laundryman,
succumbed to a chest wound after reaching the hospital. Only one On
Leong, shot in the abdomen, survived, and not for long.

Soon a squad of police descended on Hip Sing headquarters on the
Bowery. They arrested three men inside and another four found hiding on
the roof. Two had revolvers that had recently been fired; they were taken to
the hospital and identified by the wounded survivor before he died. A little
later, officers collared Mock Duck, courtesy of an On Leong informer. As
he was led away, several men cursed him. "They have threatened to stab

me," he complained to the arresting officers, who were unable to understand the Chinese epithets.

Police continued to make arrests until twenty-one Hip Sings were in custody, but they missed the two who had actually planned the executions. One, San Francisco–born Sing Dock, was known as the "Scientific Killer" because of his methodical approach to his chosen occupation. Small in stature, with a lifelong fascination for firearms, he had joined the Hip Sing Tong in California at the age of nineteen. The other was Yee Toy, who had also come from San Francisco. He had taken a job as a cook for a wealthy family when he got to New York. Yee's boldness was belied by his slight build. Known by the sobriquet "Girl Face" because of his effeminate features, he, too, knew how to handle a gun. But both Sing Dock and Yee Toy were overlooked by police after the shooting.

The On Leongs had been expecting trouble. A week earlier, Lee Toy had told a reporter he had heard that a dozen of them had been targeted by the Hip Sings for some sort of surprise attack. But no one had expected the theater, theretofore neutral ground, to be the scene of the carnage. Gin Gum told police that the men who were shot had been witnesses against Mock Duck and that the attack was an act of revenge. He also said he had seen Mock Duck lead gunmen through the theater before the shooting and leave before the play began, which was probably a lie; if true, it would certainly have put the On Leongs on alert.

Two men identified as shooters were held without bail pending a coroner's inquest. Bond was posted for the others, including Mock Duck. Although two eyewitnesses placed him at the scene, he was released on $1,000 bail.

Tom Lee served as master of ceremonies at the double funeral of the Yuck brothers on August 10. Carriages lined both sides of Mott Street, and forty policemen were on hand to keep order. But there was no further trouble from the Hip Sings as the cortege passed through Chinatown on its way to Cypress Hills Cemetery. They had already won this round.

Smarting from the assassination of four of their brethren, the On Leongs didn't let even a week go by before striking back. And in so doing, they ratcheted up the conflict to a new and previously unseen level of depravity.

The victim this time was forty-two-year-old Hop Lee, an Eleventh Street laundryman. Two policemen walking past his establishment at 1:00 a.m. on August 12 heard a racket coming from inside, and when they broke in, they came on a gruesome scene: four Chinese men had pinned Hop Lee down on his own ironing board, two at his head and two at his feet. And another was butchering him viciously with a huge meat cleaver.

Hop had been asleep, police said later, when five On Leongs forced his door, dragged him from his bed, and stretched him out on the board. They might have killed him with one blow but instead chose torture. The man wielding the cleaver delivered repeated blows to his body and his head. And in an act of pitiless savagery, he severed Hop Lee's nose from his face.

Hop's assailants fled at the sight of the police. Two of them, Charlie Joe and Lee Toy, ran upstairs to the roof of the building. After a struggle, Joe was subdued. Lee Toy, the tough who had beaten up Warry Charles in 1891 and Wong Get in 1894, leaped across a five-foot gap to a neighboring building and then jumped to a third whose roof was a twenty-foot drop from the second. He, too, put up a struggle, but he was apprehended. A third, Mon Moon, was more easily captured: he fell down a flight of stairs while escaping, fracturing several ribs.

Poor Hop Lee was taken to Bellevue Hospital, where he identified Mon Moon and Charlie Joe, but not Lee Toy, before he died. While the former recuperated at Bellevue, the coroner decided to hold Joe and set $5,000 bail for Lee Toy.

The police were certain the attack was retaliation for the theater massacre. But why Hop Lee was targeted was a mystery. He was no fighting man, nor was he known to have had a hand in the recent killings. But he was a Hip Sing and a friend of Mock Duck's, and that was apparently enough for the avenging On Leongs.

Three days after Hop Lee's murder, Tom Lee was summoned for a chat with Assistant District Attorney J. Frederic Kernochan, a young, Yale-educated attorney and Spanish-American War veteran. Kernochan wanted to discuss the recent clashes of the tongs, and Lee agreed to the meeting. He asked his attorney, David Frank Lloyd, to accompany him.

But there would be no meeting.

It had been months since a threat had been made on Lee's life, and he had relaxed his vigilance. He went alone to the corner of Centre and Franklin streets, where he was to meet Lloyd, but the lawyer was late. Suddenly Gin Gum and Charlie Boston overtook him and warned him breathlessly that Mock Duck and three other Hip Sings were "laying" for him. Two were waiting in ambush on Leonard Street, and two were posted on Franklin Street. They had somehow found out about the meeting or else had simply followed Lee to Kernochan's office.

Lee bolted into the nearby police station, his hat flying in the air. He told his story to two officers, who quickly made the rounds with him and discovered two Chinese men hiding behind a truck in the shadow of the court building. The men fled, but Lee was certain one of them was Mock Duck. He told the police he had learned that the $3,000 bounty the Hip Sings had placed on his head in February was still on offer. And he resolved never again to leave his premises without bodyguards.

Because of the attempt on Tom Lee's life, the next move belonged to the On Leongs. And this time, the targets were all members of the Huie family. Although the Huies were closely associated with the Hip Sings, not all were members. On Leongs had killed one, Huie Fong, on Mott Street in February.

The new attack on the Huies was artfully planned. At 9:00 p.m. on August 20, several On Leongs created a diversion on Mott Street by firing half a dozen shots from a roof directly across from their headquarters. It was a calculated effort to draw the police to Mott, and it worked flawlessly. Captain Eggers's headman in Chinatown hurried from his post in front of the Chinese Theatre. As he and his men searched for the shooters, the real action was taking place on Pell Street.

With Eggers's men preoccupied, police from Elizabeth Street—who no longer technically had jurisdiction over Chinatown but who still came when called—got to the third floor of 18 Pell first. They found one Huie clan member clutching his right arm, three more shrieking in agony on the floor, and eight others trying to minister to them. The room was a wreck, and the walls were riddled with bullet holes. An officer fashioned a tourniquet to stop the loss of blood from one man, probably saving his life. He and a kinsman who had been shot were taken to the hospital. Two cousins, neither seriously injured, were treated on the spot; they and five others were held as witnesses.

Eggers was furious. He dressed down his Chinatown squad. The shooting had taken place right under the nose of his headman, but the Sixth Precinct police had beaten his men to the scene. The men of the Sixth, who had seen three Chinese men killed and at least five wounded since they had lost their Chinatown franchise, had ample cause for schadenfreude.

At the arraignment, the On Leong secretary, Lee Loy, blamed the Hip Sings for the dustup. He explained unconvincingly that the Huie cousins were actually *friendly* with Tom Lee and his men, a fact that had ostensibly earned them the enmity of the Hip Sings. Mock Duck's version of the story was that the cousins, though not Hip Sings, had refused advances by the On Leongs.

"Aren't you afraid the On Leong Tong will get you sooner or later?" Mock Duck was asked.

"Not on your life," he replied. "Look, they're cowards. They're afraid of me."

Indeed they were. But the police did not think retaliation would be long in coming. A sign on the big bulletin board near the corner of Pell and Doyers proclaimed, "Members of the Hip Sing Tong on whose head a price of $1,000 is set are warned to remain off the streets this week."

It was good advice.

The massacre at the Chinese Theatre had been a watershed. Up to that point, a few Chinese men had died, but to the casual observer the incidents appeared isolated and could be dismissed as the consequence of personal grudges. But the episode on Doyers Street, and now this most recent attack on the Huies, were clearly gang shootings. There was no denying that a line had been crossed.

New Yorkers knew gang wars when they saw them; they had been going on for half a century. In recent years, the papers had reported often, for example, on the rivalry and turf battles between the Eastman Gang, a group of Jewish thugs deeply involved in prostitution and gambling east of the Bowery, and Paul Kelly's heavily Italian Five Points Gang, whose territory lay to its west. Less than two years had passed since a battle royal between the two gangs on Rivington and Allen streets, which began over a card game, had ended in carnage. It had taken five hours and all the reserves three police stations could muster to quell it, and it had spawned a great public outcry.

The Doyers Street killings made national news, in part because they occurred against the backdrop of what the New York *World* called a "great crime wave" that had gripped the city in 1905. "The present outbreak of crime is one of the worst that has occurred in New York in many years," the paper observed in August as it detailed the major thefts, holdups, and violent crimes of the prior month. Even District Attorney Jerome confirmed an uptick in criminal activity.

New Yorkers were feeling more unsafe than usual, and many blamed the massive influx of newcomers for the trouble. Immigration at the Port of New York, which accounted for about 80 percent of all arrivals in the United States, was at an all-time high; from January to April 1905, nearly 290,000 people came from abroad, an increase of more than 40 percent over the same period in 1904. On one Sunday in May, more than 12,000 foreigners landed at Ellis Island. Most of the blame for the uptick in crime fell on Italians and Jews, so the perception of a spike of violence in Chinatown felt like one more unwelcome appendage of the hydra head.

A gang shooting in Chinatown was as much a worry for the average Chinese as it was for municipal authorities. One could now no longer feel safe even in neutral territory like the Chinese Theatre. And the violence was horrible for business. Chinatown's white tourists, who spent money on food and souvenirs during their visits, would certainly find other diversions if they feared getting caught in cross fire.

"When there is trouble in Chinatown," the New York *Age* declared, "the first thought of the police is, '*cherchez* Mock Duck.'"

By 1905, Mock Duck had become larger than life. The *New-York Tribune* called him a "bogie man" whom the children of Chinatown had endowed with supernatural attributes. "His big ears can hear a pin drop a block away, his beady eyes can see around the corners ahead of him, he can read the minds that would shoot at him from under blouses [and] no yellow man's bullet can puncture his thick hide," it was said.

Mock Duck's reputation, however, was belied by the fact that there was no proof he had ever murdered anyone. Even the police admitted they couldn't pin a homicide on him, although they suspected he had masterminded more than one.

"I kill no one. You prove that I kill. I hate nobody, and I am not a bad man," Mock Duck insisted to the *Tribune,* which described him as "the picture of injured innocence" in his all-too-frequent appearances before the sergeant at the station house and the magistrate in police court.

But it was not only Mock Duck whose savagery was being exaggerated. One could say the same about the Chinese quarter in general. "Chinatown has been the synonym for vice for many years," the *Buffalo Express* wrote. "It is the most vicious of the many vicious districts of New York. It harbors the most dangerous bands of assassins, the most unbridled rings of gamblers and the most daring gangs of opium smugglers and dive keepers that ever flourished in the low life of the metropolis."

In fact, very little of that was true. There had been just over three thousand arrests in the Sixth Precinct in 1904, but nearly twice that number in the Fifth, Twelfth, and Twenty-second and three times as many in the Nineteenth; all but one of these were in lower Manhattan. That year, ninety-five arrests were made for gambling in the Sixth, a number surpassed in eleven other districts. Opium might have been more specific to the Chinese quarter, but only eighteen arrests were made for violation of the opium law. According to police statistics, 334 Chinese were arrested in New York in 1904, compared with nearly 20,000 Irishmen, more than 13,000 Italians, more than 12,000 Russians, and more than 11,000 Germans. In fact, among the twenty-three categories of "nativity of persons arrested" compiled by the police that year, China ranked second from the bottom. And although Manhattan experienced more than six hundred homicides in 1904, the death toll attributable to the conflict between the Hip Sings and the On Leongs that year had been just *one.*

Still, it was prejudice and appearances, not facts, that fueled the furor over Chinatown. The *Baltimore American* correctly complained that New York's Chinese were getting far more attention than their numbers would suggest they deserved. "The internal politics of the Syrians and the Armenians do not get into the police courts," it observed, despite their superior numbers. "But as for the Chinese, this handful of strangers, with their queer customs, their strange psychology and their halting efforts to adapt themselves to institutions which are not of their making, have managed in the past six months to involve nearly all the legal machinery of the city, including the District Attorney's office, the police courts and the detective organization at Police Headquarters, in a little private quarrel of their own."

But it was more the prejudice of whites than any goings-on in Chinatown that caused New Yorkers to single it out as the city's most vexing trouble spot. It was not so much that the Chinese themselves had "managed" to involve the legal machinery of the city as it was that that machinery was determined to intrude into Chinese lives. Whites insisted on seeing Chinatown as a quarter shrouded in mystery rather than one troubled by gangs but populated, in the main, by law-abiding people who wished only to be left alone.

When the newspapers wrote about Chinatown, the image presented was of a dangerous and sinister underworld whose perilous alleys crawled with gun-toting, opium-addled gang members. The New York *World* called it "the worst slum in the city of New York," a "municipal disfigurement," a "haven for fugitive criminals," and "a catch-basin for crime." It styled the Chinese quarter as "the successor as a crime centre of Five Points and Mulberry Bend," referring to two of the city's most notorious rough-and-tumble neighborhoods, both nearby. And it dismissed it as "a place of filth, of squalor, of Oriental tinsel and mystery."

Eagerly abetting this skewed view were some white hangers-on in Chinatown—sometimes known as *lobbygows,* a term of uncertain origin—who ran evening coach tours of the quarter and weren't above staging visits to fake gambling and opium joints, and interviews with "debased" white women of Chinatown to satisfy the prurient interests of their slumming uptown clients. Chuck Connors, one such figure, was a Tammany operative seen by outsiders as "the mayor of Chinatown" even though no Chinese would ever have called him that. He was a useful conduit to the white establishment, because he knew everybody and his fund-raisers gave him excellent access to the rich and powerful. But he made a living showing white New Yorkers and tourists the seedy and exotic Chinatown they wanted to see.

Of more immediate import than the view of the newspapers and the public was the attitude of the police, and it was, in the main, a deeply racist one. When he looked at Chinatown, Commissioner McAdoo did not see tinsel and mystery. He saw only "an ulcer spot on the face of the city which would be much better off if the whole place could be leveled and rebuilt."

New York had had half a century's worth of experience with organized crime, and the criminal wrongdoings of the Irish, Italian, and Jewish immigrant gangs were far more heinous than the tong killings in Chinatown. But the Irish-born McAdoo didn't even accept that organized Italian crime existed. "That there is such a thing as a thoroughly organized, widely separated secret society which directs its operations in all parts of the United States from some great head centre, such as the Mafia or Black Hand is pictured, I have never believed," McAdoo wrote.

But he had no doubt about the tongs: "They have a sort of trust, so as to handle the profits of Chinatown, by which they grant permission to gamble, insure protection from the police, create the impression that they

STARTS FROM NEW YORK THEATRE,
BROADWAY & 44TH ST., (OPP. HOTEL ASTOR)

Evening coach tours of Chinatown were popular with tourists, as this 1905 advertisement shows. Tong wars threatened this profitable enterprise.

have a 'pull' with the head 'Melican' men, furnish lawyers for defendants in court, and give wise advice out of court." In McAdoo's view, they were "dirty, sordid, and mean, vicious and criminal," and "grafted on Western civilization."

The situation in Chinatown was also a major concern for China's diplomats. Misbehavior among Chinese in America—almost all of whom remained subjects of the emperor—reflected poorly on China. On August 21, Shah Kai-Fu, the Chinese consul, paid a call on the district attorney to see if he could stop the warfare.

Jerome told him to discuss the matter with Commissioner McAdoo.

The fact that the level of crime in Chinatown had been greatly overstated was no guarantee that things there would *stay* quiet. After the attack on the Huie cousins, retaliation was a foregone conclusion, and Chinatown was put on virtual lockdown. Uniformed headquarters police were stationed about fifty feet apart on the principal thoroughfares, and detectives, as well as private agents employed by Consul Shah, were everywhere, watching everyone.

Local pawnshops and hardware stores nearly sold out of armaments, especially large-caliber revolvers, which many Chinese preferred, and a police dragnet in which about five hundred Chinese were searched yielded several hundred weapons, including meat cleavers and even a crude switchblade. The On Leong heavyweight Lee Toy was among those frisked, and when police found a .44-caliber revolver on him with every chamber loaded, they arrested him.

Everyone braced for bloodshed, but nothing happened for several days—due, no doubt, to the crackdown. The tong men were too canny to misbehave while under a microscope. On August 27, Captain Eggers's men heard there was likely to be trouble at the Chinese Theatre once again. It seemed like good information; it was the Hip Sings' turn to strike, and Mock Duck had again been seen in the vicinity. Eggers added five plainclothesmen to the uniformed officers already posted at the stage, in the aisles, and in front of the hall and ordered that every member of the audience be searched that night. When no guns were found, he permitted the show to go on but kept several men inside the theater just in case.

Tensions remained high, however, and there was no shortage of other rumors. Mock Duck told Eggers's men that On Leong spies posing as laundry supply dealers were staking out Hip Sing–owned laundries uptown for future attacks. And on August 28, Gin Gum went to the Sixth Precinct— which might have lacked authority in Chinatown for the moment but was still where the On Leongs had the best relations—and told the acting captain, Patrick J. Tracy, whom McAdoo had recently named to head Elizabeth Street, that five Hip Sing assassins "armed to the teeth" were en route from Philadelphia. He had learned via long-distance telephone that the men, sent to murder Tom Lee and as many of his followers as possible, were coming by train.

Tracy dispatched plainclothesmen to each of the railroad's ferry stations on the New York side of the Hudson and detailed twenty detectives to watch the headquarters of both tongs. He ordered the immediate arrest of anyone who made the slightest hostile move. Eggers sent in fifteen of his own men as reinforcements. But no Chinese thugs arrived that night. Or if they did, they were never found.

On August 29, 1905, the coroner began his inquest into the Chinese Theatre murders. Four On Leongs had been gunned down, and nine Hip Sings—including Mock Duck—were accused of complicity in their deaths. Mock Duck and Tom Lee were both present at the Criminal Courts Building but were kept apart until the proceedings began, one in the coroner's office and the other in the district attorney's. Assistant District Attorney Kernochan served as prosecutor; the attorney Eli Rosenberg appeared for the prisoners. And the first witness called was Mock Duck himself.

The wily Hip Sing denied being in the theater on the evening of August 6, and he had an airtight, not to say *inspired,* alibi: he had been at the Oak Street Police Station when the killings occurred, posting bail for friends arrested for gambling. He claimed he had heard nothing about the incident until he learned of it at the station.

"Why did you go to the station house?" Kernochan demanded.

Mock Duck replied, "To bail out my friends."

"Where did you go first in Chinatown?"

"I met Ong Lung Ong, and he asked me to go to the station. I met him in Pell Street and then got a lawyer for the men under arrest."

"Do you know the gun shop of R. J. Hartley & Co. at No. 313 Broadway?"

"No."

"Did you buy pistols there on Friday previous to the shooting?"

"No."

"Did you try to buy cartridges there on Friday previous to the shooting?"

"No. I was never in the place."

"Did you try to buy cartridges in any store on the Friday previous to the shooting?"

At this point, Mock Duck's attorney advised him not to answer to avoid possible incrimination.

Next up was the Chinese Theatre's janitor, who said he had seen Mock Duck on the premises on the night of the murders with seven or eight men carrying what appeared to be packages of firecrackers. He also identified six of the defendants. An On Leong echoed his testimony and placed all the prisoners at the scene. Mock Duck's denial of the purchase of revolvers was also contradicted. A white newspaper reporter claimed he saw him buy guns and cartridges at Hartley's on Broadway a few days before the shooting.

The coroner's jury found Mock Duck directly responsible for the killings, and he was held on $5,000 bail. And without leaving their seats, they sent four of the other eight defendants to the Tombs to await indictment as accessories. These were held without bail; the four others were held as witnesses on $500 bond each.

The trial, however, would never take place. The authorities kept Mock Duck behind bars for most of the balance of the year. They surely already knew they lacked sufficient evidence to convict him—he had not been on-site at the time of the shootings, and all of the evidence against him was circumstantial—but they were in no hurry to let him out. Finally, just before Christmas, they dropped the case.

Many in Chinatown shuddered at the news: Mock Duck was once again on the loose.

Chapter 9

✹

Profit Sharing

C hinatown was decorated with lanterns and banners on January 24, 1906, and festivities to welcome the Year of the Horse had already begun. The crackling of firecrackers could be heard throughout the quarter.

All the better to drown out the sound of gunfire.

A little before 2:00 p.m., "Black Devil" Lee Toy and three other On Leongs turned onto Pell Street and entered No. 32, a lodging house, to pay a New Year's call on friends. As soon as they disappeared inside, half a dozen Hip Sings stole into the alley next door, positioning themselves so they might watch the street without being seen. Others staked out locations on the stairway leading up from the basement of No. 28.

After the visit was over and the men emerged, a volley of shots rang out. Windows shattered, and sightseers and pedestrians ducked for cover. As the On Leongs attempted to flee, one was felled by a bullet in his chest, and another took one in his skull. When he stirred, he was mercilessly shot in the head a second time, blowing off most of his jaw. Both men were dead before the ambulance arrived. The other two were wounded but survived. Lee Toy, deeply loathed by the Hip Sings, was hit twice in the chest.

"It sounded like Gettysburg," exclaimed Captain Tracy, who had been around the corner when the first shots were fired. His officers arrested two On Leongs and four Hip Sings, including Louie Way—who had attempted to shoot the On Leong treasurer, Chu Gong, the previous March—and "Girl Face" Yee Toy, who had helped plan the Chinese Theatre shootings. All but Yee Toy were unhurt and taken to Elizabeth Street. Yee, however, had been shot through both shoulders and suffered a fractured skull. He was rushed to Hudson Street Hospital, along with the two wounded On Leongs, who were placed under armed guard lest their enemies make a second attempt at them.

When police searched the bodies of the two deceased On Leongs, they found on one of them several dollars' worth of quarters wrapped in red paper. These were New Year's gifts of "lucky money" for unlucky children who would now never receive them.

Tracy was optimistic about the chances for conviction. "If we can get a Chink or two locked up for good," he predicted, "there is a chance to stop these outbursts."

The Pell Street killings were a surprise for two reasons. First, Chinese New Year is traditionally a time of comity, when friendships are renewed, obligations discharged or wiped clean, and enmities forgiven. An act of war committed at such a time signaled blatant disrespect for Chinese conventions and sensibilities.

Chinese New Year is also a time for making amends, and the second reason the attack was unexpected was that several days earlier the local Chinese themselves had made an effort to resolve the problems between the two tongs before the New Year began. The newspapers reported that the matter had been adjudicated before a "Chinese court"—that is, the Chung Hwa Gong Shaw—and that a truce had been struck. In fact, on January 20, Captain Tracy had been invited to a meeting at Chinatown's City Hall. Although he was given no details, he had been assured the two tongs had agreed to bury the hatchet and that peace would prevail in Chinatown in the New Year.

But that was just the point. The Pell Street shootings were not technically violations of the cease-fire, because it wasn't slated to begin until the *following* day. This had been an under-the-wire attempt by the Hip Sings to clean up unfinished business while they still could. After the coroner remanded the Hip Sing offenders to the Tombs without bail, he discovered a familiar reason for the attack: the two murdered men were slated to testify the following Monday as alibi witnesses in the trial of the men who had so savagely mutilated Hop Lee, the laundryman, the previous summer. Now they would no longer be available to give the butchers a free pass. Although the grand jury indicted the men, not one was ultimately convicted.

Guests had been invited and musicians engaged for a grand banquet to mark the truce, but there was so little trust between the rival tongs, especially after the killings, that the On Leongs never appeared. The

Chinese tong men detained in connection with the January 24, 1906, Chinese New Year ambush on Pell Street were photographed together with their arresting officers on the steps of the Elizabeth Street Police Station.

newspapers speculated whether their absence had been a precautionary measure or a calculated insult that signaled war anew.

The next day, the New York *Sun* observed, brought "the most quiet New Year that Chinatown ever saw."

Dissatisfied with Captain Eggers's performance, Commissioner McAdoo had abolished his Central Office "Chink Squad," as the *New York Post* crudely described it, and transferred him to Brooklyn late in 1905. He also restored full authority over Chinatown to Captain Tracy at the Sixth Precinct. McAdoo went out of his way to humiliate Eggers when he made the announcement, telling the press that "weak men must be weeded out at once," possibly because he had gotten wind of a remark Eggers made in an unguarded moment that suggested he might have loyalties other than strict obedience to McAdoo himself.

"I will continue to be a sergeant of police," Eggers had said, "and Mr. McAdoo might not always be a Commissioner of Police."

Eggers's comment was prescient, although it didn't take a crystal ball to recognize that McAdoo was out of favor with Mayor George B. McClellan. His zeal in combating vice had been blamed for the slim margin by which the mayor had been reelected in 1905. Before the end of the year, McClellan asked for McAdoo's resignation and appointed the retired army brigadier general Theodore A. Bingham to his post. He also named Rhinelander Waldo, a Spanish-American War veteran, first deputy commissioner of police.

Bingham, a West Point graduate with government experience, was an avowed anti-Semite and a racist. Like many New Yorkers, he blamed foreigners for most of the city's crime. He reserved special enmity for Jews and called Chinatown a "plague spot that ought not to be allowed to exist." Waldo, not yet thirty, had no experience in politics, but he was a member of the Fifth Avenue smart set. Connected by blood to many old Knickerbocker families, he was already a millionaire. The plucky Waldo had served in the Philippines, "where there are more Chinese in a minute than New York has in a year," the New York *Sun* assured its readers, "so he knows something of their tricks and their manners."

On January 26, in one of his first official acts, Waldo paid a visit to Chinatown, where Captain Tracy took him on a walking tour. Their first stop was 18 Mott, still adorned with decorations to welcome the Year of the Horse, only a day old. They were received by Tom Lee, who continued to be known informally as the "mayor of Chinatown," and by Gin Gum. Offering Waldo a cigar, Lee explained that the On Leong Tong was composed of peace-loving businessmen firmly opposed to the disorder in Chinatown and assured him it was the Hip Sings who were the hatchet men and the troublemakers. Waldo politely asked that Lee use his influence to preserve peace, and Lee, of course, agreed to do his utmost.

Waldo's next stop, naturally, was 12 Bowery, where Mock Duck and Wong Get also spouted their usual propaganda: the Hip Sings were the reformers, allies of the Parkhursts, trying to stop gambling. Although one wall of the meeting hall was adorned with an image of a Chinese god, Waldo couldn't help but notice that the opposite wall bore a crayon portrait of none other than Frank Moss, who for a decade had served as the patron saint of the New York branch of the Hip Sing Tong. Waldo left them with a veiled threat: if the fighting did not stop, he would flood Chinatown with police and lock up all the troublemakers. Mock Duck appeared unperturbed.

"I want to compliment you for having your precinct so well in hand," Waldo told Captain Tracy. "I think you will be able to put down these tong wars," he added. But Tracy's tenure at Elizabeth Street was to be short-lived, because Commissioner Bingham was less impressed with him than Waldo was. Less than a month later, by Bingham's order, Tracy was transferred to Jamaica, New York, where, within a few years, he would be accused of graft and suspended. Captain Herman W. Schlottman, a twenty-one-year veteran of the force, exchanged places with Tracy and became the new warden of Chinatown.

In January 1906, a sixty-two-person delegation from China led by two imperial commissioners came to the United States to study political and social institutions. One of the delegates was thirty-one-year-old Dr. Froman F. Tong, a physician with the title of special commissioner to the United States. Tong had studied in the United States before and this time planned to stay for postgraduate work at Columbia University. He would later be named vice-consul in China's New York mission.

Together with Consul Shah Kai-Fu and several prominent Chinatown leaders, Dr. Tong approached the Court of General Sessions judge Warren W. Foster—who had once been entertained at an On Leong dinner—to ask him to mediate the conflict in Chinatown. A Tammany Democrat, Foster graciously consented to do what he could to bring about peace.

On January 30, at the Criminal Courts Building after court had recessed for the day, he met with representatives of both tongs—eleven people in all. Neither Tom Lee nor Mock Duck attended; Gin Gum, second-in-command, headed the On Leong delegation, and the treasurer Huie Gow led the Hip Sing contingent. Their lawyers were also on hand. Foster sat behind a large desk, and the attendees formed a semicircle in front of him, Hip Sings on one side and On Leongs on the other. He explained that he was sitting not in his judicial capacity but rather as a mediator who wished

Rhinelander Waldo, ca. 1908. He became
New York City police commissioner in 1911.

only to help stop the carnage. The tong leaders had been called together by
the authorities before but never by a judge and never for mediation. This
was a first.

"This business has gone on too far already, and it must be stopped at
once," he cautioned. "The rivalry between the tongs has reached such a
stage that it reflects on the good name of this city, and threatens the business of that particular section. Now, if you wish your business to go on
successfully, if you want to encourage sightseers down there, you must stop
this bloodshed. If you can't agree among yourselves, then the law will
bring about a settlement."

It was, of course, an empty threat. The law had proven quite powerless
to stop the bloodshed up to then, which was why mediation was being
tried in the first place. Attorneys for both tongs asserted that all their clients
wished was peaceful coexistence, which, after so many years of fighting,
might well have been true. Consul Shah seized on that statement and

Judge Warren W. Foster,
dubbed "the Great White
Father of Chinatown" for
his peacemaking efforts.

suggested that the two declare an immediate armistice and set the goal of agreeing on a written peace treaty in a week's time. In the meantime, both tongs would appoint commissioners empowered to sign a binding agreement.

The pact, as negotiated, forbade the purchase or carrying of deadly weapons by tongs or their members. It limited the tongs' receipts to member dues, prohibiting the levying of tribute on local businesses or the acceptance of payments for concessions or favors. It included a pledge not to interfere with each other's property. Each tong was to designate a representative to meet monthly with the Chinese consul to adjudicate any infractions and punish misconduct. And each pledged a bond of $1,000 to ensure adherence to all obligations.

That was the extent of the *public* agreement. But the two tongs had also reached a tacit understanding—not codified in the treaty and likely not even discussed in English—concerning the traditional territorial boundaries that separated them. Mott Street would henceforth be understood as the preserve of the On Leongs, and Pell would be recognized as Hip Sing territory, with Doyers Street considered neutral ground.

And although the pact was clear that no "protection" money was to be collected by anyone, there was nonetheless a widespread belief that tong business would continue more or less as usual, except that the Hip Sings would now be let in on the graft, free to exact tribute from businesses within their sphere of influence—that is, Pell Street.

"The truth of the treaty, which will be a surprise to Judge Foster," the *New York Times* confided, "is that the On Leongs have consented to share the profits derived from the protection of Chinatown's gambling industry with the Hip Sings."

Signing was set for February 6. The On Leong delegation got to the criminal court on time, but the Hip Sings did not; they arrived only after the On Leongs had left in a huff. Dr. Tong persuaded the Hip Sings to sign anyway, and Chong Pon Sing, Huie Gow, and Yip Shung, president, treasurer, and secretary, respectively, all did so. The On Leongs didn't sign until two days later. A ratification meeting, including the formal exchange of copies, was scheduled, with a celebratory banquet to follow. In the meantime, both tongs were expected to file bonds with the judge to guarantee their observance of the treaty.

As soon as the On Leongs had committed, the Hip Sings issued three hundred invitations to a New Year's banquet at the Hung Far Low Restaurant on Pell. Among those asked were the police commissioner, Bingham; the deputy commissioner, Waldo; judges of the Supreme Court of New York County and the Court of General Sessions; and, of course, the Parkhurst superintendent, McClintock. Tom Lee was also on the invitation list, together with several of his On Leong brethren, and although the On Leongs failed to show, Lee did observe the nicety of sending written regrets. Without a single On Leong in attendance, but with forty-five policemen on patrol to be sure the peace was kept, the Hip Sings turned the event into a victory celebration.

Lee's decision to boycott did not mean the agreement was void; it was surely a precautionary measure. A signed agreement notwithstanding, the On Leongs still had little reason to trust their longtime antagonists, especially in a Pell Street venue. The following night, they held a more muted affair of their own on Mott. Gin Gum insisted that Hip Sings had been invited, but even if they had wanted to come, having been snubbed by the On Leongs the night before, they could hardly have attended and preserved face.

There was now a formal accord, blessed by the authorities and backed by surety bonds, to stop the violence in the Chinese quarter once and for all, as well as a tacit agreement to divide the turf. The First Tong War was officially over, and if there was a victor, it was surely the Hip Sing Tong. By any measure, the Hip Sings had won points at the expense of their formerly omnipotent rivals; this accounted for their victorious attitude.

But even this was not terrible news for the On Leongs. The conflict had been costly and had sapped their treasury, and the closing of many gambling halls had depressed their revenues. Provided it could be done in a face-saving manner, it made good economic sense to cut the Hip Sings in if doing so would buy a measure of peace and quiet and boost profits at the same time.

Optimists predicted it would produce some quiet, at least for a time. But only the optimists in Chinatown believed that permanent peace had been achieved.

Americans who read about the peace agreement surely wondered why law enforcement had failed so miserably at quelling the violence in Chinatown and why the authorities had to resort to mediation between what were essentially two criminal organizations to accomplish it. Years later, the *New York Times* fretted about the issue this way: "It is at once irritating and humiliating that the termination of hostilities has been brought about, not by the police and our courts, through stern enforcement of the law and equally stern penalties for its violation, but because certain high-placed officials in the two societies met . . . and, after long discussion, came to terms." It went on, "The men who could issue such orders . . . showed themselves to constitute an *imperium in imperio* [literally, "a state within a state"], alien and isolated, possessing and exercising the power of life and death."

The *Times* was driving at a very basic truth: the Chinese in America seemed to be governed far less by American law than by their own rules, which stressed fealty to the orders of the bosses of their fraternal organizations over nearly everything else.

This was true in part because the Chinese who came to America had little or no experience with disinterested government officials who dispensed justice strictly according to the rule of law. They were accustomed, in the old country, to rule by fiat: in the family, by the patriarch; in the village, by the headman; and in the district, by the magistrate, who adjudicated both criminal and civil matters. Although he represented the lowest rung in a civil administration that culminated with the emperor at its top, the village head was probably the highest-ranking person with whom the mostly rural Chinese who made it to America ever dealt, and most issues were resolved within the village itself.

The China they left had never possessed a large body of laws, nor did the disputes these men were likely to encounter require an advanced legal system to resolve. Most quarrels had been arbitrated by the village head, according to his interpretation of justice and tradition, or by a committee of elders selected with the consent of the litigants. Few issues ever made it to court, and those that did were adjudicated by magistrates who were often highly corrupt themselves.

Chinese immigrants naturally sought to replicate institutions they understood and to which they were accustomed and, if new ones were needed, to create them along familiar lines. Clan associations mediated issues within families in San Francisco and New York, just as they had in Taishan. Regional associations—the mutual aid societies organized according to the counties from which the emigrants had come—settled matters among their members. Although these had no antecedents in China, they proved very useful in America. Issues outside their jurisdiction could be resolved by the Chinese Consolidated Benevolent Association, the umbrella organization that included the key regional associations. And at critical moments, Chinese diplomats—agents of the Chinese government in America—also intervened.

Given their background and experience, the Chinese strongly preferred extrajudicial solutions to their conflicts, and so as a general practice what could be settled in Chinatown was settled there, without reference to courts or civil authorities if at all possible. But issues that involved non-Chinese had to be adjudicated by the government, as were some matters—such as smuggling, gambling, drugs, prostitution, assault, and murder—in which white America insisted on asserting its authority.

Under normal circumstances, Chinese saw little benefit in bringing outsiders into intramural quarrels. But the police and the courts could be used strategically to improve one's lot or gain leverage over an enemy, and both tongs resorted to this frequently. Tom Lee's taxing of the gambling houses and paying police not to molest them was only one of the more egregious examples. Manipulating the police into molesting or arresting your enemies was a handy tactic. Lying to the authorities, fleeing from justice, suborning perjury through bribery and threats, and even murdering witnesses before they could testify—or afterward, in retaliation or as a warning to others—were also useful tools, employed with impunity when the situation required it.

The *Times*'s point was well taken, as far as it went. The Chinese *weren't* playing by American rules. But had the newspaper adopted a broader view, it might have apportioned blame more equitably. Whose fault was it that half a century after the Chinese began to arrive in New York in significant numbers, they remained—as the writer noted—"alien and isolated"?

If there had ever been a welcome mat for the Chinese in America, it was withdrawn in several stages. The Page Act of 1875, the first restrictive immigration law in American history, was aimed at stemming the flow of Asian prostitutes, but as a practical matter it slowed the immigration of *all* Chinese women to a trickle, making virtual bachelor societies of America's Chinatowns. In 1882, the Chinese Exclusion Act not only precluded the entry of most Chinese; it made it clear that the presence of those already here would be tolerated only grudgingly: they would be ineligible for citizenship, and most would not be permitted to be joined by their families. The 1888 Scott Act prohibited Chinese laborers who left the country from returning; it also spitefully stranded thousands who had gone home temporarily with the understanding they could come back. And the renewal of the Exclusion Act through the Geary Act in 1892 and again through the Scott Act in 1902, when it became permanent, imposed onerous registration burdens on the Chinese who remained and relegated to the shadows those who could not prove they had entered lawfully.

The law made it crystal clear that Chinese were *not* Americans, and—unlike all other immigrants—it gave them no hope of ever *becoming* Americans. It denied them representation at any level of government and any say in the laws that ruled them. It rendered their chief forms of recreation—including victimless crimes like gambling—illegal and punished offenders, sometimes severely. It marginalized the significant number who could not register because they could not prove legal entry, forcing them to live in fear that a chance encounter with a policeman could result in imprisonment or deportation. And it severely compromised any prospect they had of getting justice from the courts.

And what American law did not do, American society did. Chinese were made to feel like unwelcome guests in someone else's country. The fact that even many who were American-born could speak English only haltingly suggests they enjoyed little entrée into the broader society. Racial prejudice excluded them from many occupations. It wasn't exactly apartheid, but nor was there much fraternization. Americans visited Chinatowns but mostly to gape at the "debased" lifestyle of opium-addled gamblers and prostitutes; they objectified rather than befriended Chinese.

The *Times*'s editorial placed a great deal of faith in the police and the judicial system, but in practice Chinese could count on neither for a fair shake. The power New York police wielded over the Chinese in the Tammany era went mostly unchecked, and the officers—from the captains on down—were notoriously corrupt. Underpaid police shook down businesses and individuals with impunity and threatened dire consequences, including physical harm, if they were not paid. They were also highly biased against the Chinese and saw them as a scourge. Nor could Chinese who were arrested count on sympathy from prosecutors or impartiality from the courts. As long as judges and juries routinely voiced their prejudice against Chinese and trusted the testimony of white witnesses over theirs, how could justice be served?

None of this excused the brutality and murder that were going on in Chinatown, but it begins to tell the story of why so many Chinese failed to internalize American values or embrace a system whose rules were so blatantly stacked against them. It explains why any fealty they might have developed to an abstract system of justice and rule of law failed to supplant the loyalty owed to families and tong bosses. And it sheds some light on why they took a cynical approach to the courts and viewed them more as tools to accomplish their own ends than as temples in which they could rely on justice being dispensed.

•   •   •   •   •

The failure of Mock Duck to appear at the negotiations, the signing of the peace agreement, or the Hip Sing banquet was no accident. He had not been a peace advocate, and in any event several newspapers reported he was no longer on good terms even with the Hip Sings. February 13 then brought the startling news that he had allegedly organized a new tong. And allied with him in this new venture was none other than his old friend Wong Get.

Much had changed in the ranks of the Hip Sing Tong in 1905. Mock Duck had spent most of the second half of the year in jail awaiting trial for the Chinese Theatre murders, and Wong Get had returned to China in late 1904 and stayed for most of the following year. During this time, the Hip Sings had elected a new slate of officers. When Wong returned from China and demanded his office back, he was rebuffed. And as a sign of bad blood between him and his former colleagues, he blamed his recent arrest for running a gambling house not on On Leongs but on Hip Sing informants.

The news of a third warring tong was ominous. "Chinaman may cry 'Peace, peace!' but there is no peace in the bosom of Mock Duck, that handsome little Chinese person who looks like a choir boy and feels all the time like a bull terrier," the New York *Sun* quipped, borrowing a line from Patrick Henry. And as the *New York Times* pointed out, the new, unnamed tong was not a party to the recently concluded peace treaty.

Captain Schlottman, eager to make a mark during his first days on the job, staged several raids on Chinatown games on Sunday, February 18, 1906. He arrested seventeen Chinese for gambling. While the prisoners were being booked, Mock Duck entered the station house, introduced himself to the new captain, and paid $500 bond for each of the prisoners.

But that is not all he did. As arrests were being made at a policy shop at 18 Pell, he offered $20 to one detective and $50 to another if they would release his cousin and a friend, who were among those being taken into custody. The officers not only refused; they arrested him on the spot and charged him with attempted bribery. He was arraigned on February 20 at the Court of Special Sessions and held on $5,000 bail. His attorney, Daniel O'Reilly, argued unsuccessfully for a reduction in bond by claiming no crime had been committed.

"What? Do you say it is no crime for a man to offer money to a policeman to permit his prisoner to escape?" the judge demanded, incredulously.

"Well, not for a Chinaman," O'Reilly responded. "Chinks don't call that criminal."

No bondsman appeared, not the Hip Sings, and not even the Parkhursts, who could have been counted on in the past to provide bail for Mock Duck. In fact, at the arraignment, one of his attorneys intimated that the arrest had been part of a plot against Mock Duck by Superintendent Mc-Clintock *himself.* If so, it was proof positive that the Parkhursts had finally seen through him and realized he was not—and never had been—the reformer they once thought him.

If there ever was a third tong, it lacked the resources even to post bond for Mock Duck. In fact, it was never mentioned again, suggesting that it was an aborted effort or that the papers had gotten it wrong from the start. In any case, Mock Duck, who couldn't come up with the cash for his own bail, was charged with attempted bribery and sent to the Tombs—again.

Although a peace accord had been signed, the New York *World* shared the general pessimism about its durability and value. Dismissing it quite accurately as "merely an agreement to divide the district on new lines" that would permit the tongs to "carry on their criminal trade without interfering with each other," the paper put forth its own radical proposal to solve the problem once and for all: wipe Chinatown off the map entirely and turn the area into a park.

Beginning in late February, in a series of articles and editorials—it was difficult to tell the difference—the *World* made the case for the destruction of "the worst slum in the city of New York," a "municipal disfigurement" that was home to squalor, disease, and enslaved white women. Its overcrowded and dilapidated buildings housed debased people. Razing Chinatown would be, in the *World*'s words, "a work of civic purification."

Precedent could be found in the case of Mulberry Bend, formerly one of the worst sections of New York's Five Points neighborhood and a notorious breeding ground for crime and disease. It had been leveled and converted into a park in 1897 at a cost of less than $1.5 million. The displaced people, if Mulberry Bend was a guide, would mostly find new homes in the immediate area, in new tenements, built according to updated building regulations. "It is better to clean out a centre of infection and make it wholesome," the *World* concluded, "than it is to set guards about it and try to remedy and cure the evils that it breeds."

The specific proposal was to turn the area bounded by Bayard Street, the Bowery, Chatham Square, Park Row, Worth Street, and Mulberry Street into a public garden—an extension of Mulberry Bend Park. It would involve the demise of the most densely Chinese-populated blocks of Pell, Doyers, and Mott streets. The cost of acquiring the land was estimated at about $2 million. To build support, the paper sought the endorsement of Father Ernest Coppo of Mott Street's Church of the Transfiguration, who claimed that "the instrumentalities of Christianity are unable to cope with the horrible conditions that have made Chinatown what it is." Father Coppo was willing, if need be, to see his own church razed in the process.

The government had the power to condemn small sections of the city to provide open public space. On March 1, the *World* presented the case to Mayor George B. McClellan, who immediately declared his support and ordered a full investigation of the plan. The idea also garnered backing from the president of the Board of Health and from the police commissioner,

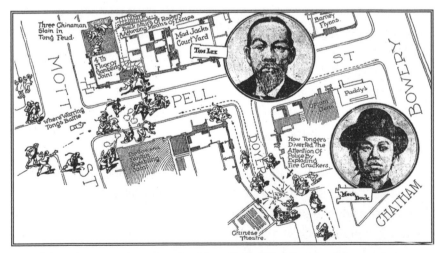

Map drawn to support the New York *World*'s campaign to raze Chinatown and turn the area into a park.

Bingham. In subsequent days, endorsements came from the Tenement House commissioner, the fire commissioner, the parks commissioner, and the city comptroller. Even Dr. Parkhurst weighed in in favor of the plan.

Consideration of the proposal moved quickly. A public hearing before the Board of Improvements was ordered for March 20 by the Manhattan borough president, and because no voices had been raised in opposition, it seemed certain to be adopted. But at city hall on that day, Chinatown's landlords and merchants spoke up for the first time.

James L. Conway, president of the Real Estate Owners' Association, argued that there were better places for a public park. "The whole east side is more congested than Chinatown," he observed. William C. Beecher, representing fifty-two Chinese merchants, maintained not only that Chinatown was no worse than other areas but that New York was home to no more law-abiding people than the Chinese. He estimated the project cost at $8 million. And Bartow S. Weeks, counsel for Chinatown property owners, argued that the law did not empower the city to condemn private property to suppress social evils or eliminate tenements. Cracking down on moral evil was the role of the police, and ameliorating unsanitary conditions that of the Tenement House Commission.

The *World* dismissed the opposition as mere "rookery owners" and quoted the Reverend Madison C. Peters, who testified on behalf of the ministers of the city: "Greed is the bottom of the opposition. Greed of the landlord, who would rent his property to the devil for a branch of hell if he could get enough ice to cool the rent money."

Even after opposition was voiced, the *World* declared the project a done deal. And after a second hearing, the Board of Improvements endorsed a trimmed-down version that was sent on to the Board of Estimate, which was responsible for budget and land-use decisions.

Rumors about what would become of New York's Chinese flew wildly. In April, residents of the Red Hook neighborhood of Brooklyn—a tough section populated by Italian and Irish dockworkers where the Five Points Gang member Al Capone got his start—were alarmed by reports that a new Chinatown would be established on its waterfront. In July, the Bronx buzzed with the story that several wealthy Chinese merchants were negotiating to purchase property at 149th Street and Morris Avenue, also an ethnic enclave and home to many German and Irish immigrants. And in August, it was said that wealthy Chinese had already bought lots at another Brooklyn site, a heavily German and Jewish area at the end of the new Williamsburg Bridge.

The Board of Estimate finally acted the following year, authorizing a park on a smaller parcel of land about an acre and a half in size, bounded by the Bowery, Pell, Doyers, and a portion of Mott Street and valued at $583,000. But predictions of Chinatown's demise were premature. In the end, it was the attorney Daniel O'Reilly, a former congressman, friend of Tom Lee's, and defender of Mock Duck in the recent bribery case, whom the Chinese had to thank. On behalf of his Chinese friends who had no wish to move—and perhaps of himself, because his Chinese clientele provided him with lucrative business—O'Reilly persuaded the Board of Estimate to revoke its approval, and by July 1907 the New York *World*'s idea was officially dead.

The efforts by Tom Lee and others to build relationships with New York's powerful had paid off in spades, and Chinatown and its tongs would remain exactly where they were.

At the end of March 1906, an eighteen-course dinner for three hundred was held at the Port Arthur Restaurant on Mott Street to celebrate peace in Chinatown. The organizers managed to get officers of both tongs to sit together at the same meal. As far as anyone could recall, it was a first.

Judge Foster, credited as the architect of the peace, occupied the place of honor, directly under a stuffed white dove suspended from the ceiling. The meal took five hours from start to finish, but despite the armistice nerves remained frayed. When a waiter dropped a tray, breaking several bowls and causing a loud crash, "every Chinaman who did not plainly see what had happened either jumped or ducked."

In mid-April, Mock Duck's attorney got his bail reduced by arguing that it had been set high not because of the nature of the charge—which, after all, was only bribery, not murder—but rather because of his record. Once bond was cut to $2,000, he was able to put up the cash. He had languished in the Tombs for two months.

Asked if he intended to honor the peace compact struck between the Hip Sings and the On Leongs, he dodged the question. But he did declare, "I'm not going to do any shooting. I'm not the bad man the police make me out to be." Tom Lee, for one, certainly wasn't persuaded. Less than an hour after Mock Duck's discharge, Lee showed up at the Criminal Courts Building, hoping to persuade a judge to secure a promise from his nemesis to keep the peace, even as a non-signatory. But the judges had all gone home for the day.

Three days later came the news of the devastating earthquake that had hit northern California. Although the mostly wooden buildings of San Francisco's Chinatown had by and large survived the tremor, they quickly succumbed to the subsequent fires that burned out of control. Many New York Chinese had friends and relatives in San Francisco, then as now the city with the largest concentration of Chinese in America, and a committee was organized to raise money for the Chinese victims. Three Chinatown merchants spearheaded a drive that raised $5,000 within five days of the initial shock. Tom Lee headed the list of donors with a contribution of $50.

Several days later, Mock Duck was once again in jail, though only briefly. On April 24, he was accused of running a gambling house at 11 Doyers and arrested, together with twenty-five other men, although all were quickly released for lack of evidence. Their defense was that the police had disrupted not gambling but a discussion about sending funds to San Francisco. In fact, there was no evidence Mock Duck was in any way affiliated with the relief committee, as Tom Lee was. Lee and the On Leongs were always ready when philanthropy was needed; the same could not be said of Mock Duck or the Hip Sings.

Chinese women, even in America and even in the twentieth century, were sometimes bought and sold. Their favors might be offered up to other men for profit, or they might be used as chattel to discharge debts. Even those who were ostensibly "married" were often not legally wed. For at least eight years, Wong Get cohabited with a white prostitute turned actress named Florence Fucci, who sometimes went by the name of Florence Wong, but he was later enumerated in the census with a Chinese-born wife named Fong Shee and two children. There is no record of either marriage.

By contrast, Tom Lee and Warry Charles married white women in for-mal, lawful ceremonies. As a practical matter, though, because fraternizing with "Chinamen" was highly discouraged among women of high station, and because most Chinese men lived at the bottom of the society anyway, Chinese in America typically chose only from among lower-class women. This often meant immigrants, most commonly Irish, English, German, or Italian ones.

Mock Duck, too, had lived with a white consort in 1902, but by 1906 the newspapers recorded him as married to a Chinese woman known as Tai Yow Chin. This, too, was probably not a legal union, and Tai Yow, five feet four inches tall and rotund, had a habit of getting into compromising situations. In March 1906, while Mock Duck was still incarcerated, she showed up in Rhode Island. One story held that she had been kidnapped by On Leongs, but Wong Get denied they had had anything to do with it. Providence police, believing she had been brought there to be sold, arrested her but released her when Mock Duck's relatives came up from New York to retrieve her. A few months later, she was picked up in a dingy room in Philadelphia. Again, local police felt sure she was being "held in captivity for immoral purposes." She had been in town for three weeks.

On learning of her arrest, Mock Duck, by then out on bail, went to Philadelphia to rescue her. Although the police didn't believe she was really his wife, they permitted him to visit her cell, where he surely coached her on what to say to the judge. The following day, the magistrate heard testimony not only from the Hip Sings but from several local On Leongs, who alleged that the woman had been brought to Philadelphia to liquidate a $1,000 debt incurred by Mock Duck and that she was not his wife. But the judge, declaring that the police had erred in arresting her in the first place, released her, and Mock Duck hustled her out of court.

When Tai Yow came to live with Mock Duck, she did not come alone. Her first husband, a jeweler named Chin Mung whom she had wed in San Francisco, had earlier been married to a white woman who had died in 1901 shortly after giving birth to a baby girl. That was when Chin Mung married Tai Yow and moved his family to Manhattan. In 1905, after he,

Portrait of Tai Yow Chin, the first
Mrs. Mock Duck, 1906.

too, had died, Tai Yow moved in with Mock Duck on Doyers Street. And
the little girl, known as Ha Oi, came with her.

Although there was never a formal adoption—indeed, there is no record of a formal marriage, either—Mock Duck effectively became Ha Oi's
stepfather. She lived with the couple in their spotless, four-room flat at
10 Doyers. The household also included an elderly cousin and an Irish house-
keeper named Bedelia who spoke English with a strong brogue and could
also manage pidgin Chinese. The little girl was, by nearly all accounts, an
adorable and well-loved child who was watched over carefully. Mock Duck
was overprotective of her, rebuffing entreaties from the teachers at the
Morning Star Mission across the street to send her to their kindergarten.
Instead, he brought in a tutor. Ha Oi was permitted to play with a few
friends but was not allowed on the street alone.

The child had some Caucasian features. Although her skin was light yellow and her dark hair was tied in knots on the top of her head, her eyes were large, round, and blue. But she was always dressed in Chinese clothing and lived in an entirely Chinese environment. She couldn't speak a word of English.

On the morning of March 19, 1907, two agents from the Society for the Prevention of Cruelty to Children, with police backup, knocked insistently on the door of No. 10. At first, Bedelia refused to let them in, protesting that the family was still asleep. But she relented when they identified themselves as officers of the law. They made their way through the flat and discovered the child asleep in the arms of the aged cousin. Then Mock Duck and Tai Yow were roused, and the agents explained the purpose of their mission.

Their society—known as the Gerry Society after Elbridge Gerry, one of its cofounders—had received a letter asserting that a six-year-old white Christian child was being kept in slavery by Mock Duck and was being beaten and abused. The letter was poorly written, and the Gerry Society believed it had been penned by a Chinese. The writer alleged that the little girl's hair had been dyed to disguise her race and demanded she be removed from the household immediately.

The couple explained Ha Oi's origins and assured the agents she was loved and well cared for and that nothing untoward went on in their home. They contended the letter writer had been one of Mock Duck's enemies and pleaded with them to leave the child be. But the men insisted on seizing the girl and told the couple she would be brought before a magistrate at the children's court, who would decide her fate.

At which point, the hard-boiled Mock Duck, the most feared highbinder in Chinatown, frequently jailed and twice tried for murder, threw himself on the child's bed and wept.

The couple attended the arraignment, at which the magistrate reviewed the charges and listened to both sides. He directed that the girl be cared for by the Gerry Society for two days while its agents investigated her background and her treatment in Mock Duck's home. This gave the couple confidence she would be restored to them, because they saw nothing wrong with the way she had come into their care or the way in which she was being raised.

When the time came for the hearing, however, the Gerry Society asked for an extension. The girl's caretakers had unbraided the child's pigtails and after washing her hair thoroughly discovered that she was, in reality, an auburn blonde. They believed she might be a full-blooded Caucasian and suspected she had been kidnapped. So they took photographs of her in both Chinese and American clothing and sent them off to San Francisco to see if their counterparts there could shed any light on her origins.

Based on nothing other than the child's appearance, the Gerry Society concluded unequivocally that "there is not a drop of Chinese blood in Ha Oi's little body." And their San Francisco colleagues—even though all birth records from that period had been destroyed in the fire that followed the earthquake—declared categorically that both of the girl's parents had been white and that her mother, a servant girl, had "abandoned her to the Chinese."

Mock Duck resolved to use every legal means possible to fight for custody. He retained counsel and filed a writ of habeas corpus. The child was then taken to the Supreme Court of New York County, where his attorney contended he and Tai Yow had taken excellent care of her and remained fit to raise her. The Gerry Society, for its part, argued that given his record Mock Duck was no proper guardian.

The judge questioned Mock Duck about his two murder indictments and the pending charge of bribery. In his final ruling on April 12, he declared that the child was Caucasian and in no way bound to Mock Duck and his wife by "ties of race" and that Mock Duck was, in any case, not a fit guardian. Ha Oi was thereupon remanded to the custody of the Gerry Society, which was to find a new home for her. She would never see Mock Duck or Tai Yow again.

In its annual report that year, the Gerry Society congratulated itself on its handling of the case. "The greatest satisfaction has been experienced in . . . the rescue of an American child from a degraded life among Chinese criminals," the report read. And public opinion was squarely behind the society. But a rare note of sympathy for the aggrieved Chinese couple in what had otherwise been a public crucifixion, and a suggestion that Ha Oi's future might not be so bright after all, was offered by a letter writer to the *New York Herald* identified only as "Cosmopolitan":

> So the courts have deprived Mock Duck of his little white foster child, Ha Oi. Well and good. That he loved her and lavished upon her all that money can buy counts for nothing, for has he not been accused or suspected of all the crimes in the code, although none has been proved? "Hath not a Jew hands, organs, dimensions, senses, affections, passions?" wrote Shakespeare. So might he have written of a Chinese, and the answer would have been equally in the affirmative. But what of that? Mock Duck has committed the crime of being born of an alien race. Happy little Ha Oi, that she has been dragged from the lap of pagan love and luxury that she may become the drudge of some Christian household and the target of its taunts.

Chapter 10

Have Gun, Will Travel

A lthough New York was at peace, it wasn't the only place where Hip Sings clashed with On Leongs.

By the turn of the century, both organizations had begun to expand into other cities in the East and the Midwest; the Hip Sings, a California import, were present in several West Coast locations as well. Chapters could form when the Chinese population in a given city was large enough to sustain them, and sometimes New Yorkers were dispatched to help organize them.

The Hip Sings, for example, had been active in Philadelphia as early as 1889; they made the newspapers there when several tried to deter witnesses from testifying in a case against gamblers through a combination of bribery and blackmail. And in 1895, Wong Get had traveled to Washington, D.C., to organize a local Hip Sing chapter, or, as the *Washington Post* put it, "to bleed resident laundrymen and Chinese merchants." He and another senior tong man threatened laundrymen with harm or false accusations unless they made weekly payments ranging from $2 to $10. The On Leongs, for their part, became particularly strong in Boston, Cleveland, and Pittsburgh, and both tongs had a sizable presence in Chicago.

While New York remained the center of gravity, the tongs continued to add locations as the twentieth century progressed. And although there had always been informal cooperation among the branches in various cities, by the early part of the century a formal coordinating structure was established. The Boston-based Meihong Soohoo took credit for establishing the On Leongs' national organization in about 1905. The Hip Sings did so somewhat later, at a 1918 national convention in San Francisco.

Each branch of the On Leong Tong elected its own president, vice president, secretary, and treasurer. The various presidents sat on a combination "executive committee and arbitration board" that constituted the supreme governing board of the national association. Charged not only with leadership but also with mediating any disputes among the individual associations, the board also elected national officers—a national president and vice president and two secretaries—who organized annual conventions. They not only helped the local branches keep in closer touch but also helped them come to one another's aid when needed.

Such aid sometimes called for the lending of hit men. When attacks and assassinations were required, common practice was to recruit *boo how doy*—"hatchet men"—from other locations. These men, who might be fellow tong members or hired guns, could be brought in, set to their deadly tasks, and spirited out of a city quickly. They were less likely than locals to be identified and arrested.

But in drawing the far-flung branches closer together, the national organizations also increased the chances that conflict in one location might spill over into others. This would become a bigger and bigger problem as the years passed and an explosive one by the 1920s.

In mid-August 1907, the New York On Leongs once again sat down for a meal with the Hip Sings. The occasion was a celebration of a full year of peaceful coexistence. Ninety people attended the costly feast at the Tuxedo Restaurant, which began at 8:00 p.m. and ran well beyond midnight before the fruit and cigars appeared at the upscale Doyers Street eatery. The district attorney's office came in full force. Chinese government representatives were also on hand, as were many men of note from New York's financial and professional worlds.

In his toast, Judge Foster, whom the New York *Sun* had dubbed "the Great White Father of Chinatown," related the events that led to the armistice and declared that the truce had been kept faithfully. He also assured the audience that recent outbreaks of violence between branches of the two tongs in Philadelphia and Boston that had been in the news had had nothing whatever to do with the New Yorkers.

On this latter point, however, he was both naive and sorely mistaken. The enmity between the Hip Sings and the On Leongs transcended geographic boundaries. Philadelphia's troubles began in 1906 and broke out for the same reasons that had caused the earlier New York war. In June, local On Leongs fired on a Hip Sing who had helped police organize an antigambling raid. Brother Hip Sings returned the fire, four men were shot, and many arrests were made. Another clash shortly afterward resulted in the shooting of three Chinese men, one fatally, as well as one of the white heads of a Christian mission in Chinatown. Two On Leongs were convicted, and a peace treaty was signed, but the feud was renewed a year later when two Hip Sings were shot to death. One of those arrested was Charlie Boston, senior functionary of the New York On Leongs, who had been lent to his Philadelphia brothers for the battle.

The Hip Sings, too, sometimes dispatched assassins from New York. After the Chinese Theatre and Pell Street shootings, "Scientific Killer" Sing Dock and "Girl Face" Yee Toy headed for Boston, where they set to planning another spectacular bloodbath. In July 1907, a dozen New York Hip Sings led by Sing and Yee arrived in Boston and rented rooms near Chinatown. Within a few days, they opened fire on local On Leongs on Oxford Place, killing three and wounding seven in the worst violence Boston's Chinese quarter had ever seen.

It was all connected. The killings were acts of revenge on Boston On Leongs believed to have been among the Philadelphia shooters. Sing Dock and Yee Toy evaded capture, just as they had after the Chinese Theatre murders, but Boston police arrested seven other Hip Sings who were held without bail for manslaughter. Of the three men who were apprehended the following day, one was reported to be Mock Duck. He had been caught in a laundry in Quincy, Massachusetts, with a revolver on his person.

New York braced for a revenge attack. Captain Robert F. Dooley, drafted by Commissioner Bingham the previous October to take over Elizabeth Street as part of the largest shake-up in New York Police Department history in which eighty-six captains were transferred, stationed ten men in Chinatown, including one ordered to frisk every patron who entered the Chinese Theatre. But he needn't have worried, at least not on account of Mock Duck's alleged capture. Strolling leisurely into the office of the *New York Times* on August 5, a smiling Mock Duck, holding a copy of the morning's *Times* detailing his supposed arrest in Boston, told a reporter, "Never been in Boston in my life. Guess some Chinaman tell 'em he's me just for fun."

Mock Duck confirmed that he had quit the Hip Sings. He blamed some of his former brethren for his arrest for the murder of Ah Fee in 1900 and, more recently, for the bribery charge. He was, he said, on bad terms with both of the tongs.

"I have to be very careful," he told the *Times*. "I watch all around me when I go out, and I stay in the house at night," he added, "so no one can kill me in the dark."

He was right to be wary. Several months later, someone tried to burn down his home. Two old petticoats soaked in oil were the cause of the fire at 42 Division Street. The men who found them extinguished the blaze before any damage was done. But oily rags had been discovered in the building on two prior occasions during the previous three weeks, and the police strongly suspected an On Leong plot. When similar cloths were again found outside Mock Duck's door a day later, and three additional attempts were made in early March 1908, they predicted a full-blown recurrence of the war.

March also brought justice in both Boston and Philadelphia. In Boston, after a twenty-nine-day trial, nine of the Hip Sings held in the August Chinatown shootings were convicted of murder in the first degree, the tenth having died in jail. Among them was their ringleader, Warry Charles, who had clashed with Lee Toy in New York many years earlier before relocating to Boston. And in Philadelphia, two On Leongs arrested the previous July were slated to be hanged.

New York was nervous. Commissioner Bingham placed fifty plainclothesmen in Chinatown. And sure enough, ten days later there was a murder on Mott Street. It happened just in front of the Church of the Transfiguration and was actually witnessed by Assistant District Attorney Theodore Ward, who happened to be passing through Chinatown that day.

The victim was Ing Mow, a tall, lanky Hip Sing. A former laundryman, he had risen in the ranks after Mock Duck left the fold. Ing was walking down Mott when three Chinese men blocked his way. They provoked an altercation, and he was shot behind the ear. He collapsed on the steps of the priest's house adjoining the church as the shooter jettisoned his gun and the attackers fled. Ward attended Ing until the ambulance arrived, but the Chinese man expired on the way to the hospital.

The consensus was that Ing was killed because he had helped police uncover evidence that led to the convictions of the Philadelphia murderers. The following day, the *New-York Tribune* put it this way: "The Hip Sing Tong already has a new and a long bill to present to its most honorable enemy, the On Leong Tong, and yesterday one more item was added to it."

It would have been easy to conclude from the newspapers that nearly everyone in New York's Chinatown was either Hip Sing or On Leong. But tong men actually always constituted only a fraction of the Chinese population. They were just the ones who got all the attention.

The tongs were free to recruit Chinese men of all stripes, but they did not have the advantage of a "built in" pool of members like the geographic and clan societies. To attract and keep members, they had to offer carrots or sticks—or both. As a result of their underworld activities and violent confrontations, membership—when it was known, because they were ostensibly secret societies—carried a certain stigma among other Chinese and certainly in the wider society.

Leong Gor Yun, in *Chinatown Inside Out,* offered some insight:

> Chinese of all classes join the tongs mostly for economic protection, sometimes for revenge. Except for the higher-ups and the hatchet-men, most of the tong members are plain victims of exploitation. They do not brag about being tong members, for there is a general feeling among the Chinese that no one would join a tong if he could help it. Among tong members the hatchet-men are considered a bad lot. It is they who start and profit by tong wars, though they take orders from the men at the top.
>
> Most of the members are recruited among the innocent, quiet Chinese; only when they have been oppressed or exploited to the limit of endurance, will they join either the tong of the oppressor to demand redress, or the rival tong for protection and revenge. Compared to the whole population, tong membership is small.

In other words, many good men joined the tongs for protection from harassment. They could affiliate with a group that was shaking them down, or they could join a rival organization. In either case, the persecution would stop.

It was easy to lose sight of Leong's points—that tong men accounted for a relatively tiny percentage of the Chinese community and that not every tong man was a killer—when the headlines suggested another story. The truth was, most Chinese were hapless bystanders who watched the wars from the sidelines but suffered along with everyone else when all Chinese were tarred by the tongs, when tourists and businesses fled Chinatown, and when draconian solutions to the problem were proposed and carried out.

The On Leongs continued to feather their nest by cementing their relationships with New York's powerful. Thomas F. Foley, a Tammany operative and saloon owner known as "Big Tom," who had attended the 1906 peace banquet, had been sworn in as sheriff of New York County in January, and Tom Lee made sure to show up at his annual picnic. He brought twenty well-dressed Chinese men to show his respect and support for Foley, with whom he had maintained a warm friendship for many years.

After the repeated attempts to burn him alive, Mock Duck went on the road. The previous year, he had gone to Chicago, where he agitated with his old Hip Sing colleagues to raise the "protection" fee charged local merchants from $20 to $60 a week. In November 1908, however, his destination was Denver. And within days of his appearance, the town seemed on the verge of its first highbinder war. The familiar cause was control of gambling. On November 19, the body of Yee Long was found in an alley in the Chinese quarter. He had been poisoned. As the local police pieced it together, Mock Duck had been summoned by a *fan tan* operator trying to muscle his way into the lottery business. Yee Long was a casualty of this battle.

After Denver, Mock Duck went on to San Francisco, and by the spring of 1909 he was back in Gotham, dripping with diamonds. The New York *Sun* took pains to describe the "dazzling" horseshoe pin that secured his tie, the "blazing" watch charm at his waist, and the four-carat rock on his finger. Word on the street, which he denied, was that he had netted $30,000 from his Denver business.

Mock Duck was not back in time for the dinner celebrating the third anniversary of the peace accord, nor would he likely have been invited if he had been. Tom Lee, however, was very much in evidence. This feast was again held at the Port Arthur, and the usual luminaries were present, including Judge Foster and the newly appointed assistant U.S. attorney David Frank Lloyd, who had previously represented the On Leongs and who presided at the dinner. The last speaker was the coroner, who noted wryly that "since they have had peace in Chinatown, there has been no call for my services."

But there would be soon enough.

Chapter 11

The Four Brothers' War

O n June 18, 1909, the half-clothed, half-decomposed body of Elsie Sigel, a twenty-two-year-old white missionary working in Chinatown, was discovered inside a steamer trunk above a chop suey restaurant on Eighth Avenue. Missing for more than a week, the young granddaughter of a Civil War hero had been strangled with a curtain cord that remained tightly wound around her neck.

Sigel's murder was quickly determined to be a crime of passion. A Chinese waiter named Leon Ling was named as a person of interest, because her corpse had been discovered in his room. The two had been having an affair over the strenuous objection of Elsie's parents. Most damning was the fact that the thirty-year-old Ling had suddenly disappeared, together with a friend.

The slaying made national news, and a manhunt was begun. New York police arrested Chu Gain, proprietor of the Port Arthur Restaurant, who had also known Sigel intimately and had been a rival for her affections. And Ling's companion was caught in Amsterdam, New York, and subjected to thirty hours of unremitting interrogation. He was firm in fingering Ling as Elsie's killer and cited jealousy over her relationship with Chu Gain as the motive. But he steadfastly maintained he had no idea where Ling was.

The police commissioner, Theodore Bingham, took a personal interest in the investigation. He could hardly have done otherwise, so salacious and relentless was the news coverage, and he ordered photographs and descriptions of Ling distributed to police departments across the country. But in early July, Bingham was summarily dismissed, his penchant for reform, his severe management style, and his frequent shake-ups having finally caught up with him. His sudden removal was blamed by some on the inability of the police to capture Elsie's slayer.

Ling was never apprehended, but his presumed crime cast a long shadow on Chinatown. The interracial nature of the affair fanned the flames of bigotry and set off a wave of hysteria. Business in Chinatown fell off sharply; Tom Lee claimed it went down 70 percent after the murder. "Sightseers seem afraid to come to Chinatown any more, or the few who do come here hesitate to go into the stores," he complained to the *New York Times*. Worse, he reported, vigilantes posing as police officers were attacking Chinese, raiding their stores, and robbing their apartments.

Sigel's murder, and the sensational newspaper coverage that followed it, had unleashed a torrent of antipathy toward Chinese everywhere. Fearing for their personal safety, New York Chinatown merchants even sent a delegation to Washington to press China's chargé d'affaires to request special protection from the federal government. This appeal was passed on to the governor of New York and, in turn, to the newly appointed acting police commissioner, William F. Baker, who was promoted after Bingham's ouster. And Baker did, indeed, augment the police presence in the Chinese quarter.

Recognizing the threat posed by the case to the welfare of Chinese in America, Wu Ting Fang, China's minister to the United States, called on all Chinese to assist in the dragnet. The Oriental Club—an association of New York's leading Chinese—offered $500 for the arrest and conviction of Elsie's murderer. And the officers of the Chee Kung Tong—the so-called Chinese Freemasons—felt so compelled to distance themselves from Leon Ling that they sent a letter to the *Times* stating that although he had once been *proposed* for membership in their organization, he had never belonged.

But Ling *had* been a member of a Chinese association, though not of the Hip Sings or the On Leongs. He had belonged to the Four Brothers' Society, which was suspected of harboring him. The Four Brothers was not a secret society like the fighting tongs; it was a clan organization, and it normally kept a low profile. But it had the resources and the moxie to defend its interests if these were threatened.

The group was known formally as the Lung Kong Tin Yee Gong Shaw (after a temple in Guangdong Province) and popularly as the See Sing Tong, meaning the "Four Surnames Society." It claimed to trace its roots back to seventeenth-century China, although such a beginning is apocryphal. It was an alliance of four numerically small families—the Lau, Kwan, Cheung, and

Chu clans—that had been formed in San Francisco and from there established itself in other North American Chinatowns. The New York branch was headquartered at 22 Pell.

The Hip Sings had clashed with the Four Brothers in 1897 when Mock Duck tried to shake down Chu Lock's Pell Street gambling house. Most members of the Chu family belonged to the society, including Chu Gain, Ling's rival for Elsie Sigel's affections, and Chu Fong, the Hong Kong–born former proprietor of the Doyers Street theater, who was its president. But something heinous was about to happen that would deeply embitter the Four Brothers' relationship not with the Hip Sings but with the On Leong Tong. And it would also involve a woman.

While the police were turning Chinatown upside down looking for Leon Ling, five of the nine Boston Hip Sings convicted of the July 1907 murders were sentenced to the electric chair. Nearly everybody feared a new tong war would result. Even with thirty uniformed officers and thirty detectives posted in the Chinese quarter, Tom Lee didn't feel safe enough to venture outside 18 Mott for several days, and he kept half a dozen men around him at all times. At one point, at the urging of nervous detectives, he retreated to his uptown home.

Mock Duck, always a person of interest when violence broke out, went to the Elizabeth Street Station voluntarily this time. He wanted the police to know that he was off for Coney Island and intended to keep out of any altercations. He even invited them to send a detective to see him off to *prove* he was leaving Manhattan. But, although he didn't say so, he wasn't out of the game forever. A newspaper report less than a week later suggested Mock Duck had buried the hatchet with the Hip Sings and had been reinstated as a "silent member" of the tong.

When no trouble broke out, the extra police were withdrawn. But the following month, tragedy struck again when, at 2:00 a.m. on August 15, 1909, a frightened Chinese man named Chin Lem raced into the street from 17 Mott, searching frantically for a policeman.

"Murder!" he screamed as he spied a bluecoat across the street. He led the officer to an outbuilding in the rear of No. 17 and up a staircase to the second floor. Unlocking a door, he revealed the mutilated body of a round-

Police detectives posted in Chinatown on July 6, 1909, in anticipation of a new tong war.

faced twenty-one-year-old Chinese woman clad in a yellow silk jacket and blue silk trousers. She was lying next to a blood-soaked bunk, a diagonal slash across her abdomen and a bloody, seven-inch hunting knife stuck upright in the floor beside her corpse. Marks on her throat and the condition of her clothing suggested she had been strangled before she was stabbed. Cuts on her hands indicated she had struggled with her assailant. She had also been gored twice through the heart.

The policeman took Chin, a thirty-one-year-old out-of-work laundryman, to the station house, where he told Michael J. Galvin, who had been made captain shortly before Commissioner Bingham's departure, that he lived across the street from the crime scene at 22 Mott in rooms belonging to the On Leong Tong, which he had recently joined. There police found a trunk, two new Colt revolvers, and six long, horn-handled hunting knives resembling the one found near the body. Inside the trunk were the dead woman's clothes, some jewelry, and photographs of herself with Chin Lem. And across the street, in the room where the body lay, were several letters, including dunning notices demanding payment for jewelry.

Chin Lem told the captain he had left the woman in her room while he went to play cards and had found her dead upon his return. Her name, he said, was Bow Kum, and she was his wife. Fighting tears, he related that she had been living in a San Francisco mission when they met and that she had rejected another suitor—a man named Lau Tong—before agreeing to marry him. He had come to New York first and sent for her later.

Three weeks earlier, Lau Tong had shown up and demanded $3,000, insisting she belonged to *him*. Chin Lem, he had asserted, had had no right to take her without compensation. Chin blamed Lau for her murder. Asked to explain why his own bloody handprint had been found on one of the house's wooden shutters, Chin explained he had bloodied it when he raised the young woman's head to determine whether she was still alive.

Over the next several days, police set about unraveling Bow Kum's tragic story. Born in China, she had been brought to San Francisco to work as a servant but had been sold upon arrival. Rescued by Donaldina Cameron, a well-known Bay Area missionary, she had been taken to the Presbyterian Home, where she remained for six months. Eventually, she was permitted to leave to marry Chin Lem, then a successful laundry owner, who had asked for her hand. It seemed that Lau Tong had not been her suitor so much as her *owner* and that he was seeking restitution of his *property*, which he claimed included Bow Kum and her jewelry.

The police asked why the couple did not share quarters, and Chin Lem did not offer a reassuring explanation: he said she had previously lived with him but had moved to No. 17, which explained why some of her belongings were still in his room but cast doubt on the nature of the relationship. They suspected Bow Kum had been working as a prostitute. Word on the street in Chinatown was that "many men had been attentive" to the young woman, and the fact that the couple lived apart seemed to bear this out.

Chin Lem was held on $5,000 bail as a material witness and a suspicious person but was not accused of murder. He made no effort to secure bond and was remanded to the Tombs, where he was watched carefully, lest he bite off his fingernails. The police planned to have a chemist examine the dried blood on them the following day to see if it was a match with that of the dead woman.

The signs pointed to another crime of passion, with Chin Lem as Bow

The only known portrait of Bow Kum, whose murder launched New York's second major tong clash, the Four Brothers' War.

Kum's killer. The police were unable to connect anyone else to the murder, and Lau Tong, the man Chin accused, had apparently not been seen in Chinatown. But unless they could uncover concrete evidence, they had little hope of securing a conviction.

The On Leongs raised several thousand dollars for Chin Lem's defense and hired an attorney. By August 18, they had collected enough to secure bail as well, and he was released. After conferring with his fellow tong men, he announced that several witnesses had come forward and would be able to identify the killer on sight, a story immediately dismissed by Captain Galvin, who believed, as most observers certainly must also have, that it was merely a ploy hatched by the On Leongs to clear their compatriot.

Gin Gum, Chin Lem's brother On Leong, arranged for a proper burial for poor Bow Kum. The next day, accompanied in the coffin by some dainty edibles, a deck of cards, a comb, a brush, and a mirror, the body of the hapless girl was taken by coach to Cypress Hills Cemetery in Brooklyn and interred there. Chin Lem alone cried bitterly over her casket.

Police questioned several Chinatown residents about Bow Kum and received reports from California, and the day after the funeral they arrested two San Francisco Chinese men. One was Lau Tong, thirty-four, and the other was a twenty-three-year-old laundryman named Lau Shong, his kinsman.

On the night of the murder, the Laus had been seen in the courtyard under Bow Kum's window and observed leaving the place together. Blood-stains were discovered on Lau Tong's shirtsleeve, and there was evidence acid had been used to remove their traces. Suddenly Chin Lem's story began to seem credible. The two men were interrogated, but neither confessed. On September 10, 1909, both were indicted for murder.

San Francisco police records revealed that Lau Tong had been accused of eight shootings and had served a prison term. They also testified that Bow Kum had been a virtual slave in his house and had been removed in a police raid instigated by a mission worker. That is when the woman was taken to the mission house, where she ultimately met Chin Lem.

When Lau Tong learned of Bow Kum's whereabouts, police discovered, he had hurried to New York to claim her, but when she refused him, he had insisted on compensation instead. He believed Chin Lem owed him for the woman and demanded $3,000; when Chin refused, he threatened to kill them both. It was only after a final meeting on the day of the murder failed to resolve the impasse that Bow Kum had been butchered.

Lau Tong and Lau Shong were Four Brothers men. When Chin Lem refused to pay, it was deemed not a personal matter but rather an issue for their respective societies to sort out. Chin had presented the problem to the leaders of the On Leong Tong, who determined that because the girl had been procured through the mission and not directly, the demand was without merit and no payment was required.

The On Leongs' decision turned out to be not only Bow Kum's death warrant but also the trigger for out-and-out war. The Second Tong War—known as the Four Brothers' War—would be fought with revolvers, pistols, and fire and would involve imported hatchet men. The Chinese Theatre would again figure in the action, as would Pell Street and an underground arcade. The whole affair would last only a little over a year, but repeated peacemaking efforts would be required to bring it to an end.

Violence broke out on the afternoon of September 12, 1909, even though Chinatown was saturated with patrolmen and detectives, when a thirty-nine-year-old Four Brothers laundryman named Gun Kee was shot in front of On Leong headquarters. His assailant, Lee Wah, was an On Leong and a cousin of Tom Lee's.

A policeman saw Lee Wah shoot his victim in the back at close range with a derringer—a pocket pistol. Gun Kee dropped to the pavement, although he suffered only a superficial wound. The officer arrested Lee Wah, who refused to discuss his motive for the shooting, though the police were certain it was related to the Bow Kum murder.

There was nothing random about the targeting of Gun Kee. Gin Gum said Gun Kee had attempted to assassinate *him* in the same location when he and several other On Leongs were being examined by the grand jury in the Bow Kum case. And the next day, Lau Tong and Lau Shong had been arraigned at Tombs Police Court for the murder of the young woman. They pleaded not guilty and were held on $3,000 bail each.

This new outbreak of hostilities had nothing to do with gambling. Indeed, there wasn't much gambling going on in Chinatown. When Commissioner Bingham promoted thirty-nine-year-old Michael J. Galvin, a seventeen-year veteran on the force, to captain and assigned him to the Sixth Precinct the previous spring, he had made it clear that cleaning up Chinatown was to be Galvin's highest priority. That meant closing down not only the gambling dens but the "disorderly houses" as well.

Galvin had set a date after which white females who could not prove they were married to Chinese—the vast majority of Chinatown's prostitutes fell into this category—had to leave the quarter. This maneuver, although highly questionable legally, was taken seriously, and by July, 125 Chinatown apartments formerly occupied by white women were vacated. The tally had reached 200 by September. In the case of the gambling houses, Galvin's opening salvo was a symbolic one: he closed down an operation at 14 Mott—On Leong headquarters—and stationed a guard outside. But he also raided a Hip Sing parlor at 22 Pell. By July, fifty-six gambling houses had been closed, about two-thirds Hip Sing clients and the rest On Leong.

Galvin was successful where others had failed, but it took a lot out of him. Between the Elsie Sigel and the Bow Kum murder investigations, he was putting in twenty-hour workdays. The chief lost forty pounds during the first few months of his command and suffered a nervous breakdown in August. Warned by his doctor that he must rest or die, he took a leave of absence. By late fall, however, he was back on the job.

Although many proclaimed the death of the peace treaty, it had not, in fact, been broken with the shooting of Gun Kee. This battle did not concern the Hip Sings; it pitted the On Leongs against an entirely different adversary. And it was an enemy smarting from three perceived wrongs: the refusal of the On Leongs to offer compensation for Bow Kum; the arrest of her two suspected killers; and now the wounding of a Four Brothers man.

Everyone braced for retaliation. Tom Lee increased his personal detail to six men. The police heard that two cases of derringers had arrived at On Leong headquarters the previous week and that the Hip Sings had received a shipment of their own. So they sent twenty-five uniformed officers and an equal number of plainclothesmen on a house-to-house search for the weapons. On September 13, they forced their way into both headquarters buildings, but the tongs were a step ahead of them. The guns had been distributed before they could be confiscated.

In mid-October, when the atmosphere was at its most tense, news came from Boston that three of the Hip Sings convicted of first-degree murder there had been put to death in the electric chair. Suddenly the Hip Sings seemed equally likely to strike a blow against the On Leongs. But it was the Four Brothers who acted, and it took only until November 5.

That evening, two On Leongs slated to testify against the Laus were seriously wounded in Chatham Square. Four out-of-town thugs recruited by the Four Brothers followed them to the foot of Doyers Street, where two drew revolvers and fired. One target was shot through the lung and fell to the pavement. The quartet was arrested and arraigned the same day.

Captain Galvin expected another attack but didn't think it would come until after the trial of Bow Kum's alleged assassins. He was certain there would be trouble if the suspects were acquitted, and the police had learned that both organizations were seeking to import gunmen from Boston. The Four Brothers had sent Chu Lock—the gambling house owner acquitted of attacking Mock Duck in 1897—there to hire hatchet men. And Boston police reported that a dozen Chinese with criminal records were on their way to New York.

Galvin hoped to head off another cycle of homicides and thought he saw an opportunity to mediate when the national president of the Four Brothers' Society, Sam Lock, who had arrived from San Francisco to arrange for the defense of the accused assassins, called on him on November 15. Galvin tried to convene a peace parley, but Tom Lee spurned his invitation. Gin Gum, however, did reassure the *New York Times* that "we are not making any threats, and if any trouble starts here the On Leong Tong won't start it."

At the end of November, however, the On Leongs *did* start trouble. They made another move against the Four Brothers, but one that involved neither bullets nor blood: they *expelled* its members. Membership in the two organizations had always overlapped; there was no perceived conflict, because one was a tong while the other was a clan society, and bad blood between the two groups had not changed that fact. But enmity had gotten so intense since the Bow Kum murder that the powers that be in the On Leong Tong decided to take preemptive action. A poster appeared at On Leong headquarters announcing that fifty-four members had been expelled for nonpayment of dues. The pretext, of course, was bogus, and nobody was fooled: *every* name on the list belonged to a Four Brothers man. Some suggested it had been a face-saving move by the On Leongs, who had been tipped off to expect a mass resignation. There was even speculation that those ousted had applied to the Hip Sings for membership.

A month later, on December 27, two Four Brothers men in their seventies were shot in a room at 30½ Pell Street. One died immediately, and the other, an officer in the society, was fatally wounded after taking three bullets. On his deathbed, he told police that four men had broken into the room and that two had stood by as the others fired. He did not identify them, but all signs pointed to the On Leongs. War between them and the Four Brothers was now in full throttle.

Three days later, Ah Hoon got his. He had been flirting with death for several years, and his time had finally come.

Ah Hoon, an On Leong, was a comedian at the Chinese Theatre, where he doubled as assistant manager. He was no favorite of the Hip Sings; they had been the butt of some of his jokes, and they had allegedly marked him for death shortly after he arrived from San Francisco in 1906. The thirty-five-year-old comic lived at 10 Chatham Square, a communal residence for actors and musicians who worked in the theater a few doors away. He died at about 2:00 a.m. in the hallway outside his fourth-floor room from a single shot to the head.

There were two theories as to why Ah Hoon was chosen. He had been a member of the Four Brothers in San Francisco and by one account had been warned to renounce his On Leong membership in New York. But the police had a more plausible notion: Ah Hoon was murdered in retaliation for the killing of the two elderly Four Brothers men and probably by shooters imported from Boston.

Ah Hoon had known he was a marked man. A death threat had been pinned to his door the day before. He had even made plans to leave town and appealed for police protection in the meantime. Captain Galvin had assigned two detectives to escort him to and from the theater and also staked out the hall itself, where it was believed a strike might occur.

On the night of his death, Ah Hoon was nervous. He didn't eat dinner, and he cut his act short. Nothing happened at the theater, but to be safe, the police saw him home by way of a back exit. They escorted him through backyards to the rear entrance of 10 Chatham Square and then up the back stairs to the fourth floor. They did not leave until he was safely in his room for the night. The murder occurred when he emerged several minutes later to clean up at the washstand across the hall. Nobody saw the shooter.

A year after the slaying of Ah Hoon, the crook in Doyers Street was first referred to as the Bloody Angle of Chinatown. But because Ah Hoon didn't die there—he didn't even set foot on Doyers the night he was murdered— the term had to refer to other events on that short alley, whose obtuse angle prevents a straight line of sight from its Pell Street end to Chatham Square. Although legend has long held that tong men used the Doyers Street bend for cover, sneaking up on one another to deal unexpected deathblows, that does not seem actually to have happened. There were far more face-offs on Mott and Pell streets than ever took place on Doyers, which was ostensibly neutral territory. Doyers did, however, provide a convenient exit for the Hip Sing killers involved in the 1905 Chinese Theatre massacre, and that incident might have been the source of the nickname.

In the wake of Ah Hoon's murder, the newspapers were full of dire proclamations that New York's tong war had been renewed and that the truce had been broken. And there was indeed a war on, but it wasn't a renewal, because the Hip Sings were not involved. But with the assassination of Ah Hoon, everybody knew there would be more trouble between the On Leongs and the Four Brothers.

With the rise to prominence of the Four Brothers came hints the Hip Sings were in decline. The latter's New York branch had been tapped for substantial financial support for their accused Boston brothers, and the attorneys' fees, especially through the lengthy appeals process, had been burdensome. This expense, coupled with a severe drop in income after Captain Galvin closed the gambling halls and ejected the prostitutes, had made a huge dent in the tong's treasury. The Hip Sings had also lost members—and their dues—after the departure of Mock Duck.

Perhaps because of this reversal in their fortunes, the Hip Sings decided to ally with the Four Brothers against their common antagonist. In early 1910, cooperation between the two groups was formalized. On January 3, a notice appeared on Chinatown bulletin boards that translates as follows:

All the companies and tongs on Pell and Doyers Streets, namely the Four Brothers' Society, the Hip Sing Tong and all the minor family [associations] in the neighborhood, have openly declared war against the great On Leong Tong of Mott Street. A few days ago, members of the On Leong Tong crept up to the rooms of two old men—the two oldest men in the Four Brothers' Society; men who did not fight and were poor and could not carry a gun—and murdered them in cold blood.

This would have posed a major challenge to the On Leong Tong had anything come of it, but nothing much did. One sign of it, though, was that not only did Sam Lock, the senior Four Brothers functionary from San Francisco, attend the trial of Lau Tong and Lau Shong, but Mock Duck did as well. After returning from the West briefly in the spring of 1909, he had gone back to Denver to tend to unfinished business that, ironically, also involved an indentured Chinese woman. He had paid $4,000 for Lilly Yem, who, like Bow Kum, had fled into the arms of Christian mission workers, and he had gone back to reclaim his "property." But he was now back in New York and back in the good graces of the Hip Sing Tong.

The attorney Terence J. McManus appeared for the defendants in the Bow Kum murder trial at the criminal branch of the New York County Supreme Court. The prosecutor, however, was the perennial Frank Moss, recently appointed first assistant district attorney. He was now working under the direction of Charles S. Whitman, the former magistrate and newly elected district attorney of New York County.

Moss began by telling the jury that the murder of Bow Kum had been one of the most brutal his office had ever prosecuted. After testimony from the coroner and several policemen, he called Charlie Boston, now the On Leong Tong president, as his first Chinese witness. He wasn't accustomed to getting support from the On Leongs, but in this case he knew he could count on a cooperative witness.

The stocky Boston, outfitted in Chinese robes, testified that the two defendants had approached him prior to the murder and asked him to urge Chin Lem to come to terms. He said he had gone to see the couple and that Bow Kum herself had expressed willingness to commit to paying Lau Tong $1,500 at some future date but that Chin Lem had refused. When Boston was asked about his own organization and he responded that the On Leong

Chin Lem, the sometime laundryman who brought Bow Kum to New York.

Tong was a merchant association that had nothing to do with gambling, however, there was an audible titter in the audience.

On cross-examination, Boston revealed that the On Leongs had convened a meeting to discuss strategies for getting Chin Lem acquitted. He stated that Tom Lee had pledged money to defend Chin Lem but had vowed he would not be party to framing anyone else for the crime.

The principal prosecution witness was Chin Lem himself, decked out in stylish Western clothing, his cropped hair parted to one side. He related how he had met Bow Kum, married her, and brought her to New York and how agents of the Four Brothers had come to reclaim her or, failing that, to demand compensation. But he didn't acquit himself well under cross-examination, which lasted a full hour. The defense made every effort to discredit him and pin the murder on him. McManus got him to admit that he had not found employment in New York and, when he couldn't account for how he had supported himself since his arrival, implied he had used Bow Kum's favors to earn his living. In the process, he established that Chin Lem had not married Bow Kum legally, because he had another wife in China.

"You know under American laws you couldn't have two wives?" McManus asked.

"I go under Chinese laws," Chin Lem replied.

"Isn't it a fact that she wanted to leave you and go to Boston because you were forcing her to lead an immoral life?" he probed.

"No," the witness protested. But the attorney's point was made.

McManus made much of the fact that Chin Lem's hands had been bloodstained when he reported the murder and that he owned knives similar to the one found next to the body.

The next day, Moss put up a parade of witnesses, all friends of Chin Lem's. So many placed the defendants at the scene of the murder in precisely the same way that the defense attorney wondered out loud whether they had been holding a mass meeting with a brass band while they waited outside the building for the crime to be committed. It was far more likely, of course, that the only meeting that took place was the one at On Leong headquarters at which the strategy for Chin Lem's defense, as well as the amount to pay the witnesses, was decided.

The defense presented its entire case in a day. The thrust was that the defendants were innocents being scapegoated by the On Leong Tong in order to shift the blame from Chin Lem. Lau Tong testified that he didn't know Chin Lem, had never seen Bow Kum, hadn't heard of her death until the morning after. Lau Shong claimed he had been unaware of the murder until his arrest. A parade of alibi witnesses, white and Chinese, supported the testimony of both that they had been elsewhere on the night the young woman died.

After summations, the case went to the jurors. As the *New York Times* put it, "A bewildered jury, after being shown a preliminary glimpse at the jealousies and ethics of a strange people, had the choice between two absolutely contradictory lines of evidence." This was often the case in Chinese trials. Honesty didn't come into the picture when friends' lives and liberty were at stake or when one side or another was willing to pay handsomely for helpful testimony.

After deliberating for several hours, the jurors returned a verdict of not guilty. And the two defendants promptly bowed to them, Chinese-style, in gratitude.

❖   ❖   ❖   ❖   ❖

The war Captain Galvin predicted if the defendants were acquitted would have broken out on January 23, 1910, had twenty-eight-year-old Yoshito Saito been the man his shooter thought he was. The hapless Saito, a Japanese valet, was shot through the back in front of 4 Doyers Street that day by a Four Brothers man named Jung Hing. It was his misfortune to be a dead ringer for an On Leong who had testified against the Laus in the Bow Kum trial.

Jung Hing was five feet six and weighed 125 pounds. He was dressed nattily in up-to-date American clothes, purple socks peering out from above the tops of his leather shoes. He dropped his revolver and fled into No. 4 but was apprehended by a patrolman. Two white *lobbygows,* hangers-on in the Chinese quarter, identified him, as did the victim before he died.

Although there had been a killing, and although the killer had been *aiming* for an On Leong, no On Leong had died, so no retaliation was required. The following month, in fact, the On Leongs gave a dinner to celebrate the end of the New Year festival and the peace compact with the Hip Sings, now four years old.

Nearly half of the police headquarters detective staff attended, a strong indication that the On Leongs had made progress in cultivating them. Even though authority over Chinatown had been returned to Elizabeth Street, headquarters police had been drawn into Chinese affairs in the past and could be again. And because the Hip Sings had made it a practice to go right to the top when they wanted the police involved—usually in a raid on an On Leong joint—better relations with Central Office staff were obviously beneficial to the On Leongs as well. Nor was there any downside to sidling up to them.

Thousands of firecrackers heralded the arrival of the guests, all of whom received white carnations to pin to their lapels—emblems of the armistice. But this was an On Leong show; if any Hip Sings or Four Brothers members were on the guest list, there is no record of it. Tom Lee, Charlie Boston, and Gin Gum, the hosts, entertained not only the police but also assistant U.S. attorneys David Frank Lloyd, who served as toastmaster, and Francis P. Garvan, who had prosecuted Ah Fee's alleged slayers in 1901 and four Hip Sings accused in the Bowery shootings three years later.

Other members of the district attorney's staff were present, as was Judge Foster and the coroner Israel L. Feinberg. It was a lovefest in which one of the guests lauded Tom Lee, who beamed through it all.

The New York *Sun* provided a succinct, tongue-in-cheek cheat sheet that explained exactly why the On Leongs were cultivating a few of the guests: "There was Coroner Feinberg, who sits on 'em; Magistrate Corrigan, who holds 'em for examination; the fifteen assistants from the District Attorney's office, who prosecute 'em and several lawyers who defend 'em." Lloyd couldn't resist a dig at the police in his remarks, illustrating the rift in the relationship between his office and the police. He observed that if the restaurant's windows had been open, "certain police captains" would hear him say there would not be half as many violent crimes in Chinatown if the police did not side with one faction over the other.

Not to be outdone, the Hip Sings held their own dinner on Pell a week later. They, too, invited guests from law enforcement, including several assistant district attorneys, police—from both the Sixth Precinct *and* the Central Office—and of course the Parkhurst Society.

All seemed relatively calm in Chinatown, but a debt between the On Leongs and the Four Brothers remained unpaid. A down payment would shortly be made on that obligation.

The first victim—and the luckiest—was forty-six-year-old Chu Moy Yen. A Four Brothers man who ranked just under Sam Lock, he didn't usually venture onto On Leong turf. But on Sunday, April 10, 1910, an errand took him to Mott Street, and when he passed the Port Arthur Restaurant at Nos. 7–9 early that afternoon, he was shot by a tall Chinese who escaped into the building. Chu took two bullets in the right thigh. Although he got a good look at his shooter, he declined to identify him to the police.

Retaliation took only a couple of hours. Even though Chinatown was immediately flooded with police after the attack, Chu Hen, an undersized but powerful Pell Street laundryman, a Four Brothers member, and a Chu kinsman, still managed to shoot and kill Chung Fook, an On Leong, at the foot of Mott Street. Chu, who inadvertently fled into the arms of a policeman and was immediately arrested, had been taking no chances: his torso was

The Port Arthur Restaurant on Mott Street in April 1910 after the shooting of Chu Moy Yen. The building to its immediate right, No. 11, was owned by Charlie Boston and housed a brothel. It was nearly blown up in 1912 in an effort to assassinate a senior On Leong officer.

wrapped in several layers of protective fabric, one of steel, three of leather, and an outer covering of silk.

Captain Richard E. Enright, a fourteen-year veteran who was named acting head of Elizabeth Street when Captain Galvin was transferred to Coney Island for his health by Commissioner William F. Baker, sent out all his reserves and requested backup from other stations. More than a hundred extra police flooded the quarter, and visitors were urged to stay out of Chinatown. Everyone waited for the next shoe to drop.

Several newspapers blamed the outbreak on the killing of Bow Kum. Others cited the suppression of Chinatown gambling and the Elsie Sigel murder. They also pointed to tensions stemming from the recent decrease in the Chinatown population. An informal census by Captain Galvin the previous year had suggested that in the wake of the closing of the gambling halls and the exile of the single white women, more than half the residents of the Chinese quarter had relocated, leaving little more than a thousand Chinese where twice that number had lived. And the decrease even in Chinese visitors to the quarter—most white tourists had stopped coming after the Elsie Sigel murder—was pronounced: out-of-towners had dwindled from five to six thousand every Sunday to fewer than a thousand. The *New-York Tribune* went so far as to predict that Chinatown would pass into history within six months.

Following the Sunday shootings, two Chinese merchants not connected with either of the feuding parties asked Judge Foster to mediate once again. The On Leongs were said to be willing; the conflict had been unwanted and bad for business, and they were eager for a settlement. But the Four Brothers refused. "I am willing to do all in my power to aid in restoring peace in Chinatown," Foster told the *New York Times*. "But the difficulty is that the Four Brothers is reluctant to be a party to such a conference. A few days will show what can be done."

It actually took more than a few days to show what could be done, and it wasn't much. Mediation lasted for the rest of April. Terence J. McManus, attorney for the Four Brothers, submitted a draft peace protocol on April 13, but no approval was forthcoming from the On Leongs.

Judge Foster, however, was not alone in his labors. Even as McManus set to work on a new treaty, parallel negotiations that did not require interpretation had begun. The Chinese minister in Washington sent the first secretary of the Chinese legation to New York to broker a settlement. Together with Yung Yu Yang, China's New York consul as of late the previous year, he met on April 14 with Tom Lee and Mott Street merchants and then headed over to Four Brothers headquarters. He told the newspapers that the legation was taking no sides in the matter. "All that is wished," he said, "is to have peace and to enforce justice."

But peace was problematical because the Four Brothers' Society was itself divided. By April 21, the two tongs were on the brink of an agreement. But when a placard announcing the impending accord was posted in Chinatown, it was ripped down by a young Four Brothers man in a calculated insult to the leadership of both tongs. This clear sign of generational dissent gave the On Leongs an opening to assert that if the Four Brothers could not control its own men, signing a treaty with it would be pointless. They now insisted on a bond from the Four Brothers as insurance against misbehavior by its younger members.

Under these conditions, despite the best efforts of the diplomats and intense pressure from Chinatown merchants, negotiations fell through and more bloodshed seemed inevitable. The Four Brothers outnumbered the On Leongs—it was said to boast a thousand members to the On Leongs' three hundred—and it believed there was still a score to be settled.

Captain Enright's tenure at Elizabeth Street had been temporary; his permanent replacement, a police veteran named William H. "Big Bill" Hodgins, arrived in mid-April. The rotund, Irish-born Hodgins, who enjoyed a reputation for being tough on street gangs, visited Tom Lee to talk the Four Brothers matter over with him, but when it was clear there would be no agreement, he doubled down the police detail in the quarter. There were so many officers on the streets that the *New York Times* commented that policemen "almost elbowed each other."

Hodgins got nowhere with Tom Lee, because Lee was right to fear the schism in the Four Brothers' Society. The organization had essentially split into two factions. The younger members—the ones, as a practical matter, who did all the shooting—were no longer loyal to the leadership, and they made up nearly half of the organization. Anathema to the On Leongs and distrusted by the senior Four Brothers men, they were in no position to make peace, even if they had wanted to. And because any pact acceptable to the On Leongs would have to be honored by *both* Four Brothers factions, no accord was forthcoming.

On June 10, 1910, Chu Hen, the Four Brothers man in the makeshift bulletproof vest charged with the April 10 retaliatory shooting of Chung Fook, was acquitted by a jury after three hours of deliberation. The verdict, reached in spite of sworn testimony by six white witnesses, enraged the On Leong Tong. But for the Four Brothers, it was cause for merriment. The society decided to hold a huge banquet to celebrate Chu Hen's freedom and the ostensible two thousandth anniversary of its founding in China.

The Four Brothers members were well aware such a gathering would be provocative, because Chu Hen's release was deeply offensive to the On Leongs. It was also dangerous, because such a large gathering offered their enemies a golden opportunity to strike. All seemed peaceful as the guests arrived at the venue, and even "Big Bill" Hodgins, on hand on Pell Street with two officers because he anticipated trouble, remarked on the quiet.

Suddenly, however, Pell Street became a shooting gallery. Half a dozen On Leongs rushed around the corner from Mott and began to fire at the guests. They were aiming for Chu Hen, the guest of honor, but he was not hit. At the first sound of gunfire, several Four Brothers men drew their own guns and gave nearly as good as they got. Broken shopwindows, shattered window casings, and nicks in the iron balconies and fire hydrants bore witness to the fracas. The victims, however, were all Four Brothers men.

The skirmish lasted less than two minutes and ended as suddenly as it had begun. Eight arrests were made. Within half an hour, a hundred uniformed policemen had invaded Chinatown, a cordon was drawn around the quarter, and visitors were barred. But there was no further trouble that night, and the banquet went on as planned.

A couple of weeks later, fifty-year-old Chu On, like his kinsmen a Four Brothers member, made the mistake of shopping on Mott Street. He had been away from New York for several months and had returned the previous day. He brushed aside warnings to avoid Mott because he didn't think anyone there would recognize him. But as he passed in front of No. 11, five shots rang out, fatally wounding him. The police were reasonably sure he had been involved in the shooting of Ah Hoon, the On Leong actor, half a year before, which would explain both his exile and the reason he was targeted.

And August saw a repeat of the Chu On incident. This time, the victim was forty-nine-year-old Chu Hin, a prosperous merchant who ran a restaurant in an underground arcade that had opened three years earlier. The

OPPOSITE: **Pell Street, ca. 1910, showing the Mon Lay Won (Chinese Delmonico) Restaurant at No. 24. Two Four Brothers men were wounded outside the establishment on June 26, 1910, and it was the site of a celebratory banquet later that year when the tongs signed a peace agreement.**

passageway began at 11 Doyers Street and ended at 20 Mott; the two lots were back-to-back. Chu had played a prominent role in the Four Brothers' councils of war and knew he was a marked man; several months earlier, a threatening note had been pinned to the door of his eatery.

He had managed to stay out of sight after that, but shortly before 8:00 p.m. on August 16 he ventured into the Mott Street half of the arcade, which proved his undoing. This stretch was considered On Leong territory. Five shots were fired—so rapidly that they sounded like one continuous round— and four bullets lodged in Chu's skull. He was dead before he hit the ground.

An unidentified Chinese merchant explained to the *New-York Tribune* why the Four Brothers had gotten the worst of the recent battles. "The On Leongs have regular gun men who receive $30 a month besides room and board. The Four Brothers consider this dispute a family calamity and have to serve as volunteers in the fight. Accordingly, they are not so effective in their battle."

The Four Brothers' Society had an additional problem: its war chest depleted by legal fees and the costs of fighting, it had been forced to dun its members to fund the conflict. Because its membership was limited to people who belonged to its four clans, recruiting additional associates was next to impossible. Nor was it in the business, as the tongs were, of shaking down vice dens. Existing members were called on to pony up as much as $50 apiece to underwrite the war. But the On Leongs were hurting too. The downturn in business and the departure of the gambling dens meant a decline in revenues available to defray the heavy costs of war.

The result was heightened efforts to broker a cease-fire, and finally, after months of talks, a notice appeared on the bulletin board outside Chinatown's City Hall on Sunday, December 18, 1910, announcing a temporary cease-fire. It was to be in force until the following Saturday. The proclamation was issued in the name of the Chinese Consolidated Benevolent Association and the Chinese consul. They had been working with the two adversaries in secret and now believed a permanent treaty was achievable within the week.

It took a little longer than that, but before year's end an accord was struck, probably due as much to exhaustion and lack of funds as to pressure from local merchants. On December 29, delegates from the two organizations—the Four Brothers factions had apparently found a way to speak with one voice again—affixed their signatures with writing brushes to a six-foot parchment that reestablished friendly relations between them. A toast followed, punctuated by a noisy volley of firecrackers and a tune from a Chinese band.

The agreement extended to branches of the two groups throughout the United States. It mandated that if future killings occurred, the murderers be surrendered to police. Blood retribution was to be forsworn in favor of financial settlements achieved through mediation. Other provisions included agreement not to interfere in pending court cases, to return confiscated property, and to settle outstanding debts—including a refund of dues to those Four Brothers men who had been ejected from the On Leong Tong.

The Four Brothers' War was over. But why had it lasted as long as it did? The peace accord "might have been accomplished long ago," one of the Chinese merchants who had advocated negotiations observed caustically, "but the police did not want peace, nor did the lawyers."

This comment was probably unfair. Certainly the attorneys could count on more business when tong men were constantly being arrested, arraigned, and tried for assault and murder and when peace talks were protracted. But there is no evidence that the lawyers ever intentionally slowed down or complicated the process for their own gain, and no one else ever accused them of this.

As for the police, they certainly had had a vested interest in keeping gambling going when a cut of the revenues made its way into their pockets. The merchant's criticism might have been appropriate to the First Tong War, in which the illicit income of the police from the gambling bosses was at stake, but not to the most recent conflict. There wasn't much betting going on in Chinatown, and in any case the Four Brothers' War hadn't been about gambling.

It had broken out over a private dispute about a woman and had been sustained by attempts to manipulate the trial of her alleged assassins. It had persisted because of a lack of trust that an agreement would be honored. Fatigue and the expense of keeping up hostilities had finally brought both sides to the table. It is hard to see what reason the police or municipal higher-ups would have had to keep this particular fight going.

But there *was* something else at stake in this war and, indeed, to a greater or lesser extent in all of the clashes in Chinatown. When one tong man was wronged or killed by a member of another tong, retribution was always required in order to preserve "face," a deeply important concept among Chinese and other Asians. Face was a tit-for-tat construct that had everything to do with honor and prestige, and holding one's head up in the society was deemed so important that it justified the expenditure of vast sums and, if necessary, the taking of lives.

In the context of the tong wars, saving face meant never absorbing the last blow. When Chu Hen killed Chung Fook, for example, avenging his death became imperative for the On Leongs. The fact that a jury acquitted him of the crime was not only irrelevant; it was galling. If they couldn't get the courts to dispense what they believed to be justice, then the On Leongs had to strike back at the Four Brothers themselves in order to save face, which is why they launched the Pell Street attack at the banquet thrown in Chu Hen's honor. They didn't get Chu's head, which would certainly have been the most desirable and appropriate prize, but that of any Four Brothers man might do, because their basic quarrel was with the organization, not just the individual.

The same principle had applied in the First Tong War, when On Leong toughs butchered poor Hop Lee on his ironing board. Hop Lee hadn't had anything to do with the Doyers Street theater killings that preceded his death, but he was a Hip Sing and one of Mock Duck's associates, and that was sufficient. When he was killed, On Leong face was preserved. Unfortunately for all concerned, preserving face in this context was generally a zero-sum game, and one blow automatically begat the next one.

Face, according to Lin Yutang, a famous Chinese author and linguist writing in the 1930s,

> is what men fight for and what many women die for. . . . It protracts lawsuits, breaks up family fortunes, causes murders and suicides . . .

and it is prized above all earthly possessions. It is more powerful than fate and favour, and more respected than the Constitution. . . . It is that hollow thing which men in China live by.

Lin observed that in matters in which face is at stake, "nothing really prevents the parties from coming together except a nice way of getting out of it, or probably the proper wording of an apology." In the world of the tongs, however, the all-too-frequent search for "a nice way of getting out of it" generally proved a tortuous, repetitive, and costly process.

As Leong Gor Yun noted, "Starting a war was simple enough, but there was no stopping it until the rivals convinced themselves that they had had revenge and the war funds were exhausted. . . . Each tong would go through a 'face-saving' process, half-heartedly threatening to renew war, but in the end they would arrange a peace banquet and issue a joint peace statement." In other words, once face had been saved—and money used up—there was no more point in conflict.

So it was with the Four Brothers and the On Leongs. The obligatory banquet that followed the signing of the accord provided an auspicious beginning to the New Year. Peace in Chinatown was not destined to last long, but the feast did mark the end of any significant role for the Four Brothers' Society, whose members were undoubtedly delighted to go back to being a fraternal, mutual aid organization.

From here on in, the battle would once again be a two-tong affair.

Chapter 12

Mock Duck's Luck Runs Out

On January 25, 1911, federal customs agents undertook a sting operation against two Seventh Avenue opium joints. Customs had been aware for months that tens of thousands of dollars' worth of the drug was being smuggled into the country and winding up in Chinese hands in several eastern cities. A tip had led agents to these two establishments, which purported to be tea and cigar shops.

To obtain evidence, undercover officers had cultivated scraggly beards, turned up their coat collars, and dabbed talcum powder on dirty faces to make themselves look like "hop fiends." Both stores sold them lychee nutshells in which cooked opium had been substituted for nut meat. Each "nut" cost fifty cents.

On the day of the raid—part of a nationwide war on the illicit opium trade—agents with search warrants surrounded the buildings and entered, revolvers drawn. Four Chinese men drew their own guns but were subdued without any shots being fired. A total of $10,000 worth of raw and cooked opium was seized, in addition to paraphernalia for processing the drug.

The more telling find, however, was a cache of letters, telegrams, ledgers, and memoranda. These hinted strongly at broad police involvement in the sordid business. Several of the documents, signed by various public officials, were letters written to the On Leong Tong kingpin Charlie Boston, a proprietor of both shops, thanking him for favors received. From police captains in Philadelphia, Boston, and Pittsburgh, there were letters of introduction written for Boston. There were also lists of New York police officials. Taken together, they suggested the existence of a broad smuggling and distribution network that extended to the nation's major cities, made possible by tacit police cooperation.

The federal agents had purposely *not* called on municipal police for assistance in the raids; they did not even inform the West Thirty-seventh Street Police Station, which had jurisdiction over that area, until after the fact. Given possible police complicity in the illegal activity, which they would have had every reason to suspect, this was prudent. Even after securing the premises, they did not allow the local police access.

Neither Charlie Boston nor the On Leong Tong was new to the opium business. As early as 1883, Tom Lee had been accused of collecting a "license fee" from local opium joints. But Boston was far more involved than that. He wasn't just *taxing* the joints; he was *operating* them, and his customers were by no means all Chinese. By 1899, he was running a place on Broadway between Sixty-sixth and Sixty-seventh streets where New Yorkers of all stripes might come in for a relaxing smoke.

The stakes, however, had recently been raised. Opium had previously been regulated at the state level and merely taxed by the federal government, but in 1909 importing it had become a federal crime. At the urging of the Roosevelt administration and in response to pressure from social reformers, temperance advocates, and missionaries, Congress had passed the Opium Exclusion Act. The new law banned the importation, possession, and use of opium for smoking—the type favored by Chinese. It did not, however, address opium used for medicinal purposes, which was more common among white Americans.

The U.S. attorney's office had a field day sorting through the confiscated correspondence. The process took days because some documents required translation. When the newspapers discovered that police officials in Boston and Pittsburgh had been implicated, they contacted their departments and printed their predictable denials. Some items shed light on how opium was getting past customs officials at the borders. Others were letters written to Charlie Boston from white women; the district attorney refused to talk about them, but the implication was that there was material in them of prurient interest. Boston, who also ran a brothel, was well-known for his eye for the ladies.

The pieces of the puzzle, once assembled, suggested the existence of a national syndicate headed by Charlie Boston that managed the smuggling and sale of opium, importing the contraband via San Francisco, Seattle, Portland, and over the Canadian border. But when federal agents, armed with a warrant, set out to arrest him, they were told he had fled to Philadelphia.

He hadn't. And after a five-day manhunt, they nabbed him on Mott Street in front of On Leong headquarters. The tong boss was dressed stylishly in Western attire, with a peaked cap pulled down over his eyes and three large diamond rings adorning his thick fingers. After a short struggle—he asked for his overcoat and for a minute to confer with Tom Lee but was denied both—they whisked him away at gunpoint to the Tombs, where he was charged with smuggling. Charlie Boston's capture was considered one of the most important arrests of a Chinese ever made in New York City.

At the Tombs, Boston admitted to partnership in the two shops that were raided but would say nothing about the sale of opium. He was arraigned the next day and released on $2,500 bail. On February 20, he was indicted by a federal grand jury for conspiracy to smuggle opium.

Although protection payments to the On Leong Tong by proprietors of local opium dens had been mentioned occasionally in the press, this was the first indication the tong leadership was involved in importing and distributing the drug. Perhaps more shocking was the suggestion that it was more than a local business. Charlie Boston was overseeing a nationwide syndicate.

The On Leongs initially suspected the tip to customs had come from the Four Brothers' Society while they were still at war with it but soon concluded it had actually been the Hip Sings, who had been attempting to break into the lucrative opium business themselves. On the strength of his police connections, Charlie Boston had presumed to dictate the terms of entry to the rival tong, reserving the lion's share of the New York business for himself. Dissatisfied with their share of the spoils, the Hip Sings had decided to fight back. And just as they had done in the 1890s, they attempted to get others—in this case, the federal government—to do their dirty work. With Boston out of the way, there would be one fewer obstacle to overcome in their entry into the opium trade.

Nobody expected peace to hold for long after Charlie Boston's arrest. He was too important a figure. Then there was the fact that the documents seized at his so-called tea and cigar shops included detailed records of payments to hired assassins in the recent tong war shootings.

The only real question in anyone's mind was when their services would be needed again.

Gambling was once again flourishing in New York. And it was the new mayor who brought it back.

William Jay Gaynor became mayor on January 1, 1910, with the support of Tammany Hall. A former state Supreme Court justice, he defeated two opponents for the office. Gaynor was his own man, however, and he didn't play the game exactly as Tammany had hoped; he was a reformer who appointed technocrats from the civil service list rather than offering patronage jobs to Tammany hopefuls. Although he was no fan of gambling, his unorthodox approach to controlling it turned out to be the best thing to happen to the gambling bosses in a long time.

Gaynor was first and foremost a civil libertarian and a strong opponent of police lawlessness. As a judge, he did what he could to put an end to warrantless raids and police brutality. He could not abide the Reverend Parkhurst, and even before he became mayor, he urged Mayor McClellan to oust Theodore Bingham, whom he accused of running roughshod over the law in his crusade against crime.

Many said Mayor Gaynor was his own police commissioner; among these was William F. Baker, who had been appointed to that job before Gaynor's arrival but had served most of his term under him. Baker, predictably, was no fan. Several years after he left office, he described the gambling situation under Gaynor.

"After Gaynor got in he said he wanted government by law and not by men. He warned me not to make arrests without legal evidence and not to enter houses without warrants." As a result, Baker recalled, "the gambling houses multiplied so fast that you could not keep track of them." But what really annoyed Baker was the June 1910 order forcing all police to wear uniforms. Gaynor issued it because he believed it was plainclothesmen who were chiefly responsible for collecting graft payments from lawbreakers. But its effect was to deprive the police of a key means of collecting evidence against gambling bosses.

"I think that order made more for chaos in the department than anything ever did," Baker recalled. "You know what chance we had to get evidence against a gambling house with uniformed men? That order played right into the hands of the gamblers."

Plainclothesmen had, of course, never been very effective in Chinatown, but under Mayor Gaynor gambling made a comeback there as well as elsewhere in the city. And more gambling, of course, meant more revenue for the tongs.

To everyone's surprise, things remained peaceful for nearly a year after Charlie Boston's arrest. The tongs even cooperated on a fair and a parade in April 1911 to raise money for famine relief in China. Hip Sings, On Leongs, and Four Brothers men marched "as though they had never sought each other's vitals," the New York *Sun* observed sardonically, and more than $7,500 was raised. Even a Fourth of July parade involving all three tongs was peaceful.

There was still some fighting going on, but it was mainly intramural. Relations had soured between Sing Dock and Yee Toy, Hip Sing partners in crime—literally—in both the Chinese Theatre and the Boston killings. Without quitting the Hip Sings, Sing Dock organized a new alliance within the Chee Kung Tong. Known as the Kim Lan Association (literally the "Golden Orchid Society"), it was described as the "cadet branch" of the Chinese Freemasons. The new group attracted about two hundred members, many of whom were disenchanted former Hip Sings. None of this sat well with "Girl Face" Yee Toy, who remained the key Hip Sing hit man, and after a heated argument he shot Sing Dock, unarmed at the time, in the stomach at close range. The wound was lethal, but the assassination did not provoke retaliation from the On Leongs, because they were not involved.

The federal case against Charlie Boston took time to prepare. He finally went on trial in mid-December, nearly a year after his arrest. His plea of not guilty was based on the argument that despite what he had said during his interrogation, the establishments had not, in fact, belonged to him. Several

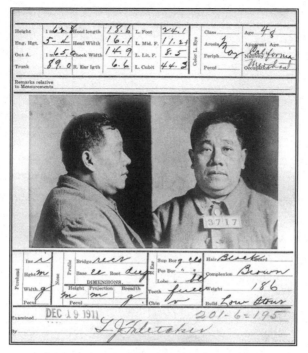

Atlanta penitentiary record of the physical
examination of Lee Quon Jung, a.k.a. Charlie
Boston, shortly after his incarceration in
December 1911.

municipal officials were subpoenaed to testify as government witnesses, because among the confiscated papers were letters and courtesy cards they had
sent to Boston. Such cards, issued by government officials to friends and
family, did not render recipients immune to arrest but did serve as subtle
reminders that those possessing them had close contacts in government.
When found in the possession of someone accused of a federal crime, they
were, at minimum, somewhat embarrassing to the givers.

Before the names of Charlie Boston's government contacts could be
read aloud in court, however, the tong kingpin suddenly changed his plea
to guilty. Lobbied by his associates, who realized that further scrutiny of
the web of relationships the On Leongs had built up with police and
politicians over the years could lead to additional revelations terribly
detrimental to their friends and to their businesses, Boston relented and

took one for the team. On December 12, he was sentenced to eighteen months in federal prison, to be followed by three years' probation. A week later, he entered the U.S. penitentiary in Atlanta, Georgia.

Some of Boston's Canadian accomplices had been arrested as well, so the Customs Office was satisfied his drug empire had been destroyed. But his conviction dealt a serious blow to the On Leong Tong in other ways. He had been a strong financial backer of the organization: an important source of funds during the Four Brothers' War and of bail money whenever members were arrested. And the connections he had assiduously cultivated with government officials were among the tong's most valuable assets.

The prospect of revenge was on everyone's mind. And given Charlie Boston's status, many assumed that when it came, it was likely to be spectacular. They would not be disappointed. The seeds of the Third Tong War had been planted.

Retaliation did not come immediately, however, thanks in part to events unfolding halfway around the world. Revolutionary forces in China were on the brink of overthrowing the Manchu overlords who had ruled their country since the mid-seventeenth century. An uprising in the central Chinese city of Wuchang on October 10 had launched a military offensive, and a rival government had been established. In a matter of months, the boy emperor Pu Yi would abdicate the throne, the Qing dynasty would fall, and the era of Republican government would begin.

In mid-December 1911, however, the revolutionaries were in dire need of funds, and they appealed for support to Chinese subjects everywhere, especially those living abroad. New York's community was determined to do its part, and at a meeting on December 12, the very day of Charlie Boston's conviction, the Hip Sing, Four Brothers, and On Leong tongs pledged $1,000 each to the cause.

At the meeting, Tom Lee spoke with what the New York *Sun* called "almost fraternal affection" for his counterparts in the other two tongs. He even had kind words for Mock Duck's patriotism. Also present was Wong Get, who had gone back to China again but had returned by 1910 and who, like Mock Duck, had reestablished himself in the Hip Sing hierarchy.

"Brethren, we have buried the hatchet in the breast of the Manchu dynasty," Lee told the gathering to a round of applause. What he did *not* say was that there were closer breasts destined for On Leong hatchets and that additional burials were not far off.

There would be one final display of comity before all hell broke loose, however. On January 1, 1912, Chinatown celebrated the birth of the Republic of China. One hundred thousand firecrackers, imported from China for the occasion, were exploded throughout the quarter. As thousands watched, Tom Lee led a procession to Chinatown City Hall, where a new Chinese flag hung for all to see and a painting of Dr. Sun Yat-sen, the father of the revolution, replaced the image of Confucius. Determined to take no chances, the police frisked everyone who looked as if he might be a gunman, just in case. But it was a day of national pride and celebration, not one to be marred by parochial grievances.

A bitter wind was blowing and the streets were deserted at 7:30 p.m. on January 5 when four men left On Leong headquarters and headed for Pell Street. Dressed in American clothing, their coat collars turned up against the breeze, they stole silently down Pell, each with a hand hidden beneath his coat. The quartet came to a stop in front of No. 21, where the lookout for the gambling parlor within had temporarily abandoned his position. There was no one to warn those inside that danger was afoot.

The men entered silently through a small foyer that opened to a large room in which about twenty Chinese men were gambling at four tables. The sentry was watching the games and had his back to the door, so he didn't see them come in. On the far left, at the table closest to the door, sat Liang You, vice president of the Hip Sing Tong, dealing *fan tan*. At the table behind him stood Chong Pon Sing, the tong president, playing *pi gow*. And the dealer at his table was none other than Mock Duck, one of the proprietors of the establishment.

The On Leongs wasted no time. They drew Smith & Wesson revolvers from under their coats and shot into the crowd. Some twenty bullets were fired, five of which penetrated the body of fifty-year-old Liang You, who slumped down, lifeless, against the wall behind him. And Chong Pon Sing, also fifty, took missiles in his chest, arm, and abdomen and dropped to the floor, fatally wounded. The shooters then discarded their revolvers and disappeared into the winter night.

When the police arrived, they found seven men milling around as if nothing were amiss. Mock Duck was among them, unhurt and seemingly unfazed by the events of the previous few minutes. No one was paying any attention to the men who had been shot, one mortally wounded under a table, the other a corpse perched against a wall. Helping himself to a cup of tea as the officers came in and demanded to know who the dead man was, Mock Duck responded indifferently that he didn't know him. The police held everyone in the hall as material witnesses and summoned an ambulance for Chong, who was still breathing.

In the meantime, a Hip Sing led officers to the On Leong building, where he identified two of the shooters. The police collared them and brought them to the hospital, where nurses propped Chong up on pillows and he fingered them as his assassins. Back at the police station, the two were placed in a lineup of fourteen men, and several arrested Hip Sings also identified them. Chong died the next day.

The On Leongs were charged with homicide and held on $10,000 bail each, but Mock Duck was accused only of maintaining a gambling house. There was no other charge to level against him; he hadn't done anything else wrong that day. The evidence, in the form of confiscated gambling paraphernalia, was damning, however, and it seemed an open-and-shut case. He insisted to the coroner that he had arrived on the scene after Liang You was already dead. He paid his $1,000 bond and was released.

The arrest and imprisonment of Charlie Boston, the On Leongs' number two man, was undoubtedly the main provocation for an attack on such high-ranking Hip Sings. But other hostile acts had contributed to the On Leongs' outrage. In November, two Hip Sings had murdered a Cleveland On Leong for refusing to pay them protection money. And a relative of Tom Lee's had been slaughtered in Chicago by a Hip Sing gunman.

Having suffered through tong wars in the past, the police wanted to avert another one if they could. They didn't know why the Hip Sings had been killed, so they turned reflexively to the old standby of suppressing gambling. Their solution was to launch the largest raid Chinatown had seen in years.

On the morning of January 9, the chief magistrate—and former commissioner of police—William McAdoo issued 221 warrants for the arrest of Chinese gamblers, each made out in the name of "John Doe Chinaman." At 5:00 p.m., under orders from the police inspector John Daly and Captain Frank A. Tierney, who had been appointed to head the Sixth Precinct in 1911, eighty policemen marched into Chatham Square, sealed off the Chinese quarter, and broke up into twenty-eight squads of two to six men each. The teams then descended, axes, clubs, and crowbars in hand, on an equal number of Pell, Mott, and Doyers Street gambling dens.

They pried open locks, smashed through doors, and shattered glass and discovered not only *fan tan* and policy paraphernalia but also three roulette wheels, previously unseen in Chinatown. To avoid the appearance of bias, they made sure to include both Mock Duck's establishment and Tom Lee's building. By midnight, about seventy-five arrests had been made with the aid of an informant, a Japanese mission worker from Boston who had infiltrated the Chinese quarter and collected evidence, undetected, for a month. Protected from identification by a face mask, he pointed out the proprietors in each house.

But the Third Tong War was on, and seventy-five arrests weren't going to stop it. Many senior tong men would be caught in the crosshairs in a battle that had begun over control of the opium trade but immediately became more about face than about anything else. It would last nearly a year and a half. The weapons employed would be the most fearsome Chinatown had ever seen. And the coming year would be the bloodiest of all.

The On Leongs surely expected retaliation for their brazen decapitation of the Hip Sing Tong, and it was not long in coming. At the end of February, seventeen-year-old Eng Hing and thirty-year-old Lee Dock shot Tom Lee's nephew right in his uncle's Mott Street building.

The men sneaked through the same underground arcade in which the Four Brothers restaurateur had met his end two years earlier. It was about

8:00 p.m., and with the brims of their slouch hats turned down and their collars turned up, they were not noticed on Mott Street. When they got to No. 18, where several On Leongs were congregating in Lee Po Ming's fruit store, they flung open the door, dropped to their knees, and opened fire. One target fell to the ground; others drew guns, answered the fire, and pursued the young men, who rushed back to the arcade. One was hit; the other managed to flee.

Lee Kay, a thirty-two-year-old nephew of old Tom Lee's, took a bullet in his stomach, although the intended target had probably been Lee Po Ming, vice president of the tong, whose demise would have been a more suitable answer to the assassination of the top Hip Sing men. Lee Kay was brought to the hospital, unconscious, together with his wounded shooter, Eng Hing, who himself had taken bullets in the left arm and the back. The second bullet had passed perilously close to Eng's lung, but the wound was not fatal. The police arrested two of Eng's attackers and charged them with felonious assault; each was held on $3,000 bail. Officers later apprehended Lee Dock, the other Hip Sing shooter, who was identified by Lee Kay from his hospital bed and held without bail.

If the attack had been calculated to alarm Tom Lee, it had its desired effect. Whether the intended victim had been his associate or his nephew, it was still bad news for him. He had not appeared in public since the shooting of the senior Hip Sings, because he fully understood that *his* head would be the most fitting price of all that the Hip Sings could exact for the murder of their leaders. He telephoned Elizabeth Street twice to ask for protection, claiming he expected to be gunned down before morning. Then he barricaded himself inside his Chinatown quarters, which had been fitted up like an arsenal.

A couple of weeks later, three top On Leongs narrowly escaped injury in a copycat attack. They had just entered a grocery at 11 Mott when four men, shielding their faces with large umbrellas, suddenly opened the door and began firing into the store. After about twenty shots, they fled, wounding one Chinese and one Italian man but no tong elders. The police arrested a pair of Hip Sings for the shootings.

The first week of April 1912 was Holy Week, and Father Ernest Coppo, pastor of Mott Street's Church of the Transfiguration, was worried his pa-

Mock Duck, 1905. He was arrested
for running a gambling establishment in
1912 and sentenced to one to two years
in Sing Sing prison.

rishioners might get caught in cross fire on their way to or from worship.
Through the good offices of some Chinatown leaders, he secured a temporary truce from the tongs. A cease-fire would prevail from April 3 to April
17, and the traditional geographic boundaries—Mott for the On Leongs,
Pell for the Hip Sings—would be suspended, with free passage permitted
to all. The agreement was posted for all to see, and there were no notable
violations.

June brought Mock Duck's trial on the gambling allegation, the only
charge the district attorney had been able to pin on him from the night the
Hip Sing leaders were assassinated. Police testified that when they arrived,
he was counting out a roll of bills and that he had admitted that both the
money and the gambling house were his. A translator took the stand to
confirm that signs removed from the premises identified three people,
including Wong Get and Mock Duck, as co-owners of the resort.

Mock Duck claimed he had been at the gambling parlor because Chong

Pon Sing, the assassinated Hip Sing president—the true proprietor of the place, he maintained—owed him a couple of hundred dollars. It never hurt to blame someone who was dead. He discovered when he arrived that Chong had been shot, he testified, but finding money on the table, he had helped himself to two $20 bills, which he claimed Chong had promised him earlier that evening.

He denied his name had appeared on the list of proprietors and maintained he had not understood when the police asked him whether he owned the place. His explanation for why his private papers had been found there was that, being illiterate, he had left them with Chong, who regularly helped him with correspondence. This couldn't have been true; he had been able to read English well enough when he visited the *New York Times* in 1907 to taunt it over a false report of his arrest in Boston. But to bolster his case that he was illiterate in both Chinese and English, and that despite having been born in San Francisco he could not understand the latter well, he testified through an interpreter throughout the trial. His testimony strained credulity, however, and it is doubtful many in the courtroom believed him. The jury did not; they voted to convict the wily defendant.

Before sentencing, the judge—who had earlier tried Mock Duck twice for homicide—remarked that the man led a charmed life: "He seems never to be able to get within the clutches of the law, and yet he is the most notorious Chinaman probably in the city." But this time, Mock Duck's luck failed him. The judge sentenced him to the maximum term for a first offender: not less than one year, nor more than two, in Sing Sing prison.

Even before the sentence was pronounced, the defense attorneys announced their intention to appeal. They petitioned the New York Supreme Court for a "certificate of reasonable doubt," a document normally issued to keep a client out of jail in cases in which error by the trial court is likely to result in a verdict being overturned on appeal. The basis for the appeal was that the rules of the Chinese policy game differed from the American kind, and it was thus supposedly not covered by the statute under which Mock Duck had been convicted. On July 6, a certificate was granted, entitling the defendant to a new hearing. But because the appellate court was out of session, he was freed on $3,500 bail until a trial could be scheduled. Chinatown immediately buzzed with the rumor that Mock Duck would head for San Francisco and then China rather than risk prison time.

A few days after Mock Duck's conviction, the On Leongs eliminated Yee Toy, a.k.a. "Girl Face," the Hip Sings' chief gunman. Yee was one of the men indicted in the 1906 murder of two On Leongs on Pell Street, one of the organizers of the Chinese Theatre and Boston massacres, and the cold-blooded murderer of Sing Dock, his brother Hip Sing. As he emerged from the Chinese Delmonico at 24 Pell, someone appeared from the doorway of No. 18 and, in full view of a policeman, shot him five times at close range, piercing his hand, abdomen, and chest.

The shooter was a China-born cook named Jung Hing. He took off for Mott Street but as he rounded the corner had the misfortune to run right into another officer. There was little doubt he was the assassin. Not only had the shooting been witnessed by an officer, but six others—several of whom were white—picked him out of a lineup.

Jung Hing, however, was no On Leong. He was the same man who had killed a Japanese valet in error for the Four Brothers in 1910. But this time, he was identified as a member of the Kim Lan Association, the branch of the Chee Kung Tong started the previous year by the late Sing Dock. And while it is possible he acted to avenge the murder of Sing Dock, the "Scientific Killer" slain in cold blood by Yee Toy the previous year, it is also likely he did it for a reward. The *New-York Tribune* reported that the bounty offered by the On Leong Tong for killing a Hip Sing, normally $500, had been raised to $4,000 for whoever took down the hated Yee Toy. And should the killer be sent to the electric chair for the crime, his family would reap the benefit.

The Hip Sings saw On Leong fingerprints all over the murder and were not about to take the loss of their deadliest hatchet man lying down, especially on top of the recent slaughter of their two top men. Regardless of who had pulled the trigger, they were certain On Leongs had bankrolled the killing, and they decided on a shocking and novel response: they set out to blow up On Leong headquarters.

On June 23, 1912, someone with a passkey infiltrated the On Leong clubhouse and, undetected, planted dynamite beneath the altar of the Joss

Hall used for worship and club rituals. The explosive was rigged with a timer set to go off shortly after 10:00 p.m., when offerings were usually made to Guan Gong, the patron deity. Something went amiss, however, and it detonated about half an hour early, while the room was still deserted.

The explosion caused panic on Mott Street. A celebration of the Feast of Saint Gonzaga at the Catholic church ended abruptly when the startled musicians cast their instruments aside and fled. A rumor passed that dozens of On Leongs had been killed, but the truth was otherwise. Although the explosion created a great hole in the floor below the altar and destroyed much of the Joss Hall and the room below it, no one was actually injured.

Nor did a second bomb find its target in the wee hours of July 1, when "Big Lou"—Louis Ling Hoa, then president of the On Leong Tong—left 11 Mott three minutes before it exploded in the building's ground-floor hallway. The On Leongs rented rooms in the rear of No. 11 from Charlie Boston, who owned the building, and often used them to meet in council, as they had that night. "Big Lou," at six feet the tallest Chinese in the quarter, had been worried by the recent spate of violence against senior tong men, because at his height any gunman would find him hard to miss. He traveled only with bodyguards and had been granted a police escort as well.

Gunpowder might have been a Chinese invention, but no Chinese in New York was known to have expertise in explosives; tong men had theretofore employed only knives, hatchets, and guns. So the On Leongs concluded the Hip Sings had probably hired Italian hit men for the job, explosives being "the Italian method of warfare," the New York *Sun* advised readers. Eddie Gong, a senior Hip Sing, wrote years later that Yee Toy, who had been experimenting with explosives, was responsible, but Yee Toy's murder had actually preceded the bombings.

Against the possibility that the explosions had indeed been the work of non-Chinese, Gin Gum posted a notice in several English-language newspapers offering a reward for the arrest of the person or persons responsible:

FIFTEEN HUNDRED DOLLARS REWARD will be paid to the party or parties securing the arrest and conviction of the cowardly assassins who on the night of the 23rd day of June, 1912, placed and exploded a bomb on the premises known as 14 Mott Street, in the city of New York, on the top floor thereof, and for the arrest and conviction of the assassins who placed and exploded a bomb on the morning of July 1, 1912 in the premises of 11 Mott Street, in the city and county of New York. Any person with information relating to these outrages may apply to Gin Gum, Secretary of the Chinese Merchants Association of the City of New York, No. 24 [sic] Mott Street, New York City.

The police believed the bombings were reprisals for the murder of Yee Toy and other senior Hip Sings. They also feared that the introduction of this new weapon might herald a more terrifying and deadly phase in the war of the tongs.

"There's a monkey dead in 13 Doyers."

That's what Moe Harris, a white resident of the Chinese quarter, told a beat officer on the evening of July 15, 1912. The officer understood the racist slur as a code word for a Chinese; had he meant a white man, Harris would simply have said "a man dead." The policeman followed the informer into the building, where they passed through several narrow halls until they came to a door that was ajar.

Inside was the half-naked body of Hun Kem Yun, the Hip Sings' chief gunman since the death of Yee Toy. An expert *fan tan* dealer, he had been one of Mock Duck's most trusted comrades. Hun hadn't been seen in Chinatown for days. Bullets had pierced his arm, his heart, and his temple.

Hun had known he was on the On Leongs' hit list. Indeed, he was walking around with the evidence. His autopsy revealed that apart from the fatal blows administered that evening, he had been nursing an older bullet wound for weeks. The police believed he had been involved in the attempt to blow up On Leong headquarters and been "on ice" since then, but the On Leongs, bent on retribution, had discovered his hiding place and struck. Because 13 Doyers backed up to On Leong territory, police speculated his assassin had climbed onto the roof of the building and descended via the fire escape.

Another Hip Sing met his doom before the end of the month. Thirty-year-old Jow Chuck, a cook, had joined the tong after resigning from the

On Leong Tong, which might have been his undoing. The tongs did not take kindly to resignations, still less to defections. He was peeling potatoes in the back of a restaurant at 11 Pell when a marksman hit him from a Doyers Street building behind the eatery. Five bullets sailed through the kitchen window; two entered his neck, and a third pierced his head. The police assumed On Leongs had eliminated him out of concern over possible betrayal of their secrets.

The next big melee, which the *New York Herald* labeled the "most spectacular and disastrous battle in the history of Chinatown," occurred on Pell Street in mid-October, soon after the Hip Sing gunman Louie Way was released from Sing Sing.

Louie Way had been involved in the attempted murder of the On Leong treasurer, Chu Gong, on Pell Street in 1905. He had been convicted only of assault in the first degree, however, and only, the Hip Sings believed, because the On Leongs had fabricated evidence against him. A little more than two years into his nine-and-a-half-year sentence, he had been pronounced insane and transferred to Dannemora State Hospital to serve out a shortened term. After unsuccessful attempts to secure a new trial and, failing that, to be deported to China, he was finally released in mid-August 1912, having served just over six years.

Sane or not, he didn't waste much time exacting revenge. Just before 3:00 p.m. on October 14, Louie Way stepped out of Hip Sing headquarters and shot an On Leong emerging from 23 Pell Street. Within five minutes, a no-holds-barred gunfight broke out. Three bands of On Leongs opened fire simultaneously from different locations along Pell, and Hip Sings responded in kind. One Hip Sing shooter, perched on the balcony of the Chinese Delmonico, fell dead in the first volley of shots. Another dropped to the street as he fired.

When the police arrived, they, too, began shooting, and Chinese gunmen returned fire. Calm was eventually restored, but the battle was most notable for its collateral damage. A twenty-nine-year-old Russian Jewish locksmith lay dead on the street, as did another, unidentified man. A fifty-eight-year-old Jersey City freight conductor was critically injured and eventually died, as did two Hip Sings.

Ten other people, including two women, were wounded. Bullets had even injured two horses. Shards from windowpanes in half a dozen buildings on both sides of Pell lay on the pavement. The police arrested two Hip Sings and three On Leongs and held all for murder.

The proximate cause of the scuffle, the district attorney believed, was the murder indictment the day before of Eng Hing and Lee Dock, the men accused of shooting Tom Lee's nephew Lee Kay the previous February. Lee Kay had died of his wounds in June.

November saw the trial of Jung Hing, the Kim Lan Association marksman who slaughtered Yee Toy, the Hip Sings' top gunslinger. There were several eyewitnesses, so conviction ought to have been a sure bet. But the defense attorney argued it was a case of mistaken identity and that accusing Jung had been a Hip Sing plot. After ten hours of deliberation, one juror refused to convict, and the trial ended in a hung jury. Jung, well-known to the police, was retried in December, however, and this time the vote for conviction was unanimous.

Captain Tierney sent reinforcements into Chinatown. Armed with a search warrant—Mayor Gaynor insisted on these—they forcibly entered Hip Sing headquarters on December 7. Their worst fears were confirmed when they discovered a small arsenal: seven .38-caliber revolvers, freshly oiled and fully loaded, and a double-barreled Winchester rifle. The police felt sure they had nipped "a good sized tong shooting" in the bud.

On December 13, the judge sentenced Jung Hing to die in the electric chair during the week of January 20, and he was immediately spirited off to Sing Sing, where the execution was to take place. But on appeal, his lawyers got his sentence reduced to a term of not less than seven and a half, nor more than nineteen and a half, years.

Mock Duck did not leave for China, as many had expected he would in order to avoid the possibility of incarceration, but his wife did. In fact, Tai Yow went to China in December 1911, a month before his arrest. Whether she ever returned is unclear, but Mock Duck was finished with her in any case. Without benefit of a divorce—if indeed he had ever legally married her in the first place—on January 16, 1913, in Pittsfield, Massachusetts, the thirty-four-year-old took another wife. His new bride was the eighteen-year-old Manhattan-born Frances Toy, the mixed-race daughter of Cuban-born Josephine Mendry, a white woman, and the late Charles Toy, a Chinese merchant.

Not much of a honeymoon was possible, because just over a month after his wedding, on February 28, 1913, his guilty verdict was affirmed, and in early March the new groom was off to Sing Sing.

Then something remarkable happened. Gin Gum, secretary of the On Leong Tong and a fifty-year-old widower, fell in love, too—with thirty-seven-year-old Josephine Toy, Frances's widowed mother and thus Mock Duck's new mother-in-law. The story was later told that Gin Gum approached his archenemy through an intermediary to ask for her hand. Although Josephine worked as an interpreter and had income of her own, she was probably living with Mock Duck and Frances, and given the views of women at the time—they were generally considered to be under the care of men—such a conversation might actually have occurred.

If Mock Duck was consulted, he likely raised no objection, because on April 29, 1913—when he was already imprisoned in Ossining, New York—Gin Gum tied the knot with Josephine Toy in the Central Methodist Episcopal Church in Toledo, Ohio. In so doing, the On Leong became the Hip Sing's stepfather-in-law.

The end of May 1913 brought an announcement that peace was at hand.

The impetus for the latest round of negotiations had come from the Chinese consul, who met with the On Leongs, the Hip Sings, and the Kim Lans. But he failed to bring them to closure, so he appealed to District Attorney Charles S. Whitman, who decided to play hardball. Whitman threatened to prosecute for blackmail and conspiracy anyone who would *not* sign a truce.

Negotiations continued with the assistance of the Chinese Merchants Association, as well as Captain Tierney and the perennial Judge Foster. The Kim Lans held out for a large indemnity from the Hip Sings, who had killed several of their members, but eventually agreement was reached. On May 21, placards spelling out the accord were posted in Chinatown over the seals of all three societies and the Merchants Association.

There were several reasons that agreement, so elusive in the past, was achieved this time. Raids on opium dens had cost Chinatown dearly, and not only in money: drugs, weapons, and paraphernalia had been seized. Three Chinese—two Hip Sings and an On Leong—had been condemned to death and were awaiting execution. And the relative calm in Chinatown in the months since the Pell Street shootings, coupled with the return of gambling, had resulted in an upturn in business. Everyone wanted things to stay that way.

The treaty, signed on May 28 in Judge Foster's chambers, ostensibly put an end to the Third Tong War. Gin Gum, who came with four colleagues, signed for his society. Tom Lee never showed up for such events; although he was always the ultimate authority in the tong, he had not held the office of president for some time. Five Hip Sings, led by the national president, Fong Foo Leung, a thirty-six-year-old China-born physician, represented their organization, and three officers of the Kim Lans were present as well. All wore Western clothing, and only two or three signed in Chinese. Times had changed since the fall of the dynasty, and these were strong indications that the men had begun to see themselves not as Chinese so much as Chinese Americans.

The agreement opened all of Chinatown to members of all the societies; there would theoretically be no more On Leong or Hip Sing spheres of influence. It mandated that property taken from one tong by another be returned and that tong members avoid creating disturbances and refrain from interfering in pending court cases. It also provided for dispute resolution by the Chinese Merchants Association and, failing that, adjudication by the police captain.

A large dinner to celebrate the peace was set for June 12, and because the pact struck in New York also extended to other cities, delegates from Chicago, St. Louis, Pittsburgh, Boston, Philadelphia, and other eastern cities were invited to Manhattan. A sixty-one-course banquet for several hundred had been arranged at the Port Arthur Restaurant on Mott Street.

Apart from representatives of the tongs themselves—even Charlie Boston, recently released from the penitentiary, was there—many New York luminaries came to Chinatown for the event. The district attorney had another commitment, but half a dozen of his assistants attended. Judge Foster, of course, was present, as were Vincent Astor, the son of the millionaire

John Jacob Astor IV and a businessman and philanthropist in his own right; the suffragettes Inez Milholland and Cora Carpenter; the U.S. congressman Henry M. Goldfogle; the New York County sheriff, Julius Harburger; and the prominent attorneys Abraham Gruber and Edward Lauterbach. And of course, the Chinese consul was there, beaming throughout the evening.

Even before the banquet, however, people began to express doubts about the treaty's staying power. The district attorney's office got an earful from some Chinatown figures about the role of the Chinese Merchants Association, which was to be the sole arbiter of differences but was not universally viewed as a neutral party. Although the On Leong Tong sometimes went by that English name, this was a different organization. But Chinatown wasn't that large, and the membership of any organization of merchants would almost by definition overlap substantially with that of the On Leong Tong. The concern that it could not be counted on to be fair was therefore quite possibly justified.

There was also an issue with the arbitration section of the accord, which violated the oaths tong members took upon joining in several respects, and hence was likely to be ignored, especially when brother tong members were in trouble with the law. And finally, there was fear the fragile agreement would be unable to withstand the execution of a tong member by the government.

Even the police were pessimistic. They welcomed the news, but they did not relax their vigilance. Bluecoats remained visible throughout Chinatown.

Chapter 13

Chinatown: Renovated, Disinfected, and Evacuated

After a disgruntled former city employee shot Mayor William Jay Gaynor in the summer of 1910, John P. Mitchel, president of the Board of Aldermen, assumed his duties temporarily. It didn't take long for the acting mayor to clash with the police commissioner, William F. Baker, and in October, Gaynor—who would live out his remaining three years with a bullet lodged in his throat—returned to a written report alleging incompetence and insubordination on Baker's part. Among the accusations were his failure to suppress lawlessness and vice in Coney Island and a resumption of the use of plainclothesmen, which Gaynor had expressly forbidden.

Within days, Baker stepped down. In his place, Gaynor appointed James C. Cropsey, a Brooklyn lawyer who was a personal friend. But it didn't take long for Cropsey, who had no experience in law enforcement, to run afoul of the mayor. He did not obey instructions to choose officers from the civil service lists, and he, too, was out of office in a few months. So Gaynor, who must have been embarrassed at the quick turnover in department heads, turned to a known commodity: Rhinelander Waldo, who had served as first deputy commissioner under Theodore Bingham.

Waldo had earlier been appointed fire commissioner by Gaynor, and he had performed well in the position. He had adhered strictly to the civil service list in filling positions in his department, one of Gaynor's requirements, and was credited with doing away with graft and favoritism. He assumed his new position on May 23, 1911.

Determined to make his mark, the new police commissioner immediately appointed a special twenty-man team to break up gangs and prevent crime. Known popularly as the Strong-Arm Squad, they soon became infamous for cruel and abusive treatment of those they arrested. They were not notably active in Chinatown, but their excesses came back to haunt Waldo after one of their members was reported to have gunned down a former business partner to stop him from testifying against him in court. Although no one accused Waldo of personal corruption, persistent reports of graft in the department eventually engendered calls for his resignation for incompetence and dereliction of duty. Prominent among Waldo's critics was District Attorney Charles S. Whitman.

Waldo was between a rock and a hard place. He would lose credibility if he did not defend the men under his command, but he certainly realized he had a serious corruption problem in his department. So he decided to counterattack and try to shift the blame.

If graft remained a problem on the force, he asserted, it was because policemen were underpaid. A first-year officer earned only $800 a year—about $20,000 in 2016 dollars—less 2 percent earmarked for his pension. It was simply not enough for a married officer to make ends meet. By one estimate, he would need to earn at least $1,000 just to meet expenses and $1,400 to permit him to amass a modest nest egg. "Their lives are such as to tend to make bad men of them," wrote one observer. "The pressure to become a grafter is there." In his 1913 budget, therefore, Waldo requested a starting salary of $1,000 for new officers and an increase of $100 per year for those already on the force. And he brazenly requested that his own salary of $7,500 be doubled.

Waldo also struck back at Whitman. He asserted publicly that there would be far less gambling if the judges and the district attorneys would do *their* jobs. To make that case, he took the unusual step of publicizing a list of nearly four hundred gambling resorts raided by the police the previous year. The inventory was notable for the small number of convictions that followed. He named not only the gambling bosses but also the owners of the properties where they were operating—some of whom were prominent New Yorkers. The implication was that it was the *judicial* system that was failing to act, and for the wrong reasons.

Waldo's list included several Chinatown properties, and it offered a rare window on who was actually behind the gambling dens. Although some establishments continued to be run in the names of individual owners, as in the past, the list made clear that the tongs themselves had gotten into the business in a big way.

The Chinatown establishments listed were

Chu Company: Nos. 12, 14, and 19 Doyers Street and Nos. 20½ and
  24 Pell Street
On Leong Tong: No. 15 Doyers Street, Nos. 15, 16, 17, 24, 26, and 32
  Mott Street
Hip Sing Tong: No. 17 Doyers Street and Nos. 8, 10, 16, and 19 Pell
  Street
Chu Lock: Nos. 16 and 18 Doyers Street and Nos. 23 and 25 Pell
  Street
Mock Duck: Nos. 21 (two joints) and 22 Pell Street
Four Brothers' Society: Nos. 13 and 20 Pell Street

The tongs' earlier role had been only to exact protection money from
individually held gambling halls. The fact that *ownership* of many of them
was now in their hands, and possibly had been for some time, was significant. Because Hip Sing–owned parlors were certainly not paying tribute to
the hated On Leongs, the cause of the friction between the groups had
changed. The matter of who would stand between the police and the gambling halls was no longer the main bone of contention.

The On Leongs' monopoly was now clearly a thing of the past. But in
any event, recent clashes had been about other things: "ownership" of a
young woman; arrests of compatriots; elimination of informers and tong
leaders; and the heading off of potentially damning court testimony. Graft
would still be a fact of life, but future battles would center on defections,
protecting their brethren, and saving face. And most would break out on
their own, without any formal declaration of war.

In the eyes of the men of the Chinese Merchants Association, charged with
refereeing the May truce, another tong war would have a devastating effect
on business. But like the police, they still stubbornly believed the best way
to ensure quiet was to suppress gambling. The summer of 1913 saw an
initiative to accomplish just that.

For several weeks, members of the association gathered evidence against
what seemed a growing number of betting parlors in the Chinese quarter.

And in early August, its head, Lee Frank, presented the information to Assistant District Attorney Aaron J. Conlon. Accompanying him were nine Chinese men willing to testify that the establishments were indeed gambling houses.

This effort was actually part and parcel of the association's responsibilities under the treaty. In cases in which the law was being violated, the organization was obliged to aid in prosecuting the offenders. And to demonstrate that they were acting evenhandedly, the merchants made sure their list of eighteen establishments—which must have been quite similar to Waldo's list—included both On Leong and Hip Sing properties.

Conlon pledged to secure warrants to search the dens, although it is not clear whether any raids took place. The following month, however, came the news that Mayor William Jay Gaynor had collapsed of a heart attack on a transatlantic voyage and died. It had been Gaynor, a Democrat, who had promoted Waldo. But the mayor's immediate successor, the Republican Ardolph L. Kline, had no love for him, and the police commissioner was widely expected to be fired, although Kline made no immediate move to do so. He was only slated to be in office until Gaynor's term expired in just over a hundred days.

The gambling bosses could hardly wait to see the end of Waldo. They anticipated that his departure might end the campaign being waged against them. The commissioner, however, was determined to keep up the pressure as long as he remained in office.

Two weeks after Gaynor's death, Waldo made a surprise visit to Chinatown and didn't like what he saw. Showing up unannounced just before midnight on September 25, he got out of his car and walked around. At 18, 26, and 28½ Pell Street, there was unmistakable evidence of gambling. When he ran into Captain Tierney, he led him and two of his officers to No. 18, where access was blocked by three "icebox" doors. These were fashioned out of several layers of new wood, nailed together with the grains crossing; it was impossible to split one with a single blow. By the time such a door could be demolished, the gamblers inside would have had ample time to hide the evidence and flee.

"Well, what shall we do, Commissioner?" Tierney asked. "Break it in?"

"No," Waldo replied coldly. "If that door isn't opened legally within five minutes, you will cease to be a police captain."

He was serious. After two years in the Sixth Precinct, Tierney had become lax in going after gamblers. Waldo's insinuation, of course, was that the casino was operating with his tacit approval and that it would therefore take only a word from him for the owner to open the door. A few minutes later, Waldo looked at his watch and said, "You have just one minute left."

Thirty seconds later, a key materialized.

No arrests were made; the gamblers had had sufficient time to cover their tracks. But Waldo had seen enough. He ordered Tierney and the two officers back to the station. There he stripped them of their badges, ordered them to remove the police insignias from their uniforms, and suspended them on the spot. The next day, he installed Captain Dominick Riley as interim station head.

Riley, transferred from the Greenwich Street Station, took the example of his predecessor to heart. But a tactic that had served him well on the West Side—disguising undercover policemen as players to collect evidence against gambling houses—was useless in Chinatown. There were no Chinese on the force, and it was impossible to disguise white officers as Chinese. Reconnaissance in Chinatown required the cooperation of Chinese stool pigeons, and these were not easy to come by, nor could they necessarily be trusted.

Riley decided to undertake raids personally. His first foray took him to half a dozen Hip Sing–run resorts, and to show that he was not in the pocket of the On Leongs, he hit two of theirs next. On the evening of October 2, spying an "icebox" door ajar at 11 Mott, he slipped inside and discovered forty Chinese gamblers at play. Although he was in civilian clothes, he was recognized.

As Chinese men scurried for the exits, he demanded, "Who owns all this?" Everyone there knew it was Charlie Boston's place, but nobody dared open his mouth. So when he got no answer, Riley announced, "If nobody owns all this, it must be abandoned property." And with that, he let the Chinese men leave, blew his whistle, and ordered his policemen to confiscate

Captain Dominick Riley, ca. 1910–1915.
His tenure in the Sixth Precinct proved too
much for him and marked the end of his
career in the police department.

the eight *fan tan* tables, twelve thousand policy tickets, and two iron safes in the room. A repeat performance at his next stop, 16 Mott, yielded seven *fan tan* tables and the attendant paraphernalia.

Riley's tenure at the Sixth Precinct was intense, but it was also very short. Like Captain Galvin before him, he couldn't handle the pressure. The eighteen-hour days were too much for him, and on the evening of November 9, not even two months into his assignment, he collapsed on the job. He was taken home to Brooklyn, and although his condition was not judged grave, it marked the end of his career in the police department.

Chinatown had done him in.

The first trial of Eng Hing and Lee Dock, the Hip Sings charged with the murder of Tom Lee's nephew, had ended in a hung jury. But the men were convicted in a second trial early in 1913 and sent to Sing Sing, where they were scheduled for electrocution. The executions were postponed, however, because of pending appeals. In late November, their attorney, Terence J. McManus—who had represented the Four Brothers men accused of killing Bow Kum—announced he would submit evidence to the state Supreme Court that two of the witnesses against the men had perjured themselves at the behest of the On Leong Tong.

McManus had engaged a private investigator who had befriended, and then secretly recorded, a twenty-seven-year-old white Chinatown hanger-on known as Rubber. His real name was Frank Treglia, and he was a private detective in the employ of the On Leong Tong. The investigator installed a Dictograph in a Thirty-fourth Street apartment and connected it by wire to an adjoining room, where two stenographers were hiding. He then invited Rubber there for a party. Rubber supplied the opium, and the investigator brought two young, attractive girls who had been instructed to flatter him and get him to talk.

After a few tokes of the pipe, Rubber got expansive and began to discuss the trial. The girls steered him to the subject of "Chinese Flossie" Wong and Grace Mack, two white women whose testimony had helped convict the defendants.

"The girls went down there and they never seen a thing," Rubber volunteered. "They just went down there and swore that they seen these Chinamen."

"And they didn't see them? But who told the girls to tell that?"

"The Chinamen did that. . . . The girls lived with On Leong Tong men . . . and they were got to swear that they saw these young men shoot, and they did swear. They naturally knew that it was one of the On Leong Tongs that shot him, and it makes no difference to them as long as he is arrested whether he is guilty or not."

"But what about these girls?"

"They testify to everything," Rubber declared. "Them girls have been witnesses in every case in which they could be."

"How do they do that?"

"Because in every case they can be brought up here. They can be taught. It can be explained to them."

The two women who had apparently lied under oath were *also* secretly taped on another occasion, and McManus submitted all the Dictograph records as evidence. In December, he asked for a new trial on the grounds that the testimony that had convicted his clients had been perjured.

Surprisingly, this plea was denied, but the defendants were accorded a series of reprieves to permit their lawyers to marshal additional evidence for a second application. A motion was heard by Judge Thomas C. T. Crain at the Court of General Sessions in early October 1914; Grace Mack appeared and admitted she had lied but said she had done so out of fear for her life. "That," she explained, "is the reason other white girls in Chinatown do not come forward and tell the truth."

But the state produced Lillie Wilson, another white woman, to impeach Grace Mack. In the end, the judge decided that even given the new evidence, the case against the defendants remained strong, and he denied the appeal. On the specific allegation that On Leongs had coached and threatened witnesses, he wrote, "If On Leong Tong influence was exerted to further the conviction of the defendants, Hip Sing Tong efforts have been made to secure their acquittal and discharge." Whether or not the judge was being fair, he was surely correct in this observation.

The executions were rescheduled for November 2, 1914—but the attorneys got Governor Martin H. Glynn of New York to delay them again. And on January 28, 1915, just a few days before the prisoners were to be put to death, the lawyers again went before Judge Crain to seek a new trial.

"We believe absolutely that they are innocent men, and we will not remit our efforts until we have done everything to save their lives." The speaker was none other than Frank Moss, who, even as late as 1915, had not ended his blind, two-decade-long love affair with the Hip Sing Tong, despite repeated demonstrations that it was entirely unworthy of his admiration or protection and the fact that even his former colleagues at the Parkhurst Society were apparently no longer supporting it. Moss had been working with the other attorneys on the appeals throughout the previous year.

Moss produced four new witnesses—all white—to poke holes in the case. But the judge wasn't moved, and he offered another insight about the perjury allegation:

> Now, if the On Leong Tong were desirous of convicting the Hip Sing Tong men in order to revenge the killing of Lee Kay, without any definite knowledge on the part of the On Leong Tong as to particular individuals who had done the shooting, it appears to me that they would have picked out men prominent in the Hip Sing Tong society, and that they would not have chosen as a party to wrongfully accuse, a young man like Eng Hing . . . and a man like Lee Dock, who, while a member of that Tong, was an inconspicuous member, who had only recently arrived from Philadelphia.

Their motion denied and their appeals exhausted, the defendants had only one avenue left: executive clemency. Moss took the lead in contacting the governor. The petition, submitted in November 1914, included letters of support for the defendants, affidavits of witnesses, and even a record of Gin Gum's 1898 California forgery conviction, because it had been he who had allegedly suborned perjury on the part of the witnesses in the original trials.

Nothing if not persistent, and determined to fight to the bitter end, Moss followed up the clemency plea with a telegram seeking a last-minute stay. He was able to secure a respite until early February, but that was as far as the governor was willing to go. Eng Hing and Lee Dock finally ran out of luck early in the morning of February 5, 1915, when, at Sing Sing prison in Ossining, New York, each received three lethal 1,850-volt shocks in the electric chair.

Upon Captain Riley's departure, Commissioner Waldo brought the seventeen-year veteran Lieutenant John L. Falconer to Elizabeth Street and promoted him to captain. But Falconer himself soon had a new boss. On December 31, 1913, the last day of his administration, Mayor Kline finally removed Rhinelander Waldo and installed Waldo's deputy, Douglas Imrie McKay, as police commissioner. But Alderman John P. Mitchel had succeeded Kline as mayor, and McKay didn't get along with him any better than Baker had, so he lasted only five months in the job. He was a reformer, however, and during his short time in office he made a valiant effort to suppress street gangs and eliminate vice.

Taking his cue from McKay, Captain Falconer sought to crack down hard on Chinatown. In February 1914, after McKay heard a rumor of an imminent resumption of tong hostilities, Falconer initiated a raid on a Hip Sing lodging house at 16 Bowery. His men weren't looking for gambling gear, though; they were seeking weapons. And they discovered a cache of hatchets, daggers, and revolvers and five hundred pounds of cartridges. Two Hip Sings were arrested.

That was just the beginning. Falconer was relentless. In the first year and a half of his two years at the Sixth Precinct, he destroyed more than a hundred *fan tan* tables. He posted detectives everywhere and recruited not only a Chinese plainclothesman but two Japanese stool pigeons to infiltrate the gambling halls. Under the pressure of unremitting raids and destruction of property, many den owners took the path of least resistance. They picked up stakes and moved. Newark, New Jersey, was a favorite destination.

With their departure went a lot of local business, because without gambling once again Manhattan's Chinese quarter ceased to be the weekend destination for the area's Chinese that it had been. There was an attendant downturn in the opium business and in prostitution as well. Even the white tourist trade, which had rebounded since the Elsie Sigel murder but still subsisted on its ability to show outsiders the squalid side of Chinatown life, suffered. And by mid-1915, the police reckoned as many as two thousand Chinese had moved out of the quarter. More than a few tenements once filled with Chinese men were now being rented to immigrant Italian and Jewish families. As the New York *Sun* put it, "Chinatown is being renovated, disinfected, civilized, Christianized and consequently evacuated," adding that "chop suey is giving way to spaghetti and gefuelte fisch."

Among those lamenting the decline was old Tom Lee. "Things very dull," he said with a sigh to a *New-York Tribune* reporter. "No business. No white people come to visit. Chinamen all leaving. Laundrymen used to come Saturday night. See friends, smoke pipe, gamble little, maybe. Now Chinamen go to New Jersey for fun. Stores all closing. Never saw things so dull. Soon be no Chinatown at all."

Tom Lee, ca. 1913.

Lee placed the blame squarely at the feet of overzealous policemen. "It is not because gambling has ceased," he said. "The Chinese stopped that and were glad to do it. It only brought trouble and death. But it is because the police will not leave us alone that Chinatown is dying. Here, there and in Pell Street and in Doyers, shops have been closed. The merchants are driven out by the police when they are trying to conduct an honorable business."

Under Falconer, the police had gotten so aggressive that some Chinese began to push back. In April 1915, the Mott Street merchants Hor Pooh and Yee Loy went to court to get a restraining order against Commissioner Arthur Woods—another reformer, who had been appointed by Mayor Mitchel to succeed McKay—as well as Inspector George R. Wakefield and Captain Falconer. They accused the officials of harassment by constantly dispatching detectives to "inspect" their places of business. Counsel for the city countered by documenting several raids there during the previous six months that had yielded gambling paraphernalia. The judge ruled against the two Chinese, and his decision was affirmed on appeal without explanation.

A similar suit was filed by Lee Yick You, whose Wing Woh Chong Company at 34 Pell, in business for thirty years, had also become a frequent target of police persecution. In excellent English, he told the judge that police were camping out in front of his store, interrogating his customers, and unlawfully searching his premises at all hours of the day and night. Officers had threatened him and intimidated his subordinates but had never accused him of any illegal acts. The judge, however, who had been told by someone that the "interference had been dropped," also denied the application.

In late October, an association of thirty Chinatown property owners— many if not most of them white—lodged a formal protest with the mayor. Their ox, too, was getting gored by the police, because harassment was causing high vacancy rates in Chinatown, and because each time doors were smashed or windows broken in a police raid, it was their property that got destroyed. City hall quickly bucked the complaint to police headquarters, which ostensibly launched an investigation, but there is no record of any action by the police on the complaint apart from a hearing by the third deputy police commissioner. Nor could the mayor's office have reasonably expected that those who were complaining would get satisfaction when he sent them right back to the police department, the very source of their troubles.

The police had begun to behave as if *all* Chinese were criminals. Innocent Chinese were being harassed, and all routes to redress seemed blocked. Not even the courts, which consistently sided with the police, seemed to offer the Chinese meaningful recourse.

The government was speaking with one voice. It was sick and tired of the tong wars. If eliminating them meant abusing the innocent majority and even destroying Chinatown in the process, then so be it.

Time was catching up with the old lions of the On Leong Tong. Although only fifty-two, Gin Gum, the longtime secretary, consigliere, interpreter, spokesman, and peace negotiator, succumbed in mid-1915, not to a Hip

Sing bullet, but to a weak heart. He died in his room at 24 Mott during a national On Leong convention in Philadelphia. When fellow tong men learned of his death, many stopped in New York to pay their respects before heading for home.

The On Leong Tong organized the funeral, the largest Chinatown had seen in many years, and in deference to the wishes of his widow, Josephine, a Christian service was arranged. Branch by branch, On Leongs approached and bowed deeply as a sign of respect for their old comrade. All Chinatown watched as the 128-carriage cortege passed onto the Bowery on its way to Cypress Hills Cemetery in Brooklyn. Ten coaches were actually chartered by the Hip Sing Tong, and one carried the On Leongs' archenemy, Mock Duck, who had become Gin Gum's stepson-in-law two years earlier. Out of deference to the On Leongs, he and his wife, Frances, did not attend the service, but they did join the procession. He explained, "We can pay honor to Gin Gum at the cemetery."

Tom Lee wasn't well, either. In 1913, his son Frank, who had left in 1906, returned to New York to visit his aging father, now in his mid-sixties. Frank had gone to China to study and had remained there, engaged in Baptist educational work until 1911, when he was appointed to Guangdong Province's Foreign Affairs Bureau. Frank had joined Dr. Sun Yat-sen's Guomindang Party, and when Sun fled China in 1913 to escape political enemies, Frank arranged for a one-year stay in America as a commercial commissioner. He had married and was a father of three, and he surely wanted his father and his brother, Tom junior—a sometime circus acrobat turned chauffeur—to meet his family.

Old Tom remained active through 1916, but by early 1917, after the death of his wife, he was so feeble that few were permitted to see him. And on January 10, 1918, nearing seventy, the genteel mayor for life of New York's Chinatown passed away quietly in his bed, ending a reign of nearly four decades.

Lee's body, in a silk brocade shroud, was laid out in a metal casket in his third-floor office at 18 Mott. It rested on a crepe-swathed bier flanked by candelabra. Bouquets filled the chamber and overflowed into two adjacent rooms. For two days, mourners from all walks of New York life—merchants and waiters, bankers and laundrymen, Caucasians and Chinese, Hip Sings,

Business was suspended in Chinatown for the funeral of "Mayor" Tom Lee. His January 14, 1918, cortege, the largest ever seen in Chinatown, included three marching bands, five buses, and 150 carriages.

On Leongs, and Four Brothers men—lined up to pay their respects to the man whose word had been law in the Chinese colony for as long as anyone could remember. Among the callers were leading lights of the Tammany organization such as "Big Tom" Foley, former sheriff and leader of the Second Assembly District; and Al Smith, who would go on to become governor of New York in 1923 and the Democratic Party's presidential nominee in 1928.

The funeral was put off until January 14 to give mourners from afar time to get to New York. A brief service by the New York chapter of the Chee Kung Tong—the Chinese Masons—which Lee had helped found as the Loon Yee Tong so many years earlier, was held in the morning. This was followed by a Christian ceremony organized by his sons. Then, as the casket was carried down the narrow staircase to the street by members of the Lee clan, an Italian brass band struck up a rendition of "Nearer, My God, to Thee."

Business was suspended in Chinatown when Tom Lee's funeral procession, which outshone all that had preceded it, left Mott Street at 2:00 p.m. Thousands lined the streets as three marching bands, five buses, and 150 carriages made two passes through the Chinese quarter. Then, headed by a hearse drawn by six black horses, the cortege took off for the Williamsburg Bridge and went on to Cypress Hills.

Tom Lee had never been universally liked, but he had been deeply respected. The newspapers ran numerous obituaries following his death, but perhaps none was so moving as this tribute, a wire dispatch that appeared in several papers around the country:

> Now that the last columns have been written of his gorgeous Chinese funeral, two generations of reporters who covered Chinatown affairs are recalling the calm counsel that old Tom Lee always had to offer on every conceivable twist and turn of life. If this Chinese patriarch had been born an American, everyone who really knew him believes he would have filled the real mayor's chair much better than many men who do not wear queues.

But now the mayor was gone, and so was the old Chinatown.

Under Mayor Mitchel and Commissioner Arthur Woods, a lot of progress was made in reforming and professionalizing the police department and fighting crime citywide. Woods, a Harvard graduate and a sociologist, kept politics out of the department. He instituted a merit system and got his officers pay raises and longer vacations. In his first three years, homicides took a nosedive—from 265 in 1913 to 186 in 1916. "While it is impossible to attribute this to any one cause," he said, "the fact remains that the decrease has been regular and has . . . been concurrent with our practical elimination of organized bands of gangsters and gunmen and our sustained efforts to prevent the illegal carrying of revolvers and other dangerous weapons."

The quiet in Chinatown about which Tom Lee had complained, which was part and parcel of Woods's efforts, continued in the run-up to World War I. Even after Mitchel lost to John F. Hylan in 1917 and Tammany Hall returned to power, Chinatown remained at peace for several years.

After the United States declared war on Germany in 1917, a draft was instituted for men between the ages of eighteen and forty-five. Even noncitizens were required to register, although they were exempt from induction into the service. Chinese who were citizens, however, were fair game. Fully 30 percent of America's Chinese were native born by 1920, and more than a hundred Chinese New Yorkers fought under the Stars and Stripes. Chinese men did not generally see combat; most were assigned to officers' messes and other menial tasks, but they had nonetheless served, if only food. Nationwide, the On Leong Tong contributed thirty-eight men to the war effort.

Chinatown also did its part in other ways. A wire service photograph that appeared in newspapers around the country in 1917 showed the New York On Leong president, Lou Fook, signing an application for a $50 Liberty Bond, and he was not alone. Chinese merchants throughout the country were doing the same, even though few of them were actually American citizens. The New York *World* carried a notice in April 1918 of a Chinese American Liberty Loan Rally on Mott Street, which featured music and "entertainment of the Orient showing real American patriotism."

In April 1919, Hip Sings, On Leongs, and Four Brothers men met together to plan a welcome for the Chinese New Yorkers who had served the United States in World War I. There was even a bona fide local Chinese hero: the California-born Sing Kee, an On Leong who had moved to New York early in the decade. The only American of Chinese descent to receive the Distinguished Service Cross, he had been honored for "extraordinary heroism" by operating his regiment's message center single-handedly even as Germans gassed and bombarded it. He and others were feted with a parade down Fifth Avenue and a huge Chinatown feast.

OPPOSITE: The opening of the new On Leong Tong headquarters at 41 Mott Street, completed in 1921 at a cost of $150,000. The building was mortgaged a decade later to raise funds for members put out of work by the Great Depression.

It wasn't exactly a lovefest, but nor was it war. In late 1921, when the On Leongs brought two thousand of their brethren from around the nation to Manhattan for an eleven-day celebration to dedicate their sumptuous new $150,000 headquarters building at 41 Mott, local Hip Sings were among the guests. And when Dr. Fong Foo Leung, former president of the Hip Sing Tong, died of cancer in July 1922, the On Leongs sent a ten-foot floral tribute.

"Chinatown is a joke! Not enough pep to chase a cat," a veteran patrolman remarked early in 1922. "Five years ago there was a lot of queer doings down here, but Doyers Street now is just like a sidewalk in Woodlawn Cemetery. Opium? Not enough to fill a pipe. Gunmen? Well, they may come down here but they don't operate on my beat, see?" He attributed the cessation of the violence to the well-publicized execution of Eng Hing and Lee Dock seven years earlier. "That's it—the electric chair. That's what scared the bad men."

The newspapers had the same impression: that it had been the example of the two dead prisoners that had stopped the killing. But memories were short. The peace agreement had actually predated their execution by two years. In the aftermath of World War I, the tongs had remained relatively quiet; they went about their business and actually cooperated from time to time. And even when provocations did occur, no broad conflict broke out.

Not even the cold-blooded murder of Ko Low, the national president of the Hip Sing Tong, was sufficient to start a new confrontation, despite predictions to the contrary from all quarters. Forty-two-year-old Ko Low was gunned down on Pell Street on the night of August 7, 1922. He had been dining at the Chinese Delmonico with two Chinese men and two white women. Just before the party left the restaurant, one of the men excused himself, went out on the restaurant's balcony—most Chinatown restaurants were on the second floor, and most had shallow balconies protruding over the sidewalk—and mopped his brow with his handkerchief. It was probably a signal. When Ko Low, immaculately well-groomed in his freshly pressed English tweeds, emerged on the arms of the two women and headed toward his home at the corner of Doyers Street, two gunmen, one armed with a Luger automatic pistol, fired a dozen bullets at him.

Only one hit Ko Low, but it caused a mortal wound. He declined to describe his assailant to the police on the way to Beekman Street Hospital, and he died the next morning. But it was clear the shooting had been personal: neither the $1,000 in cash nor the thousands of dollars' worth of jewelry Ko Low sported on his person was touched.

The newspapers assumed On Leongs were behind the hit; the *New York Times* even jumped the gun with an article headlined "Tong War On." But if the papers rushed to judgment, the Hip Sings did not. Lee Yee Hong, the local president, wisely chose to investigate before pointing fingers.

Aided by Chinese informers, police detained two Brooklynites: thirty-two-year-old Tom Yee, a student; and James Chuck, thirty-three, owner of a chop suey restaurant. Both were identified by witnesses. Yee had suffered two fractured ribs at the end of June at the hands of one of Ko Low's cousins and had just been released from the hospital. He wasn't an On Leong. Revenge was assumed to be his motive.

Ko Low's funeral was nearly as elaborate as Tom Lee's had been. After lying in state at Hip Sing headquarters, he, too, enjoyed a grandiose procession out of Chinatown, which swarmed with police. To demonstrate that they had not been involved, the On Leongs sent an ostentatious display of flowers. And any doubt was removed when notices appeared on the bulletin board at the corner of Pell and Doyers bearing the seals of both the Hip

A cache of weapons seized by police from Hip Sing Tong headquarters in a preemptive raid on December 1, 1922.

Sing *and* the On Leong tongs. The dual proclamation was unprecedented. It declared that the death of Ko Low had been discussed amicably by the two societies, which had jointly concluded it had not been a result of enmity between them.

The police, however, were not convinced that fresh attacks were off the table. Undercover officers in Chinatown noted that Lee Yee Hong never appeared without two bodyguards and that he had ceased to use the main entrance to Hip Sing headquarters. Lee had taken to coming and going via the roofs of neighboring buildings, which suggested he was anticipating trouble. And when the police noticed Hip Sing men furtively ferrying bundles into their headquarters by night, they were nearly certain something was up.

On December 1, local police and federal officials staged a preemptive raid on Hip Sing headquarters. They arrested Lee Yee Hong and his bodyguards and confiscated more than fifteen pistols, a box of daggers and brass knuckles, and thousands of rounds of ammunition. And in a hollowed-out idol in the assembly room, they found fourteen packages of opium and a hundred poppy heads, from which the drug is extracted. More opium was found under the floorboards. Officials valued the cache in the thousands of dollars.

Perhaps because the Hip Sings had been disarmed, or more likely because there was no will on either side for more conflict, there would be no new tong war in New York.

For the time being.

Chapter 14

The Defection of Chin Jack Lem

By the 1920s, the On Leongs and the Hip Sings had established branches in most of the cities of the East and the Midwest with significant Chinese populations. Both tongs had formed chapters in Philadelphia, Chicago, Pittsburgh, Cleveland, Washington, Minneapolis, Newark, and Schenectady. The On Leongs were also active in Boston, Baltimore, Hartford, Detroit, Providence, and at least half a dozen other cities. The Hip Sing Tong, of course, remained strong in the West, from whence it had come; Hip Sing branches existed in San Francisco, Seattle, Portland, Denver, Boise, Butte, and Spokane, among other places. The New York–born On Leong Tong, by contrast, had never attempted to expand beyond the Midwest.

Members of these local organizations were linked together in a network under the aegis of national umbrella organizations, which governed the tongs, organized annual conventions in various cities around the country, adjudicated differences, and generally performed a coordinating role. The downside of closely linked branches, however, was that conflict in one city could easily foment trouble in another. The various local On Leong branches had inherited enmity for Hip Sings—and vice versa—from their New York brethren, and the result was a tinderbox that could easily be set aflame by an incendiary event anywhere in the network. As the individual branches became larger, they acted more independently. Brush fires became more frequent, and the national leadership had a harder time extinguishing them. Finally, they lost the ability to do so.

The spark that caused the fourth and final tong war was a defection, but the conflict would take on a life of its own, spread to a dozen cities, and continue, in fits and starts, for nearly a decade. Persistent but uncoordinated flare-ups throughout the East and the Midwest, sometimes employing imported hit men and automatic weapons, would produce more carnage than any of the previous three wars. Reining it in would prove too much for any single police department, prosecutor, or mediator, and even for the national tong leaders. And it would grow so large and so out of control that it would ultimately trigger spectacular and unprecedented intervention by an impatient federal government fed up with the tongs and all too willing to summarily rid the country of Chinese, tong members or not, to stop the violence.

When the peace that prevailed until 1924 finally ended, it wasn't the New York branches of the tongs that broke it. The instigator of the Fourth Tong War was a hard-boiled restaurateur and sometime opium dealer named Chin Jack Lem. A big fish in the On Leong pond, he had directed the Chicago branch for nearly two decades and had once headed the national organization as well.

In April 1924, when the On Leongs held their annual convention in Pittsburgh, Chin and thirteen others were ousted from the tong in a bitter factional dispute that involved accusations of mishandled funds. Resentful but undaunted, Chin secretly applied to the Hip Sing Tong for membership, promising he could bring a hundred On Leongs along with him, including the entire membership of the Pittsburgh and Cleveland chapters, who he insisted were loyal to him.

The Hip Sings were divided. Chin was privy to all the On Leongs' secrets and vulnerabilities, so everybody knew the tong could not sit idly by and allow him to join the enemy camp. A vote was put off until the annual Hip Sing convention, slated for September in Spokane, and in the interim Chin and his followers relocated to Cleveland. But their application to the Hip Sings became known, and the On Leongs mobilized for battle. They went after the recently ousted president of their Cleveland branch, a member of Chin's faction. Ambushed in front of his Ontario Street store, he took five bullets but miraculously did not die of his wounds.

Then Wong Sing, the treasurer of the Cleveland On Leongs, who remained loyal to the tong, filed a complaint with the police against Chin Jack Lem and his men. He accused them of attempting to force him at gunpoint to sign over local tong property valued at $70,000. This was plausible, given Chin's boast that he could essentially replace the On Leong marquee in Cleveland with a Hip Sing sign if the tong accepted him. He was indicted on July 1 and released, but he jumped his $500 bail and returned to Chicago. Shortly afterward, an anonymous letter arrived at Cleveland On Leong headquarters. It was a death threat against On Leong officers in Cleveland, Pittsburgh, and Chicago.

The radioactive question of admission of the expelled On Leongs was high on the Hip Sings' convention agenda. The head of the New York branch opposed accepting them, it was whispered, because he had been bribed to vote no by the On Leongs, who were desperate to derail the defection. But his delegation overruled him, and New York voted yes, which turned out to be the majority position. The Hip Sings would accept the refugees, a verdict that amounted to a declaration of war.

Everyone saw it coming, and the Chinese Consolidated Benevolent Association in New York even tried to broker a peace resolution in *advance* of a breakout of hostilities, but the Hip Sings wouldn't sign. New York police summoned the leaders of both tongs to headquarters, but the Hip Sings didn't show. They were gearing up for war.

The opening salvo of the Fourth Tong War was the murder of a New York On Leong at a Delancey Street restaurant on October 8. On the eleventh, a Hip Sing laundryman was shot in Brooklyn, a Dayton tong man was slain, and another was shot in Chicago. On October 12, the body of a Chinese man who had been shot, strangled, and clubbed to death was discovered on a New Jersey roadside fifteen miles from Manhattan. This prompted Newark police to raid every house in the city's Chinese quarter. Similar reports of violence came in from Pittsburgh, Boston, and Schenectady and, within the next few days, from Philadelphia, Detroit, and Milwaukee as well.

On October 15, Chin Jack Lem, armed with an automatic weapon, was apprehended in Chicago. He needed it for protection, he explained to the police, because the On Leong Tong had put a $15,000 price on his head, and he flashed a badge to prove he had been appointed a deputy sheriff and could legally carry a gun. But he was still wanted in Cleveland, so he was arrested. Inexplicably, however, he was then released on $5,000 bail, and

Chin Jack Lem, expelled On Leong kingpin
who joined the Hip Sings and single-
handedly caused the Fourth Tong War.

he disappeared *again*. Both the appointment and the release were, no doubt, evidence of the powerful friends in the Chicago firmament Chin had culti-vated over the many years he had ruled the On Leongs there.

Over the next couple of days, a thirty-year-old New York On Leong was mortally wounded in his Allen Street flat, and a sixty-four-year-old On Leong was slashed to death in the chop suey restaurant he managed in Queens. It was a gruesome scene: his head had nearly been detached from his body, which bore fourteen slash marks left by a meat cleaver. A Hip Sing arrested in Yonkers in connection with that killing told police that a cook in the restaurant had offered him $500 to assist him in the murder.

In New York, the Chinese consul, Ziang-Ling Chang, huddled with the police commissioner, Richard E. Enright, who had briefly manned the

Elizabeth Street Station in 1910 and been appointed commissioner in 1918 after twenty-two years on the force. Together with the Chinese Consolidated Benevolent Association, they made several efforts to organize a parley.

Peace agreements, of course, had come and gone over the years and never seemed to stick. But a truce still seemed the best hope for stopping the bloodshed, because the authorities didn't really know what else to do. This battle had nothing to do with gambling, drugs, or women, so going after the vice dens wouldn't accomplish anything. By the end of the month, they had achieved a two-week armistice, which was to extend to November 13 and apply not just to New York but to the rest of the country as well. Although four bullets fired just outside the negotiation venue killed a Hip Sing and broke up the meeting, the agreement was eventually signed.

Then New York police got word that Chin Jack Lem was heading for Manhattan. Five plainclothesmen posted at Pennsylvania Station spotted him on his arrival on November 9 and nabbed him. He was arraigned the next day and held on $20,000 bail, pending receipt of extradition papers from Cleveland. Following his detention, Consul General Chang announced that the two tongs had agreed to extend the cease-fire for another two weeks.

The police thought his capture might end the war. They couldn't have been more wrong.

On the morning of October 26, 1924, a taxicab pulled up to the corner of Pell and the Bowery and unloaded three suspicious-looking Chinese men. At the sight of two police detectives, they fled, and the officers, believing they were tong gunmen, pursued and nabbed them. Shortly afterward, another cab discharged seven Chinese passengers at the corner of Mott and Pell. Some of the men were in very poor shape and had to be carried on the backs of the others. They, too, were chased, and after several shots were fired, they were arrested.

At the police station, the men admitted they were all Hip Sings. Only three were local, however; the other seven were imported hit men, brought in to supplement the depleted ranks of Hip Sing shooters. But they had not been recruited from Boston, Philadelphia, or any of the usual locations. A month earlier, these men had all been in Hong Kong. Summoned to New

York—probably by the national Hip Sing association—to fight the On Leongs, paid $200 apiece, and promised two meals a day and work once they reached America, they had stowed away on a cargo ship, the SS *Gaelic Prince,* packed two to a wooden crate.

The men, near collapse from malnutrition and beriberi, were taken to the hospital. Only half were thought likely to survive. One died that same night, and another succumbed a few days later. The three accused of smuggling them in were indicted by a federal grand jury.

The Hip Sings were reaching far and wide not only for foot soldiers but also for munitions. Acting on a tip, police raided an uptown Chinese eatery on October 28. They arrested Long Wong Chue, a Hip Sing waiter, and confiscated two tear gas grenades that had been shipped to him from a manufacturer in Pittsburgh. Long denied the weapons were intended for use against the On Leongs; he said they were samples he intended to ship to China, but the police didn't believe him. They knew Long; he had been arrested the previous month for running an opium den and was out on $1,000 bail.

Dr. Carlton Simon, special deputy police commissioner, told reporters that if one of the bombs had ignited in a confined space, everyone in the room would surely have been killed.

A few days before the two-week extension was due to expire, the Reverend Lee Tow, a sixty-one-year-old Baptist minister and former president of the Chinese Consolidated Benevolent Association, joined an effort by Christian Chinese to end the turmoil. But during a passionate speech at the Port Arthur Restaurant, Lee was suddenly stricken with paralysis. He never regained consciousness and was regarded as another martyr in the war of the tongs, which resumed with a vengeance on Thanksgiving Day.

That day, the son of an On Leong perished in his Brooklyn laundry in a volley of bullets shot from automatic weapons by Hip Sing assailants. The next day, two more New Yorkers fell: a forty-three-year-old Hip Sing laundryman and a forty-year-old On Leong, stabbed in his Eldridge Street bed. He had struggled with his assailant and plunged through a window to his death.

In the meantime, Chin Jack Lem was fighting extradition. He was being sought by *two* states: by Ohio for extortion, and by both Ohio and Illinois for jumping bail. Governor Al Smith of New York signed extradition papers for Ohio, but Chin's lawyers initially blocked the move. Finally, on November 29, the prisoner was handed over to the custody of Cleveland detectives. Before they even left the courthouse, however, they were served with a writ from the state Supreme Court admitting Chin to $30,000 bail— even though he had already jumped bail *twice*. The argument was that he should first be sent back to Chicago, the jurisdiction from which he had fled to New York.

Hostilities continued, fueled by the defections, which were intolerable to the On Leongs, and sustained by the imperative of retaliating for every killing. Rumors of hatchet men pouring into New York from other cities abounded. One held that Hip Sings were importing seventy gunmen. Eng Ying "Eddie" Gong, the national Hip Sing secretary who had relocated to New York in 1921, dismissed the report out of hand. "It is ridiculous to think that we would pay $200 cash to bring 70 men from the Pacific coast," he said, although the Hip Sings had in fact already imported shooters from much farther away than that. "We have no money in our organization," he continued, "but if gunmen are being imported, it behooves us to be on the alert." So he applied to the New York police for protection. So did Henry Moy and Charlie Boston, now the top local On Leongs. All also acquired bulletproof vests.

While Chin remained in New York, the seven accused of cooperating with him in the Cleveland extortion attempt were convicted. Their sentences varied from three to twenty-five years. A week later, all his legal remedies exhausted, Chin was finally extradited to Ohio, shackled hand and foot to a detective. When he got to Cleveland, he appeared in court in a heavy steel vest and pleaded not guilty. Astoundingly, he was not remanded but *again* freed—this time on $15,000 bond.

The killings continued. In Chicago, the going rate for murder for hire was $1,000 a head; if one succeeded only in wounding a victim, $350 would be paid by the rival tong. Shooting up someone's place of business fetched $50. The head of Chicago's dominant Moy clan was shot on

Christmas Day by two Hip Sings. Another Chicago Chinese was found slain on January 3, 1925. This was followed by an attack by assailants wielding sawed-off shotguns on two Chicago laundrymen while they were ironing.

In New York, it was open season on the Chin family. On December 14, 1924, forty-year-old Chin Song, a fruit vendor who belonged to neither tong, had his head blown off in his Mott Street room. Then, on January 4, 1925, Chin Hing, a Hip Sing restaurant worker, was gunned down by an On Leong, and three days later a Chinese dentist and Columbia graduate, thirty-five-year-old Dr. Wah S. Chan, was discovered in his Mott Street office, his jugular vein severed. Chan was not a tong man either, but all the victims were members of the Chin clan, which was not coincidental: so was Chin Jack Lem.

He finally went on trial on February 9 with the indispensable Wong Get as his interpreter. His defense was that he had not been in Cleveland when the alleged extortion took place, which was true. But he was found guilty and sentenced to fifteen years in the Ohio Penitentiary by a judge who called him "a thoroughly desperate character and a bad man." Chin Jack Lem was taken to the county jail and his bond increased to $25,000, pending an appeal. Unable to make bail this time, he was incarcerated in the Ohio Penitentiary at Columbus on February 23.

"The verdict means the end of warfare between the two tongs, which in the last six months has cost 41 lives," William P. Lee, secretary of the Chicago On Leongs, told the press. Like earlier predictions, it was overly optimistic. But the judgment—coupled with a brutal cleaver attack on a Hip Sing on Orchard Street on March 3 and the March 20 shooting death of an On Leong baker—did result in the convening of yet another peace parley, this one entirely Chinese-driven.

Nineteen members of the Chinese Consolidated Benevolent Association from different cities converged on New York to assist the Chinese consul, Ziang-Ling Chang, in mediation, and after two weeks of shuttle diplomacy an agreement "for lasting peace between the On Leongs and Hip Sings in all parts of the United States" was reached. It was signed on March 26, 1925, at Chinatown's City Hall by the heads of both tongs as twenty New

York policemen looked on and another hundred patrolled the streets, just in case.

Among the terms were pledges by the On Leongs not to bring further charges against Hip Sing men and not to provide additional witnesses against them in court proceedings. They also agreed to refrain from molesting their former brethren who had joined the other tong. For their part, the Hip Sings were enjoined from organizing in certain cities. The On Leongs had insisted on this because they did not wish to see their rivals make additional inroads into territory in which they had traditionally held sway.

After the signing, senior members of both tongs not seen in public for months because they were obvious targets emerged from their hiding places. Banquets were planned—each tong gave a dinner for the peacemakers— and peace did, indeed, break out.

For five months.

The 1925 agreement didn't end the conflict; there was still plenty more carnage ahead. What it *did* end was *declared* wars between the tongs. But relations would remain so tenuous and fragile that just about any incident could prove incendiary.

Trouble broke out again in late August 1925. This time it started in Boston, where an On Leong felt a Hip Sing had been too attentive to his wife. The two exchanged gunfire, and both were wounded. News of the shooting spread rapidly, although the personal nature of the quarrel wasn't part of the message. And shortly after word reached New York, an On Leong cook was felled by a vengeful Hip Sing in the basement of a Doyers Street chop suey joint. Homicides followed in Pittsburgh, Chicago, Baltimore, and Minneapolis, and Chinese elsewhere were nervous. Washington, D.C., police arrested forty-eight Chinese in a weekend raid and placed detectives in the capital's tiny Chinatown. At a Jersey City subway station, police nabbed three Chinese for carrying revolvers. And a Newark Hip Sing was so petrified by repeated, ominous thumping on his door that he bounded through a window, severely lacerating himself in the process.

The peace agreement had been held together only by what one newspaper called "gossamer threads," and while the Boston incident was the proximate cause of its violation, its demise was probably inevitable. The key point of dissatisfaction on the part of the Hip Sings was the territorial restriction. The two tongs were about even in number in New York and Chicago, but the On Leongs were particularly powerful in Cleveland, Pittsburgh, Baltimore, Philadelphia, Washington, St. Louis, and Boston, and they wished to preserve their prerogatives in those cities and in the East generally. Under the treaty, the Hip Sings were permitted to organize in additional locations in the West, but they chafed at being enjoined from expanding in eastern cities, especially Boston. They had, in fact, quietly begun to establish themselves there in violation of their pledge.

After the fighting resumed, Hip Sing and On Leong leaders in New York stoked the coals with telegrams warning their brethren around the country to be alert for enemies. In the vain hope of containing the nascent resumption of the war, police in several cities strengthened their presence in their respective Chinatowns. Within just a couple of days, more than a hundred Chinese were arrested in eight cities.

Because the agreement did not appear to be holding, the authorities turned up the heat. First, immigration officials in Washington announced that all Chinese incarcerated for tong shootings would be deported upon the expiration of their prison terms. Then Philadelphia police began rounding up all Chinese who could not produce registration certificates, which had been required of all alien Chinese in America since 1892. Seventy-five men were hauled into police headquarters, although all but fifteen were eventually released. And in New York, bluecoats and plainclothesmen flooded Chinatown; 150 reinforcements were sent in to augment the regular police presence, and patrolmen were stationed fifteen feet apart. A house-to-house search for weapons was also undertaken.

New York police attempted to bring the two sides together for another summit. Detectives fetched the tong leaders, who sat in separate rooms at police headquarters for four hours as two police captains ferried between them. Suspicion and enmity ran so deep, however, that they were unable to persuade the delegates even to sit in each other's presence, let alone to renew the shattered truce. In the end, they secured only a promise to meet the following day at the office of the district attorney. And even that was achieved only by threatening them with arrest for conspiracy.

The Chinese Consolidated Benevolent Association summoned Meihong Soohoo for the next day's discussions. Soohoo, founder of the Boston chapter of the On Leong Tong, was also its national president; his imprimatur would be necessary for a new treaty. District Attorney Joab H. Banton, a Tammany appointee, presided over the meeting, which also included Soohoo's Hip Sing counterpart and attorneys for both tongs. The one point on which both sides concurred at once was that the breach had come not as a result of a declaration of war but rather as the unfortunate consequence of a personal quarrel.

After two hours, agreement was secured to form a joint committee to fix responsibility for violation of the treaty. The two sides also came together on what Banton called "practically a truce" that was to last until Monday, August 31. That day, a smaller group reconvened and decided to scrap the earlier agreement and go back to the drawing board. Because there had been dissatisfaction with the terms of the March 26 accord, this seemed the only way forward. They pledged to cease hostilities until a new accord was drafted. And they issued a general call to tong branch leaders throughout the country to meet in New York with Chang Lee Kee, president of the Chinese Consolidated Benevolent Association, to ratify it.

Barely two days later, however, nineteen-year-old Sam Wing, who had arrived with several other On Leong gunmen a few days earlier, fatally shot Tom Wong, a Hip Sing, in his Brooklyn laundry. Revenge was swift; the following day, a fifty-year-old On Leong laundryman was killed in Manhattan by a Hip Sing who also wounded his two sons.

The district attorney would not comment publicly on these shootings. But he did reveal his intention to proceed speedily with the cases against the gunmen and his plan to call yet another conference. Wong Get, asked point-blank whether he considered the truce to have been broken, also declined to offer an opinion. But the On Leongs, who had borne the brunt of the recent killings, saw an opportunity to seize the high ground. The tong secretary issued a statement pointing out that since the renewal of hostilities five On Leongs had been slain, but the tong had attempted no reprisals. "We shall not do so," he announced, "unless driven to it in self-defense."

On September 8, with the police commissioner, Richard E. Enright, and the Chinese consul at his elbow, Banton assembled the parties for a "final ultimatum." He spoke for the five district attorneys of the city and intimated that he had the federal government behind him as well. "I am appealing to you for the sake of the reputation of the good Chinese in this country, whose rights are being jeopardized by the tong men," he said, quite accurately. "It is the duty of the leaders of the Chinese here to tell the contending tongs that they must live in peace in this country or get out of it."

Such appeals had proven futile in the past, however, and Washington was getting impatient. Federal officials had already vowed to begin deporting imprisoned tong men when their sentences were up. But with the obvious failure of the tongs, the consul, the Benevolent Association, and the police to stop the shooting, they were poised to up the ante.

The evening after Banton's "final ultimatum," two Hip Sings lay dead in New York. Exasperated, the police decided to make good on the threat to hold the tong chiefs accountable for further violence. Accordingly, Lee Gee Min, the national secretary of the On Leong Tong, and Henry Moy, the local secretary, were arrested and accused of complicity in one of the deaths. It was the first time tong leaders not on the scene had been held personally responsible for a murder.

At the arraignment, however, the gaping flaw in the strategy became clear. Counsel for the defense called the arrest "the most outrageous ever made in New York," because there was no evidence the men had had any involvement in the shooting or in planning for it. The magistrate agreed and discharged the tong officers.

New York police, who couldn't think of anything else to do, then returned to staging raids on Chinatown. They confiscated weapons and opium and made a few arrests of men carrying pistols. In one altercation, detectives exchanged fire with several men on a Mott Street rooftop. And the violence elsewhere continued: a Hip Sing was killed in New Kensington, Pennsylvania, and an On Leong severely beaten in Chicago.

With local authorities at their wit's end and the Chinese killings front-page news throughout the country, the federal government concluded it was time to step in. In a drastic measure, Emory R. Buckner, U.S. attorney for the Southern District of New York, declared his intention to deport every Chinese found who was unable to prove his eligibility to remain in the United States. On September 11, he warned the tong bosses that "every Chinaman we mark for deportation will go back to the Orient and all the funds and power you have, all the lawyers and pull you may think you have, will not stop us."

Under the terms of the 1902 Scott Act, which extended earlier Chinese exclusion legislation indefinitely, each alien Chinese residing in America was required to register with the U.S. government and receive a certificate to be carried on his or her person at all times. Because registration required applicants to prove they had entered the country legally, however, many Chinese could not qualify and therefore did not attempt to register.

Buckner threatened to use this fact to begin wholesale deportation of Chinese in order to suppress the tongs, although it was a blunt instrument that could not help but target multitudes of peaceful, non-tong members as well. He was not bluffing, however; nor was he acting alone. He had secured the cooperation of the U.S. commissioner general of immigration and four departments of the federal government. He had Washington, fed up with the machinations of the Chinese tongs, squarely behind him.

The raids began late on September 11 and extended into the wee hours. Federal agents acting under Buckner's orders rounded up Chinese who could not immediately produce residence permits and brought them in paddy wagons to Manhattan's Federal Building. After the first few dozen arrests, of course, word spread and the streets quickly emptied of people. Chinese fled to Newark, Jersey City, Hoboken, Long Island City, the Bronx, and elsewhere. A total of sixty-eight were caught, however, and were brought before officials and questioned individually through interpreters.

Six were able to prove they were legal residents, and another fourteen claimed they could do so if permitted to fetch their papers. Five others were turned over to the police for carrying weapons. Most of those remaining were Chinese seamen who had overstayed the sixty-day limit allowed for foreign sailors. They were placed under arrest, arraigned, and sent to Ellis Island, where they were held without bail to await deportation.

The federal government's heavy-handed intervention provided the impetus the tong leaders needed to come to terms. On September 14, at the Chinese consulate on Astor Place, the two tongs concluded a new peace compact. One sticking point, whether individuals would be permitted to defect from one tong to another, was resolved by a commitment to official notifications between tongs before transfers would be valid. The agreement was sealed at midnight and the news wired immediately to local tong headquarters across the country.

But the Feds didn't care. The raids continued. Local police placed a cordon around Chinatown, and federal agents descended on restaurants, gambling houses, joss houses, theaters, and tenements. If Chinese stayed off the streets, they would drag them from their beds. Everyone they found who looked Chinese was picked up; six hundred more were detained. The lights at the Federal Building burned through the night as each was examined by a federal officer.

In the end, 134 were found to be in violation of the Scott Act and taken to the Tombs to await expulsion. "The violators of the immigration laws are the trouble makers through whom the tongs have fought their recent wars," the *New York Post* declared, citing not a shred of evidence for this preposterous claim. The fact was, there was no shortage of legal residents among the tong men and no proof that it was men who were out of status who were the "trouble makers."

The following day, Buckner asserted that not even the signing of a new peace pact would stop additional federal raids. "If the Hip Sings and the On Leongs are going to get along without killing, well and good," he said, "but the immigration law is the immigration law . . . whether there is or is not a tong war in progress. Those found unlawfully here will be deported," he vowed.

Chinatown didn't stay subdued for long, because whatever the government was doing had no effect on the continued enmity between the tongs. On September 18, 1925, a thirty-year-old Hip Sing tailor was killed instantly as he emerged from his shop. His murderer, a thirty-two-year-old On Leong cook, had been hiding in a doorway on the border of Little Italy. He was grabbed by an Italian real estate agent who worked nearby. He struggled mightily, but the man restrained him as several bystanders who had witnessed the shooting yelled, "Lynch him!" Finally, a policeman arrived and pacified him with a sharp blow to the jaw. It had been an act of retaliation; several hours earlier, the man's cousin, an On Leong laundryman, had been shot, killed, and mutilated by three assassins in his laundry in a Pittsburgh suburb.

On the same day, the newspapers reported that the two tongs were continuing to negotiate because declaration of the new treaty had been premature. Although a document had apparently been signed, the Hip Sings now balked at revealing the names of their members who had deserted the On Leong Tong. As many as three hundred men would have been on such a list, and the Hip Sings had concluded that releasing it would violate their charter, which guaranteed secrecy. A meeting adjourned without resolving the issue.

Raids by federal agents and police continued unabated, and that evening, in addition to business establishments and tenements, the Hip Sing and On Leong buildings and even the Chinese Consolidated Benevolent Association were searched. At Hip Sing headquarters, someone hurled a hatchet at the officers, but it lodged in a door frame, narrowly missing them. Arsenals of revolvers, daggers, hatchets, and cleavers were seized in several locations. Patrol wagons carried 352 more Chinese to the Federal Building, the On Leong heads Henry Moy and Charlie Boston among them. Of that number, 72 were held for deportation. The 352 did not include 200 more who were able to produce their credentials on the spot. Assistant U.S. attorneys had actually conducted impromptu status hearings on the *sidewalks* of Chinatown.

Although there was no outright resistance, there was an unmistakable air of hostility on the part of the Chinese. Federal agents also faced protests by several angry white women whose husbands were among the detainees. Some were able to prove the men were legal or at least that they were their lawful spouses; several Chinese men secured release this way. Objections also came from the owners of Chinese restaurants and laundries and importers who saw a huge threat to their businesses in the possible wholesale loss of their workforce.

Detainees were held on the third floor of the Federal Building until the police could spare wagons to transport them to lockup. Some slept, others smoked, and while some seemed unperturbed, many wept. All the detainees were to be held for ten days to give them the opportunity to seek writs of habeas corpus, but federal officials predicted few would qualify. They pledged to continue the raids, the *New York Post* wrote, "until every undesirable Chinese in the city is in custody and started back to China."

On September 21, the Chinese consul, Ziang-Ling Chang, and the Chinese Consolidated Benevolent Association president, Chang Lee Kee, presided over the signing of an "eternal peace pact" at the Waldorf Astoria. Lee Gee Min signed for the On Leongs and Wong Get for the Hip Sings. Then the men shook hands—in American fashion—as a police captain looked on.

New York would now be quiet for a while, although altercations would continue in other cities. But only the naive took the "eternal" nature of the pact at face value.

In the 1890s, when the Hip Sings failed in their attempts to horn in on the On Leongs' lucrative shakedowns of Chinatown's gambling halls, Mock Duck, Wong Get, and their colleagues had cleverly conned the Parkhurst Society into carrying water for them. They had tried the same tactic in 1900–1901 with the Committee of Fifteen. Appealing to the white establishment had worked brilliantly in the past, and given the new peace agreement and the government's crackdown, returning to the old strategy seemed worth a try. This time, however, there would be a new twist: they would try to get the federal government—which, by the latest count, had slated 264 New York Chinese for deportation—to go after the On Leongs, and the On Leongs alone.

The U.S. attorney's office had been working hand in glove with federal labor, narcotics, and immigration officials in a coordinated effort to eliminate New York's undocumented Chinese population. The Hip Sings, however, decided to appeal to a different department: the Federal Trade Commission. The imaginative strategy they hatched was to accuse the On Leong Tong of unfair competition.

On September 24, 1925, two enterprising attorneys for the national Hip Sing Tong appeared before the commission and charged the On Leong

Tong with specific acts of conspiracy, intimidation, and violence in interstate and foreign commerce against nine Hip Sing importers and retail merchants in New York, Philadelphia, Pittsburgh, Cleveland, Chicago, Boston, and Seattle. According to the Hip Sings, the On Leongs had raised $1.5 million to force them out of business.

The action took not only the On Leongs but even the Hip Sings' New York chapter by surprise. The latter's attorney, Charles W. Gould, asserted that none of the local tong members had been informed of the action and even speculated that "some smart lawyer has invented a new way of earning a fee."

The On Leongs' attorney pointed out the absurdity of the charges. "It's preposterous and unthinkable that the Hip Sing group should bring the Federal Trade Commission into this," he held. "Our group is strictly a fraternal, social organization. The On Leong members, though they are all merchants, are not banded together for business purposes and they do not, as a group, carry on an interstate business. They are incorporated under the laws of New York as a social club."

The claim, while creative, was clearly without merit, and the commission declined to pursue an investigation.

Police joined two hundred tong men at the inevitable peace banquet on October 14, 1925. In general, however, Chinatown took news of the latest treaty with a grain of salt. Most saw it as a signal not that war was over but that there would be at least some respite from the bullets.

Though there was quiet, it was punctuated by occasional jitters, and by early 1927 peace was again a memory. The first blood was shed in Brooklyn, when two kitchen workers, one of whom was a Hip Sing, were gunned down at King's Tea Room on March 24. Then the horror spread quickly. Before the end of the day, killings were recorded in Newark, Chicago, and Manchester, Connecticut, and shootings in Pittsburgh and Cleveland.

Some two hundred Hip Sings who had gone to Newark the night before to smoke and gamble found themselves stranded after the trouble broke out. It was a Boston Hip Sing who had been killed there, shot twenty-nine times. After that, the rest were terrified to show their faces. New York Hip Sing leaders had to hire a private detective to organize a fleet of automobiles to ferry the frightened men back to Manhattan in safety.

The first question on everyone's mind was whether the outbreak had anything to do with what was going on in China. The newspapers were full of headlines about the military arm of the nationalist Guomindang Party, then in the process of capturing the city of Nanjing. Soldiers and civilians had looted the homes and businesses of alien residents, and several foreigners, including one American, had been killed on the very day the shooting began in America. But there was no evidence to link events on the two continents.

In Chicago, where two more men were assassinated the next day, Frank Moy, the local On Leong head, gave his own analysis of the situation: "The On Leongs are the wealthy organization. . . . The Hip Sings . . . are made up largely of small merchants, laundrymen and waiters, at whose head are a group of men little removed from blackmailers. Although the On Leongs are numerically stronger, because of their holdings and business interests, they will not go to the lengths the Hip Sings will. Hence they have often been forced to purchase peace." He went on to reveal that the previous war had ended only when the On Leongs paid the Hip Sings somewhere between $250,000 and $500,000 in gold. "Now that the Hip Sings have spent this money, they have adjourned the truce and the guns have started to blaze."

Back in New York, an exasperated District Attorney Banton warned that he would send tong men "back to China by the shipload" if the killing didn't stop. Late on March 25, 1927, after more Chinese lost their lives in Washington and Cambridge, Massachusetts, the chieftains of both tongs, who continued to deny that war had been declared, signed a letter affirming that the 1925 truce was still in effect and urging all tong men to respect it. And for his part, Banton stated that he believed the tong leaders innocent of responsibility for the outbreak.

No doubt they were. It came out later that one of the Brooklyn restaurant workers who were the first to die was a cousin of Chin Jack Lem, who was so radioactive a figure that it had simply been *assumed* that the killing of his kinsman had been tong related. The man had actually been murdered for other reasons, and the On Leongs had had nothing to do with it. But the peace was so fragile that many lives were lost as a result of the misunderstanding.

Tranquillity more or less reigned for the next year and a half, though enmity from the defections festered and the atmosphere remained uneasy. The New York columnist O. O. McIntyre noted of Chinatown that "even the children play with a listless half-heartedness in the gutters." Nobody felt that the last shoe had dropped.

Suddenly, on the evening of October 14, 1928, six men were murdered in Chicago, Philadelphia, New York, and Washington. Several others were wounded. A few days later, a fifty-three-year-old Hip Sing was shot in his Eighth Avenue laundry. Because this outbreak, like the last one, had not been authorized by either tong, it was relatively easily adjudicated. Dr. Samuel Sung Young, the new Chinese consul in New York, issued a statement that the violence had stemmed from a personal feud. The document urged Chinese in America "not to be swayed by alarming rumors" and promised that "peaceful pursuit of everyone's business will be continued as before."

Peaceful pursuits did continue for another nine months. It wasn't until early August 1929 that more murders occurred, first in Chicago, Newark, and Boston and then in New York. The same day, the U.S. attorney Charles H. Tuttle had the police round up the rival tong leaders and, in the presence of Dr. Young, took a page from his predecessor's book and warned that if shooting continued, federal agents would raid Chinatown, including the headquarters of the tongs, and deport every Chinese unable to produce credentials. The tong leaders protested once again that the conflicts were unauthorized and that no war had been declared.

But less than two hours after Tuttle's warning, another New York Chinese was assassinated, and two Hip Sing deaths were reported in Boston. The authorities were now plainly worried. It appeared as if the kingpins themselves had lost control of the situation and were *unable* to rein in the shooters. To stave off more police roundups of undocumented Chinese, the leaders agreed on a truce until 10:00 that evening, at which time they sat down to negotiate a peace pact. Most of Chinatown had closed down any-way, because few Chinese dared venture onto the streets for fear of a police dragnet. By the following morning, thanks to arbitration by Consul Young, an accord was struck, and tong leaders signed it in Tuttle's presence.

The accompanying announcement blamed the troubles on "misunder-standings" and ordered all tong branches to abstain from violence. The ac-tual pact contained much language borrowed from previous agreements but differed from them all in one fundamental way: it committed the tongs to binding arbitration by the Chinese consul general in any future conflict.

Initially, it was unclear whether this was a true armistice. It was by no means certain every branch, or every tong member, would feel bound by the new accord. In Chicago, a Hip Sing was critically wounded by an On Leong well after negotiations were under way. A knife battle took place in Newark soon after. And in Boston, the locals defied both the police and their leaders and refused to affirm a cease-fire at all, although there was no immediate renewal of conflict.

In the end, the truce held. For a while. With the onset of the Depression, the Chinese, like everybody else, had other things on their minds. But the antagonism between the tongs had not abated, and in no way was the Fourth Tong War over.

Chapter 15

✺

Coexistence

The Great Depression delivered a body blow to America's Chinese community, and New York's Chinese were no exception. It wasn't the October 1929 stock market crash per se that did it; few Chinese had invested in equities. But the businesses they ran and worked in were ultimately dependent on those who had. Before long, customers stopped coming, and by one estimate more than 150 Chinese restaurants, in and out of Chinatown, were forced to close in 1930 alone. By the next year, as many as 25 percent of all the Chinese in America were jobless, and by the middle of 1932 fully four thousand of those in New York had lost their livelihoods.

Many were hungry, but even so, more than one observer remarked that Chinese did not patronize the soup kitchens organized by white charities, even when these facilities were established in Chinatown. The *Christian Science Monitor* noted admiringly that although an uptown emergency relief organization had opened a station on Doyers Street, only white and black people from the Bowery had appeared in line—not a single Chinese. And a Pell Street kitchen set up to service the Chinese community closed after less than a week for want of patrons.

Local Chinese looked instead to their mutual aid organizations—which included not only the family circles and the regional associations but also the tongs—for aid, which in some cases meant food and shelter. The tongs began to feel the strain. This was no time for battle. "The warring tongs," the Presbyterian reverend I. S. Caldwell wrote in 1932, "ceased their rivalry and devoted themselves to the common tasks of mercy." This was an overstatement, however; although there was cooperation and temporary quiet, in no way had rivalry truly ended.

Charlie Boston didn't have to worry about the Depression; 1930 brought the death of the On Leong Tong's last remaining éminence grise. A member since the 1890s, he had assumed leadership of the New York branch—and some said the honorific of "mayor of Chinatown"—following Tom Lee's death in 1918 but had recently been in ill health. The body of the rotund boss lay in state for a week in a handsome bronze casket to give relatives and friends time to arrive for the funeral. Chinatown wondered what sort of send-off Boston would be given—Christian or traditional Chinese. And his son ruminated about whether to send his body back to China, speculating that because Boston had become so acculturated, "perhaps he would prefer to stay in America."

In the end, the affair, underwritten in part by his family and in part by the On Leong Tong, was a Presbyterian rite with some Chinese touches. Local Chinese organizations and On Leong branches from around the country were represented, although there was no mention of the Hip Sings, who had hated him. After the service, a cortege of more than a hundred cars, led by marchers carrying his portrait and innumerable floral wreaths, made its way to Brooklyn in the drizzling rain. There Boston was interred at Cypress Hills Cemetery, his grave piled high with offerings of chicken, rice cakes, and wine, as firecrackers were set off to ward off evil spirits.

Even before Boston's passing, however, a generational shift in the leadership of the tongs had occurred. Tom Lee and Gin Gum were gone. The Hip Sings, too, had seen a changing of the guard. Wong Get had returned to China in 1927, and Mock Duck was nowhere to be seen.

Both tongs marched peacefully in the 1930 Chinese New Year parade, but any altercation in just about any Chinatown in which there were branches of both tongs threatened to bring them back at each other's throats, and it wasn't always easy to distinguish personal grudge killings from tong hits. Two Chinese were arrested for the murder of a Hip Sing in mid-February; the On Leongs denied responsibility. In early June, a Hip Sing warrior was gunned down in his fourth-floor room on Allen Street. The next day, Cheong Fook was fatally slashed in the abdomen with a bread knife in front of 104 Hester Street by twenty-one-year-old Tei Get, and forty-three-year-old Lui Sing, shot five times, was found dead in the rear of his Brooklyn laundry.

The newly appointed police commissioner, Edward P. Mulrooney, a thirty-four-year veteran who had most recently headed the detective division, wasn't sure what was causing the killings or even if the tongs were responsible for them. He called on New York County's new district attorney, none other than Thomas C. T. Crain, who had been the judge in the murder case against the executed Hip Sings, Eng Hing and Lee Dock. The two men decided to summon the heads of the tongs the next morning in what was becoming an all-too-familiar ritual. The Chinese consul also paid a predictable visit to U.S. Attorney Tuttle to discuss yet another peace conference.

Mulrooney, who had picked up pidgin Cantonese during his years as a lieutenant in the Sixth Precinct, was wise in the ways of the tongs. After the meeting, he was frank with the press. "Whatever caused this outbreak," he declared, "we are treating it as a tong war. These things are like fires. Unless they are checked at once they are apt to spread. We hope to get a peace agreement between the heads of On Leong Tong and Hip Sing Tong. Evidently On Leong is on the defensive with Hip Sing taking the provocative attitude. We don't know yet what the grievance is: gambling propensities and high play, desertion of one tong for another and betrayal of secrets, blackmail and, nowadays, a little racketeering, white man style."

But the situation was more complex than it appeared. Cheong Fook turned out to be a member of the Tung On Society, an organization with roots in China made up primarily of sailors. And it appeared that his alleged slayer, Tei Get, was a member of the same group. Eddie Gong—the national Hip Sing secretary who had just authored a tell-all book on the tong wars—told police it had been a private dispute. But it appeared that the Tung On Society had become a new player in the complex and seemingly perpetual fight.

A treaty was signed on June 7, copies of which were posted in Chinatown and telegraphed to other cities. But the ink was scarcely dry when a report came of the murder of Charles Wong, twenty-five, in his Harlem laundry. Wong had left the Hip Sings two weeks earlier and joined the On Leong Tong; his killing was likely a result of his defection, which was as intolerable on the local level as it was on the national level with Chin Jack Lem.

Tong leaders disavowed the violence, but it now appeared as if they had truly lost control. In previous times, they had had the ability to sign agreements and calm things down, even if things didn't stay calm. Now even this authority was in doubt. When news came of the killing of a Hip Sing in Minneapolis and alleged orders by branches in Pittsburgh and Chicago to renew warfare, New York Hip Sing leaders warned their members that the treaty did not seem to be holding and that they should therefore again be on their guard against On Leongs.

Once again the kingpins were hauled back to a parley—this time by the Chinese consul—and after two hours they succumbed to pressure and signed yet *another* accord to supersede the previous one. It bore the same date and included this text, translated for the press by Consul Young:

> The On Leong Merchants Association and the Hip Sing Association have on account of misunderstandings broken peaceful relations. Now, as the result of the mediation of Consul-General Young and the directors of the Chinese Consolidated Benevolent Association, they have settled their differences and resumed peace. This is to notify all Chinese citizens that their minds may be relieved and that they may continue the pursuits of their various occupations. Signed and sealed this seventh day of June, 1930.

The new agreement was referred to as the Kellogg Peace Pact—a jocular reference to the Kellogg-Briand Pact, an international agreement sponsored by France and the United States concluded two years earlier in which signatory states renounced the use of war as an instrument of national policy.

In July, Chinese were slaughtering one another again. A Chinese theater was once again a killing field; this one was located on the Bowery. In the middle of a play on July 9, five shots were fired from the rear of the house. The hall quickly emptied, and when police arrived, they found the body of Chang Wah Hung in one of the seats.

But this time there was a change in the cast of characters. Chang was neither a Hip Sing nor an On Leong. He was president of the Tung On Society—the same group to which both Tei Get and his recent victim, Cheong Fook, belonged. The man suspected of his murder, however, *was* an On Leong. In retaliation, two On Leongs were killed on Mott Street by Tung Ons, and bullets were fired into the windows of On Leong Tong headquarters. The following night, nine bombs containing enough nitroglycerine to blow up an entire city block were found in a rooming house in a Chinese neighborhood in Brooklyn.

The cause of the trouble was an opium deal gone bad. The Tung Ons had failed to deliver $140,000 worth of the drug promised to the On Leongs. Four Tung Ons were later arrested in New York for offering young men a $500 bounty for each On Leong corpse they could produce.

But this was not to say all was well between the Hip Sings and their traditional rival. More shootings followed, and although no one was killed, Eddie Gong told police he believed the On Leongs were out to murder as many Hip Sings as they could. Once again, Commissioner Mulrooney and District Attorney Crain delivered an ultimatum. Mulrooney summoned a dozen leaders from the On Leongs, the Hip Sings, the Tung Ons, and several other groups and assembled them in his office on August 18. He told them he would recognize no further treaties and oversee no further mediation efforts. He would, however, ask federal authorities to begin mass deportations in a week's time if the trouble didn't stop.

But there *was* another treaty, negotiated under orders from the Chinese minister in Washington and slated to be signed on August 19. This pact was to have six signatories—On Leongs, Hip Sings, Tung Ons, and three smaller organizations. It stated explicitly that in the event of a violation, the signatories would cooperate with police to punish the offender. But it took until September 2 to be ratified. The sticking point had been a demand that each group put up $50,000 in "earnest money" to be forfeited to charity in the event of a violation. It was ultimately dropped because the smaller organizations could not afford it.

The final twenty-article agreement, placed in U.S. Attorney Charles H. Tuttle's safe, contained a provision appointing a committee of representatives of all the signatories, chaired by the Chinese consul, to settle disagreements. In the event they became deadlocked, the police commissioner, Mulrooney, would cast the deciding vote.

The New York *Sun* was perhaps to be forgiven for its skepticism: "In spite of the fact that assassination has invariably followed other such treaty-makings, either very soon afterward or within no great period of time, the white peacemakers appeared to think they had solved the problem, just as General Sessions Judge Warren W. Foster thought he had solved it well nigh twenty years ago. No such opinion is current throughout Chinatown, however, among men who know the tongs and their ways."

But a year of quiet followed. Even before the stock market crashed, Manhattan's Chinatown had slowly been morphing into a center for legitimate business and tourism, vice having, in the main, moved out. "Sightseeing buses dump their customers for a roam through three or four streets and then the tourists go back home to tell what a wicked place they saw," the New York *Sun* wrote in 1931. "But there is little really bad in the Chinatown of New York today." Whether because gambling was mostly gone or because the Great Depression had taken its toll, the *Sun* now found the Mott Street area "quiet as a side street in Brooklyn."

New York's Chinese population now numbered about eighty-four hundred. Most of those not unemployed were running or working in restaurants, laundries, and other businesses elsewhere in Manhattan or the other boroughs. Chinatown, however, remained the focal point of the community. Most Chinese organizations kept their headquarters there, including the On Leongs at 41 Mott and the Hip Sings at 13 Pell. And in 1931, both decided to hold their national conventions there.

In fact, they held their caucuses at precisely the same time. The Hip Sings deliberately changed the date of their fourteenth annual national meeting, which was to have been held earlier, to coincide with the twenty-seventh gathering of the On Leongs on April 27. It was a provocative act. Never before had both tongs met in the same city at the same time, and the police braced for trouble as several thousand Chinese of both stripes from dozens of cities descended on lower Manhattan. The *Brooklyn Daily Eagle* noted ominously that the tongs would be meeting "a knife's throw from each other."

The convocations, used to plan programs, discuss problems, and elect officers, generally lasted for a few weeks. That year both tongs would deliberate above all else not on how to annihilate each other but on the

The Hip Sing Tong and the On Leong Tong both held conventions in New York City in 1931. This April 27, 1931, photograph shows the Hip Sings on parade down Pell Street, considered Hip Sing territory. An On Leong banner, partially obscured but visible in the background, was seen by the Hip Sings as a deliberate provocation.

grim question of how to provide relief for those of their brethren who had lost their livelihoods in the Great Depression.

Tens of thousands of red, white, blue, green, and yellow electric bulbs were strung across Pell, Mott, and Doyers streets, and innumerable Chinese and American flags and buntings hung from balconies and were draped around window frames. Looking up, one saw buildings festooned with colorful banners welcoming delegates; looking down, one could not help but notice dozens of policemen, revolvers at the hip, intent on preventing them from slaughtering one another.

The first issue that arose was whether the Hip Sing parade, with its thousand banner-wielding tong men and dragon dancers, would be permitted to pass in front of On Leong headquarters. There was a long delay as the marshals discussed with police whether it would be too confrontational an act, but in the end the procession did pass 41 Mott, and while they encountered no cheering crowds there—indeed, one newspaper noted a "distinct and sinister feeling of antipathy"—there was also no foul play.

The On Leongs, however, had hung a banner across Pell Street, traditionally Hip Sing territory, a predictably incendiary move, and the Hip Sings sent a note to the On Leongs asking that it be removed. The plea was ignored, of course, because its very purpose had been to tweak the Hip Sings' noses. A Hip Sing vice president approached a police officer to complain about it, but the On Leongs had trumped them: they had secured a permit for the banner.

Both tongs held banquets on the evening of April 27, and many of their members attended a performance afterward at the Chinese Theatre on the Bowery. Somewhere between eight and nine hundred people, including about fifty women and a hundred children, were there. Police did arrest three men for carrying loaded revolvers under their overcoats, but otherwise there was no trouble. The quadrupled police guard in Chinatown might have had something to do with it. The New York *Sun* described the scene at the theater:

> . . . eight gigantic cops whose shoulders loomed over the heads of the tallest Chinese in the theater. Their nightsticks, significantly battered and scarred, zipped and zuttered as they twirled them. They lounged in the tiny lobby and every tongman who entered passed under the cold blue eye of a policeman big enough to pick him up and snap him in two. Another cop strolled the sidewalk in front of the theater. Three or four haunted the dark corners in the alley back of the long, narrow building. . . . There were cops back stage, outside front and back and in the lobby, and half a dozen cold-eyed detectives gave the impression of being everywhere.

The reality was that the tongs were in no mood, and no position, for violent confrontation. They had serious issues to resolve and were truthful when they assured authorities they had no plans to attack each other. With a quarter of the Chinese in America unemployed, both tongs were focused on how to provide food and shelter for these unfortunates and how to go about settling their debts. Delivering calculated insults like the Hip Sing parade on Mott Street and the On Leong banner on Pell was as far as anybody was prepared to go.

At 9:30 p.m. on February 28, 1932, a Chinese man was shot through the fleshy part of his neck as he stepped out the door of 64 Mulberry Street in Newark. The bullet had come from a shooter in a passing automobile. Had it deviated from its course, the victim would surely have died. His assailant, another Chinese, fled the scene.

The man was taken to Newark City Hospital for treatment of his wound, which turned out to be superficial, and then to police headquarters for questioning. He spoke English well. He gave his name to the police as Mock Sai Wing and would say no more, although he did allow that it was a Hip Sing who had shot him and that he had done so over a gambling debt.

The police detectives thought they recognized him, however. Although he wouldn't admit it, they were pretty certain he was Mock Duck, the legendary scourge of New York's Chinatown from the previous generation who had dropped out of view after his release from Sing Sing nearly twenty years earlier.

There had actually been a few sightings of Mock Duck in the interim. He and his wife had attended the funeral of Gin Gum, his stepfather-in-law, in 1915, and he was said a few years later to be running a small business on Pell Street. He had been named in a Pittsburgh newspaper in 1928 as a mediator between warring factions within the local Hip Sing chapter. And it had been he who had signed the letter to the On Leongs asking them to remove their banner from Pell Street the previous year. Mock Duck had otherwise played no public role in years, however, and many thought he had died.

But Mock Duck hadn't died, and Mock Sai Wing was just playing with the police. Sai Wing was his formal name; the two were one and the same.

The police made an attempt to arrest the shooter, but they were less concerned about finding him than they were that the reemergence of Mock Duck—and especially a wounded Mock Duck with a new grievance—might spell wider trouble. But in fact this was hardly a "reemergence." Mock Duck might have been keeping a low profile, but the police soon discovered he had been quietly calling the shots as national president of the Hip Sing Tong since 1929. From a hideaway in Coney Island, he had dictated the tong's nationwide strategy in the most recent war. Now that they knew he was back in charge, police feared that the longtime Hip Sing warrior might have more mischief up his sleeve.

Amity—or at least quiet—prevailed for the balance of 1932 as problems far larger than control of Pell and Mott streets loomed. Many Chinese were finding it impossible to make a living in a depressed America and needed help. And all eyes were on China, which Japan had invaded late the previous year. In the face of war and civil unrest in their ancestral homeland, the tong men were first and foremost patriotic Chinese, concerned about the future of their native land and the family members they had left behind.

The greatest contribution Chinese in America could make to the cause was to dig into their pockets, and despite the bad economic times the tongs did their share. Funds over and above those needed for basic activities and salaries were divided between assistance to needy countrymen in America and relief for areas of China laid waste by Japanese forces.

Putting aside their differences, the two tongs had even joined together to participate in the new Patriotic League of Chinese. Money was collected by Eddie Gong of the Hip Sings, who met regularly with the On Leong brass, an arrangement unthinkable in earlier times. By mid-March, New York's Chinese had already raised $1 million, and similar efforts were taking place elsewhere. "There are no tongs as far as we are concerned now," Gong declared expansively. "We are all Chinese who feel that we must support our country."

Even the Chinese New Year celebration of January 1933 was amicable. Although the tongs did not join in a single ceremony, they actually paid their respects to each other, after a fashion. Both sponsored dragon dances; these were typically used to raise funds for charitable efforts. Houses along

A 1933 photograph of Eng Ying "Eddie" Gong (fourth from left), national secretary of the Hip Sing Tong, posing with fellow tong members. A portrait of Dr. Sun Yat-sen is visible on the wall at right.

the parade routes hung red envelopes filled with cash outside for the drag-ons to collect. But this year, the Hip Sing dragon also danced up Mott Street, and the On Leong beast ventured onto Pell. It even bowed three times in front of Hip Sing headquarters in an unmistakable gesture of respect.

When, on July 21, a Hip Sing man was shot and killed in a Boston opium den, the local branch handled the death with restraint. It appealed to New York, where tong elders asked a mediator, George Chintong, English secretary of the Benevolent Association, to determine whether the assailant had been an On Leong. Chintong declared his expectation that peace would be maintained until the investigation was concluded, but he was wrong in predicting forbearance.

News came from Pittsburgh on July 23 of the assassination of a Chinese there. And then, shortly after midnight on July 29, despite an augmented police presence in Chinatown, forty-year-old Wing Gin, an On Leong carpenter, was shot seven times as he mounted the stairway of a tenement at 15–17 Doyers Street. Wing died soon after reaching the hospital. Police nabbed forty-six-year-old Lee Bow as he fled the scene. Lee denied being a member of any tong, but the police were pretty certain he was a Hip Sing.

Later that day, Sing Kee, the local On Leong secretary and decorated World War I veteran, appeared at the police station. "There is trouble in Chinatown," he said flatly. Asked to elaborate, he replied, simply, "Use your own imagination." But the situation didn't require imagination. The drill was all too familiar. The police stationed every available man—thirty detectives and fifty-one bluecoats—in Chinatown. And they notified the U.S. attorney George Z. Medalie, whose predecessors had ordered the rounding up and deportation of illegal immigrants, to brace himself for a renewal of Tong warfare.

Just as the earthly remains of Wing Gin were making their way to Brooklyn's Evergreens Cemetery, Medalie, in what had become a grindingly familiar ritual, asked the police to bring the leaders of the two tongs to his office for a talk. Mindful of the fact that the efforts of his predecessors to give civics lessons to men barred from citizenship had proven quite useless, however, he had a different tack in mind. When Sing Kee and George Howe, secretary of the Hip Sings, appeared at the Federal Building late in the afternoon of July 31, 1933, they were told that although they were not personally under suspicion, they might possess information that could be helpful in stopping the problem. Each was then served with a subpoena to appear before a federal grand jury.

The ostensible purpose of the grand jury inquiry, which began the next day, was to determine whether the recent killings were connected with violations of the immigration or narcotics laws, both areas under federal jurisdiction. Howe, in response to a subpoena, had brought along membership records and other official documents related to the Hip Sing Tong, and the On Leongs were instructed to produce similar papers the following day.

There is no record of any action by the grand jury, but on August 17 the predictable truce was declared, even though both tong men insisted there was not, and had never been, a war. Koliang Yih, the new Chinese consul general, announced the accord, which was brief and to the point. In translation, it read,

AGREEMENT.
On Leong Tong and Hip Sing Tong.

Aug. 16, 1933.

We the authorized representatives of the above named tongs do hereby and unqualifiedly pledge our respective tongs to maintain peace and quiet and to engage in no acts of lawlessness from this day on.

We solemnly agree that the settlement of any disputes of whatever nature or of whatever origin which may arise between us shall be submitted to the Chinese Consul General, the Chinese Benevolent Association and the local authorities for arbitration.

(SIGNED FOR THE HIP SING TONG)
Eddie Gong
George Howe
(SIGNED FOR THE ON LEONG TONG)
Howard Lee
Sing Kee

In describing the pact, the consul general maintained that the tongs were burying the hatchet "to hasten the prosperity of recovery." It wasn't true, but it made for a good sound bite. The police had a different view that was less patriotic. They believed the pressure brought to bear by the federal government by hauling the leaders before a grand jury and examining their records—even though no indictments followed—had prompted the accord. "This was many degrees more unwelcome to the tongs than the simple deportation proceedings that had imposed law and order in the past," the *New York Times* observed.

Leong Gor Yun, in his 1936 book, *Chinatown Inside Out,* had an even simpler take on the truce that might have been closest to the truth. The conflict was short-lived, he wrote, "because the Hip Sing was short of funds, and the On Leong short of hatchet men. Both tongs consequently were eager to make concessions."

❖   ❖   ❖   ❖   ❖

Despite all the odds, this round turned out *not* to be just another chapter in the unending cycle of conflict, punctuated by peace agreements of varying and uncertain duration. It marked the end of the Fourth Tong War. Wing Gin would be the *last* victim of New York's celebrated tong wars. But it was far more than enhanced federal scrutiny of their archives or the sanctity of the perfunctory, two-paragraph accord their leaders signed that finally accomplished what armies of policemen, prosecutors, judges, and diplomats working assiduously for decades had utterly failed to do: cause the tongs to lay their guns down and put their decades-long conflict behind them.

Anyone who was keeping score might have noted that with the possible exception of the On Leong–Tung On conflict over a drug deal gone bad in 1930, there actually had not been a single *declared* tong war for nearly a decade, when Chin Jack Lem set off the On Leongs with his decision to seek Hip Sing membership. To be sure, there had been plenty of killing since then, but most of the time the impetus had been a personal quarrel, or at least nothing demonstrably tong-driven, even though the tongs usually got drawn in. Longtime resentments and hostilities had made Chinatowns tinderboxes that ignited far too easily when Chinese men clashed over vice, court testimony, turf, or "face," but in no case since the mid-1920s had tong leaders actually made an affirmative decision to do battle.

Then, too, the Chinatown of the 1930s was a dramatically different place from that of the 1880s, when Tom Lee came, or the 1890s and the first decade of the twentieth century, when the problems had begun. Back then, the lion's share of New York's Chinese ate, slept, worked, and played in the tiny triangle formed by Mott and Pell streets and the Bowery. Those who did not usually visited the area in the course of a typical week to purchase foodstuffs or supplies for their laundries, to relieve the drudgery of the workweek with opium or female companionship, or to gamble away a week's earnings.

Although America's overall Chinese population diminished in the decades following the 1882 Chinese Exclusion Act, the number of Chinese inhabitants in the East generally grew during this period. New York City's Chinese population dipped slightly in the first decade of the twentieth century, but it rebounded, reaching just over five thousand in 1920, eighty-four hundred by 1930, and more than ten thousand by 1933. Some of this was due to relocation from the West. Some was the result of the natural growth of families, because more Chinese were marrying and having children in America. And some was caused by undocumented Chinese smuggled in via Canada, Mexico, Cuba, and elsewhere—some of the same people the federal government sought to deport in the mid-1920s as a means of suppressing the wars.

Only a minority of the eighty-four hundred Chinese counted in New York City in the 1930 census actually lived in the Chinese enclave; most resided elsewhere, and that didn't count those in upstate towns or across the river in New Jersey. Even those in the city proper had spread out; Chinese restaurants, more and more dependent on non-Chinese patrons, had followed their customers to the neighborhoods in which they lived and worked, where competition was not as fierce as in Chinatown. As early as the late teens, more than half of New York's Chinese restaurants were located outside the quarter.

So, too, had Chinese laundries sprung up throughout the five boroughs. It was convenient to live near work—or even *at* work, because Chinese laundrymen worked late and generally bunked in the rear of their establishments. This meant Chinatown was no longer the pressure cooker it had once been. Although it was still the nerve center of the Chinese community, most Chinese spent far less time there than had once been the case. Nor was Chinatown the vice mecca it had been. *Fan tan* and opium smoking still went on, but the constant police raids had had a profound effect. Most of the action had moved across the Hudson and had not returned, and in any event there was a lot less disposable income available for wagering.

Another cause was the decline of Tammany Hall. Franklin Delano Roosevelt, who had tolerated Tammany during his term as governor of New York, took action to strip the machine of political power after he became president in 1933. That same year, Fiorello La Guardia was elected mayor on an anticorruption and antiracketeering platform, and he, too, endeavored to weaken Tammany's grip on New York politics. The organization did not disappear, but it never regained the vigor it had possessed in earlier days, and it ceased to be a potent player in regulating whatever vice remained in Chinatown.

Yet another factor was the changing nature of the Chinese population. By 1930, fully 41 percent of America's Chinese were born in the United States. This, of course, was mostly a function of the exclusion laws, which had imposed draconian limits on immigration, but one of its effects, intended or not, was acculturation. More and more Chinese were growing up outside Chinatown and going to American schools. They spoke English natively and had far more contact with non-Chinese than earlier generations. Despite continued prejudice, Chinese were becoming more American as each year passed, more apt to marry in America and to lead more normal family lives than earlier immigrants. They were consequently less subject to traditional Chinatown rivalries and less likely to see a need to join tongs.

The Depression also made its mark. During prosperous times, the tongs had been able to collect as much as $500 in a day just from tribute paid by gambling halls, but this revenue had diminished drastically by the 1930s. Although the On Leong Tong, which represented the merchants, was always in a stronger financial position than the Hip Sing Tong, both experienced extraordinary economic pressure. The On Leong Tong even filed a petition with the New York State Supreme Court in 1931 to mortgage its decade-old headquarters building at 41 Mott Street for $45,000 to raise funds to help its needy members, many of whom struggled to afford even their membership dues.

Then there were China's needs. Most of the Chinese in America—unwelcome to naturalize in their adopted country—considered themselves patriotic citizens of the Chinese Republic. And they were infuriated at the incursions Japan was making in their homeland. Reports of Japanese terror bombings provided strong incentive to support their embattled countrymen, and Chinatowns throughout North America pulled together to do what they could. Working together against a common enemy, the tongs began to see their differences as of decidedly secondary importance.

Tong wars were expensive propositions. Weapons had to be purchased in quantity, and guns, explosives, and tear gas were far more costly than hatchets and cleavers had been. Gunmen had to be recruited and paid, and their escape—or their legal defense, should they be apprehended—had to be underwritten. For these reasons, even though they frequently found themselves fighting, neither tong had shown much appetite for full-blown war for more than a decade.

The Hip Sings had long since established themselves in former On Leong territory, and the tong wars had become less about tangibles and more about an eye for an eye. The high cost of saving face, however, was measured in the killing and the maiming not only of tong soldiers but also of innocents, and over time it had a terrible effect on the Chinese population at large. It took a horrible toll on the local economy when tourists and frightened Chinese stayed away in droves.

Then, too, the titans who had declared and directed the early wars had mostly faded into history. Although Mock Duck, after a long period in eclipse, once again held sway at the Hip Sing Tong, he lacked the vigor of his youth and had been remarkably quiet. Wong Get had gone home to China, and other warriors like Tom Lee, Gin Gum, Charlie Boston, and James Wang had passed from the scene. The men whose word had been law within their tongs were gone, and the generation that followed lacked the stature and the power to see that their will was always carried out, especially by the far-flung branches of their tongs. They also had other, more pressing matters on their minds than a dance of death with the rival tong.

In the run-up to World War II, labor and political movements would take center stage in Chinatown. New, left-wing organizations, like the Chinese Hand Laundry Alliance, formed in 1933 to oppose a new city law aimed at driving Chinese out of the laundry business, and the Anti-imperialist Alliance, which opposed Japanese incursion into Chinese territory and Chiang Kai-shek's anemic response to it, would become major forces that occupied people's time and attention.

The tongs wouldn't cease to exist, nor even entirely change their ways, but they would turn a corner. In 1936, Leong Gor Yun tentatively noted a transformation that, he believed, looked "salutary for their future." He wrote,

> With the sharp decrease in their income, fighting has almost ceased, and most of their professional fighters have been forced to take up a

trade. Public opinion, too, has had its part in bringing the tongs to their senses. They have gradually disarmed, and have participated in patriotic movements to help China in her fight against Japan. . . . The reformation of the Tongs does not seem entirely hopeless, though it is too early to predict their future.

In fact, it wasn't hopeless at all. The tongs would persevere, even though the graft that had sustained them in early years had largely disappeared with most of Chinatown's vice dens. Over time, Hip Sing and On Leong tong men would move into more legitimate businesses and their tongs morph into more conservative, mainstream organizations. Having finally laid down their arms, they would become more respected, and Chinatown more willing to forgive their occasional forays into extralegal businesses like drug trafficking, prostitution, and smuggling.

On February 14, 1934—Chinese New Year—both tongs paraded their dragons through the streets of Chinatown as hundreds stood on the sidelines and cheered. The two processions began simultaneously at precisely noon, the Hip Sings from their Pell Street headquarters and the On Leongs from theirs on Mott. Men wore red sashes and beat gongs and drums. Each parade was led by youths carrying colorful banners, with a large tong flag behind them. But an experienced squad of police made sure the parades were always kept at least a block apart.

Rivalry between the On Leongs and the Hip Sings would continue to be a fact of life, but the two tongs had finally learned to live with each other.

Epilogue

The body of **Tom Lee,** buried at Cypress Hills Cemetery in Brooklyn on January 14, 1918, was disinterred three months later. As Lee had wished, his remains were sent back to China. A hearse and two taxicabs carried his exhumed casket and a few family members back to Mott Street and then on to Grand Central Terminal, where it proceeded by rail to Utica, Montreal, and Vancouver and then to Hong Kong by steamer. From there it was transferred, under the supervision of his son Frank, to a final resting place in his ancestral village in Guangdong Province.

Frank William Lee, Tom Lee's second son and an ordained Baptist preacher, returned to the native land of his father to work as a missionary. He allied himself with Dr. Sun Yat-sen and served as the latter's secretary in 1917, chief of the political department in China's Ministry of Foreign Affairs from 1918 to 1920, representative of the Republic of China to the United States in the late 1920s, and eventually acting foreign minister in the early 1930s. He also served as China's minister to Mexico, Poland, Czechoslovakia, and Portugal. He died in 1956.

Chin Jack Lem, who single-handedly caused the 1924 tong war, had been sentenced to fifteen years in the Ohio Penitentiary for extortion but served less than half that time. Despite "unruly" and even "rebellious" behavior on his part while behind bars, his sentence was commuted in 1931 by the governor against the recommendation of the warden and the parole board. The condition was that he leave Cleveland forever. Chin met a bloody end in 1937 when an assassin fired four shots into his chest at close range outside a Chicago chop suey house. The proximate cause of his murder was his alleged theft of $600 donated by his Hip Sing colleagues for war relief in China.

Sue Sing, condemned to life in prison after pleading guilty to the 1900 murder of Ah Fee, did hard time at Sing Sing until he contracted tuberculosis, whereupon he was transferred to the Clinton Correctional Facility in Dannemora, New York. In several petitions to the governor of New York for clemency, he proclaimed his innocence, fingered Mock Duck as Ah Fee's true killer, and blamed Wong Get for threatening him with death if he did not take the fall.

Chin Lem, who had brought Bow Kum to New York, joined her at Cypress Hills Cemetery in February 1914. Eleven carriages and three automobiles paid for by his brother On Leongs were required to transport the thirty-six-year-old's mourners from Mott Street to Brooklyn, where police stood guard lest his final rites ignite a new tong clash. His send-off, to the music of an Italian band and the banging of gongs, included flowers, incense, roast pig, and the burning of faux paper money to see to his needs in the next world.

The indefatigable **Frank Moss,** associated with most of New York's celebrated anticorruption efforts during his long career, never saw through his Hip Sing friends, even after joining the district attorney's office. His visceral distaste for the On Leongs put him on the side of their sworn enemies well after the rest of New York had concluded they were anything but the reformers they portrayed themselves to be. Moss died in 1920 at the age of sixty.

William McAdoo, asked to resign as commissioner of police in 1905, returned to the private practice of law until he was appointed by Mayor William Jay Gaynor as chief of the city magistrates' courts, first division. He served until his death in 1930. He is buried in Woodlawn Cemetery in the Bronx.

After serving for eight years, District Attorney **William T. Jerome,** a staunch anti-Tammany figure, gave up politics and went into private practice. But he came out of political retirement to stump for reform candidates during the Depression, noting that the only difference between 1901 and 1933 was that "the stealing is more refined." He made a fortune by investing in Technicolor, then a new technology, and died of pneumonia in 1934.

Wong Aloy, the Hip Sing interpreter who guided a Committee of Fifteen investigator through Chinatown's brothels, opium dens, and gambling houses in 1900–1901, was named special assistant to the district attorney of New York County and went on to serve as a Chinese interpreter for the U.S. Immigration Service. In 1922, however, at the age of fifty-four, he was shot and killed in a Chicago poolroom in what was rumored to be an On Leong hit.

Chinatown had proven too much for Captain **Michael J. Galvin,** who was transferred to Coney Island for health reasons after heading up the Sixth Precinct for only about a year. But he continued working overtime there, determined to crack down on tight-fitting bathing suits and dance halls. Within five months, he succumbed to chronic kidney disease, leaving behind a widow and five children.

Meihong Soohoo, longtime national president of the On Leong Tong who signed off on the 1925 peace accord, allied himself with Dr. Sun Yat-sen and was instrumental in raising money for Sun's revolution and the anti-Japanese war. In the 1940s, he attempted to convert the Chee Kung Tong into a political party and was offered a seat in the Guomindang's National Assembly. He opted instead for the rival Communists' United Front, however, and was ultimately appointed to China's National People's Congress.

Rhinelander Waldo, New York police commissioner until the end of 1913, took issue with the statement that he had been "removed" from office and successfully appealed to the state supreme court to have the word changed to "resigned," because he had tendered his resignation before he was replaced. He remained politically active and, in 1924, renounced Tammany Hall and joined the Republican Party. He died at age fifty of septic poisoning and is buried in Sleepy Hollow Cemetery in New York's Westchester County.

Ha Oi, the half-Chinese, half-Caucasian child removed from the custody of Mock Duck and Tai Yow Chin at age six in the spring of 1907, was given the new name of Helen Francis. Due to the wide publicity given her case, the Gerry Society received many offers of adoption from white couples across the country eager to give her a proper Christian upbringing.

She was presumably placed with one such couple, but her records remain sealed to this day.

Edward P. Mulrooney, the Cantonese-speaking police commissioner who had cut his teeth at Elizabeth Street and helped broker tong peace in 1930, served the department until 1933. He became the first chairman of New York State's Alcoholic Beverage Control Board following the repeal of Prohibition. He was subsequently named state commissioner of correction and effected several improvements in New York's penal system.

Charles S. Whitman, the magistrate who locked Mock Dock up for assault in 1905 and who, as district attorney, came down heavily on the tongs in pursuit of a truce in 1913, was bound for more important endeavors. After earning fame for exposing the corrupt relationship between the New York police and high-profile underworld figures, he went on to become governor of the state in 1915. He served until 1918, when he was defeated by Tammany Hall's candidate, Al Smith—a friend of Tom Lee's.

Joab H. Banton, the New York County district attorney who called in the federal government to suppress the tong wars in 1925, served in that role until 1929. In 1927, he prosecuted the actress Mae West for staging an obscene production; she was fined and jailed for ten days. The following year, he headed the prosecution of the accused murderer of the Jewish mobster Arnold "the Brain" Rothstein. Banton returned to private practice in 1929 and helped establish a law firm that bore his name. He died in 1949.

Warry Charles, head of the Boston Hip Sings who was convicted of murder, had been sentenced in 1909 to die in the electric chair. But the attorney Frank Moss interceded with Massachusetts authorities and asked for clemency. Charles was never pardoned, but his sentence was commuted to life in prison, where he died of heart trouble in 1915.

The graves of **Bow Kum, Gin Gum, Charlie Boston, Eng Hing,** and **Lee Dock,** all supposedly located at Brooklyn's Cypress Hills Cemetery, are nowhere to be found today. It is possible that their remains were exhumed and returned to China, but the cemetery has no record of either burial or disinterment for any of them.

Mock Duck died of tuberculosis on July 23, 1941, leaving his second wife, Frances. He was interred in Cypress Hills Cemetery, where a double marker was erected over his grave. But neither Tai Yow, his first wife, nor Frances rests next to him. That honor goes to Pang Ah Woo (1876–1951), a divorced, China-born ship steward who was later an employment agent for a merchant shipping line. Pang's relationship to Mock Sai Wing—Mock Duck's formal name—is unclear, but the two men share a headstone and will rest together for eternity.

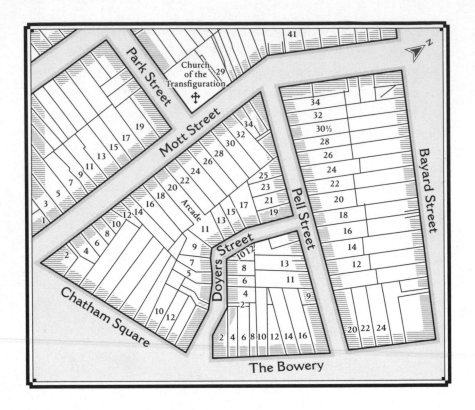

KEY LOCATIONS

Mott Street

2. Tom Lee's variety store (1880)

4. Tom Lee's cigar and tobacco shop (1880)

5. On Leongs trick Hip Sings in basement gambling raid (1904)

7–9. Port Arthur Restaurant (1897); Four Brothers member Chu Moy Yen gunned down (1910)

8. Wo Kee's store (1883)

11. Annie Gilroy's brothel (1890); Chu On, a Four Brothers man, killed (1910); Hip Sings fire on On Leong men (1912); On Leong president "Big Lou" nearly blown up (1912); police destroy Charlie Boston's gambling hall (1913)

14. On Leong Tong headquarters (1897); Mon Far Low Restaurant (1905); Four Brothers laundryman Gun Kee attacks On Leong Gin Gum and is shot by gun-

man Lee Wah the following week (1909); Charlie Boston arrested for conspiracy to smuggle opium (1911); Hip Sings dynamite building's Joss Hall (1912)

16. Chinatown City Hall and Joss House (1884)

17. Tuck Hop's store and gambling hall (1883); Hip Sing Huie Fong gunned down (1905); Bow Kum brutally murdered in an outbuilding in back (1909)

18. Loon Yee Tong headquarters (1881); Ah Chung's opium joint (1883); Gamblers' Union (1886); Lee Toy's gambling hall (1894); Lone Tai gambling hall (1900); Hip Sing gunmen kill Lee Kay (1912)

20. First New York home of Tom Lee and family (1878); Chin Tin's business establishment (1891)

24. On Leong Ah Fee falls (1900); Gin Gum dies (1915)

28. On Leong fugitive Lee Toy, at large for two months, captured by police (1894)

29. Hip Sing police informer Ing Mow gunned down in full view of an assistant district attorney (1908)

34. Wo Kee's store and headquarters of the Polong Congsee (1880)

41. On Leong Tong headquarters (1921)

Pell Street

9. Hip Sing laundryman Lung Kin, first casualty of the tong wars, assassinated (1900)

11. Jow Chuck, a Hip Sing cook and former On Leong, shot to death through kitchen window (1912)

12. Wong Get's gambling hall (1895)

13. Headquarters of the Hip Sing Tong (1912)

16. Suspicious grease fire at Hung Far Low Restaurant kills Sin Cue, principal witness in the Ah Fee murder trial (1901)

18. Mock Duck gunned down (1904); On Leongs mount surprise attack on Huie family (1905)

19. Wo On Chinese Merchandise Shop, site of Ah Fee attack (1900)

21. Tom Wing's *fan tan* hall (1905); On Leong gunmen assassinate top Hip Sing Tong officers (1912)

22. Mock Duck attempts to shake down Chu Lock's policy shop, and a brawl ensues (1897); Four Brothers' Society headquarters (1909)

23. Mock Duck hits innocent bystanders in attempt to kill Sin Cue (1900); gunfight between Hip Sings and On Leongs (1912)

24. Mon Lay Won (Chinese Delmonico) Restaurant (1894); Yee Toy, Hip Sing gunman, assassinated at behest of On Leongs by Jung Hing of the Kim Lan Association (1912)

30½. Two elderly Four Brothers men assassinated (1909)

32. Hip Sings stage Chinese New Year ambush of On Leongs (1906)

Doyers Street

2. Tuxedo Restaurant (1907).

4. Yoshito Saito, a Japanese man, is shot in a case of mistaken identity (1910).

5–7. Chinese Theatre massacre (1905)

8–10. The Bloody Angle

10. Ha Oi, a half-Caucasian child, seized from Mock Duck's home (1907)

11. Four Brothers man Chu Hin shot to death in underground arcade connecting to 20 Mott Street (1910)

13. Hip Sing gunman Hun Kem Yun killed (1912)

15–17. Wing Gin, an On Leong carpenter, shot by Lee Bow; last man to die in the tong wars (1933)

The Bowery

10. John Baldwin shot to death (1904)

12. Hip Sing Tong headquarters (1904)

Chatham Square

10. On Leong actor Ah Hoon murdered (1909)

12. Mike Callahan's saloon (1901).

ACKNOWLEDGMENTS

This book was already in production when news came of the untimely death of my dear friend Dr. Raymond D. Lum (1944–2015), late of the Harvard University Library. Ray, whom I met in the course of my research, was a source of both inspiration and practical assistance in the creation not just of this book but of two of my previous works. Nor am I alone in being the fortunate beneficiary of his wisdom, scholarship, talent, and generosity; countless others have Ray to thank in the same way. Ray reviewed the manuscript for this book and offered his usual insights, comments, and criticisms, all of which helped make it a better work. Accordingly, I would like to dedicate it to his memory.

Several others also devoted a great deal of time and effort to reading and commenting on this book at various stages of its development, and I am most grateful to them for valuable criticism and also for encouragement. I owe a huge debt of gratitude to Marsha Cohan, Madelyn Ross, Marc Abramson, Ben Bronson, Renqiu Yu, Ling-chi Wang, Charlotte Brooks, and Harvey Solomon. Marsha did double duty: together with Deborah Strauss, she also helped me understand the terminology and procedures in the many legal cases mentioned in the book.

Lester Lau helped me a great deal with the Chinese-language sources, translations, and names; so did Ping Liang, Charles T. Wu, Jane Leung Larson, Zhongping Chen, Nicky Yu, Ema Fu, Bell Yung, Ram Moy, and the late Dora Y. Lee.

I am grateful to Bill Trigg and Victor Chang of the Huie Kin Family Association for providing a copy of the Reverend Huie's memoirs; to John Jung, Chuimei Ho, Howard Spendelow, Corky Lee, Ira Belkin, Nicholas Chen, Timothy Liang, Philip Chin, and Henry Tom for helping me with various queries that came up along the way; to William L. Gao for research assistance; and to Peter Bernstein, Amy Bernstein, and Anne Thurston for expert help on the book proposal.

Works such as this generally owe a huge debt to archivists and librarians, who seldom get the recognition they richly deserve. I am especially indebted to Kenneth Cobb, assistant commissioner of the New York City Department of Records and Information Services, who cheerfully fielded my repeated requests for obscure court case files, armed only with approximate dates and the questionable spellings of names of plaintiffs and defendants willed us by long-dead reporters. I would also like to doff my hat to unsung heroes and heroines of the National Archives and Records Administration, including Marian L. Smith in Washington; Angela Tudico, Greg Plunges, and Irina Tsiklik in New York; Zina Rhone in Atlanta; Joseph Sanchez in San Bruno; and Joe Keefe in Boston.

Thanks also to Barbara Natanson, Jeffrey Bridgers, Amber Paranick, and Lara Szypszak of the Library of Congress; Bruce Abrams of the New York County Clerk Record Office; Jessica M. Herrick of the California State Archives; Kathleen Collins and Ellen Belcher of the City University of New York; Marci Reaven of the New-York Historical Society; Jack Cunningham of the Federal Trade Commission; Kate Cordes, Weatherly Stephan, and Tal Nadan of the New York Public Library; Shirlene Newman of the District of Columbia Public Library; and Carolina Padin of Cypress Hills Cemetery.

Last but not least, I want to express my gratitude to the folks at Viking. First, to editor Wendy Wolf, for her confidence in me, her crackerjack editing skills, and her expert counsel on how to make my first draft into a far better book. I'm also appreciative of her assistant Georgia Bodnar's unflagging efforts to keep the trains running on time, and the beautiful design work of Francesca Belanger. And my thanks also to production editor Bruce Giffords and copy editor Ingrid Sterner for wrestling with my endnotes, smoothing out the rough passages, catching inconsistencies, and even educating this English teacher's son on a fine grammatical point or two.

CHRONOLOGY

1878 Sent by the Six Companies of San Francisco, Tom Lee arrives in New York.

1880 The Loon Yee Tong is established. Tom Lee is appointed deputy sheriff of New York County.

1882 The Chinese Exclusion Act places a ten-year moratorium on the immigration of Chinese laborers into the United States and prohibits naturalization of Chinese.

1883 Tom Lee and others stealthily acquire Mott Street property, alarming existing tenants. Lee is indicted for extortion and keeping a gambling house.

1886 First mention in the press of the Chinese Gamblers' Union, which eventually becomes the On Leong Tong.

1892 The Geary Act extends the Chinese Exclusion Act for ten years and requires Chinese to register under penalty of imprisonment and deportation.

The Reverend Dr. Charles H. Parkhurst begins a crusade against Tammany Hall.

1894 The Lexow Committee is established to investigate the New York police. Wong Get testifies about graft between the police and the On Leong Tong.

1895 Theodore Roosevelt is appointed New York City police commissioner and institutes reforms.

Mock Duck appears in New York.

1897 The Hip Sings clash with the Four Brothers' Society. Mock Duck and others are wounded.

Tom Lee gives a dinner for Tammany Hall operatives in anticipation of their return to power and the consolidation of the governments of the five boroughs.

1900 The Hip Sing laundryman Lung Kin is shot to death, ushering in the First Tong War. The On Leong tailor Ah Fee is killed by Sue Sing in retaliation.

1901 Sue Sing is sentenced to life in prison, but others, including Mock Duck, are also charged with murder. Sin Cue, principal witness in the case, is killed.

1902 Mock Duck's murder trial ends in a hung jury. A retrial ends the same way.

1904 Goaded into action by the Parkhurst Society, the police stage raids on On Leong gambling halls. Mock Duck is wounded by Lee Sing in a failed assassination attempt. On Leongs stage an attack in front of Hip Sing headquarters on the Bowery.

1905 Hip Sings put prices on the heads of On Leong officers. A Hip Sing informant is brutally murdered, and Tom Lee's cousin is shot by a Hip Sing. Tom Lee goes into hiding until Mock Duck is taken into custody for assault.

Police stage massive Easter Sunday raid on twelve Chinatown gambling establishments. Tom Lee is arrested and charged with graft; he later engineers a Decoration Day police raid on Hip Sing gambling halls.

Hip Sing gunmen massacre On Leongs at the Chinese Theatre on Doyers Street. Mock Duck and others are arrested and charged with murder.

On Leongs stage the gruesome murder of the laundryman Hop Lee. An attempt is made on Tom Lee's life. On Leong gunmen attack members of the Huie family.

1906   Two On Leongs are killed by Hip Sings in a Chinese New Year ambush on Pell Street.

Judge Warren W. Foster negotiates a peace treaty. Mock Duck breaks from the Hip Sings and is arrested for bribery.

The New York *World* launches a campaign to raze Chinatown and replace it with a public park.

1907   Six-year-old half-Caucasian Ha Oi is removed from the home of Mock Duck and his wife and put up for adoption.

Tongs clash in Philadelphia and Boston.

1908   Several attempts are made to burn down Mock Duck's home, and he leaves town.

Boston Hip Sings are convicted of first-degree murder. Philadelphia On Leong shooters are sentenced to death. A New York Hip Sing informer is killed on Mott Street.

1909   The body of the white missionary Elsie Sigel is discovered in a trunk. A manhunt is launched for her presumed killer, a member of the Four Brothers' Society. Then the corpse of twenty-one-year-old Bow Kum, strangled and slashed to death, is found in a Mott Street outbuilding. Two Four Brothers men are charged with the murder.

The Four Brothers' War breaks out with the On Leong Tong. The On Leong actor Ah Hoon is murdered after a Chinese Theatre performance.

1910   Hip Sings ally with the Four Brothers against the On Leong Tong.

Four Brothers defendants are acquitted in the Bow Kum murder trial.

Truce negotiations falter and killing continues, but a peace accord is finally struck, ending the Four Brothers' War.

1911   Federal agents raid two New York opium joints, and the On Leong kingpin Charlie Boston is arrested. To avoid revealing the network of On Leong government contacts, he pleads guilty and is sentenced to eighteen months in a federal penitentiary.

An uprising in Wuchang heralds the beginning of the end of the Qing dynasty and the establishment of a republic in China.

1912   On Leong gunmen assassinate the president and the vice president of the Hip Sing Tong as the Third Tong War begins. Mock Duck is charged with running a lottery. Hip Sing gunmen kill Tom Lee's nephew.

Mock Duck is convicted and sentenced to one to two years at Sing Sing. The Kim Lan Association gunman Jung Hing murders "Girl Face" Yee Toy, chief Hip Sing gunman, likely at the behest of the On Leongs.

Hip Sing agents attempt to blow up On Leong headquarters and a senior On Leong functionary. Louie Way, a Hip Sing gunman, is released from prison and causes a gunfight on Pell Street. Jung Hing is sentenced to die in the electric chair for the killing of Yee Toy, though the sentence is later reduced to jail time.

1913   Mock Duck remarries without benefit of divorce. He later begins serving a sentence at Sing Sing.

On Leongs, Hip Sings, and Kim Lans sign a truce. Police launch a series of raids of Chinatown gambling resorts.

1914   Relentless police raids drive many gambling halls and Chinese residents out of Chinatown.

1915   The Hip Sing gunmen Eng Hing and Lee Dock, convicted of murdering Tom Lee's nephew, die in the electric chair at Sing Sing prison.

1918 Tom Lee dies and after a huge funeral is buried at Cypress Hills Cemetery in Brooklyn.

1922 The Hip Sing national president, Ko Low, is gunned down on Pell Street; On Leongs are exonerated.

1924 Chin Jack Lem and others are ousted from the On Leong Tong and seek membership in the Hip Sings. On Leongs accuse him of extortion. Hip Sings vote to admit him and usher in the Fourth Tong War. A negotiated armistice lasts only a few weeks.

1925 Chin Jack Lem is convicted of extortion and sentenced to prison. A peace agreement is signed and prevails for five months. Then killings occur in Pittsburgh, Chicago, Baltimore, and Minneapolis. Police threaten to arrest tong leaders for conspiracy. A new treaty is signed, but violence continues.

The New York County district attorney issues a "final ultimatum." Tong chiefs are arrested, but cases are thrown out. The federal government threatens to deport all undocumented Chinese. Roundups and hundreds of arrests begin. Raids, killings, and peace negotiations all continue. Tongs sign "eternal peace pact."

1927 A new wave of killings occurs in Brooklyn, Newark, Chicago, and elsewhere. The New York district attorney, Joab H. Banton, warns that the federal government will send tong men "back to China by the shipload" if war continues. Tongs declare truce to be still in effect.

1928 Personal feuds result in a string of murders in Chicago, Philadelphia, New York, and Washington. Tongs reaffirm peace.

1929 Killings resume in Chicago, Newark, Boston, and New York. To stave off immediate roundups of undocumented Chinese, leaders agree on a truce.

1930 Tongs march peacefully in Chinese New Year parade, but hostilities resume. Hip Sings are gunned down in New York and Newark. The Tung

On Society is blamed. Tong leaders disavow violence but appear to be losing control.

Tung Ons, allied with Hip Sings, clash with On Leongs over a drug deal gone bad. The Chinese consulate oversees the signing of a multilateral peace treaty.

1931 Hip Sings and On Leongs hold annual meetings in New York at the same time. Violent confrontation is predicted but fails to materialize.

1932 Mock Duck is shot in Newark over gambling debts by a Hip Sing assailant.

1933 Amity prevails as tongs undertake common philanthropic projects. The shooting of a Boston Hip Sing ushers in a new wave of murders. The U.S. attorney hauls tong leaders before a grand jury and subpoenas membership lists. Tongs insist there had not been a formal declaration of war. A cease-fire is declared, ending the Fourth Tong War.

1934 Both tongs parade through the streets of Chinatown in New Year celebration as hundreds of Chinese stand on the sidelines and cheer.

GLOSSARY AND GAZETTEER

Pinyin equivalents for traditional spellings and standard Chinese characters are provided where known.

Bin Ching Union (*Bingzheng Gongsuo*) 秉正公所. An early name for the Gamblers' Union that eventually became the On Leong Tong. It translates as "Upholding Fairness Society."

Bloody Angle. *See* Doyers Street.

boo how doy (*futou zai*) 斧頭仔. A hatchet man, or an enforcer. *See* highbinder.

Celestial. A term referring to overseas Chinese derived from *Tianchao* (天朝), a traditional name for China that translates as "Celestial Empire."

Chee Kung Tong (*Zhigong Tang*) 致公堂. An organization with roots in early Qing dynasty China often referred to as the Chinese Masons, a term that erroneously implies an association with the Western Masonic tradition. New York's Loon Yee Tong adopted this better-known name at about the turn of the twentieth century. *See* Hongmen.

Chinese Consolidated Benevolent Association. *See* Chung Hwa Gong Shaw; Six Companies.

Chinese Delmonico Restaurant. *See* Mon Lay Won.

Chung Hwa Gong Shaw (*Zhonghua Gongsuo*) 中華公所. The Chinese Consolidated Benevolent Association. Formed as the New York branch of the Six Companies, it served as the central governing body of the Chinese community. *See* Six Companies.

Doyers Street (*Duoye Jie*) 多也街. Narrow street in the heart of New York's Chinatown that runs from Pell Street to Chatham Square. Its obtuse angle, which prevents a straight line of sight, is popularly known as the Bloody Angle because of the legend that warring tongs could sneak up on one another there without being detected.

fan tan 番攤. The "spread and turn over game." A popular Chinese game of chance.

Four Brothers' Society (*Longgang Qinyi Gongsuo*) 龍岡親義公所. A Chinese clan association encompassing four families: Lau (*Liu*) 劉, Kwan (*Guan*) 關, Cheung (*Zhang*) 張, and Chu (*Zhao*) 趙. Also known as the See Sing Tong.

Guangdong 廣東. A coastal province in southeast China from which the majority of America's early Chinese immigrants hailed. Traditionally rendered as Kwangtung, or Canton Province.

Guan Gong 關公. A virtuous third-century general and hero whose effigy was worshipped in many Chinese joss houses. Traditionally rendered as Kwan Kung.

Guangxu 光緒. The ninth Qing dynasty emperor to rule China. His official reign lasted from 1875 to 1908.

Guangzhou 廣州. The capital of Guangdong Province. Traditionally rendered as Canton.

Guomindang 國民黨. The Chinese Nationalist Party. Traditionally rendered as Kuomintang.

He Shen 和珅. Manchu official who enriched himself and his family through graft and extortion.

highbinder. Gangster or hatchet man; archaic term derived from the name of an early nineteenth-century, non-Chinese New York City gang later used to describe a member of a Chinese American triad.

Hip Sing Tong (*Xiesheng Tang*) 協勝堂. A Chinese secret society associated with underworld activities whose name translates as the "Chamber United in Victory." Emerged on the West Coast and established itself in the East in the late 1880s.

Hong Kong (*Xianggang*) 香港. Coastal city abutting Guangdong Province. A British crown colony between 1841 and 1997.

Hongmen 洪門. A secret society formed in China early in the Qing dynasty to restore the Chinese-ruled Ming dynasty often erroneously seen as a Masonic order. It went by different names in different American cities, including the Loon Yee Tong, and later the Chee Kung Tong, in New York. Traditionally rendered as Hung Mun.

Hung Far Low (*Xinghua Lou*) 杏花樓. Restaurant located at 16 Pell Street.

joss. A term for a Chinese idol, believed to be a corruption of the Portuguese *deus,* meaning "God."

Kim Lan Association (*Jinlan Gongsuo*) 金蘭公所. The "cadet branch" of the

Chee Kung Tong, some members of which were former Hip Sings. *See* Chee Kung Tong.

Liu Jin 劉瑾. A corrupt Ming dynasty eunuch who used his high position for personal gain.

lobbygow. A hanger-on in Chinatown; often a tour guide or messenger.

Loon Yee Tong (*Lianyi Tang*) 聯誼堂. *See* Chee Kung Tong.

Lung Kong Tin Yee Gong Shaw. *See* Four Brothers' Society.

Manchu (*Manzhouren*) 滿洲人. An ethnic group from Manchuria, a region in the northeast of China, that ruled the Chinese Empire as the Qing dynasty between 1644 and 1912.

Ming dynasty (*Ming Chao*) 明朝. China's ruling dynasty from 1368 to 1644.

Mon Far Low (*Wan Hua Lou*) 萬花樓. Restaurant located at 14 Mott Street.

Mon Lay Won (*Wan Li Yun*) 萬里雲. Restaurant located at 24 Pell Street.

Mott Street (*Wu Jie*) 勿街. Principal avenue in New York's Chinatown.

Nanjing 南京. Historical capital of China located on the lower Yangtze (*Yangzi*) River. Traditionally rendered as Nanking.

Ning Yeung Society (*Ningyang Huiguan*) 寧陽會館. Association of former residents of Taishan.

On Leong Tong (*Anliang Tang*) 安良堂. A Chinese secret society organized in New York in the late 1880s and incorporated in 1897 as the Chinese Merchants Association. Its name translates as "Chamber of Peaceful Conscientiousness."

pak kop piu (*baige piao*) 白鴿票. The "white pigeon ticket" game of chance popular among Chinatown residents. Popularly known among Americans as policy.

Pell Street (*Pilu Jie*) 披露街. Avenue in New York's Chinatown.

pi gow (*paijiu*) 牌九. A Chinese gambling game that makes use of dominoes.

policy. *See pak kop piu.*

Polong Congsee (probably *Baoliang Gongsi*) 保良公司. A mutual aid society formed by New York Chinese in the 1870s.

Port Arthur Restaurant (*Lüshun Lou*) 旅順樓. Restaurant located at 7–9 Mott Street.

Qing dynasty (*Qing Chao*) 清朝. China's last imperial dynasty, which ruled from 1644 to 1912. Also called the Manchu dynasty. Traditionally rendered as Ch'ing.

Sam Yup Benevolent Association (*Sanyi Huiguan*) 三邑會館. Association of former residents of three counties near Guangzhou.

See Sing Tong (*Sixing Tang*) 四姓堂. "Four Surnames Society." *See* Four Brothers' Society.

Shandong 山東. A coastal province in north China. Traditionally rendered as Shantung.

Six Companies (*Liu Da Gongsi*) 六大公司. Umbrella organization that governed Chinatowns throughout the United States and served as the voice of America's Chinese. Eventually renamed the Chinese Consolidated Benevolent Association. *See* Chung Hwa Gong Shaw.

Taishan 臺山. A district in Guangdong Province's Pearl River delta from which the majority of nineteenth-century Chinese in America emigrated. Traditionally rendered as Toisan and Sunning (*Xinning*).

tong (*tang*) 堂. Chamber or hall. Used colloquially to describe a Chinese organization, most often a "triad," or Chinese secret society.

Tung On Society (*Dongan Huiguan*) 東安會館. A society with roots in China made up primarily of seamen. Its name translates as "Eastern Peace."

Tuxedo Restaurant (*Caihua Jiulou*) 採花酒樓. Restaurant located at 2 Doyers Street.

Wei Zhongxian 魏忠賢. A corrupt Ming dynasty eunuch who rose to a high position and manipulated the emperor for his personal gain.

NOTES

Abbreviations

The following abbreviations have been employed below for the names of newspapers cited most often.

BA	Baltimore American	NYP	New York Post
BDE	Brooklyn Daily Eagle	NYPR	New York Press
BDS	Brooklyn Daily Star	NYS	New York Sun
BH	Boston Herald	NYT	New York Times
BJ	Boston Journal	NYTGM	New York Telegram
BS	Baltimore Sun	NYTGP	New York Telegraph
BSU	Brooklyn Standard Union	NYTR	New-York Tribune
CPD	Cleveland Plain Dealer	NYW	New York World
CSM	Christian Science Monitor	PI	Philadelphia Inquirer
CT	Chicago Tribune	SDT	San Diego Tribune
DP	Denver Post	SFB	San Francisco Bulletin
DPP	Daily People	SFC	San Francisco Chronicle
IS	Idaho Statesman	SJ	Syracuse Journal
KCS	Kansas City Star	SR	Springfield Republican
MT	Macon Telegraph	TT	Trenton Times
NHR	New Haven Register	WH	Washington Herald
NYC	New York Call	WP	Washington Post
NYG	New York Globe and	WS	Washington Star
	Commercial Advertiser	WT	Washington Times
NYH	New York Herald		

Introduction

xi **other contemporary sources:** Bonner, *Alas! What Brought Thee Hither?*, 169; Lai, *Chinese American Transnational Politics*, 86; Chen, *Being Chinese, Becoming Chinese American*, 185n.

xi **"About 6000 B.C.":** "Chinese Fighting Armor in Court," *NYTGM*, Nov. 26, 1904.

xii **"Two Chinamen were shot":** Neal O'Hara, "Telling the World," *Baton Rouge Advocate*, June 25, 1930.

xii **For example, Herbert Asbury:** Asbury, *Gangs of New York*, 282, 288.

Chapter 1: An "Army of Almond-Eyed Exiles"

2 **There was bias against all newcomers:** "Chinese Immigration: Letter from Senator Blaine," *NYTR*, Feb. 24, 1879; John Swinton, "The New Issue: The Chinese-American Question," *NYTR*, June 30, 1870.

2 **In Manhattan, many early migrants:** Helen Campbell, *Darkness and Daylight; or, Lights and Shadows of New York* (Hartford: Hartford Publishing, 1896), 557; Tchen, *New York Before Chinatown*, 225; "The Chinese in New York," *NYTR*, June 21, 1885; "Chinese in New York: How They Live and Where. Their Club House," *NYT*, Dec. 26, 1873; "Mongolian Immigrants," *Fairport (N.Y.) Herald*, Oct. 3, 1879; "Little China," *NYP*, May 10, 1880.

2 **Wo Kee's shop:** "In the Chinese Quarter," *NYS*, March 7, 1880.

3 **Out of the same location:** Passport Application of Wong Achon, Sept. 13, 1880, Passport Applications, 1795–1905, General Records of the Department of State, Record Group 59, National Archives, Washington, D.C.; "The Chinese New Year," *NYH*, Feb. 27, 1874.

3 **In 1875, state census takers:** "The Chinese in New York," *NYT*, March 6, 1880; Gyory, *Closing the Gate*, 281.

3 **"A person unacquainted":** "The Work of Enumeration," *NYH*, June 3, 1880.

3 **Most of New York's Chinese:** Ibid.; "The Chinese Boarding House," *Harper's Weekly*, Dec. 1, 1888.

4 **Diligent laborers with few deadbeats:** Wong Chin Foo, "The Chinese in New York," *Cosmopolitan*, Aug. 1888, 297–98.

4 **But Chinese worked in other trades:** "In the Chinese Quarter"; "Chinese in New York," *NYT*, March 6, 1880; "Our New York Letter," *Utica Sunday Tribune*, May 6, 1883; "Mongolian Immigrants."

5 **By early 1880, Chinese had leased:** "Fleeing Celestials," *NYH*, March 3, 1880; "Chinese in New York," *NYT*, March 6, 1880.

5 **In May, Chinese tenants:** *Buffalo Evening Republic*, May 10, 1880; "Little China."

5 **His name wasn't *actually* Tom Lee:** "On Leong Tong Chieftain Dies Quietly in Bed," *NYTR*, Jan. 11, 1918; "Tom Lee, Mayor of Chinatown, Dies," *NYS*, Jan. 11, 1918; "Tom Lee's Perplexity," *NYH*, July 15, 1880; Naturalization record of Wung A. Ling, Records of the St. Louis Criminal Court, March 9, 1876, Missouri State Archives, Jefferson City, MO.

6 **Although Lee adopted Western dress:** "The Richest Chinaman in New York," *Richfield Springs (N.Y.) Mercury*, July 30, 1881.

6 **Just before coming to New York:** Ancestry.com, "1900 United States Federal Census Online Database," accessed Aug. 4, 2015, http://search.ancestry.com/search/db.aspx?dbid=7602; "Death in the House of Tom Lee," *NYS*, Jan. 22, 1883.

7 **Minnie bore two daughters:** "Tom Lee's Son and Heir," *NYS*, April 2, 1882.

7 **It took two restaurants:** Various accounts of the celebration appeared in "A Chinese Christening," *NYT*, April 2, 1882; "Tom Lee's Son and Heir"; "A Chinaman's Heir," *Truth*, April 2, 1882.

7   **From the moment they arrived:** "In the Chinese Quarter"; "Situations Wanted, Males," *NYH*, Dec. 12, 1873; "Judge Dinkel and the Chinese," *NYH*, April 27, 1880; "Mongolian Immigrants"; "New China," *NYH*, Dec. 11, 1878; "Civic Centre Projects May Claim Old Chinatown," *NYS*, Aug. 3, 1913.

8   **The Six Companies was the congress:** Him Mark Lai, *Becoming Chinese American* (Lanham, Md.: Altamira Press, 2002), 39; "The Chinese in America," *NYT*, April 10, 1876; Bennet Bronson and Chuimei Ho, *Coming Home in Gold Brocade: Chinese in Early Northwest America* (Seattle: Chinese in Northwest America Research Committee, 2015), 139–40.

9   **In the late 1870s:** "Mongolian Immigrants."

9   **That most local Chinese:** Him Mark Lai, "Historical Development of the Chinese Consolidated Benevolent Association/*Huiguan* System," in *Chinese America: History and Perspectives, 1987,* ed. Chinese Historical Society of America (San Francisco: Chinese Historical Society of America, 1987), 13–51.

9   **Tom Lee relished:** "Making Citizens of Chinamen," *NYS*, Nov. 30, 1878; "The Chinese New Year in New York," *Los Angeles Herald,* Jan. 29, 1879.

9   **No sooner had Lee settled:** "Celestial Dining," *NYH*, Aug. 11, 1878; "Celestial Dining," *NYH*, Feb. 5, 1879.

10 **Tom Lee quickly became:** "Making Citizens of Chinamen"; "The Heathen Chinese," *NYTGM*, Jan. 29, 1879.

11 **On September 15, 1881, he arranged:** "A Chinese Clam-Bake," *NYT*, Sept. 15, 1881; "Sports of the Celestials," *NYTR*, Sept. 16, 1881.

12 **The guests assembled:** "Celestials at Chowder," *New York Evening Express,* Sept. 16, 1881; "Mongolian Chowder Party," *Truth,* Sept. 16, 1881.

12 **They arrived to a Western breakfast:** "Chinese Clam-Bake"; "Mongolian Chowder Party"; "A Chinese Picnic," *NYS*, Sept. 17, 1881; "Morning Dispatches," *SFB*, Sept. 16, 1881; "Celestials Making Merry," *NYT*, Sept. 16, 1881.

12 **"Not only are they":** "Mongolian Chowder Party."

12 **Lee quickly eclipsed:** "Fleeing Celestials"; "Chinese Ostracism in Brooklyn," *NYH*, Jan. 20, 1881.

13 **The Hongmen had gotten:** Stewart Culin, "The I Hing or 'Patriotic Rising': A Secret Society Among the Chinese in America," Nov. 3, 1887, *Report of the Proceedings of the Numismatic and Antiquarian Society of Philadelphia, for the Years 1887–1889* (Philadelphia: printed for the society, 1891), 2–3.

13 **Broadly speaking, the Loon Yee Tong:** "Chinese Ostracism in Brooklyn"; "Flying from San Francisco," *NYH*, March 4, 1880.

13 **The Loon Yee Tong soon occupied:** "Chinese Ostracism in Brooklyn."

13 **Like all Hongmen chapters:** "The Highbinders," *Daily Alta California,* March 17, 1891; "Chinese Mafia," *Logansport Pharos,* June 19, 1893; "Highbinders," *Chatham Record,* Feb. 16, 1888.

14 **"before the next Presidential":** "Chinese Ostracism in Brooklyn."

14 **Shortly after the Loon Yee Tong:** "Prosperous Chinese Arrested for Voting," *NYT*, Aug. 17, 1904.

14 **"the Celestials are delighted":** "The Chinese Colony," *NYH*, May 21, 1880.

14   **But not all of New York's "Celestials":** "Deputy Sheriff Tom Lee Brings Suit Against Lee Sing and Loses His Case," *NYW,* Oct. 18, 1881; "Tom Lee Goes to Law in Vain," *NYS,* Oct. 18, 1881.

16   **When the case was heard:** "Chinese in the Courts," *NYT,* Oct. 18, 1881; "Tom Lee Goes to Law in Vain."

16   **There was nothing professional:** Lardner and Reppetto, *NYPD,* 35, 59–60; Kelly, *History of the New York City Police Department.*

16   **One superintendent:** Roundsmen patrolled the districts; it was their job to keep tabs on the patrolmen. Doormen were maintenance men responsible for the upkeep of the station houses.

16   **There were also detectives:** Costello, *Our Police Protectors,* 266–67, 287.

17   **"one of the greatest":** Ibid., 268–69.

17   **Tammany Hall demanded:** Lardner and Reppetto, *NYPD,* 65.

Chapter 2: The Gamblers' Union

19   **Tom Lee's businesses:** "Chinese in New York," *NYT,* March 6, 1880; "The Metropolis," *Auburn News and Bulletin,* Jan. 10, 1881.

19   **Even if that was an exaggeration:** "Chinese in New York," *NYTR,* June 21, 1885; "Real Estate Purchases by Chinamen," *NYTR,* April 28, 1883; "Chinese Monopoly," *Truth,* April 10, 1883; "Chinatown Excited," *NYT,* April 7, 1883; "Monopoly in the Chinese Colony," *NYTR,* April 8, 1883.

19   **The day after the announcement:** "Monopoly in the Chinese Colony"; "Chinese Monopoly."

20   **When the new landlords:** "Harmony in Chinatown," *NYT,* April 12, 1883.

20   **But in fact nothing:** *NHR,* April 25, 1883; "War Clouds in Mott Street," *NYTR,* April 25, 1883; "Tom Lee Loses His Place," *NYT,* April 25, 1883.

20   **Before the month of April:** "Tom Lee Loses His Place."

20   **"the Chinese Jay Gould":** "Chinatown in an Uproar," *NYT,* April 24, 1883; "War News from Chinatown," *NYS,* April 24, 1883.

20   **Meyers handed a list:** "Tom Lee Accused," *NYH,* April 25, 1883; "Taking Charge of His Precinct," *NYTR,* April 18, 1882; "Capt. Petty Dead," *NYT,* Dec. 15, 1889; "Citizen Tuck Hop," *NYS,* July 23, 1883.

21   **"When Chinamen come to New York":** Court of General Sessions of the Peace of the City and County of New York in the case of the *People v. Tom Lee,* Municipal Archives of the City of New York, box 103, folder 1101, May 1, 1883.

22   **To defend himself:** "Tom Lee's Denial," *Truth,* April 26, 1883.

22   **While both sides:** "The Troubles of Tom Lee," *NYT,* April 26, 1883.

22   **"respectable Chinese merchants":** "Tom Lee's Denial."

22   **On May 1, Lee:** "Tom Lee Gives Bail," *NYT,* May 3, 1883; "Tom Lee in Court," *NYH,* May 3, 1883.

23   **Then, on May 12:** "Rooting Out the Evil," *NYH,* May 12, 1883; "City and Suburban News," *NYT,* May 15, 1883; Court of General Sessions of the Peace of the City and County of New York in the case of the *People v. Ah*

Chung, Municipal Archives of the City of New York, box 73, folder 820, Aug. 18, 1882.

23 **Meyers angrily brandished:** "Tom Lee Discharged," *NYT,* May 17, 1883.

23 **"Tom has lost his badge":** "The Chinese Jay Gould," *BH,* April 30, 1883.

24 **The attack on Tom Lee:** "Banqueting the Chinese Consul," *SFB,* June 7, 1883.

24 **"Au Yang Ming . . . came to New York":** "The New Chinese Consul," *NYH,* June 18, 1883.

24 **Not all of Lee's Loon Yee Tong:** "The 'Big Flat' Raided," *NYT,* Dec. 8, 1884.

24 **Those remunerations came:** "The Mongolians in New York," *Daily Alta California,* July 29, 1884; "A Chinese Quarrel," *NYT,* Jan. 28, 1886; "'Big Flat' Raided"; "Opium Smokers Arrested," *NYT,* Dec. 9, 1884.

26 **He even raised eyebrows:** "Tom Lee a Guest of Tommy Maher," *NYS,* July 21, 1886.

26 **"Of the 9,000 Chinamen":** "New York Chinatown," *SFB,* July 19, 1887.

26 **By early 1884:** "New York Chinese," *SFB,* March 10, 1884.

26 **Apart from prostitutes:** Chao Longqi [潮龙起], "Weixian de yuyue: Zaoqi Meiguo huaqiao dubo wenti yanjiu, 1850–1943" [危险的愉悦: 早期美国华侨赌博问题研究, 1850–1943 年], *Overseas Chinese History Studies* [华侨华人历史研究], no. 2 (June 2010): 41–42.

27 **In what little leisure time:** Wong, "Chinese in New York," 306.

27 *Pi gow,* **once dubbed:** "Chinatown as It Really Is," *BA,* May 28, 1905.

28 **It was a compulsion:** George W. Walling, *Recollections of a New York Chief of Police* (New York: Caxton Book Concerns, 1887), 422; "The Game of Fan Tan," *Jackson Citizen Patriot,* May 13, 1887.

28 **The promise of profits:** Beck, *New York's Chinatown,* 97.

29 **By 1886, Tom Lee had organized:** "Chinese Gamblers," *Cincinnati Tribune,* July 19, 1887; *NYW,* July 19, 1887; "Chinese Gamblers' Union," *Sacramento Daily Union,* Aug. 21, 1887; "Hard to Deal with Chinese Gamblers," *NYH,* July 19, 1887; "Lured by the Highbinders," *NYW,* July 26, 1887.

29 **"Dr. Thoms is now in the custody":** "Highbinders After Thoms," *NYS,* July 18, 1887.

29 **The court proceedings bordered:** "Want to Swear Their Own Way," *NYH,* July 22, 1887.

30 **Thoms pleaded not guilty:** "Thoms and the Highbinders," *NYS,* July 21, 1887.

30 **Like gambling, opium:** "Opium Dens Resuming," *NYH,* May 18, 1883; Allen S. Williams, *Demon of the Orient* (New York: by author, 1883), 12.

30 **The drug, imported from Asia:** "Opium Pays No Toll," *NYS,* Sept. 23, 1894; "How Opium Is Smuggled," *NYS,* March 18, 1888.

31 **The reporter Wong Chin Foo:** "Product of the Poppy," *Tombstone Epitaph,* June 16, 1888.

32 **A hop fiend:** Walling, *Recollections of a New York Chief of Police,* 420–22. Walling was New York's chief of police from 1874 to 1885.

32   **It was easy for the police:** "Chinese in New York," *SFC*, May 27, 1883; "Opium Dens Shut," *Syracuse Standard*, May 12, 1883; "In the 'Big Flat,'" *Rockford Gazette*, July 7, 1884; "The Talk of New York," *NHR*, Dec. 14, 1884; "Opium Smokers Arrested."

32   **Citywide, more than $3 million:** Gustavus Myers, "Tammany and Vice," *Independent*, Dec. 6, 1900, 2924–27; "This City's Crying Shame," *NYT*, March 9, 1900.

33   **Gambling parlors were charged:** "This City's Crying Shame."

34   **In 1888, he worked energetically:** "Hallison and Molton," *LaPorte City Progress*, July 4, 1888, quoting the *New York Star;* "Chinese for Harrison," *St. Paul Daily Globe*, Aug. 23, 1888.

34   **In early 1889, when flooding:** "Chinamen to the Rescue," *NYH*, March 5, 1889; *NYW*, June 7, 1889; *American Missionary*, July 1889, 186.

34   **When Yuet Sing:** "Yuet Sing's Bride," *NYH*, Sept. 30, 1888; "Joss Saw Their Nuptials," *PI*, Oct. 1, 1888; "General Lee Yu Doo's Funeral," *NYH*, Oct. 30, 1888; "A Chinaman's Funeral," *Forest Republican*, Dec. 19, 1888; "Yung Chee Yang's Funeral," *Kansas City Times*, May 11, 1890. By one account, however, the so-called general was simply a poor clerk who "had won the regard of the entire Chinese community by the probity of his character," and his military service was a myth. See Stewart Culin, "Chinese Secret Societies in the United States," *Journal of American Folklore*, Jan.–March and July–Sept. 1890, 41–42.

35   **When Lee took sick:** Virginia Sánchez Korrol, *From Colonia to Community: The History of Puerto Ricans in New York City* (Berkeley: University of California Press, 1983), 67–68; "Tom Lee Is Ill," *NYT*, Aug. 16, 1887.

35   **"a powerful Republican factor":** "They'll Naturally Vote for Ben," *NYW*, Nov. 4, 1888.

Chapter 3: "A Clear Case of Corruption"

36   **"the Bloody Sixth":** "Seven Police Captains Lose Their Commands," *NYH*, Jan. 24, 1891; "Police Circles Startled," *NYT*, Jan. 24, 1891.

36   **When he got to Chinatown:** "Silent Are the Fan-Tan Dens of Mott Street," *NYH*, Jan. 30, 1891; "They Played Fan Tan," *NYH*, Feb. 2, 1891.

36   **Members of the Gamblers' Union:** "Wirepulling in Chinatown," *NYS*, June 6, 1891; Moss, *American Metropolis*, 2:426–29.

37   **After the *New York Herald*:** "Gambling with Shells While Police Look On," *NYH*, Jan. 20, 1891; "Seven Police Captains Lose Their Commands"; "Police Circles Startled."

37   **Brooks, for his part:** "The New Police Captains," *NYT*, July 1, 1887; "Inspector Brooks Looks Back over His Forty Years on the Force," *NYT*, Dec. 25, 1904; "Biographical Sketches of Greater New York Police," *Tammany Times*, Jan. 15, 1900, 22.

37   **Tom Lee immediately:** "Silent Are the Fan-Tan Dens of Mott Street."

38   **"Readers: Because of cheating":** Original Chinese notice is illustrated in Moss, *American Metropolis*, 2:427. Translation courtesy of Lester F. Lau.

38   **"eliminating despots":** The Chinese expression is "除暴安良" (*Chubao An-liang*). Another interpretation is "to rob from the rich and give to the poor."

38   **for many generations:** Arthur Bonner, "The Chinese in New York, 1800–1950," in *Chinese America: History and Perspectives, 1993* (San Francisco: Chinese Historical Society of America, 1993), 142; McKeown, *Chinese Migrant Networks and Cultural Change*, 187; "An Umbrella Aeronaut," *NYW,* June 20, 1894; Ling, *Chinese Chicago*, 133.

38   **Peace, however, would turn out:** "Sheriff Lee Back from China," *NYH,* Dec. 14, 1891; "New York Republicans to Get Down to Work," *PI,* Dec. 14, 1891; "Chinese Rise in Protest," *NYW,* Aug. 11, 1892; "Chinamen Are Good and Handy Patrons of Bowery Shooting Galleries," *NYW,* Sept. 5, 1888.

38   **But New York, by contrast:** Wang, *Surviving the City,* 136.

39   **Smuggling Chinese into the United States:** "The Smuggling of Chinamen," *NYT,* July 27, 1893; "Chinamen Evading," *Salt Lake Herald,* Sept. 10, 1889.

39   **"organized bodies of men":** "The Highbinders," *Oregonian,* Oct. 2, 1887.

39   **The tong began to establish:** "Chinese Anarchists," *NYS,* Aug. 24, 1888; "Chinatown Excited," *PI,* Aug. 30, 1889; "Chinese Blackmailers," *PI,* Aug. 29, 1889.

40   **In New York, the fault line:** "Chinatown," *Havana Journal,* July 30, 1887.

40   **"Here is the headquarters":** Ibid.

40   **In addition to being Tom Lee's nephew:** "Loie Sung's Murder Was All a Mistake," *NYT,* Oct. 19, 1905.

40   **Sometimes known as Black Devil Toy:** "Mary Chung's Romance," *NYW,* Oct. 9, 1892; "Wicked Celestials They," *NYW,* April 24, 1894; "Two Chinese Women in Court," *NYT,* March 27, 1895.

41   **When the gambling bosses:** "Done by the Hatchet Gang," *NYW,* Oct. 12, 1891; "Lee Toy Smote Two Men," *NYW,* Oct. 11, 1891.

42   **Price had also defended:** "Bought Unstamped Opium," *NYH,* Jan. 22, 1891.

42   **The defense alleged:** "Good Wages for Murderers," *NYS,* Nov. 20, 1891; "Hatchet Mob Rebuked," *NYW,* Dec. 2, 1891.

42   **On April 8, 1894, police raided:** Deposition of Wong Gett before Immigration Inspector F. S. Pierce, Dec. 19, 1911, in Chinese Exclusion Act Case File for Mrs. Duck Mok, Record Group 85, box 323, Case Nos. 95, 146, Immigration and Naturalization Service, National Archives and Records Administration—Northeast Region, New York; "Wicked Celestials They."

43   **Wong had been pummeled:** "Pursued by a Mob of Chinamen," *NYPR,* April 11, 1894; "Chinamen in Combat," *NYW,* April 16, 1894.

43   **"It is a clear case":** "Wicked Celestials They."

43   **The rotten system:** "The Golden Prime of Tammany," *NYT,* Oct. 28, 1917.

44   **"The mayor and those associated":** Fred A. McKenzie, "Tammany," *Eclectic Magazine,* Jan. 1898, 128–35.

44   **Challenged for proof:** Sloat, *Battle for the Soul of New York,* 18–27; Gardner, *The Doctor and the Devil,* 35–39.

45   **The vehicle created:** "Prosperous Chinese Arrested for Voting"; "Umbrella Aeronaut"; "Raiding Chinese Dens," *NYW,* Aug. 27, 1894.

46 **There was considerable irony:** Peter Baida, "The Corrupting of New York City," *American Heritage,* Dec. 1986; "A Palace of Plunder," *NYT,* Dec. 6, 1913.

47 **Wong Get, who did not require:** "A Chinaman's Evidence," *NHR,* June 28, 1894.

47 **"Is not Tom Lee generally considered":** *Report and Proceedings of the Senate Committee Appointed to Investigate the Police Department of the City of New York* (Albany, N.Y.: J. B. Lyon, 1895), 2:2240–66.

49 **Wong Get was determined:** "Chinamen in a Fight," *NYT,* Dec. 4, 1896; "Battle in Chinatown," *NYS,* Sept. 26, 1897.

50 **"lucrative and influential job":** "Mayor Tom Lee Boycotted," *NYS,* July 9, 1894.

51 **Two could play:** "Protection in Chinatown," *NYS,* July 29, 1894.

51 **"organized for the sole purpose":** "Hired Assassins," *Utica Observer,* Aug. 4, 1894.

Chapter 4: The Chinese Parkhursts

52 **The committee favored making:** "Lexow's Final Summing Up," *SR,* Jan. 18, 1895.

53 **The most prominent:** Richard D. White Jr., "Theodore Roosevelt as Civil Service Commissioner: Linking the Influence and Development of a Modern Administrative President," *Administrative Theory and Praxis* 22, no. 4 (Dec. 2000): 696–713.

53 **It is easy to understand:** "Mayor Strong Acts," *BJ,* April 2, 1895; "Mr. Kerwin Refuses," *NYH,* May 5, 1895.

53 **"I was appointed":** Roosevelt, *Autobiography,* 185.

53 **During his relatively brief tenure:** Kelly, *History of the New York City Police Department;* Roosevelt, *Autobiography,* 198–211.

54 **Roosevelt made short work:** "Parkhurst Finds Fault," *NYT,* Jan. 1, 1895; "Byrnes Retires with a Pension," *NYH,* May 28, 1895; Peter Hartshorn, *I Have Seen the Future: A Life of Lincoln Steffens* (Berkeley, Calif.: Counterpoint Press, 2011), 44.

55 **The Hip Sings, sensing:** "Roosevelt's Chinese Ally," *NYS,* July 19, 1895.

55 **In March 1895, Lee Toy finally:** "Wang Get, a Lexow Witness, Wins," *NYT,* March 24, 1895.

55 **"The conviction of Lee Toy":** "Lee Toy's Great Pull," *NYW,* March 26, 1895.

55 **Tom Lee—who surely:** "Murder the Talk in Chinatown," *NYW,* March 31, 1895.

56 **Despite mounting evidence:** "Police and Fan-Tan," *WS,* June 28, 1894.

56 **This rise to respectability:** Bonner, *Alas! What Brought Thee Hither?,* 139; Deposition of Chu Fong before Immigrant Inspector H. R. Sisson, April 24, 1905, in Chinese Exclusion Act Case File of Chu Fong, New York District Office of the U.S. Immigration and Naturalization Service, National Archives and Records Administration—Northeast Region, New York.

56　**The young man's name:** "Chinamen Alleged to Be Smuggled In," *NYTGM,* Sept. 9, 1896; "Strong in Chinatown," *NYW,* April 5, 1895; "The Mayor in Chinatown Late at Night," *NYTR,* April 5, 1895; "A New Temple for Chinatown," *NYTR,* May 14, 1895.

56　**In August 1895, officers raided:** "Colin Orders a Raid," *NYW,* Aug. 11, 1895; "Chinese Spies Cause a Raid," *NYS,* Aug. 11, 1895; "Only Three Chinamen Held," *NYW,* Aug. 12, 1895.

57　**"I am not through":** "Only Three Chinamen Held."

57　**"to establish and maintain":** "To Make Chinatown Moral," *NYT,* Nov. 8, 1896.

58　**Not to be outdone:** "Mott Street's New Club," *NYS,* Feb. 18, 1897; Certificate of Incorporation, Chinese Merchants Association, Feb. 4, 1897, New York State Department of State, Division of Corporations.

58　**To mark the occasion:** "On Leong Tong Celebration," *NYT,* Feb. 18, 1897; "Mott Street's New Club."

59　**"He is bold, plucky, resolute":** Moss, *American Metropolis,* 2:413–14.

59　**In court, the attorney:** "Dong Fong Says He Knows Moss," *NYTGM,* April 26, 1897; "Dong Fong Paid a Fine," *NYTGM,* April 28, 1897; "Has a Pull with Moss," *NYW,* April 27, 1897.

59　**But there was dissent:** "Chinese Parkhurstites," *NYS,* Sept. 2, 1897; "Odd Incidents by Chinamen," *NYW,* Sept. 2, 1897; "Dong Fong in Disgrace," *NYT,* Sept. 6, 1897; "Battle in Chinatown."

61　**"the spirit of a tiger":** Deposition of Mok See Duck (Mock Duck) before Immigration Inspector F. S. Pierce, Sept. 8, 1911, in Chinese Exclusion Act Case File for Mrs. Duck Mok, Record Group 85, box 323, Case Nos. 95, 146, Immigration and Naturalization Service, National Archives and Records Administration—Northeast Region, New York; W. O. Inglis, "The Golden Hegira of Mock Duck," *Saturday Evening Post,* May 27, 1905.

61　**The "shining light":** "Knives to Stop Chinese Reform," *NYH,* Sept. 26, 1897.

61　**On September 21, Mock Duck:** "Battle in Chinatown"; "The People, *etc.* in Complaint of *Leung Tai v. Chu Luck,*" City Magistrate's Court, First District, City and County of New York, Municipal Archives of the City of New York, Sept. 30, 1897; City Magistrate's Court, First District, City and County of New York in the case of the People, on the Complaint of *Chu Lok v. Leung Tai, Mock Tuck, and Wong Get,* Municipal Archives of the City of New York, Oct. 20, 1897; Court of General Sessions of the Peace of the City and County of New York in the case of the *People of the State of New York v. Wong Get* and the case of the *People of the State of New York v. Leung Tai,* Municipal Archives of the City of New York, Jan. 11, 1898; "Three Alleged Highbinders on Trial for Assault," *NYW,* Nov. 23, 1897.

62　**some seventy others spent the evening:** Among them were the New York state senator Jacob A. Cantor; the attorney Thomas McAdam; Thomas F. Smith, secretary to the outgoing Tammany head, John C. Sheehan, who was about to become clerk of the city court; John W. Keller, shortly to become

commissioner of public charities; the Brooklyn attorney and former congressman Daniel O'Reilly; and the police justice Joseph Koch.

62   **And because Tammany:** "Chinatown Honors Tammany," *NYTR,* Nov. 24, 1897.

62   **"We are living here":** "Notes from Gotham," *Bay City Times,* May 21, 1899; "Lees' Fete in Chinatown," *NYT,* April 18, 1899.

64   **"every one of whom is an expert":** Beck, *New York's Chinatown,* 122–33.

Chapter 5: The War Begins

66   **The first to die:** "Murder in Chinatown," *NYT,* Aug. 13, 1900; "Chinese Armed to Kill Another," *NYPR,* Aug. 13, 1900; "Chinese Allege Assassins' Plot," *NYTGM,* Aug. 13, 1900; "Chinaman Killed in Faction Fight," *NYH,* Aug. 13, 1900; "Homicide in Chinatown," *BSU,* Aug. 13, 1900; "Riot in Pell Street. One Chinaman Killed," *NYW,* Aug. 13, 1900.

66   **According to the rumor mill:** "Chinese in Gotham Meet and Riot Follows," *CT,* Aug. 13, 1900.

66   **The plan, police learned:** "Murder in Chinatown"; "Riot in Pell Street"; "Shooting in Chinatown," *NYT,* Aug. 17, 1900.

66   **Lung Kin's assassination initiated:** For the numbering convention for the New York tong wars, I am grateful to Arthur Bonner, author of *Alas! What Brought Thee Hither?* His book provided an invaluable road map to the conflicts in New York's Chinatown.

67   **Charged with homicide:** "Feud Renewed in Chinatown," *NYTGP,* April 21, 1901; "Chinese Murderer Held," *NYTR,* Aug. 14, 1900; "Goo Wing Ching Arraigned," *NYT,* Aug. 14, 1900.

67   **"I go die":** Testimony of Officer Henry Touwsma, the *People v. Mock Duck,* Criminal Branch of the Supreme Court of New York County, Minutes of the First Trial, New York Public Library, 1902.

67   **Ah Fee had no pulse:** "Chinaman Killed in a Fight," *NYTR,* Sept. 22, 1900; "Death Ends Chinese Riot," *NHR,* Sept. 22, 1900; "Ah Fee's Slayer in the Tombs Isn't Talking," *DPP,* Sept. 23, 1900.

68   **Tom Lee confirmed:** "Death Ends Chinese Riot"; "Highbinders in Chinatown," *NYTR,* April 14, 1901; "Feud Renewed in Chinatown."

69   **He took note when Asa B. Gardiner:** "Col. Gardiner Is Removed," *NYT,* Dec. 23, 1900; "Philbin Is Now in Office," *NYT,* Dec. 25, 1900; "Philbin After Big Game," *NYT,* Feb. 20, 1901; "Gamblers Do Business with Great Caution," *NYT,* April 9, 1901.

69   **Philbin inherited the Chinatown:** "Life Sentence for a Chinaman," *NYTR,* April 16, 1901; "Sue Sing Sent Up for Life," *BSU,* April 15, 1901.

69   **In the meantime, the Hip Sings:** "Highbinders After Tom Lee," *NYT,* April 21, 1901; "Highbinders After Life of Tom Lee," *NYH,* April 21, 1901.

70   **"They are after me now":** "New York Daily Letter," *CPD,* April 24, 1901; "Tom Lee Packs a Two-Foot Gun," *Salt Lake Telegram,* Feb. 5, 1902.

70   **Philbin and Garvan pursued:** "Five Chinamen in Murder Plot," *NYW,* June 11, 1901; "Three Chinamen Killed in Fire in Manhattan," *BSU,* Sept. 3, 1901.

70   **The men bolted:** Testimony of Detective John Farrington, Court of General Sessions of the Peace of the City and County of New York, Part II in the case of the *People v. Mock Duck,* Minutes of the Second Trial, New York Public Library, 1902.

70   **"I've been working hard":** "To Try Mock Duck for Murder," *NYS,* June 12, 1901.

71   **But before any trials:** "Boston Chinaman to Be Tried Here," *NYTR,* July 11, 1901; "Three Chinamen Killed in Fire in Manhattan"; "Chinamen Indicted," *DPP,* June 12, 1901; "Mock Duck Tried for Murder," *BS,* Feb. 20, 1902.

71   **The man was thirty-nine-year-old:** "Joy in Chinatown: Sing Cue Is Dead," *NYH,* Sept. 4, 1901; "Chinese Burned to Death," *NYT,* Sept. 4, 1901.

71   **The authorities believed the fire:** "Three Chinamen Killed in Fire in Manhattan"; "Chinese Burned to Death."

71   **"I think we can convict":** "Three Chinamen Killed in Fire in Manhattan."

71   **The election of Mayor Van Wyck:** Hazlitt Alva Cuppy and Merwin Bannister, *Our Own Times: A Continuous History of the Twentieth Century* (New York: J. A. Hill, 1904), 1:209.

71   **The nonpartisan, blue-ribbon panel:** Other members were the scholars Felix Adler and Edwin R. A. Seligman, the publisher George Haven Putnam, the former police commissioner and onetime mayoral candidate Joel Erhardt, and the prominent businessmen John Stewart Kennedy, Alexander E. Orr, and J. Harsen Rhoades.

72   **When it came to Chinatown:** "Items," *CT,* Aug. 12, 1890.

72   **"This woman solicited me":** Arthur E. Wilson, Report on Chinatown, n.d., reel 3, Committee of Fifteen Records, Manuscripts and Archives Division, New York Public Library.

73   **Most of the women:** U.S. census figures are quoted in McIllwain, *Organizing Crime in Chinatown,* 123.

73   **The few Chinese prostitutes:** Lucie Cheng Hirata, "Free, Indentured, Enslaved: Chinese Prostitutes in Nineteenth-Century America," *Signs* 5, no. 1 (Autumn 1979): 13–15.

74   **"are owned by powerful":** Leong, *Chinatown Inside Out,* 224–30.

74   **"Wong Aloy is a man":** "Highbinder Against Highbinder," *NYS,* Jan. 8, 1888; Wilson, Report on Chinatown.

75   **The Chinese New Year celebration:** "Chinatown's New Year," *NYT,* Feb. 18, 1902; "Officials in Chinatown," *NYTR,* Feb. 18, 1902; "The Man in the Street," *NYT,* Feb. 23, 1902.

76   **The dinner was inaugurated:** "Chinatown Greets Jerome," *Atlanta Constitution,* Feb. 18, 1902; "Chinatown's New Year"; "Officials in Chinatown."

76   **The day after the banquet:** The *People v. Mock Duck,* Criminal Branch of the Supreme Court of New York County, Minutes of the First Trial, New York Public Library, 1902.

76   **The first hurdle:** "Objections to Chinamen," *NYT,* Feb. 19, 1902; "New York Daily Letter," *CPD,* Feb. 21, 1902.

76   **"If this jury business":** "New York Daily Letter," *CPD,* Feb. 21, 1902.

76   **The jury box:** "Highbinder Case in Court," *NYT,* Feb. 22, 1902; "Highbinders Influence Murder Case," *DPP,* Feb. 23, 1902; Testimony of Emma Wing, Court of General Sessions of the Peace of the City and County of New York, Part II in the case of the *People v. Mock Duck,* Minutes of the Second Trial, New York Public Library, 1902.

77   **"You last Friday make witness":** "Threatens to Kill Witness of Murder," *NYH,* Feb. 26, 1902; "A Chinese Warning," *DPP,* Feb. 26, 1902.

77   **For whatever reason:** "Mock Duck Jury Disagrees," *DPP,* April 3, 1902.

78   **"If it be so":** Frank Moss, Esq., Summing Up for the Defense, Court of General Sessions of the Peace of the City and County of New York, Part II in the case of the *People v. Mock Duck,* Minutes of the Second Trial, New York Public Library, 1902.

79   **"I declare to you":** Ibid.

79   **In his summation:** Assistant District Attorney Arthur C. Train, Summing Up of the People, Court of General Sessions of the Peace of the City and County of New York, Part II in the case of the *People v. Mock Duck,* Minutes of the Second Trial, New York Public Library, 1902.

80   **"Could any man":** Ibid.

80   **After an overnight session:** "Mock Duck's Jury Disagrees," *BDE,* April 2, 1902.

80   **Mock Duck was released:** "Mock Duck Out Again," *Rochester Democrat and Chronicle,* April 4, 1902; "Mock Duck Free: No Third Trial," *NYTGM,* April 28, 1902; "Mock Duck at Liberty," *NYP,* April 28, 1902.

81   **Two weeks later, a banquet:** "Highbinder Flag Afloat in Pell Street," *NYW,* May 12, 1902.

Chapter 6: "A Regular Highbinder, Six-Shooter War Dance on the Bowery"

82   **At 1:30 in the morning:** "Feud in Chinatown," *NYG,* Nov. 3, 1904; Gong and Grant, *Tong War!,* 160.

82   **The drama continued:** "Chosen by Lot to Kill Victim," *NYW,* Nov. 3, 1904.

82   **At Hudson Street Hospital:** "Chinaman Shot," *Lowell Sun,* Nov. 3, 1904; "Chinatown Reformer Shot," *BDE,* Nov. 3, 1904; "Chinaman Murdered," *Rock Rapids Reporter,* Nov. 10, 1904; Ancestry.com, "1900 United States Federal Census Online Database."

83   **The Irish-born McAdoo:** "New York's New Chief," *DP,* Jan. 5, 1904; "McAdoo and New York Police Force," *San Jose Mercury News,* Jan. 3, 1904.

83   **Armed with warrants:** "Parkhurst Men Raid over Police Heads," *NYT,* July 22, 1904; "'Graft' in Chinatown," *NYTR,* July 22, 1904.

83   **But the interests of McAdoo:** "'Graft' in Chinatown"; "M'Adoo Tours Chinatown," *NYS,* July 23, 1904.

84 **Newspapers across the country:** "Chinese Assassin's Work," *NYS*, Nov. 4, 1904.

84 **Several papers suggested:** "Chinaman Shot"; "Chinatown Reformer Shot"; "Chosen by Lot to Kill Victim"; "Chinese Assassin's Work"; "Takes Vengeance on Chinese Spy," *NYTGM*, Nov. 3, 1904; "Assassins," *Newark Advocate*, Nov. 4, 1904.

84 **"Quite as deadly":** "Rival Chinese in Deadly Feud," *NYW*, Nov. 4, 1904.

85 **"somewhere in the dark labyrinths":** Ibid.

85 **By 1904, some sixty *fan tan* parlors:** "Chinese Lid Off," *NYG*, May 16, 1904.

85 **Fifty cents of each payment:** McIllwain, *Organizing Crime in Chinatown*, 94–95; Yu, *To Save China, to Save Ourselves*, 17.

85 **Another half dollar went:** "Call Tong Truce a Blind," *NYT*, May 31, 1913. The *Times* maintained that there were two organizations called the Chinese Merchants Association and distinguished *both* from the On Leong Tong in 1913. One was listed as headquartered at 14 Mott Street and the other at No. 16; the On Leong Tong, the *Times* said, was domiciled at No. 18. In fact, On Leong headquarters was at No. 14, and the Chinese Consolidated Benevolent Association was at No. 16; No. 18 was a building owned by Tom Lee. In most references, the Chinese Merchants Association was listed as being domiciled at 16 Mott, and it is clear it was a distinct organization from the On Leong Tong and affiliated—though not synonymous—with the Chinese Consolidated Benevolent Association.

85 **The system amounted to:** Riordon and Plunkitt, *Plunkitt of Tammany Hall*, 3–4, 20.

85 **Tom Lee had never been guilty:** McIllwain, *Organizing Crime in Chinatown*, 112.

86 **The trouble in New York's Chinatown:** "Rival Chinese in Deadly Feud"; "Warnings for Highbinders," *NYS*, Dec. 1, 1904.

86 **"We invite you to meet":** "Chinatown Gambling Feud," *NYS*, Nov. 8, 1904.

87 **If it was an olive branch:** "On Leongs Have Stolen the Hep Sings' Crest," *NYT*, Nov. 27, 1904.

87 **"a regular highbinder":** "Highbinders Fight in Mail," *NYS*, Nov. 27, 1904.

87 **The fusillade lasted:** "Chinese in Pistol Duel," *NYTR*, Nov. 26, 1904; "Chinese Fighting Armor in Court," *NYTGM*, Nov. 26, 1904; "Armor Clad Chinese Battle on the Bowery," *NYT*, Nov. 26, 1904.

87 **None of the Chinese involved:** "Chinamen in Coats of Mail," *BA*, Nov. 28, 1904; "Gambling Causes Chinatown Feud," *NYW*, Nov. 26, 1904.

87 **For his part, Mock Duck:** "Mock Duck Back, Chinatown Fears," *NYTGM*, March 18, 1905.

88 **"prepared to spend every penny":** "Police Graft in Chinatown," *NYW*, Dec. 12, 1904.

88 **"There will be murders":** "Moss Accuses Police," *NYTR*, Dec. 11, 1904.

88 **"You appear here in behalf":** "Police Graft in Chinatown," *NYW*, Dec. 12, 1904; "Moss Accuses Police."

88 **"For a week, every Hip Sing":** "Graft from Chinese," *NYS,* Dec. 12, 1904.

89 **"In the present crisis":** "Police Graft in Chinatown."

89 **"thugs, murderers, dealers":** "Graft from Chinese."

89 **"I do not want to say":** "Wants Real Detectives," *NYTR,* Dec. 12, 1904.

90 **The Hip Sings got wind:** "Chinamen Taken in Raid," *NYT,* Dec. 12, 1904; "Hip Sing on Top, Leong on Run," *NYS,* Dec. 13, 1904.

90 **The *Sun* observed:** "Hip Sing on Top, Leong on Run."

91 **"There'll be three":** "15 Hip Sing Tongers Soaked," *NYS,* Dec. 27, 1904; "Raid Ends in Sub-cellar," *NYT,* Dec. 27, 1904.

91 **"You can never convict":** "Chinaman's Shot Fatal," *NYTR,* Nov. 27, 1904; "Chinese in Coats of Mail," *BS,* Nov. 27, 1904.

92 **But death threats:** "Swear Missing Chinese Was Mock Duck's Slayer," *NYTGM,* Dec. 6, 1904.

92 **The trial went on:** "Accused of Murdering Mock Duck in Chinese Feud—No Evidence," *NYTR,* Jan. 19, 1905.

Chapter 7: A Price on Tom Lee's Head

93 **"flopping like a landed trout":** "Hip Sing Life for Each Raid," *NYS,* Feb. 1, 1905.

93 **"for every raid":** Ibid.

93 **At Yee's arraignment:** Deposition of Lee Loy before Immigration Inspector F. W. Berkshire, April 6, 1904, in Chinese Exclusion Act Case File for Lee Loy, Record Group 85, box 323, box 10, Case No. 14/3504, Immigration and Naturalization Service, National Archives and Records Administration—Northeast Region, New York; "Detective Is Real Thief," *NYS,* April 4, 1905.

94 **"Four highbinders from Boston":** "Price Put on Tom Lee's Head," *NYW,* Feb. 2, 1905.

94 **The China-born Gin Gum:** "Gin Gum Convicted of Forgery," *San Francisco Call,* May 7, 1898; "A New Trial for Gin Gum," *SFC,* Aug. 29, 1900; "Charlie Lee Is Free," *SFC,* Aug. 30, 1900.

94 **Tom Lee applied to his friends:** "Offer $3,000 to Kill Tom Lee," *NYW,* Feb. 3, 1905; "Chinese Hatchets Buried for a Day," *NYH,* Feb. 4, 1905.

95 **"The 'Melican people":** "Frenzied Finance 'Midst Chinese New Year Fun," *NYW,* Feb. 4, 1905.

95 **"They argue that if they pay up":** "Chinese Prisoners Let Go," *NYS,* Feb. 14, 1905.

96 **Like most of New York's Chinese:** "Chinatown as It Really Is."

96 **Ching Gong, a Hip Sing:** "Warfare of Tongs Claims New Victim," *NYT,* Feb. 9, 1905; "Murdered by Highbinders," *NYW,* Feb. 9, 1905.

96 **In retaliation:** "Chinatown Feud Shooting," *NYT,* Feb. 25, 1905; "Old Chinaman Shot in Feud of the Tongs," *NYT,* Feb. 25, 1905.

96 **If the On Leongs were depressed:** "Mock Duck Back, Chinatown Fears."

97 **"When Mock Duck ducked":** "'I'm a Dead Man,' Says the Mayor of Chinatown," *NYTGP,* March 19, 1905.

97 **The Hip Sings were serious:** "New Terror in Chinatown," *NYS*, March 19, 1905.

97 **Tom Lee vanished:** "Mock Duck Back, Chinatown Fears"; "Mock Duck, He Velly Bad," *NYT*, March 19, 1905.

98 **Louie Way and Lung Gow were held:** "Mock Duck Arrested," *Deseret News*, March 18, 1905; "Bad Mock Duck in Jail: His Enemy in Hiding," *NYT*, March 21, 1905; "Frank Moss and Jerome in Tiff over Mock Duck," *NYTGM*, March 22, 1905.

98 **"I don't care":** "Bad Mock Duck in Jail."

98 **Mock Duck's reemergence:** "Doomed by Highbinders," *CPD*, March 20, 1905; "Killing Overadvertised," *NYP*, March 20, 1905; "Bad Mock Duck in Jail."

98 **"I don't want to kill anybody":** "Mock Duck Now in a Tombs Cell," *NYH*, March 21, 1905.

98 **But only after Mock Duck:** "Mock Duck's Wings Clipped," *NYS*, March 21, 1905.

99 **"A few months ago":** "Frank Moss and Jerome in Tiff over Mock Duck"; "Hot Words in Courtroom Between Jerome and Moss," *BDE*, March 22, 1905.

99 **"This simple, angelic creature":** "Frank Moss and Jerome in Tiff over Mock Duck."

100 **"I am very glad to see you":** "Jerome Warns the Tongs," *NYT*, March 22, 1905; "Mr. Jerome Warns Gin Gum," *NYH*, March 22, 1905; "Jerome's Cure for the Tong War," *NYS*, March 22, 1905.

101 **It took five days:** "Mock Duck Is Free," *NYS*, March 28, 1905; "Mock Duck Released on Bail," *NYT*, March 28, 1905.

102 **"These shops pay money":** "Chinese Lid Off."

102 **"At present time the Detective":** "Detective Is Real Thief."

103 **"Of course any man":** Ibid.

103 **"The detectives who do":** Ibid.

104 **"You think it was written":** "Mock Duck: Evil Genius," *NYP*, April 4, 1905.

Chapter 8: The Chinese Theatre Massacre

106 **At a quarter to eight:** "300 Arrested in Chinatown Raid," *Utica Herald-Dispatch*, April 24, 1905.

106 **But it was Easter Sunday:** "Police Snare Hundreds in Spectacular Raid on Nine Chinatown Resorts," *NYPR*, April 24, 1905.

107 **It was the largest:** "213 Pigtail Prisoners Arraigned in the Tombs," *BDE*, April 24, 1905; "300 Arrested in Chinatown Raid."

107 **The Parkhurst superintendent:** "Police in Carriages Descend on Chinatown," *NYT*, April 24, 1905; "Chinatown Raided," *Corning Journal*, April 26, 1905; "Why Chinatown Was Raided," *NYP*, April 24, 1905.

107 **McAdoo reiterated:** "Hold 400 Chinese for Gambling," *BH*, April 23, 1905; "All Chinatown in Court," *NYP*, April 24, 1905.

108 **But anyone naive enough:** "400 Arrested in Chinatown Raid," *NYH*, April 24, 1905.

109   **"two white women":** "Made Murder Signs in Court," *NYS*, April 25, 1905.

109   **By noontime, placards:** "On Leongs All Alike," *NYTR*, April 25, 1905; "Made Murder Signs in Court."

110   **Later that day, McAdoo:** "Chinatown Mayor Is Under Arrest," *NYH*, April 27, 1905; "Chinatown Mayor Now in Police Toils," *NYT*, April 27, 1905.

110   **At 1:00 a.m. the following day:** "Cops Astray in Chinatown," *NYS*, April 29, 1905; "Eggers Fan Tan Raid a Farce," *NYS*, May 10, 1905; "Chinatown Graft Stories," *NYS*, May 12, 1905.

111   **Dong Fong, the Hip Sing:** "Dong Fong Gets Off Lightly," *NYW*, May 15, 1905; "Shot Tom Lee's Cousin," *NYS*, May 16, 1905.

112   **In the afternoon of May 30:** "Hip Sing Gets Eggers' Axe Now," *NYS*, May 31, 1905.

112   **"Fine day for Decoration Day":** "Avenging On Leongs Descend on Hip Sings," *NYT*, May 31, 1905.

112   **Less than a month later:** "Says Jim Wang's a Grafter," *NYS*, June 23, 1905; "Chinese Gamblers Paroled," *NYP*, May 31, 1905; "Wang, Reformer, Jailed," *NYP*, June 22, 1905; "Alleged Chinese Blackmailer," *BDE*, June 22, 1905.

113   **"strange, curious and grotesque":** "Chinese Drama a Mighty Serious Matter," *NYS*, Feb. 12, 1905.

113   **Suddenly, during a dramatic moment:** "Three Shot Dead in Chinese Theatre," *NYT*, Aug. 7, 1905.

114   **Soon a squad of police:** Gong and Grant, *Tong War!*, 74–77, 112–30, 158–69.

115   **The On Leongs had been expecting:** Ibid.; "Mock Duck Held for Murder," *NYS*, Aug. 8, 1905; "Chinese in Battle; 3 Dead," *CT*, Aug. 7, 1905; "Highbinders in Battle," *Binghamton Press*, Aug. 7, 1905.

115   **Bond was posted:** "Mock and His Friends Are Remanded," *NYTGM*, Aug. 7, 1905.

115   **Tom Lee served as master:** "The Yucks Buried," *NYT*, Aug. 11, 1905.

115   **Smarting from the assassination:** "Tong Midnight Murder Squad," *NYS*, Aug. 13, 1905.

116   **Poor Hop Lee:** "Chinamen Wield Cleaver, Kill Their Countryman," *BDE*, Aug. 12, 1905.

116   **The police were certain:** "Tong Midnight Murder Squad."

116   **Three days after Hop Lee's murder:** "$3,000 on Tom Lee's Head," *NYT*, Aug. 15, 1905.

117   **Because of the attempt:** "Tong War Worries Eggers," *NYS*, Aug. 22, 1905.

118   **At the arraignment:** "Four Shot in Chinatown," *NYS*, Aug. 21, 1905; "Tongs Fight Again; Four Shot This Time," *NYT*, Aug. 21, 1905.

118   **"Aren't you afraid":** "Tong War Worries Eggers."

118   **New Yorkers knew gang wars:** "Fatal Riot in New York," *NYT*, Sept. 17, 1903; "To End Shooting Affrays," *NYT*, Sept. 18, 1903; "Greene Takes Up Riots," *NYT*, Sept. 24, 1903; "Pistol Carriers Fined," *NYT*, Sept. 21, 1903; Lardner and Reppetto, *NYPD*, 125–28.

119 **"The present outbreak of crime":** "Great Crime Wave Puzzles Jerome," *NYW,* Aug. 26, 1905.

119 **New Yorkers were feeling:** "All Immigration Records Broken," *NYS,* May 10, 1905.

119 **A gang shooting in Chinatown:** "Outbreak of Crime in New York the Worst for Years," *NYW,* Sept. 4, 1905; "Great Crime Wave Puzzles Jerome."

119 **"When there is trouble":** "The Heathen Chinese," *New York Age,* Aug. 10, 1905.

119 **"His big ears can hear":** "Reign of Terror in Chinatown Now," *NYTR,* Aug. 13, 1905.

120 **"I kill no one":** Ibid.

120 **"Chinatown has been the synonym":** "To Clean Up Chinatown," *Buffalo Express,* Aug. 20, 1905.

120 **There had been just over:** *Report of the Police Department of the City of New York for the Year Ending December 31, 1904* (New York: Martin B. Brown, 1906), 41–43, 46, 48–49, 58.

121 **"The internal politics":** "Chinatown as It Really Is."

121 **"the worst slum in the city":** "Chinatown a Pest: Shame to the City; 'Clean It Up,'" *NYW,* Aug. 25, 1905; "Wipe Out Chinatown," *NYW,* March 2, 1906.

121 **Eagerly abetting this skewed view:** McIllwain, *Organizing Crime in China-town,* 105–6.

122 **"an ulcer spot":** McAdoo, *Guarding a Great City,* 170.

122 **"That there is such a thing":** Ibid., 151, 175.

123 **The situation in Chinatown:** "Tong War Worries Eggers."

123 **Local pawnshops:** "A Chinatown Roundup," *KCS,* Aug. 23, 1905; "Chinese Fear a New Tong War," *Pawtucket Times,* Aug. 23, 1905.

123 **Everyone braced for bloodshed:** "Chinatown Asks for Peace," *NYS,* Aug. 29, 1905; "Five Chinese Coming to Kill Tom Lee," *NYW,* Aug. 29, 1905.

124 **On August 29:** "Damaging for Mock Duck," *NYP,* Aug. 29, 1905; "Coroner Holds Mock Duck," *NYS,* Aug. 30, 1905; "Mock Duck Held in Murder Case," *NYH,* Aug. 30, 1905; "Mock Duck Held for Killing of Four Chinese," *NYTGM,* Aug. 29, 1905.

125 **The trial, however, would never:** "Mock Duck Let Go," *NYS,* Dec. 21, 1905.

Chapter 9: Profit Sharing

126 **A little before 2:00 p.m.:** Court of General Sessions of the Peace of the City and County of New York in the case of the *People v. George Tow,* impleaded with Louie Way and Yee Toy, Municipal Archives of the City of New York, box 10327, folder 106458, March 20, 1906.

127 **When police searched:** "Two Killed in Ambush in Chinatown Battle," *NYT,* Jan. 25, 1906.

127 **"If we can get":** "Lull in the Tong Gun Play," *NYS,* Jan. 26, 1906.

127 **The Pell Street killings:** "Two Killed in Ambush in Chinatown Battle."

127 **The Pell Street shootings were not:** "Chinese Killed Were to Testify at Murder Trial," *NYW,* Jan. 25, 1906; "Five Held for Tong War," *NYH,* Jan. 26, 1906; Court of General Sessions of the Peace of the City and County of New York in the case of the *People v. Charlie Joe and Mon Moon,* Municipal Archives of the City of New York, box 10315, folder 106446, Oct. 13, 1905.

128 **"the most quiet New Year":** "Tongs in Battle; Two Dead," *NYS,* Jan. 25, 1906.

128 **"weak men must be weeded out":** "Eggers Taken from Vice Squad; Sent to Brooklyn," *NYPR,* Oct. 17, 1905.

129 **"I will continue to be":** "Topics in New York," *NYT,* Oct. 17, 1905.

129 **Eggers's comment was prescient:** "Just the Truth," *DP,* Nov. 11, 1905; "Gen. Bingham Dies at Summer Home," *NYT,* Sept. 7, 1934.

129 **"plague spot that ought not":** Theodore A. Bingham, "Foreign Criminals in New York," *North American Review* 188, no. 634 (Sept. 1908): 383–84, 391–94; "Waldo Visits Chinatown," *NYS,* Jan. 27, 1906.

129 **On January 26, in one:** "It Happened in New York," *WP,* Jan. 29, 1906; "Deputy Waldo Now Wears Gold Shield on Duty," *NYTGM,* Jan. 26, 1906; "He Scolded Lee and Duck," *NYP,* Jan. 26, 1906; "Waldo Visits Chinatown and Sees the Tongs," *NYW,* Jan. 26, 1906.

130 **"I want to compliment you":** "Mr. Waldo Visits Tongs," *NYTR,* Jan. 27, 1906; "Transfers Captain Tracy," *NYT,* Feb. 18, 1906.

131 **"This business has gone on":** "Truce in Chinatown," *NYTR,* Jan. 31, 1906.

131 **Attorneys for both tongs:** "Chinatown's Warriors Agree to Real Peace," *NYT,* Jan. 31, 1906; "Tongs Hold Peace Confab," *NYS,* Jan. 31, 1906; "Truce in Chinatown."

132 **The pact, as negotiated:** "War of the Tongs Breaks Out Afresh," *NYT,* April 17, 1910.

133 **"The truth of the treaty":** "Peace of Chinatown Is Merely a Merger," *NYT,* April 1, 1906.

133 **Signing was set:** "Hip Sings Sign Treaty," *NYT,* Feb. 7, 1906; "On Leong Tongs Sign," *NYT,* Feb. 9, 1906.

133 **As soon as the On Leongs:** "Police Pinch Mock Duck," *NYS,* Feb. 21, 1906; "On Leongs Sign; Tong War Over," *NYS,* Feb. 9, 1906; "Peace of Chinatown Is Merely a Merger"; "On Leongs Dodge Peace Banquet," *NYH,* Feb. 12, 1906.

133 **Lee's decision to boycott:** "There's a New Tong in Chinatown Now," *NYT,* Feb. 13, 1906.

134 **"It is at once irritating":** "Topics of the Times," *NYT,* March 27, 1925.

135 **highly corrupt themselves:** Philip C. C. Huang, *Civil Justice in China: Representation and Practice in the Qing* (Redwood City, Calif.: Stanford University Press, 1996), 21–50.

135 **Chinese immigrants naturally sought:** Chu Chai, "Administration of Law Among the Chinese in Chicago," *Journal of Criminal Law and Criminology* 22, no. 6 (Spring 1932): 806.

138 **February 13 then brought:** "There's a New Tong in Chinatown Now."

138 **Much had changed:** Chinese Exclusion Act Case File for Wong Gett, Record Group 85, box 325, Case Nos. 95, 580, Immigration and Naturalization Service, National Archives and Records Administration—Northeast Region, New York; "Mock Duck Head of a New Tong," *NYH*, Feb. 13, 1906.

138 **The news of a third warring tong:** "Mock Duck Starts New Tong," *NYS*, Feb. 13, 1906; "There's a New Tong in Chinatown Now."

138 **Captain Schlottman, eager to make:** "Mock Duck Bails Prisoner," *NYS*, Feb. 19, 1906.

139 **"What? Do you say":** "Mock Duck Goes to the Tombs," *NYTGM*, Feb. 21, 1906.

139 **No bondsman appeared:** "Mock Duck Held in $5,139 for Trial," *NYW*, Feb. 24, 1906.

139 **"merely an agreement":** "Local Board Calls Hearing on Chinatown Park Plan," *NYW*, March 6, 1906.

139 **"the worst slum in the city":** "Wipe Out Chinatown."

140 **"It is better to clean out":** "Tear Down the Dens of Chinatown and Make a Park of New York's Darkest Spot," *NYW*, Feb. 28, 1906; "Some of the Plague Spots in Chinatown That Should Give Way for a Public Park," *NYW*, March 1, 1906.

140 **"the instrumentalities of Christianity":** "Calls a Public Hearing on Park for Chinatown," *NYW*, March 5, 1906; "Some of the Plague Spots in Chinatown That Should Give Way for a Public Park."

140 **The government had the power:** "Wipe Out Foul Crime Dens—Make a Park," *NYW*, March 2, 1906; "Calls a Public Hearing on Park for Chinatown"; "Dives Must Give Way to Chinatown Park," *NYW*, March 24, 1906.

141 **"The whole east side":** "Rookery Owners Oppose Chinatown Park Plan," *NYW*, March 20, 1906.

141 **"Greed is the bottom":** "Scores Men Who Shelter the Dens of Chinatown," *NYW*, March 20, 1906; "Argue on Chinatown Park," *NYT*, March 21, 1906.

141 **Even after opposition:** "Fight to Wipe Out Chinatown for Park Good as Won," *NYW*, March 21, 1906; "For a Chinatown Park," *NYP*, May 1, 1906.

141 **Rumors about what would:** "A Chinatown in Brooklyn?," *NYT*, April 27, 1906; "Chinatown in the Bronx," *NYT*, July 25, 1906; "Chinatown May Move Over to Williamsburg," *NYT*, Aug. 6, 1906.

142 **The Board of Estimate finally acted:** "A Park in Chinatown," *NYT*, Feb. 9, 1907; "'Dan' O'Reilly Celestial Hero," *WT*, June 27, 1907.

142 **"every Chinaman who did not":** "Tong Killings Pause and Chinatown Feasts," *NYT*, March 29, 1906; "Feast for Tongs' Treaty," *NYPR*, March 29, 1906; "Eighteen Course Dinner to Celebrate Peace in Chinatown," *BDE*, March 29, 1906.

142 **In mid-April, Mock Duck's attorney:** "Mock Duck's Bail Reduced," *NYT*, April 13, 1906.

143 **"I'm not going to do":** "Mock Duck Is Free," *NYT*, April 15, 1906; "Mock Duck Is Free," *NYS*, April 15, 1906.

143   **Three days later came the news:** "Our Chinese Aiding 'Frisco," *NYT,* April 23, 1906.

143   **Several days later:** "Police Get Mock Duck Again," *NYP,* April 24, 1906.

143   **For at least eight years:** Testimony of Florence Bendorff and Emma Wing, Court of General Sessions of the Peace of the City and County of New York, Part II in the case of the *People v. Mock Duck,* Minutes of the Second Trial, New York Public Library, 1902; Ancestry.com, "1910 United States Federal Census Online Database," accessed Aug. 4, 2015, http://search.ancestry.com/search /db.aspx?dbid=7884.

144   **In March 1906:** Testimony of Chin Hen Leon, Court of General Sessions of the Peace of the City and County of New York, Part II in the case of the *People v. Mock Duck,* Minutes of the Second Trial, New York Public Library, 1902; "Mock Duck Says the Girl Is His Wife," *PI,* May 25, 1906; "Hostile Chinese Factions in Court," *PI,* May 26, 1906; "Mock Duck's Wife Was Lost," *NYS,* March 9, 1906.

144   **On learning of her arrest:** "Hostile Chinese Factions in Court."

144   **When Tai Yow came to live:** "Mock Duck's Child Seized," *NYP,* March 19, 1907.

145   **Although there was never:** Ibid.; "Mock Duck Bereft of His Joy," *NYS,* March 20, 1907.

146   **The child had some:** "Mock Duck's Child Seized."

146   **On the morning of March 19:** "Cruelty Sought at Mock Duck's," *NYT,* March 20, 1907.

146   **Their society—known:** "Mock Duck Bereft of His Joy."

146   **The couple explained:** "Call Mock Duck's Stepchild a Slave," *NYH,* March 20, 1907.

146   **At which point, the hard-boiled:** "Mock Duck Bereft of His Joy."

146   **The couple attended the arraignment:** "Ha Oi Still a Captive," *NYP,* March 22, 1907; "Ha Oi Is Lost to Chinatown," *NYS,* March 23, 1907.

147   **Based on nothing other:** "Ha Oi Is Lost to Chinatown"; "Current News of the World," *Sausalito News,* April 6, 1907.

147   **The judge questioned Mock Duck:** "Law Takes Ha Oi from Mock Duck," *NYH,* April 13, 1907; "Mock Duck Loses Little Ha Oi," *NYS,* April 13, 1907.

147   **"The greatest satisfaction":** New York Society for the Prevention of Cruelty to Children, *Thirty-third Annual Report* (New York: Offices of the Society, 1908), 33–34.

148   **"So the courts have deprived":** "Mock Duck and Ha Oi," *NYH,* April 15, 1907.

Chapter 10: Have Gun, Will Travel

149   **Although New York was at peace:** "Bad Chinamen These," *PI,* Dec. 1, 1889; "Sing's Romantic Career," *WT,* Jan. 13, 1896; "Paid Them Blackmail," *WP,* July 20, 1895.

149 **The Boston-based Meihong Soohoo:** Meihong Soohoo, *Wo tonghen Meidi: Qiao Mei qishinian shenghuo huiyilü* [我痛恨美帝—侨美七十年生活回忆录; I bitterly hate imperialist America: Reminiscences of a seventy-year sojourn in the United States] (Beijing: Guangming Daily, 1951), 39–47; Gong and Grant, *Tong War!*, 244–45.

149 **Each branch of the On Leong:** "500 Chinese Here from 20 Cities to Attend Convention," *WP*, Sept. 2, 1924.

150 *boo how doy:* Chinese translation courtesy of Ram Moy.

150 **In mid-August 1907:** "The Peace of Pell Street," *NYT*, Aug. 23, 1907; "Tongs, at Peace, Dine in Chinatown," *NYH*, Aug. 22, 1907; "Eat Because Tongs Are Quiet," *NYS*, Aug. 22, 1907.

150 **"the Great White Father":** "Chinaman Killed in Street," *NYS*, Mar. 2, 1908.

150 **On this latter point:** "Chinese Tongmen Battle and Four Are Injured," *Omaha World Herald*, June 6, 1906; "Celestials at War Among Themselves," *SDT*, July 5, 1906; "Chinese Feud On Again," *CPD*, July 5, 1906; "Marked for Death," *Grand Rapids Press*, July 7, 1907; "Chinamen Shot in Philadelphia," *Augusta Chronicle*, July 8, 1907; "Chinatown Tongs Engage in Fight," *Harrisburg Patriot*, July 8, 1907.

151 **The Hip Sings, too:** "Battle of Rival Chinese Societies," *Oswego Palladium*, Aug. 3, 1907; Gong and Grant, *Tong War!*, 175–80; "More Arrests in Hep Sing Killing," *BH*, Aug. 4, 1907.

151 **Captain Robert F. Dooley:** "Biggest Shake-Up in Police History," *NYT*, Oct. 26, 1906.

151 **"Never been in Boston":** "War Cloud in Pell Street," *NYTR*, Aug. 4, 1907.

152 **"I have to be very careful":** "No More Tong Wars Here for Mock Duck," *NYT*, Aug. 6, 1907.

152 **He was right to be wary:** "Mock Duck's Home Afire," *NYTGM*, Feb. 28, 1908; "Tenement Fire in Tong War," *NYT*, Feb. 28, 1908; "Smoking Out Mock Duck," *NYT*, Feb. 29, 1908; "Eight Fires Now at No. 42," *NYT*, March 9, 1908.

152 **March also brought justice:** "Nine Chinese Guilty of Feud Murders," *NYT*, March 8, 1908; "Charles, the Vice Sleuth," *NYT*, March 9, 1908; "Two Chinese to Be Hanged," *NYT*, March 8, 1908.

152 **New York was nervous:** "Police Guard Against Tong War," *NYT*, March 16, 1908.

152 **The victim was Ing Mow:** "Murder in Tong War," *WP*, March 28, 1908; "Chinaman Killed in Street," *NYS*, March 28, 1908; "Boston Tong Trial Inspires Murder in New York," *BJ*, March 28, 1908.

153 **"The Hip Sing Tong already":** "Killed by Rival Tong," *NYTR*, March 28, 1908.

153 **"Chinese of all classes":** Leong, *Chinatown Inside Out*, 68–69, 80–81.

154 **The On Leongs continued to feather:** "G'long Now, Danny Riordan," *NYS*, Sept. 5, 1908; "Foley Gives Big Outing," *NYT*, Aug. 30, 1902.

154 **After the repeated attempts:** "Mock Duck in Chicago," *NYS*, Oct. 9, 1907; "Undesirable Citizens," *Huntington Herald*, Oct. 8, 1907; "Wily Mock Duck,

Fan-Tan King, Tells Why He Is Here," *DP*, Nov. 12, 1908; "Mock Duck, Old Denizen, Angry at 'Fake,'" *DP*, Nov. 19, 1908; "Mock Duck Leaves Denver Mysteriously," *DP*, Nov. 7, 1908; "Chinatown in Denver Sees Deadly War," *Salt Lake Telegram*, Nov. 20, 1908.

154 **After Denver, Mock Duck:** "Mock Duck Back A-glitter," *NYS*, May 24, 1909.

155 **"since they have had peace":** "Tom Lee Never Winked," *NYS*, Feb. 2, 1909.

Chapter 11: The Four Brothers' War

156 **On June 18, 1909:** For a complete and thought-provoking account of the Sigel murder and its broader significance, see Lui, *Chinatown Trunk Mystery*.

156 **Sigel's murder was quickly:** "Find Miss Sigel Dead in Trunk," *NYT*, June 19, 1909; "Police Hunt in Washington," *NYT*, June 20, 1909; "Arrest Friend of Miss Sigel," *NYT*, June 20, 1909; "Chong Saw Ling Kill Sigel Girl," *NYT*, June 23, 1909; "Chong Admits Lying About Sigel Murder," *NYT*, June 24, 1909.

156 **The police commissioner, Theodore Bingham:** "Arrest Friend of Miss Sigel"; "Police Neglect, due to Mayor's Shakeup, Let Ling Get Away," *TT*, July 4, 1909.

157 **"Sightseers seem afraid":** "Chinese Merchants Ask for Protection," *NYT*, July 4, 1909.

157 **Sigel's murder, and the sensational:** "Says Ling Escaped in Cousin's Wagon," *NYT*, July 6, 1909.

157 **Recognizing the threat:** "Minister Wu Joins Hunt," *NYT*, June 23, 1909; "Elsie Sigel's Death," *Montreal Globe*, June 23, 1909; "Chinese Freemasons," *NYT*, July 4, 1909; "Cunning of the East Beats Western Wit," *WT*, July 3, 1909; "Police Neglect, due to Mayor's Shakeup, Let Ling Get Away."

157 **The group was known formally:** Lai, "Historical Development of the Chinese Consolidated Benevolent Association/*Huiguan* System," 31–32; James S. L. Jung, "A Concise History and Development of the Lung Kong Organization," Pan American Lung Kong Tin Yee Association Web site, accessed Aug. 4, 2015, http://www.palungkong.org/concise%20lk%20history.htm.

158 **While the police were turning:** "Five Boston Chinamen Must Die in Chair," *DP*, July 3, 1909; "Tong War Threatened," *BS*, July 6, 1909.

158 **Mock Duck, always a person:** "Says Ling Escaped in Cousin's Wagon"; "A 40-Course Chinese Banquet," *NYT*, July 12, 1909.

158 **When no trouble broke out:** "Chinese Girl Murdered," *Watertown Daily Times*, Aug. 16, 1909; "Chinese Girl Slain in New York City," *Amsterdam Evening Recorder*, Aug. 16, 1909.

159 **The policeman took Chin:** "Chinese Girl Murdered," *NYS*, Aug. 16, 1909.

160 **Chin Lem told the captain:** "Chinese Girl Murdered," *Watertown Daily Times*, Aug. 16, 1909.

160 **Over the next several days:** "Clue in Bloody Fingers," *SJ*, Aug. 16, 1909.

160　**The police asked why the couple:** "Girl Murdered, Chinaman Held," *NYC,* Aug. 16, 1909; "Murder of Woman Puzzles Chinatown," *NYPR,* Aug. 16, 1909; "Suspect Chin Len," *Syracuse Herald,* Aug. 17, 1909.

160　**The signs pointed to another:** "Chin Len Caught in Tangle of Stories," *Utica Observer,* Aug. 17, 1909; "Think Chin Len Killed Girl," *NYS,* Aug. 17, 1909; "Chin Len Bailed Out," *Utica Observer,* Aug. 18, 1909; "Says He Saw Man Murder Bow Kum," *WT,* Aug. 18, 1909.

162　**Gin Gum, Chin Lem's brother:** "Bow Kum Laid to Rest," *NYC,* Aug. 20, 1909.

162　**Police questioned several:** "Arrests in Chinatown Case," *NYP,* Aug. 20, 1909; "Chinamen Are Indicted," *SR,* Sept. 11, 1909.

162　**San Francisco police records:** "Arrests in Chinatown Case"; "May Be Murderers," *WS,* Aug. 20, 1909.

162　**When Lau Tong learned:** "Hatchet Men in Case," *BS,* Aug. 21, 1909.

163　**Violence broke out:** "Aims at Tom Lee's Lieutenant but Hits Wrong Man," *NYS,* Sept. 14, 1909.

163　**A policeman saw Lee Wah:** "Police Feast with Hip Sings," *NYS,* May 17, 1909; "Chinatown Going Fast," *NYTR,* July 12, 1909; "Captain Galvin Tired Out," *NYTR,* Aug. 25, 1909.

164　**Galvin was successful:** "Chinatown Wrecks Galvin," *NYPR,* Aug. 25, 1909; "Captain Galvin Tired Out."

164　**Everyone braced for retaliation:** "Hostile Tongs Prepare for War," *NYT,* Sept. 15, 1909; "Gun Play in Mott Street," *NYTR,* Sept. 13, 1909; "Human Target for Tong War Practice," *NYPR,* Sept. 13, 1909; "Fearing Tong War, Arrest 19 Chinese in Raid," *NYTGM,* Sept. 14, 1909.

164　**In mid-October:** "Three Chinese Tong Murderers Killed in Chair," *NYTGM,* Oct. 12, 1909.

164　**That evening, two On Leongs:** "New Chinatown Warfare," *NYP,* Nov. 6, 1909.

165　**"we are not making":** "Marked for Death by Chinese Tongs," *NYT,* Nov. 17, 1909.

165　**At the end of November:** "Gotham Chinese Make Odd Move; Trouble Feared," *New Orleans Item,* Nov. 26, 1909; "Tong Expulsion Not Real," *NYS,* Nov. 25, 1909; "It All Began with Bow Kum," *NYS,* Dec. 29, 1909.

165　**A month later:** "Deadly Tong War Claims Two More New York Victims," *Salt Lake Telegram,* Dec. 28, 1909; "New York Trying to Prevent Tong Outbreak," *Deseret Evening News,* Dec. 28, 1909.

166　**Three days later, Ah Hoon:** "Chinese Killed Were to Testify at Murder Trial"; "Tong War Is Renewed," *Marion Daily Mirror,* Dec. 30, 1909.

166　**There were two theories:** "Police Hold Chinese Woman as Witness in Tong Murder," *NYTGM,* Dec. 30, 1909.

166　**Ah Hoon had known:** "Chinese Clown Acts While He Knows Highbinders Are Waiting to Kill Him," *NYH,* Dec. 31, 1909.

166　**On the night of his death:** "Ah Hoon's Death Warning," *NYP,* Dec. 30, 1909; "Police Trying to Stop Tong Fight in New York," *Cincinnati Post,* Dec. 30, 1909; "Tong War Closes Theater," *NYS,* Dec. 30, 1909.

167 **A year after the slaying:** The first mention in the press of the Bloody Angle on Doyers Street appears to be in "His Fourth Attempt to Die," *NYT,* Dec. 25, 1910.

167 **With the rise to prominence:** "War of the Tongs Breaks Out Afresh."

167 **"All the companies and tongs":** "Tongs United to Fight On Leong," *Detroit Free Press,* Jan. 4, 1910.

168 **This would have posed:** "Mock Duck at Bow Kum Trial," *BH,* Jan. 5, 1910; "Mock Duck Comes to Denver," *DP,* Sept. 5, 1909; "40-Course Chinese Banquet."

168 **The attorney Terence J. McManus:** "Chinese Murder Trial," *BDE,* Jan. 4, 1910.

168 **Moss began by telling:** "Bow Kum Trial On," *NYC,* Jan. 6, 1910; "Accuse Witness on Stand of Slaying Girl," *NYH,* Jan. 6, 1910; "A Chinese Love Tragedy," *BA,* Jan. 6, 1910.

169 **On cross-examination:** "Bow Kum's Man Is Grilled," *NYS,* Jan. 6, 1910.

169 **The principal prosecution witness:** "Bow Kum Case In," *NYTR,* Jan. 7, 1910; "Heard Two Chinamen Make Death Threat," *Pawtucket Times,* Jan. 7, 1910; "The Two Laus May Go Free," *NYS,* Jan. 7, 1910.

170 **The defense presented:** "Chinese on Stand," *NYTR,* Jan. 8, 1910; "Chinese Trail Still Blind," *NYS,* Jan. 8, 1910.

170 **"A bewildered jury":** "Acquit Chinamen of Killing Bow Kum," *NYT,* Jan. 11, 1910.

170 **After deliberating for several hours:** "Two Chinese Freed," *NYTR,* Jan. 11, 1910.

171 **The war Captain Galvin:** "Shot in the Back in Chinatown Feud," *NYT,* Jan. 24, 1910; "Chinese Kills a Japanese," *NYS,* Jan. 24, 1910.

171 **Nearly half of the police:** "Chinese Entertain," *NYTR,* Feb. 22, 1910.

172 **"There was Coroner Feinberg":** "On Leongs Very Peaceful," *NYS,* Feb. 22, 1910.

172 **Not to be outdone:** "Chinese New Year Dinner," *NYT,* Feb. 28, 1910.

172 **The first victim:** "Items of Interest from Busy Gotham," *SFC,* April 18, 1910.

172 **Retaliation took only:** "Killed in Tong War," *NYTR,* April 11, 1910.

173 **Captain Richard E. Enright:** "Chinaman Slain in Tong Outbreak," *WH,* April 11, 1910; "New Head Detective M'Cafferty Is Out," *NYT,* April 1, 1910; "Big Crowd at Galvin's Funeral," *NYTR,* Sept. 2, 1910.

173 **Several newspapers blamed:** "Bloody Tong War May Sweep East," *Niagara Falls Gazette,* April 11, 1910; "War over Slain Girl Costs Lives of Six," *Salt Lake Herald-Republican,* April 11, 1910; "War of Tongs Fatal to Five in Two Cities," *Syracuse Post-Standard,* April 11, 1910; "Chinatown Going Fast"; "It All Began with Bow Kum."

174 **"I am willing to do all":** "Another Chinaman Shot in Tong War," *NYT,* April 13, 1910.

174 **It actually took more than:** "Tong War in New York," *Salt Lake Herald-Republican,* April 13, 1910; "Judge as Tong Arbiter," *NYTR,* April 14, 1910.

174   **"All that is wished":** "Peace Envoy in Chinatown," *NYT,* April 15, 1910; "Chinese Envoy Steps In," *NYTR,* April 19, 1910.

174   **But peace was problematical:** "Peace Again in Chinatown," *NYPR,* April 22, 1910; "Treaty to End Tong War," *NYT,* April 22, 1910; "Tong Peace to Be Signed," *NYS,* April 22, 1910; "No Peace Yet of the Tongs," *NYS,* April 23, 1910; "Chinese Tongs to Fight Some More," *Detroit Free Press,* April 23, 1910.

175   **Under these conditions:** "Tong War Goes On; Mediation Fails," *NYT,* April 23, 1910.

175   **"almost elbowed each other":** "Bingham Shakes Up Police Again," *NYT,* Nov. 7, 1907; "Old Tom Lee Balks Efforts at Peace," *WT,* April 23, 1910; "Tong War Goes On."

175   **Hodgins got nowhere:** "Big Bill Working on Chinese Puzzle," *WT,* May 4, 1910; "Two Tongs Within a Tong," *NYS,* May 2, 1910.

175   **On June 10, 1910:** "Chu Hen Acquitted of Murder," *NYS,* June 10, 1910; "One Dead, One Dying in Chinese Shooting," *NYTR,* June 27, 1910.

176   **The Four Brothers members:** "Three Shot Down in Chinese Feud," *NYC,* June 27, 1910.

176   **Suddenly, however, Pell Street:** "War Under Big Bill's Nose," *NYS,* June 27, 1910; "Four Brothers Man Slain, Two Mortally Wounded When the On Leongs Open Fire on Deadly Enemies," *NYH,* June 27, 1910.

176   **A couple of weeks later:** "Chinaman Crosses Dead Line and Dies," *Pawtucket Times,* Aug. 17, 1910; "Chinamen Held for Coroner," *NYTR,* Aug. 18, 1910; "Another Chinese Murder," *Harrisburg Patriot,* Aug. 17, 1910; "Tong War Expected," *BS,* Aug. 18, 1910; "Tong War Again Breaks One Victim in New York," *MT,* Aug. 21, 1910.

178   **"The On Leongs have regular":** "The Tongs at War Again," *NYTR,* July 28, 1910.

178   **The result was heightened:** "Peace of Tongs Only Temporary, Chinese Assert," *NYW,* Dec. 20, 1910.

178   **It took a little longer:** "Tongs Sign Peace Pact," *NYTR,* Dec. 30, 1910; "Chinese Sign a Treaty of Peace," *Evening Standard,* Dec. 30, 1910; "Chinese Tongs End Their War," *Daily Capital Journal,* Dec. 30, 1910; "Tongs and the Wars They Waged in the Palmy Days of Chinatown," *NYS,* Aug. 10, 1919.

179   **"might have been accomplished long ago":** "Chinese Hold a Love Feast," *NYTR,* Jan. 1, 1911.

180   **"is what men fight for":** Lin, *My Country and My People,* 190–91.

181   **"Starting a war":** Leong, *Chinatown Inside Out,* 76.

Chapter 12: Mock Duck's Luck Runs Out

182   **On January 25, 1911:** "Opium Raids in Tenderloin," *NYS,* Jan. 26, 1911; "Letters, &c., from Opium Dens," *NYS,* Jan. 27, 1911.

183   **Neither Charlie Boston:** "Rooting Out the Evil"; "Opium Smokers Arrested," *NYT,* Aug. 11, 1899.

183 **The U.S. attorney's office:** "Opium Raids in Tenderloin"; "Letters, &c., from Opium Dens."

183 **The pieces of the puzzle:** "Alleged Opium Chief Held," *WP,* Jan. 31, 1911; "Henkel Nabs Charley Boston," *NYTR,* Jan. 31, 1911; "Hold Chinaman as Head of Opium Ring," *NYT,* Jan. 31, 1911.

184 **At the Tombs, Boston:** "Peace Treaty of Tongs in Danger," *Pittston Gazette,* Feb. 1, 1911; "Charley Boston Indicted," *BA,* Feb. 21, 1911.

184 **Although protection payments:** "The Tongs at War," *Honesdale Citizen,* Feb. 3, 1911; "Opium King's Arrest Cause of Tong War," *NYS,* Jan. 7, 1912.

185 **Nobody expected peace:** "Tong Aided Slayer Elsie Siegel Escape," *MT,* Feb. 12, 1911.

185 **Gaynor was first and foremost:** Mayor Gaynor's activities with respect to the police department are well described in Johnson, *Street Justice,* 100–107.

185 **"After Gaynor got in":** "Gambling Revival Blamed on Gaynor," *NYT,* Sept. 29, 1914; "Gaynor Throws Out Plain-Clothes Men," *NYT,* June 22, 1910; "Mayor Gaynor's Career," *BS,* Aug. 10, 1910.

186 **To everyone's surprise:** "High Honors for Chu Tom," *NYS,* Feb. 20, 1911; "Chinatown's Tongs Raise Peace Banner," *NYH,* April 4, 1911; "Chinese Dragon on Parade," *NYS,* April 9, 1911; "Day of Amity in Chinatown," *NYS,* July 5, 1911.

186 **There was still some fighting:** Gong and Grant, *Tong War!,* 203; "New Tong War Element," *NYTR,* Aug. 4, 1912; Van Norden, *Who's Who of the Chinese in New York,* 91; "Shot by Old Enemy," *WS,* March 13, 1911; "Sing Dock Mortally Shot," *NYTR,* March 13, 1911.

186 **The federal case against:** "Charley Boston Case Takes Officials East," *Gazette Times,* Dec. 12, 1911; "Sale of Opium Is Admitted by Boston," *Gazette Times,* Dec. 13, 1911.

188 **Some of Boston's Canadian:** "Boston Pleads Guilty," *NYTR,* Dec. 13, 1911.

189 **"Brethren, we have buried":** "Chinese Here Bury Hatchet," *NYTR,* Dec. 13, 1911.

189 **There would be one final:** "Hankow Is Bombarded," *Springfield Daily News,* Jan. 1, 1912; "Chinese Cheer Republic," *NYTR,* Jan. 2, 1912.

189 **A bitter wind was blowing:** "Chinese Tongs in Bloody Encounter," *North Tonawanda Evening News,* Jan. 6, 1912.

189 **The On Leongs wasted no time:** "One Dead, One Dying in Tong Feud," *NYH,* Jan. 6, 1912.

190 **When the police arrived:** "One Dead, One Dying in Tong War Raid," *NYS,* Jan. 6, 1912.

190 **In the meantime, a Hip Sing:** "Chinese Tong War Denied," *BS,* Jan. 7, 1912; "Two Chinese Held on Murder Charge," *NYH,* Jan. 7, 1912.

190 **The arrest and imprisonment:** "Opium King's Arrest Cause of Tong War."

191 **On the morning of January 9:** "Axe Men Invade Chinatown," *NYT,* Jan. 10, 1912; "Gamblers Captured in Chinatown Raid," *NYS,* Jan. 10, 1912; "Masked Chinaman Led Police Raid," *NYH,* Jan. 10, 1912; "Raid 20 Chinese Gambling Resorts," *NYTR,* Jan. 10, 1912.

191   **The On Leongs surely expected:** "Hip Sing Boys Attack Men in Raid; Two Shot," *NYS,* Feb. 28, 1912; "Two Chinamen Shot in a Tong Battle," *NYT,* Feb. 28, 1912.

192   **A couple of weeks later:** "Fusillade in Chinatown," *NYT,* March 13, 1912.

193   **June brought Mock Duck's trial:** "Court Gets Lesson on Chinese Policy Game," *NYS,* June 7, 1912; "Mock Duck on Trial," *NYTR,* June 7, 1912; "Try Mock Duck on Policy Charge," *NYH,* June 7, 1912.

194   **"He seems never to be able":** The Honorable Edward Swann Jr., Presentencing Remarks, Court of General Sessions of the Peace of the City and County of New York, Part IV in the case of the *People of the State of New York v. Mock Duck,* Lloyd Sealy Library, John Jay College, June 6, 1912.

194   **Even before the sentence:** "Mock Duck Escapes Again," *NYP,* July 6, 1912; "Mock Duck to Appeal," *BDE,* July 6, 1912; "Mock Duck Wins a Point," *NYS,* July 7, 1912; "Mock Duck Going Home," *NYS,* July 12, 1912.

195   **A few days after Mock Duck's:** Gong and Grant, *Tong War!,* 13, 206.

195   **The shooter was a China-born:** "Riddled Yu Toy from Pell Street Doorway," *NYS,* June 18, 1912.

195   **Jung Hing, however:** "New Tong War Element"; Van Norden, *Who's Who of the Chinese in New York,* 91; "Tongs to Reward Gun Man," *NYTR,* June 19, 1912.

195   **On June 23, 1912:** "Chinese Bomb Timed to Kill Packed Tong," *NYT,* June 24, 1912.

196   **Nor did a second bomb:** "Chinatown Shaken by Another Bomb as Feud Re-opens," *NYW,* July 1, 1912.

196   **Gunpowder might have been:** "They're After Big Lou, Head of the On Leong," *NYS,* July 2, 1912; Gong and Grant, *Tong War!,* 191–93.

196   **"FIFTEEN HUNDRED DOLLARS":** "They're After Big Lou, Head of the On Leong." In this case, "Chinese Merchants Association" clearly meant the On Leong Tong, of which Gin Gum was secretary. The address at the end of the notice was incorrect; the On Leong Tong was located at 14, not 24, Mott Street.

197   **"There's a monkey dead":** "Hip Sing Gun Man Slain in His Bunk," *NYH,* July 15, 1912; "Mock Duck Dealer Slain in His Bunk," *NYT,* July 15, 1912.

197   **Another Hip Sing met:** "Shot Dead in Chinese Feud," *NYT,* July 27, 1912.

198   **Louie Way had been involved:** "9 Years for Tong Shooting," *NYT,* May 29, 1906.

198   **Sane or not, he didn't:** "Four Slain and Eleven Wounded in Chinatown Battle," *NYH,* Oct. 15, 1912; "Four Dead in Street in Chinatown Battle," *NYS,* Oct. 15, 1912; "Death List Now Has Total of Five," *NYW,* Oct. 15, 1912; "Chinese Gunmen Held," *NYS,* Oct. 16, 1912.

199   **The proximate cause:** "Four Dead in Street in Chinatown Battle."

199   **November saw the trial:** "Chinaman Found Guilty of Murder in War of Tongs," *NYW,* Dec. 7, 1912; "Chinaman Guilty of First Degree Murder," *NYS,* Dec. 8, 1912.

199   **Armed with a search warrant:** "Seek Opium, Find Firearms," *NYH,* Dec. 8, 1912; "Chinaman Guilty of First Degree Murder."

199   **On December 13, the judge:** "Chair for Chinaman; First Case in 30 Years," *NYC,* Dec. 14, 1912; "Chinese Murderer Sentenced," *NYTR,* Jan. 23, 1913.

199   **Without benefit of a divorce:** "Chinese Couple Married," *SR,* Jan. 17, 1913; Ancestry.com, "Massachusetts, Marriage Records, 1840–1915," accessed Aug. 4, 2015, http://search.ancestry.com/search/db.aspx?dbid=2511.

200   **Then something remarkable:** FamilySearch.org, "Ohio, County Marriages, 1790–1950," accessed Aug. 4, 2015, https://familysearch.org/.

200   **The end of May 1913:** "Chinese Tongs End War," *NYT,* May 22, 1913.

200   **There were several reasons:** "Chinese Tongmen Sign 'Peace Forever' Treaty," *NYTR,* May 29, 1913.

201   **The treaty, signed:** "Chinatown Signs Treaty of Peace Among All Tongs," *NYW,* May 28, 1913.

201   **The agreement opened all:** "Sign Chinatown Peace Pact," *NYS,* May 29, 1913; "Paint Brush and Steel Pen Bring Tong War to End," *IS,* May 29, 1913.

201   **Apart from representatives:** "Sketches at Love Feast," *NYW,* June 13, 1913; "Chinese Tong Men See Millennium in Peace Banquet," *NYW,* June 13, 1913.

202   **Even before the banquet:** "Call Tong Truce a Blind"; "Peace Irks Tongs: War Likely in Chinatown," *NYTR,* May 31, 1913.

202   **Even the police were pessimistic:** "Police Distrustful of Chinatown Peace," *NYS,* May 31, 1913.

Chapter 13: Chinatown: Renovated, Disinfected, and Evacuated

203   **After a disgruntled:** "Mitchel Again Asks for Baker's Head," *NYT,* Oct. 4, 1910; "Mayor Drops Police Heads; New Men In," *NYT,* Oct. 21, 1910; "Waldo in the Lead for Police Head," *NYT,* May 22, 1911; Bernard Whalen and Jon Whalen, *The NYPD's First Fifty Years: Politicians, Police Commissioners, and Patrolmen* (Lincoln, Neb.: Potomac Books, 2014), 67–70.

203   **Waldo had earlier:** "Gaynor Puts Waldo in Cropsey's Place," *NYT,* May 24, 1911.

203   **Determined to make his mark:** "Strong Arm Squad a Terror to Gangs of New York," *NYT,* Aug. 20, 1911; "Whitman Openly Says Police Let Gunmen Escape," *NYT,* Aug. 22, 1912.

204   **If graft remained a problem:** "Inspectors Underpaid," *DPP,* Aug. 20, 1912; "Find Underpay Creates Graft," *DPP,* March 10, 1913.

204   **Waldo also struck back:** "Waldo Gives Record of 13 Sam Paul Raids," *NYS,* Aug. 6, 1912; "Vice Haunt Owners," *NYT,* Aug. 28, 1912; "Gambler Who Defied Police Is Shot Dead," *NYT,* July 16, 1912.

204   **Waldo's list included:** "Houses Used for Gambling and Names of Owners," *NYTR,* Aug. 28, 1913.

205   **For several weeks, members:** "Chinatown to Stop Its Own Gambling," *NYTR,* Aug. 2, 1913; "Chinese Traders to Fight Gambling," *NYT,* Aug. 2, 1913; "Chinese Merchants Name Tong Gamblers," *NYS,* Aug. 2, 1913.

206 **Conlon pledged to secure:** "Lid Not to Lift While Waldo Stays," *NYS,* Sept. 27, 1913.

206 **Two weeks after Gaynor's death:** "Nice Day Says Tom Lee; Have Cup Tea?," *NYTR,* April 30, 1916.

206 **"Well, what shall we do":** "Waldo Suspends a Chinatown Captain," *NYS,* Sept. 26, 1913; "Lid Not to Lift While Waldo Stays"; "Raid Leads to Changes," *NYTR,* Oct. 2, 1913.

207 **Riley, transferred from the Greenwich:** "Riley Makes Raid Alone," *NYW,* Oct. 3, 1913; "Capt. Riley Raids Chinatown Alone," *NYT,* Oct. 5, 1913.

208 **Riley's tenure:** "Chinatown Cleanup Too Much for Riley," *NYTR,* Nov. 10, 1913; "Captain Riley's Respite at Richmond Hill," *NYW,* Nov. 12, 1913; "Say Ex-capt. Riley Took $1,000 Bribe," *NYT,* Dec. 3, 1913; "Riley Charge Dropped," *NYTR,* Nov. 28, 1914.

208 **The first trial of Eng Hing:** "Chinese to Die for Murder," *Bismarck Daily Tribune,* March 23, 1913; "Captain of Death House," *Keowee Courier,* Sept. 3, 1913.

209 **McManus had engaged:** "Dictograph Records Tong War Evidence," *NYS,* Nov. 27, 1913.

210 **"That," she explained:** "Girl Braves Tong to Save Chinese," *NYTR,* Oct. 6, 1914.

210 **"If On Leong Tong influence":** Opinion of the Court of General Sessions of the Peace of the City and County of New York in the case of the *People v. Eng Hing and Lee Dock,* Oct. 28, 1914, Executive Clemency and Pardon Case Files for Eng Hing and Lee Dock, Records of the Department of Correctional Services, New York State Archives, Series A0597-78, box 91, folder 27.

210 **The executions were rescheduled:** "Tong Men Cheat Little Green Door at Eleventh Hour," *NYW,* Oct. 31, 1914.

211 **"Now, if the On Leong Tong":** Motion for a New Trial on Newly Discovered Evidence, Court of General Sessions of the Peace of the City and County of New York in the case of the *People v. Eng Hing and Lee Dock,* Jan. 28, 1915, Executive Clemency and Pardon Case Files for Eng Hing and Lee Dock, Records of the Department of Correctional Services, New York State Archives, Series A0597-78, box 91, folder 27.

211 **Eng Hing and Lee Dock finally:** "Two Chinese Gunmen Are Electrocuted," *Elkhart Truth,* Feb. 5, 1915.

211 **On December 31, 1913:** "Kline Ousts Waldo; Calls Him Childish," *NYT,* Jan. 1, 1914.

212 **In February 1914:** "Raid Tong Headquarters," *NYT,* Feb. 20, 1914.

212 **With their departure:** "Ban on Fan Tan Routs Chinamen," *NYTR,* Feb. 1, 1914; "Chinatown Vanishing," *Duluth Herald,* July 9, 1915; "New York's Chinatown Annexed to the United States," *NYS,* Feb. 8, 1914.

212 **"Things very dull":** "Old Tom Lee Mourns; Chinatown 'Velly Dull,'" *NYTR,* Feb. 5, 1915.

213 **Under Falconer, the police:** "Chinese Rebel, Ask That Court Keep Police Off," *NYTGM,* April 13, 1915; "Appellate Court Decisions," *NYS,* June 26, 1915.

214 **A similar suit was filed:** "Chinaman Asks Police Curb," *NYS*, Oct. 13, 1915; "Chinaman Asks Injunction," *NYT*, Oct. 13, 1915; "Chinese Denied Injunction," *NYPR*, Oct. 17, 1915.

214 **In late October, an association:** "Too Many Police, Chinatown Plaint," *NYT*, Oct. 23, 1915.

214 **Although only fifty-two:** "Gin Gum Dies in Bed After Stormy Life," *NYS*, April 21, 1915; "Gin Gum's Funeral Brings Tong Peace," *NYT*, April 25, 1915; "Tongs at Peace at Jim Gun's Bier," *NYH*, April 25, 1915.

215 **In 1913, his son Frank:** "Tom Lee's Son Back as Chinese Official," *WT*, Jan. 23, 1914; "Pell Street Boy Here as Official," *WH*, Jan. 4, 1914; *Who's Who in China: Biographies of Chinese Leaders* (Shanghai: China Weekly Review, 1936), 136–37.

215 **Old Tom remained active:** "Arousing Interest of Chinese in America's Liberty Loan," *Greensboro Daily Record*, May 21, 1916.

215 **Lee's body, in a silk brocade shroud:** "Tom Lee, Mayor of Chinatown, Dies"; "On Leong Chieftain Dies Quietly in Bed," *NYTR*, Jan. 11, 1918; "Chinatown Chief's Body Lies in State," *NYTR*, Jan. 14, 1918; "Chinatown to Bury Mayor with Honor," *NYS*, Jan. 14, 1918; "Chinatown's Patriarch Buried, Soul Commended by 2 Faiths," *NYTR*, Jan. 15, 1918.

217 **"Now that the last columns":** "What Goes On in Gotham Now," *Riverside Enterprise*, Jan. 30, 1918.

217 **"While it is impossible":** "Woods Reviews His Police Work," *NYT*, Dec. 28, 1917.

218 **Chinese who were citizens:** Tsai, *Chinese Experience in America*, 97.

218 **"entertainment of the Orient":** "Chinese Leaders Buy Bonds While Tongmen Enlist," *Salt Lake Telegram*, April 27, 1918; "Arousing Interest of Chinese in America's Liberty Loan"; "Back the Fighting Lad with the Fighting Loan," *NYW*, April 26, 1918.

218 **In April 1919, Hip Sings:** "Chinatown Forgets Feuds to Arrange Soldiers' Welcome," *NYTR*, April 14, 1919; "Chinese Leaders Buy Bonds While Tongmen Enlist"; *History of the Seventy-seventh Division, August 25th, 1917, November 11th, 1918* (New York: Seventy-seventh Division Association, 1919), 44.

220 **In late 1921:** "Rival Tongs Join in Fete," *KCS*, Oct. 2, 1921; "2,000 Chinese Arrive to Open Club House," *NYW*, Sept. 30, 1921; "2 Chinese Held as Assassins of Tong Leader," *NYTR*, Aug. 9, 1922; "Chinatown Mourns Death of Dr. Fung, Tong Chief," *NYW*, July 12, 1922.

220 **"Chinatown is a joke!":** "'Chair' Makes Good Chinese; Tong Wars End," *Riverside Enterprise*, Feb. 14, 1922.

220 **Not even the cold-blooded murder:** "Police Fear Tong War Is on as Head of Hip Sing Is Shot," *NYW*, Aug. 8, 1922; "Tong Leader and Woman Shot in Feud," *NYTR*, Aug. 8, 1922; "2 Chinese Held as Assassins of Tong Leader," *NYTR*, Aug. 9, 1922.

221 **The newspapers assumed:** "Tong Leader and Woman Shot in Feud," *NYTR*, Aug. 8, 1922; "Tong War On," *NYT*, Aug. 8, 1922.

221 **Aided by Chinese informers:** "2 Chinese Held as Assassins of Tong Leader"; "Identify Tom Yee as Man Who Shot President Ko Low," *NYW*, Aug. 9, 1922.

221 **Ko Low's funeral:** "Ko Low to Be Buried with Christian Service," *NYTR,* Aug. 12, 1922; "Chinese Tong Leader Buried," *Boston Globe,* Aug. 14, 1922; "Tongs Arbitrate Ko Low Crime at Peace Table," *NYTR,* Aug. 15, 1922.

222 **The police, however:** "New York Police Seize Many Guns; Tong War Feared," *Anaconda Standard,* Dec. 2, 1922; "Tong War Nipped by Arms Seizure," *PI,* Dec. 2, 1922.

Chapter 14: The Defection of Chin Jack Lem

223 **By the 1920s:** "500 Chinese Here from 20 Cities to Attend Convention"; "Hip Sings Meeting," *Bellingham Herald,* Sept. 27, 1926; "Tong Men Meet in Parley Here," *Spokesman-Review,* Sept. 19, 1924.

224 **In April 1924:** Gong and Grant, *Tong War!,* 250–51.

224 **The Hip Sings were divided:** Ibid., 247–55; "Tong of Chinese Merchants Will Meet Here Next Week," *WP,* Aug. 27, 1924; "Arrest Chinese, Blame Rivalries in Tong Shootings," *CPD,* May 30, 1924.

224 **Then Wong Sing:** "Freed of Tong Death Threat," *CPD,* Aug. 28, 1924.

225 **Everyone saw it coming:** Gong and Grant, *Tong War!,* 253–54.

225 **The opening salvo:** "Steps Taken to Prevent More Chinese Trouble," *Biloxi Daily Herald,* Oct. 9, 1924; "New York Slaying," *Rockford Morning Star,* Oct. 12, 1924; "Tong War Brings Second Slaying," *CT,* Oct. 12, 1924; "Dayton Chinese Slain in Tong Feud," *CPD,* Oct. 12, 1924; "Tong War Worries Police of Big Cities," *Rockford Republican,* Oct. 13, 1924; "Eastern Tong Killings Stir Up Police Here," *CT,* Oct. 15, 1924; "Another Chinese Slain by Tongs," *NYS,* Oct. 13, 1924; "Mexico Scene of Fatal Tong Feud," *CPD,* Oct. 22, 1924.

225 **On October 15, Chin:** "Seize Tong Man; Find He's Also Deputy Sheriff," *CT,* Oct. 16, 1924; "Mysteries on Tong War," *Biloxi Herald,* Nov. 4, 1924; "Chin Jack Lam Jailed When Caught Armed," *SJ,* Oct. 16, 1924.

226 **Over the next couple:** "Fifth Chinese Slain in Tong Feud Here," *NYT,* Oct. 17, 1924; "Tong Hatchetmen Believed Slayers of Elderly Chinese," *BDS,* Oct. 18, 1924; "Tong Seeks Release of Murder Suspect," *BDE,* Nov. 8, 1924; "Chinese Tells Court He Was Offered $500 to Kill Corona Man," *BDS,* Nov. 11, 1924.

227 **By the end of the month:** "Warring Chinese Sign Armistice Ending Tong War," *San Diego Union,* Oct. 31, 1924; "New Tong Murder Halts Peace Talk," *TT,* Oct. 30, 1924; "Tong Murder Prelude to an Armistice," *CT,* Oct. 31, 1924.

227 **Then New York police got word:** "Seize Tong Leader as Cause of War," *NYT,* Nov. 10, 1924; "Peace Treaty of Tongs Extended," *CPD,* Nov. 13, 1924.

227 **On the morning of October 26, 1924:** "Chinese Dies After Voyage in a Box," *NYT,* Oct. 27, 1924; "Smuggled Suspects Tong Feud Recruits According to Police," *Tampa Tribune,* Oct. 29, 1924; "Peace Is Expected in Tong War Here," *NYT,* Oct. 30, 1924.

228 **Acting on a tip, police raided:** "Tear Bombs Seized in Raid on Chinese," *NYT,* Oct. 29, 1924; "Chinese Waiter Taken with Bomb," *BH,* Oct. 29, 1924.

228 **But during a passionate speech:** "Rev. Lee Tow Dies, Chinatown Mourns," *NYT,* Nov. 24, 1924.

228 **That day, the son:** "Police Guard Chinese Shops to Avert Tong War," *CT,* Nov. 27, 1924; "Two Chinese Murdered at Hartford," *SR,* Nov. 27, 1924; "Truce of Tongs Broken Ere It Officially Ends," *CPD,* Nov. 28, 1924; "Seven Slain as Truce of Tongmen Ends," *PI,* Nov. 29, 1924.

229 **In the meantime, Chin Jack Lem:** "Takes Chinese to New York," *CPD,* Nov. 28, 1924; "Tong Strife in New York Rages Again," *Buffalo Morning Express,* Nov. 29, 1924.

229 **Hostilities continued:** "Police Ready to Foil New Tong Shootings," *NYP,* Dec. 7, 1924; "Tongs Appeal to N.Y. Police," *BH,* Nov. 30, 1924.

229 **While Chin remained:** "7 Chinese Guilty in Tong Case," *CPD,* Dec. 13, 1924; "Chin Jack Lem on Way to Cleveland," *CPD,* Dec. 19, 1924; "Chin Jack Freed on $15,000 Bond," *CPD,* Dec. 21, 1924.

229 **In Chicago, the going rate:** "Murder Price List Established in Tong Warfare," *Queens Daily Star,* Feb. 12, 1925.

230 **He finally went on trial:** "Chin Jack Guilty; Armistice in Tong War Is Forecast," *CPD,* Feb. 19, 1925; "Chin Jack Off to Pen," *CPD,* Feb. 24, 1925.

230 **"The verdict means":** "Gashed by Cleaver in Tong War," *NYS,* March 3, 1925; "Killing May Mean Tong War Resumed," *SR,* March 23, 1925; "Convict Tong Leader; Means End of 'War,'" *WP,* Feb. 19, 1925; "County-Wide Tong War Ends as Rival Leaders Sign Truce," *Buffalo Courier,* March 27, 1925.

231 **Among the terms were pledges:** "County-Wide Tong War Ends as Rival Leaders Sign Truce"; "Tong Peace Signed, Chinatown Happy," *NYT,* March 27, 1925.

231 **Trouble broke out again:** "Tongs on Verge of Peace Pact," *BH,* Sept. 6, 1925; "Last Honors for Lee Kue Ying," *NYS,* Aug. 24, 1925; "Three Wounded in Tong Fight," *SR,* Aug. 25, 1925; "Tong War Renewal Seen in Killing," *NYT,* Aug. 25, 1925; "Chinese Tongs Renew Strife in Five Cities," *NYS,* Aug. 25, 1925; "Eastern Cities See Renewal of Tong Warfare," *IS,* Aug. 26, 1925.

232 **The peace agreement:** "Boston Tong Fight Brings New Warfare," *SR,* Aug. 26, 1925; "3 Chinese Killed in New Outbreak of Rival Tongs," *Queens Daily Star,* Aug. 25, 1925; "Tong War Renewal Seen in Killing."

232 **Because the agreement did not:** "Fifth Chinese Slain in War of Tongs," *NYP,* Aug. 26, 1925; "Tong War Claims Its 5th Victim; Scores Arrested," *BDE,* Aug. 26, 1925; "Tong War Spreads into Five States," *NYT,* Aug. 26, 1925.

232 **New York police attempted:** "Tongs in Peace Talk, One More Is Killed," *NYT,* Aug. 27, 1925.

233 **The Chinese Consolidated Benevolent Association summoned:** "Call Leader of Tong to End War," *SDT,* Aug. 28, 1925; Soohoo, *Wo tonghen Meidi,* 39–47.

233 **After two hours:** "Tong Men to Call on Pecora Today," *NYT,* Aug. 28, 1925; "Banton Lines Up Tong Leaders," *NYS,* Aug. 29, 1925; "Rival Tong Chiefs Agree on a Truce," *NYT,* Aug. 29, 1925; "Tong Officers Pledge Peace," *CPD,* Sept. 1, 1925; "Tong Forces Call Meeting to Make Universal Peace," *Kingsport Times,* Sept. 2, 1925.

233 **Barely two days later:** "Tongs to Sign New Peace Pact," *Boston Globe,* Sept. 1, 1925; "Chinese Slain, Peace Broken," *CPD,* Sept. 3, 1925; "Tong Peace Broken by a Shooting Here," *NYT,* Sept. 3, 1925; "One More Is Killed in Tong War Here," *NYT,* Sept. 4, 1925.

233 **The district attorney would not:** "Plan Swift Justice for Tong Killers," *NYT,* Sept. 5, 1925; "Tongs Are Warned Killings Must Stop," *NYT,* Sept. 9, 1925.

234 **"I am appealing to you":** "Demands Tong Truce," *NYP,* Sept. 8, 1925; "Tong Chieftains Called on Carpet," *CPD,* Sept. 9, 1925.

234 **The evening after Banton's:** "Two Killed as Dread Chinese Gunmen Act," *SJ,* Sept. 10, 1925.

234 **At the arraignment:** "Murder Indictment in Tong Outbreak," *NYT,* Sept. 11, 1925; "Tong Leaders Are Released in New York," *CPD,* Sept. 11, 1925.

234 **New York police, who:** "Murder Indictment in Tong Outbreak"; "Tongs Are Warned Killings Must Stop."

235 **In a drastic measure:** "200 Chinese Arrested Here in Federal Raids," *NYS,* Sept. 12, 1925; "Federal Drive on to End War of Tongs," *NYT,* Sept. 13, 1925; "U.S. Lands Chinese Who Began Last War," *NYP,* Sept. 12, 1925; "40 Chinese Seized; 1 Picked as Killer in New Tong War," *BDE,* Sept. 12, 1925.

236 **But the Feds didn't care:** "134 Chinese Taken in Raid Here to Be Deported by Government," *NYS,* Sept. 15, 1925; "134 Chinese in Tombs After U.S. Tong Raid Await Deportation," *NYP,* Sept. 15, 1925; "450 Chinese Seized, Tong Peace Signed," *NYT,* Sept. 15, 1925.

236 **Chinatown didn't stay subdued:** "On Leong Tong Member Is Murdered in His Laundry," *North Tonawanda Evening News,* Sept. 18, 1925; "New Tong Murders; 500 Chinese Seized," *NYT,* Sept. 19, 1925; Inmate Record of Jung Fung, Sing Sing Prison, Series B0143, Sing Sing Prison Inmate Admission Registers, 1842–1852, 1865–1971, New York State Archives.

237 **On the same day:** "Chinese Is Slain as Truce Is Signed," *NYS,* Sept. 18, 1925.

237 **Although there was no:** "72 More Chinese Here Ordered Deported," *NYS,* Sept. 19, 1925; "Raids Net 400 More Chinese; To Deport 72," *BDE,* Sept. 19, 1925; "New Tong Murders; 500 Chinese Seized."

237 **Detainees were held:** "U.S. Raiders Arrest 354 in Tong Roundup; To Deport 74 More," *NYP,* Sept. 19, 1925; "72 Chinese Held for Deportation," *PI,* Sept. 20, 1925.

238 **On September 21:** "'Real Peace' in New York," *BH,* Sept. 22, 1925; "Warring Tongs Sign 'Eternal' Peace Pact," *NYP,* Sept. 22, 1925.

238 **The Hip Sings, however:** "Federal Tong Probe Asked by Hip Sings," *NYP,* Sept. 25, 1925; "Hip Sing Tong Asks Trade War Probe," *WS,* Sept. 25, 1925; "Mask Off at Last in Tong Wars Among U.S. Chinese," *St. Petersburg Independent,* Sept. 26, 1925.

239 **"It's preposterous":** "Federal Tong Probe Asked by Hip Sings."

239 **Police joined two hundred:** "Rival Tongs at Peace Dinner Agree to 'Bury the Hatchet,'" *BDE,* Oct. 15, 1925; "Tongs Have Peace Dinner," *NYT,* Oct. 15, 1925.

239 **The first blood was shed:** "5 Slain, 3 Shot as Tongs Renew War in 6 Cities," *BDE,* March 24, 1927.

240 **"The On Leongs are the wealthy":** "Extortion Called Basis of Tong War," *NYP,* March 25, 1927.

240 **Late on March 25:** "Tong Chiefs Order Slaying Stopped; Two More Killed," *BDE,* March 26, 1927; "Tong Leaders Warn Fellows of No Warfare," *Canton Repository,* March 26, 1927.

240 **No doubt they were:** "Warring Tongs Announce Truce," *IS,* March 27, 1927.

241 **"even the children play":** "New York Day by Day," *Lexington Leader,* Aug. 30, 1927.

241 **Suddenly, on the evening:** "Tongman Is Killed in Laundry Attack," *NYP,* Oct. 19, 1928; "Chinese Succumbs to Feud Wound," *BDE,* Oct. 19, 1928; "Tong Strife Ends," *Bellingham Herald,* Oct. 26, 1928.

241 **It wasn't until early August:** "Chicago Police Patrol Chinatown," *Edwardsville Intelligencer,* Aug. 5, 1929; "Chicagoans Fear New Tong Clash," *MT,* Aug. 5, 1929; "Fear Serious Tong Outbreaks," *Richmond Times Dispatch,* Aug. 5, 1929; "Chinese Chiefs Have Orders to Stop," *Bellingham Herald,* Aug. 5, 1929; "Guns Roar, Tong War Spreading in East," *SDT,* Aug. 5, 1929; "Tuttle Threatens Chinese Roundup," *NYP,* Aug. 6, 1929.

241 **But less than two hours:** "Two Wounded as Tong War Reaches City," *BSU,* Aug. 5, 1929; "Chinatown Raids On Today Unless Tongs Quit War," *BDE,* Aug. 6, 1929; "Tuttle Threatens Chinese Roundup."

242 **The accompanying announcement:** "A New Peace Treaty," *Lexington Herald,* Aug. 7, 1929; "Tongs Sign New Treaty Early Today," *Baton Rouge Advocate,* Aug. 7, 1929.

242 **Initially, it was unclear:** "Chicago Tongman Critically Wounded," *SR,* Aug. 7, 1929; "New York Armistice Has No Effect on Rivals Here," *BH,* Aug. 7, 1929; "Chinatown Raid Amuses Crowds," *BH,* Aug. 8, 1929; "Stabbing Follows Tong Peace Pact," *NYP,* Aug. 13, 1929.

Chapter 15: Coexistence

243 **The Great Depression delivered:** Song, *Shaping and Reshaping Chinese American Identity,* 50; "Tongs of Chinatown United by Necessities of Relief," *CSM,* July 12, 1932; Tsai, *Chinese Experience in America,* 108–9.

243 **Many were hungry:** "Tongs of Chinatown United by Necessities of Relief"; "Bowery Now at Odds on Winter Breadlines," *BDE,* Aug. 6, 1931.

243 **"The warring tongs":** "Let's Think This Over," *Augusta Chronicle,* May 27, 1932.

243 **Charlie Boston didn't have to worry:** "Chinatown's Patriarch Buried, Soul Commended by 2 Faiths"; "Brewing Chinatown Tong War May Dethrone Charley Boston," *NYTR,* May 21, 1921; "Chinatown to Bury Boston on Sunday," *NYP,* Jan. 7, 1930; "About Burying Charlie Boston," *NYS,* Jan. 8, 1930.

244 **In the end, the affair:** "Charlie Boston Finally Buried," *NYS,* Jan. 13, 1930.

244 **Even before Boston's passing:** Harry R. Sisson to Chinese Inspector in Charge, New York, Feb. 21, 1927, and Deposition of Wong Gett before Immigration Inspector P. A. Donahue, March 1, 1927, in Chinese Exclusion Act Case File for Wong Gett, Record Group 85, box 325, Case Nos. 95, 580, Immigration and Naturalization Service, National Archives and Records Administration—Northeast Region, New York; "Tongs Sign New Peace Pact," *NYS*, June 7, 1930.

244 **Both tongs marched peacefully:** "Murder Charges to Two Chinese," *SR*, Feb. 13, 1930; "Hostile Tongs Bar Census of 500 Chinese in Newark," *NYP*, April 18, 1930; "Raid Chinatown After Rumor of Tong Wars," *CT*, May 19, 1930; "Chicago's War of Gangsters Goes Oriental," *Seattle Times*, June 5, 1930; "Outbreak of Tong War in New York Feared Following Rumors of Strife Among Chinese in the Middle West," *Bellingham Herald*, June 5, 1930; "Brooklyn Chinese Shot Dead," *NYS*, June 6, 1930.

245 **"Whatever caused this outbreak":** "Brooklyn Chinese Shot Dead."

245 **But the situation was more complex:** "Two Heads Hunted, Two More Die Here," *NYT*, June 7, 1930; "Chinatown War Still Going On," *MT*, June 7, 1930; "Tong Toll Now 6; Peace Parley On," *NYP*, June 7, 1930.

245 **A treaty was signed:** "Tongs Sign New Peace Pact"; "Another Chinese Is Shot to Death," *MT*, June 8, 1930; "Blame Hip Sing Desertions in New Tong War," *CT*, June 8, 1930.

245 **Tong leaders disavowed:** "Hip Sing 'Reveres' Quizzed by Police," *NYP*, June 9, 1930; "Report Chicago Tongs Will Defy N.Y. Peace Pact," *CT*, June 9, 1930.

246 **"The On Leong Merchants Association":** "Tong Chiefs Sign Treaty of Peace," *SR*, June 10, 1930.

246 **Kellogg Peace Pact:** "Men and Events," *China Weekly Review*, June 14, 1930.

246 **In July, Chinese were slaughtering:** "Chinese Warned to End Killings," *Reading Times*, Aug. 19, 1930; "Tong War Flames Forth in New York," *Tonawanda Evening News*, July 31, 1930.

247 **The cause of the trouble:** "Alleged £100 Offer for Murder," *Manchester Guardian*, Aug. 16, 1930; "Chinese Warned to End Killings."

247 **More shootings followed:** "Boost Patrols to Curb Tong Warfare," *SDT*, Aug. 12, 1930; "Five Chinese Hurt in New Tong War: Poolroom Shot Up," *BDE*, Aug. 18, 1930; "Five Chinese Shot in Pell St. Ambush," *NYT*, Aug. 18, 1930; "Chinese Warned to End Killings."

247 **The final twenty-article agreement:** "Chinese Societies to Sign Pact Ending New York Tong Wars," *Tampa Tribune*, Aug. 19, 1930; "Mulrooney Named Arbiter as Tongs Accept Peace Pact," *BDE*, Sept. 2, 1930; "Tongs Sign Another Peace Pact," *NYS*, Sept. 2, 1930.

247 **"In spite of the fact":** "Tongs Sign Another Peace Pact."

248 **"Sightseeing buses dump":** "Canaries Warn Chinese of Raid Peril," *NYS*, April 21, 1931.

248 **In fact, they held their caucuses:** "Chinese to Gather Here," *NYS*, April 22, 1931; "The Heathen Chinee Is Peculiar," *NYS*, April 24, 1931; "Two Tongs Convene," *BDE*, April 27, 1931.

249   **Tens of thousands of red:** "Trouble Feared as Tongs Meet," *NYS*, April 27, 1931; "Chinatown in Ominous Quiet as Big Tongs Prepare Parley," *BSU*, April 28, 1931.

250   **The On Leongs, however:** "Police Watch Hips of Hips and Leongs," *NYP*, April 28, 1931.

250   **Both tongs held banquets:** "Rival Tongs at Play Together," *NYS*, April 28, 1931; "Tongs Under Guard Plan Aid for Idle," *NYT*, April 29, 1931.

251   **At 9:30 p.m. on February 28:** "Old Tong Leader Is Shot," *NYS*, Feb. 29, 1932; "Shooting Revives Mock Duck Legend," *NYT*, Feb. 29, 1932.

251   **There had actually been a few:** "Gin Gum Dies in Bed After Stormy Life"; "Gin Gum's Funeral Brings Tong Peace"; "Tongs at Peace at Jim Gun's Bier"; "Chinatown Turns: Seeks Aid of Law," *NYTR*, April 8, 1915; "Bankruptcy Notices," *NYT*, Nov. 30, 1917; "Police Watch Hips of Hips and Leongs"; "Hip Sing Heads Called to End Local Dispute," *Pittsburgh Post-Gazette*, March 10, 1928.

251   **The police made an attempt:** "Old Tong Leader Is Shot"; "Profiles: Tong Leader," *New Yorker*, Dec. 30, 1933.

252   **The greatest contribution:** "Tongs of Chinatown United by Necessities of Relief."

252   **Putting aside their differences:** Ibid.; "So They Say," *Miami Daily News-Record*, Feb. 29, 1932; "Chinese Throughout the U.S. Work and Sacrifice for War Stricken Homeland," *Columbus Daily Enquirer*, March 13, 1932.

252   **Even the Chinese New Year:** "Rival Tong Dragons Greet Chinese Year," *NYT*, Jan. 27, 1933.

253   **When, on July 21:** "Chinatown Guarded as Tong Man Is Slain," *NYT*, July 23, 1933; "Denies Tong Mediation," *NYT*, Aug. 4, 1933; "Tong Slayers Fool Police," *SJ*, July 29, 1933; "Chinese Shot to Death; N.Y. Tong Feud Blamed," *BS*, July 29, 1933.

254   **Later that day, Sing Kee:** "New Tong War Spreads Here in Shooting," *NYS*, July 29, 1933; "Chinatown Fears Tong War Start," *TT*, July 30, 1933.

254   **Just as the earthly remains:** "May Avert Tong War," *NYS*, July 31, 1933; "Tong War Inquiry Begun by Medalie," *NYT*, Aug. 1, 1933.

255   **In describing the pact:** "Tongs in Truce After Killings," *NYP*, Aug. 17, 1933; "Tong Peace Signed; NRA Is Credited," *NYT*, Aug. 18, 1933.

255   **"This was many degrees":** "Tong Peace Signed; NRA Is Credited."

255   **"because the Hip Sing":** Leong, *Chinatown Inside Out*, 79.

256   **Then, too, the Chinatown of the 1930s:** Carlos E. Cortés, ed., *Multicultural America: A Multimedia Encyclopedia* (Thousand Oaks, Calif.: Sage, 2013), 1:489; Wang, *Surviving the City*, 69–81.

257   **Another cause was the decline:** Charles LaCerra, *Franklin Delano Roosevelt and Tammany Hall of New York* (Lanham, Md.: University Press of America, 1997), 84.

258   **Yet another factor:** Sue Fawn Chung, "Fighting for Their American Rights: A History of the Chinese American Citizens Alliance," in *Claiming America: Constructing Chinese Identities During the Exclusion Era*, ed. K. Scott Wong and Sucheng Chan (Philadelphia: Temple University Press, 1998), 96.

258 **The Depression also made:** Tsai, *Chinese Experience in America,* 108–9; Leong, *Chinatown Inside Out,* 74.
258 **Then there were China's needs:** "So They Say."
259 **In the run-up:** Yu, *To Save China, to Save Ourselves,* 42–45; Kwong, *Chinatown, New York,* 55.
259 **"With the sharp decrease":** Leong, *Chinatown Inside Out,* 82–84.
260 **On February 14, 1934:** "Chinatown Lions on Parade," *NYS,* Feb. 15, 1934.

Epilogue

261 **The body of Tom Lee:** "Tom Lee Is Going to Grave in China," *NYS,* April 4, 1918.
261 **Chin Jack Lem:** "Deposed Tong Tyrant Slain," *NYS,* Nov. 2, 1937; "Governor White Commutes Former Tong's Sentence," *Coshocton Tribune,* Nov. 20, 1931; "Not So Good," *CPD,* Nov. 21, 1931; Alan F. Dutka, *Asiatown Cleveland: From Tong Wars to Dim Sum* (Charleston, S.C.: History Press, 2014), 68.
262 **Sue Sing:** Executive Clemency and Pardon Case Files for Sue Sing, Inmate No. 6033, Records of the Department of Correctional Services, New York State Archives, Series A0597-78, box 73, folder 32.
262 **Chin Lem:** "Chin Lem Buried with Full Rites," *NYH,* Feb. 22, 1914; "Deadly Tongman Is Quiet Forever," *TT,* Feb. 22, 1914.
262 **William McAdoo:** McAdoo, *Guarding a Great City,* 175–76.
262 **William T. Jerome:** "Jerome Dies at 74," *NYT,* Feb. 14, 1934.
263 **Wong Aloy:** *Twenty-first Report of the State Civil Service Commission* (Albany: Oliver A. Quayle, State Legislative Printer, 1904), 154; "Blame Tong War for Poolroom Death Mystery," *CT,* April 28, 1922; "Fear Tong War," *IS,* Jan. 13, 1923.
263 **Meihong Soohoo:** Him Mark Lai, "China and the Chinese American Community: The Political Dimension," in *Chinese America: History and Perspectives, 1999,* ed. Marlon K. Hom (San Francisco: Chinese Historical Society of America, 1999), 7.
263 **Rhinelander Waldo:** "Col. Waldo, 50, Dies of Septic Poisoning," *NYT,* Aug. 14, 1927.
264 **Edward P. Mulrooney:** "Edward Mulrooney, 85, Dead; Police Commissioner 1930–33," *NYT,* May 1, 1960.
264 **Joab H. Banton:** "Indict Actors on Charge of Giving Indecent Play," *IS,* March 3, 1927; "Star in 'Sex' Goes to Jail," *IS,* April 20, 1927.
264 **Warry Charles:** "Warry Charles, Chinese 'Lifer,' Dies in Prison," *BJ,* Aug. 10, 1915; "To Ship Body of Warry Charles to Brooklyn," *BJ,* Aug. 13, 1915.
264 **Mock Duck:** Ancestry.com, "1920 United States Federal Census Online Database," http://search.ancestry.com/search/db.aspx?dbid=6061; "1930 United States Federal Census Online Database," http://search.ancestry.com/search/db.aspx?dbid=6224; "1940 United States Federal Census Online Database," http://search.ancestry.com/search/db.aspx?dbid=2442, all accessed Aug. 4, 2015.

SELECTED BIBLIOGRAPHY

Anbinder, Tyler. *Five Points: The 19th-Century New York City Neighborhood That Invented Tap Dance, Stole Elections, and Became the World's Most Notorious Slum.* New York: Free Press, 2001.

Asbury, Herbert. *The Gangs of New York: An Informal History of the Underworld.* New York: Thunder's Mouth Press, 2001. Original work published 1928.

Beck, Louis J. *New York's Chinatown: An Historical Presentation of Its People and Places.* New York: Bohemia, 1898.

Bonner, Arthur. *Alas! What Brought Thee Hither? The Chinese in New York, 1800–1950.* Madison, N.J.: Fairleigh Dickinson University Press, 1997.

Chan, Sucheng. *Chinese American Transnationalism: The Flow of People, Resources, and Ideas Between China and America During the Exclusion Era.* Philadelphia: Temple University Press, 2006.

Chang, Iris. *The Chinese in America: A Narrative History.* New York: Viking Press, 2003.

Chen, Shehong. *Being Chinese, Becoming Chinese American.* Urbana: University of Illinois Press, 2002.

Coolidge, Mary Roberts. *Chinese Immigration.* New York: Henry Holt, 1909.

Costello, Augustine E. *Our Police Protectors: History of the New York Police from the Earliest Period to the Present Time.* New York: by author, 1885.

Crouse, Russel. *Murder Won't Out.* Garden City, N.Y.: Doubleday, Doran, 1932.

Dillon, Richard H. *The Hatchet Men: The Story of the Tong Wars in San Francisco's Chinatown.* New York: Coward-McCann, 1962.

Freeland, David. *Automats, Taxi Dances, and Vaudeville: Excavating Manhattan's Lost Places of Leisure.* New York: New York University Press, 2009.

Fronc, Jennifer. *New York Undercover: Private Surveillance in the Progressive Era.* Chicago: University of Chicago Press, 2009.

Gardner, Charles W. *The Doctor and the Devil; or, Midnight Adventures of Dr. Parkhurst.* New York: Vanguard, 1931.

Gilfoyle, Timothy J. *A Pickpocket's Tale: The Underworld of Nineteenth-Century New York.* New York: W. W. Norton, 2006.

Gong, Eng Ying, and Bruce Grant. *Tong War! The First Complete History of the Tongs in America; Details of the Tong Wars and Their Causes; Lives of Famous Hatchetmen and Gunmen; and Inside Information as to the Workings of the Tongs, Their Aims and Achievements.* New York: N. L. Brown, 1930.

Gyory, Andrew. *Closing the Gate: Race, Politics, and the Chinese Exclusion Act.* Chapel Hill: University of North Carolina Press, 1998.

Hall, Bruce Edward. *Tea That Burns: A Family Memoir of Chinatown*. New York: Free Press, 1998.

Ho, Chuimei, and Soo Lon Moy. *Chinese in Chicago*. Charleston, S.C.: Arcadia, 2005.

Huie Kin. *Reminiscences*. Peiping, China: San Yu Press, 1932.

Jeffers, H. Paul. *Commissioner Roosevelt: The Story of Theodore Roosevelt and the New York City Police, 1895–1897*. New York: J. Wiley & Sons, 1994.

Johnson, Marilyn. *Street Justice: A History of Police Violence in New York City*. Boston: Beacon Press, 2003.

Kelly, Raymond W. *The History of the New York City Police Department*. New York: New York City Police Department, 1993.

Kinkead, Gwen. *Chinatown: A Portrait of a Closed Society*. New York: HarperCollins, 1992.

Kwong, Peter. *Chinatown, New York: Labor and Politics, 1930–1950*. New York: New Press, 2001.

Lai, Him Mark. *Chinese American Transnational Politics*. Urbana: University of Illinois Press, 2010.

Lardner, James, and Thomas A. Reppetto. *NYPD: A City and Its Police*. New York: Henry Holt, 2000.

Leong, Gor Yun. *Chinatown Inside Out*. New York: B. Mussey Books, 1936.

Lin, Yutang. *My Country and My People*. London: William Heinemann, 1936.

Ling, Huping. *Chinese Chicago: Race, Transnational Migration, and Community Since 1870*. Redwood City, Calif.: Stanford University Press, 2012.

Lui, Mary Ting Yi. *The Chinatown Trunk Mystery: Murder, Miscegenation, and Other Dangerous Encounters in Turn-of-the-Century New York City*. Princeton, N.J.: Princeton University Press, 2007.

McAdoo, William. *Guarding a Great City*. New York: Harper, 1906.

McIllwain, Jeffrey Scott. *Organizing Crime in Chinatown: Race and Racketeering in New York City, 1890–1910*. Jefferson, N.C.: McFarland, 2004.

McKelway, St. Clair. *True Tales from the Annals of Crime and Rascality*. New York: Random House, 1951.

McKeown, Adam. *Chinese Migrant Networks and Cultural Change: Peru, Chicago, Hawaii, 1900–1936*. Chicago: University of Chicago Press, 2001.

Moss, Frank. *The American Metropolis: From Knickerbocker Days to the Present Time: New York City Life in All Its Various Phases: An Historiograph of New York*. Vol. 2. New York: P. F. Collier, 1897.

Ostrow, Daniel. *Manhattan's Chinatown*. Charleston, S.C.: Arcadia, 2008.

Qin, Yucheng. *The Diplomacy of Nationalism: The Six Companies and China's Policy Toward Exclusion*. Honolulu: University of Hawai'i Press, 2009.

Riis, Jacob A. *How the Other Half Lives: Studies Among the Tenements of New York*. New York: Dover, 1971. Original work published 1890.

Riordon, William L., and George Washington Plunkitt. *Plunkitt of Tammany Hall: A Series of Very Plain Talks on Very Practical Politics*. New York: Signet Classics, 1995. Original work published 1905.

Roosevelt, Theodore. *An Autobiography*. New York: Macmillan, 1913.

Sloat, Warren. *A Battle for the Soul of New York: Tammany Hall, Police Corruption, Vice, and Reverend Charles Parkhurst's Crusade Against Them, 1892–1895*. New York: Cooper Square, 2002.

Song, Jingyi. *Shaping and Reshaping Chinese American Identity: New York's Chinese During the Depression and World War II*. Lanham, Md.: Lexington Books, 2010.

Tchen, John Kuo Wei. *New York Before Chinatown: Orientalism and the Shaping of American Culture, 1776–1882*. Baltimore: Johns Hopkins University Press, 1999.

Tow, Julius Su. *The Real Chinese in America; Being an Attempt to Give the General American Public a Fuller Knowledge and a Better Understanding of the Chinese People in the United States*. New York: Academy Books, 1923.

Tsai, Shih-shan Henry. *The Chinese Experience in America*. Bloomington: Indiana University Press, 1986.

Tung, William L. *The Chinese in America, 1820–1973: A Chronology and Fact Book*. Dobbs Ferry, N.Y.: Oceana, 1974.

Van Norden, Warner M. *Who's Who of the Chinese in New York*. New York: by author, 1918.

Wang, Xinyang. *Surviving the City: The Chinese Immigrant Experience in New York City, 1890–1970*. Lanham, Md.: Rowman & Littlefield, 2001.

Yu, Renqiu. *To Save China, to Save Ourselves: The Chinese Hand Laundry Alliance of New York*. Philadelphia: Temple University Press, 1992.

INDEX

Note: *Italic* page numbers refer to illustrations.

on Fourth Tong War, 226, 230, 234,
241, 242, 245, 246, 247, 255
role of, 29, 135
on Third Tong War, 200, 202
and Froman Tong, 130–31, 133
Chinese criminal syndicates, 39, 182, 188
Chinese Delmonico Restaurant. *See* Mon
Lay Won.
Chinese Exclusion Act (1882), 2, 11, 14, 26,
34, 38, 136, 256, 271
Chinese Hand Laundry Alliance, 259
Chinese Hospital, 85, 86
Chinese immigrants
arrest statistics on, 120
citizenship eligibility of, 2, 10, 11, 14,
26, 136–37, 218, 254
clothing and dress of, 4, 6
dialects spoken by, xv, 7
ethics of, 64
illegal entry via smuggling industry, 39,
56, 228, 257
laundry business associated with, 4, 13,
28, 96, 257, 260
mutual aid societies of, 7–9, 39, 135, 243
prejudice against, xi, xii, 2, 76, 79–80,
92, 110, 120–21, 122, 136–37,
147–48, 157, 258
ratio of men to women, 73–74, 136
registration of, viii, 136, 232, 235, 237, 241
returning to China, ix, 1, 4, 8, 10, 26,
74, 86, 136,
and rule of law, 92, 134–37, 170, 180
and saving face, ix, 133, 134, 165,
180–81, 191, 205, 256, 259
stereotypes of, xii, xiii, 2, 3, 5, 12, 28, 76
targeting of, viii–ix
U.S. population of, 38, 257–58
Chinese Journal, xi
Chinese laborers, ix, 1, 2, 4, 6, 34, 136, 271
Chinese language, dialects of, xv, 7
Chinese Merchants Association
and negotiations in Third Tong War,
200, 201, 202, 205, 206
and On Leong Tong, 58, 75, 85, 293n, 307n
Chinese Theatre
and First Tong War, 113–15, 118, 119,
123, 124–25, 151, 167, 180, 268, 273
and Four Brothers' War, 163, 166, 167
photograph of, *114*
Chinese women
buying and selling of, 143, 144, 160
ratio of men to women, 73–74, 136

Ching Gong, 95–96
Chin Hing, 230
Chin Jack Lem
arrests of, 225, 227, 275
defection to Hip Sing Tong, xviii,
223–25, 245, 256, 275
extradition fight of, 229
incarceration in Ohio Penitentiary,
230, 261
killings related to, 240–41
murder of, 261
On Leong Tong's bounty on, 225, 230
photograph of, *226*
trial of, 230
Chin Lem
death of, 262
as laundryman, xviii, 160
murder report of, 158–61
portrait of, *169*
testimony in Bow Kum's murder trial,
169–70
Chin Mung, 144–45
Chin Song, 230
Chin Tin, 24, 41, 42, 267
Chintong, George, 253
Chong Pon Sing, 133, 189–90, 193–94
Chow Yong, 109
Christian Science Monitor, 243
Chu, Y. K., xi
Chuck, James, 221
Chu Company, 205
Chu family, 61, 158
Chu Fong, xviii, 56, 158
Chu Gain, 156, 158
Chu Gong
gathering evidence on Hip Sing
gambling houses, 111–12
Hip Sing Tong's assault on, 97, 98
Hip Sing Tong's bounty on, 94
identity of, xiii
as On Leong Tong treasurer, xviii,
58, 97
and Louie Way, 97, 98, 126, 198
Chu Hen, 172–73, 175, 176, 180
Chu Hin, 176, 178, 268
Chu Lock, xix, 61, 158, 165, 205, 267
Chu Moy Yen, 172, *173,* 266
Chung, Ah, 23, 267
Chung Fook, 172, 175, 180
Chung Hwa Gong Shaw
as governing body, 9, 85, 135, 277
headquarters of, *63,* 85, 293n